The Second Cold War

Toward the end of the Cold War, the last great struggle between the United States and the Soviet Union marked the end of détente, and escalated into the most dangerous phase of the conflict since the Cuban Missile Crisis. Aaron Donaghy examines the complex history of America's largest peacetime military buildup, which was in turn challenged by the largest peacetime peace movement. Focusing on the critical period between 1977 and 1985, Donaghy shows how domestic politics shaped dramatic foreign policy reversals by Presidents Jimmy Carter and Ronald Reagan. He explains why the Cold War intensified so quickly and how—contrary to all expectations—U.S.–Soviet relations were repaired. Drawing on recently declassified archival material, *The Second Cold War* traces how each administration evolved in response to crises and events at home and abroad. This compelling and controversial account challenges the accepted notion of how the end of the Cold War began.

Aaron Donaghy teaches U.S. foreign relations history and modern international history at University College Dublin. He is the author of *The British Government and the Falkland Islands, 1974–79* (2014).

Cambridge Studies in US Foreign Relations

Edited by
Paul Thomas Chamberlin, *Columbia University*
Lien-Hang T. Nguyen, *Columbia University*

This series showcases cutting-edge scholarship in US foreign relations that employs dynamic new methodological approaches and archives from the colonial era to the present. The series will be guided by the ethos of transnationalism, focusing on the history of American foreign relations in a global context rather than privileging the US as the dominant actor on the world stage.

Also in the Series

(Continued after the Index)

The Second Cold War

Carter, Reagan, and the Politics of Foreign Policy

AARON DONAGHY

University College Dublin

CAMBRIDGE
UNIVERSITY PRESS

University Printing House, Cambridge CB2 8BS, United Kingdom

One Liberty Plaza, 20th Floor, New York, NY 10006, USA

477 Williamstown Road, Port Melbourne, VIC 3207, Australia

314–321, 3rd Floor, Plot 3, Splendor Forum, Jasola District Centre, New Delhi – 110025, India

79 Anson Road, #06–04/06, Singapore 079906

Cambridge University Press is part of the University of Cambridge.

It furthers the University's mission by disseminating knowledge in the pursuit of education, learning, and research at the highest international levels of excellence.

www.cambridge.org
Information on this title: www.cambridge.org/9781108838030
DOI: 10.1017/9781108937016

First published 2021

A catalogue record for this publication is available from the British Library.

ISBN 978-1-108-83803-0 Hardback

To my parents, Paula and Tom, and my brother, Cian

Contents

Acknowledgments

The roots of this book date back to 2015, with the award of a Marie Skłodowska-Curie Global Fellowship from the European Union. Since then I have incurred a string of debts, individual and institutional. At Harvard University, Fredrik Logevall has been a terrific source of intellectual insight and encouragement. Fred kindly agreed to support my EU application, despite not knowing me or my work previously. I am deeply grateful that he did. John Young (University of Nottingham) has been extremely generous with his guidance and expertise ever since serving as my PhD examiner. His help is enormously appreciated. My early mentors at University College Dublin, Richard Aldous (now Bard College) and William Mulligan, have been unswerving in their support over the years. I am indebted to them both. Prior to joining Harvard, I enjoyed a six-month stint at Cornell University. Matt Evangelista served as my adviser and I wish to thank him here. I also want to acknowledge the vital support of the European Union, which funded my research on either side of the Atlantic.

As an Irishman, settling in Boston was not difficult. It was made even easier by the kindness of Joe and Marina McCarthy. Few know the Harvard scene better, and none are more generous with their time. I am indebted to them beyond measure. Harvard's Center for European Studies was the perfect environment in which to work. For their hospitality I wish to thank Elaine Papoulias, Charlie Maier, Mary Sarotte, Grzegorz Ekiert, Art Goldhammer, Laura Falloon, Elizabeth Johnson, Roumiana Theunissen, Filomena Cabral, Gila Naderi, and my fellow visiting scholars. My thanks also go to the Harvard History Department, especially Kimberly O'Hagan and Daniel Lord Smail.

At Boston College, Rob Savage and Oliver Rafferty were great company and always kind with their time. I would like to thank them both. For their hospitality I wish to acknowledge Judith Weinraub, Heather Campion, Sean Rowland, and Peter Ubertaccio, Dean of Arts and Sciences at Stonehill College. I would also like to express my thanks to Ambassador David Aaron and Ambassador Jack Matlock, who provided candid recollections of the Carter and Reagan years, respectively. For the time they gave me in Washington, DC, I am grateful to Brian Cahalane of the Irish Embassy and Michael Murphy (Office of the Historian of the House of Representatives). A number of excellent people made my stay at Cornell enjoyable: among them were Matt Evangelista, Lisel Hintz, Dawn Alexandrea Berry, Agnieszka Nimark, Judith Reppy, Nishi Dhupa, and Elaine Scott.

This project also took me to Great Britain. A John Antcliffe fellowship sponsored my research on the Margaret Thatcher/Cold War era at the University of Cambridge, Churchill College. I wish to thank Andrew Riley, Allen Packwood, David Reynolds, Barry Phipps, and Dame Athene Donald. At the University of Nottingham, John Young, Sarah Badcock, Paul McGarr, Bevan Sewell, Tracy Sisson, and the late Sandra Winfield were very kind with their time, and I would like to thank them all. A mention, too, for colleagues at University College Dublin—past and present—for their help in various ways: William Mulligan, Richard Aldous, Robert Gerwarth, Christoph Müller, John McCafferty, Diarmuid Ferriter, Sandra Scanlon, Paul Rouse, Declan Downey, Judith Devlin, David Kerr, Maurice Bric, Robert Strong, Catherine Hynes, Suzanne D'Arcy, Kate Breslin, Emma Lyons, Kate O'Hanlon, Richard McElligott, Mark Jones, Laura Kelly, Susan Grant, James Matthews, Marie Leoutre, Keith McLoughlin, Jennifer Farrell, Niamh Wycherley, Ezequiel Mercau, Conor Tobin, Elaine Pereira Farrell, Conor Mulvagh, and Jennifer Keating.

I have benefited from the assistance of archivists at many different libraries and institutions. Special thanks go to the staff at the Ronald Reagan Presidential Library, the Jimmy Carter Presidential Library, and the UK National Archives, who retrieved vast quantities of documents, often at short notice.

It has been a pleasure to work with Cambridge University Press. I am especially grateful to Cecelia Cancellaro, my editor in New York, for agreeing to publish the book at a time when the world was upended by the viral pandemic. I wish to thank editorial assistant Rachel Blaifeder, former editor Debbie Gershenowitz, content manager Thomas Haynes,

and the book series editors, Lien-Hang Nguyen and Paul Thomas
Chamberlin. I also want to express my gratitude to the anonymous
reviewers, whose insights and criticisms improved the quality of the book.

Above all, I want to thank my family. Caroline, Mary, Paddy, and Tina
Donaghy have been unceasingly kind and helpful over the years. My
greatest debts by far are owed to my parents, Paula and Tom, and my
brother, Cian, for all their devoted support and encouragement. It is to
them that this book is dedicated, with love and gratitude.

This project has received funding from the European Union's
Horizon 2020 research and innovation program under the Marie
Skłodowska-Curie grant agreement No. 659369.

Abbreviations

ABC	American Broadcasting Company
ABM	Anti-Ballistic Missile
ACDA	Arms Control and Disarmament Agency
AFL-CIO	American Federation of Labor and Congress of Industrial Organizations
ALCM	Air-launched Cruise Missile
ASAT	Anti-satellite Weapons
AWACS	Airborne Warning and Control System
BMD	Ballistic Missile Defense
CBS	Columbia Broadcasting System
CDE	Conference on Disarmament in Europe
CDM	Coalition for a Democratic Majority
CDU	Christian Democratic Union (Federal Republic of Germany)
CIA	Central Intelligence Agency
CNN	Cable News Network
CPAC	Conservative Political Action Conference
CPD	Committee on the Present Danger
CPSU	Communist Party of the Soviet Union
CSCE	Conference on Security and Cooperation in Europe
EEC	European Economic Community
ERW	Enhanced Radiation Weapon
FBI	Federal Bureau of Investigation
FCO	Foreign and Commonwealth Office (United Kingdom)
FEMA	Federal Emergency Management Agency
FIFA	International Federation of Association Football
FRG	Federal Republic of Germany (West Germany)

GDP	Gross Domestic Product
GDR	German Democratic Republic (East Germany)
GNP	Gross National Product
GOP	Grand Old Party (The Republican Party)
GRU	*Glavnoye Razvedyvatelnoye Upravlenie* (Chief Intelligence Office)
ICBM	Intercontinental Ballistic Missile
INF	Intermediate-Range Nuclear Forces
IOC	International Olympic Committee
JCS	Joint Chiefs of Staff
KAL 007	Korean Airlines Flight 007
KGB	*Komitet Gosudarstvennoy Bezopasnosti* (Committee for State Security)
LSG	Legislative Strategy Group
MAD	Mutual Assured Destruction
MBFR	Mutual and Balanced Force Reductions
MFN	Most Favored Nation
MIRV	Multiple Independently Targetable Reentry Vehicle
MI6	Military Intelligence, Section 6 (British Secret Intelligence Service)
MX	LGM-118A Peacekeeper Missile (Missile Experimental)
NAACP	National Association for the Advancement of Colored People
NACIPG	Nuclear Arms Control Information Policy Group
NAE	National Association of Evangelicals
NATO	North Atlantic Treaty Organization
NBC	National Broadcasting Company
NORAD	North American Aerospace Defense Command
NSA	National Security Agency
NSC	National Security Council
NSDD	National Security Decision Directive
NSPG	National Security Planning Group
OMB	Office of Management and Budget
OPEC	Organization of Petroleum Exporting Countries
PAC	Political Action Committee
PD	Presidential Directive
PDPA	People's Democratic Party of Afghanistan
PFIAB	President's Foreign Intelligence Advisory Board
PRC	People's Republic of China
RDF	Rapid Deployment Force

RYAN	*Raketno-Yadernoe Napadenie* (Nuclear Missile Attack)
SACPG	Senior Arms Control Policy Group
SALT	Strategic Arms Limitation Talks (also Strategic Arms Limitation Treaty)
SANE	National Committee for a Sane Nuclear Policy
SCC	Special Coordinating Committee
SDI	Strategic Defense Initiative
SIOP	Single Integrated Operational Plan
SLCM	Sea-launched Cruise Missile
SPD	Social Democratic Party (Federal Republic of Germany)
START	Strategic Arms Reduction Talks (also Strategic Arms Reduction Treaty)
TASS	*Telegrafnoye Agentstvo Sovietskovo Soyuza* (Telegraphic Agency of the Soviet Union)
TNF	Theater Nuclear Forces
UK	United Kingdom
UN	United Nations
USSR	Union of Soviet Socialist Republics

Introduction

Never, perhaps, in the postwar decades was the situation in the world as explosive and hence, more difficult and unfavorable, as in the first half of the 1980s.[1]

    – Mikhail Gorbachev, February 25, 1986

"The main issue Kennedy is raising is leadership," Carter mused. "The weekend newspapers were unbelievable, practically anointing Kennedy as the president and claiming the 1980 election is already over." It was September 17, 1979, and "the Kennedy challenge" was on Carter's mind.[2] An ABC–Harris Poll showed the Massachusetts senator leading the president by 61–34 percent in the race for the Democratic nomination.[3] Carter's prospects were cast into further doubt on November 4, when sixty-six Americans were taken captive in Iran. At the suggestion of his secretary of state, Cyrus Vance, Carter forwent a holiday tradition. The great Christmas tree south of the White House was left unlit to signify sorrow for the hostages' plight. It seemed to cap a miserable year, which saw inflation and interest rates spiral amid a major oil crisis. Fuel shortages led to long queues at gas stations across America. Gallup polls in June and October gave the president an approval rating of 28 percent.[4] Christmas brought little festive cheer. On December 25, Carter learned of another foreign emergency: the Soviet 40th Army had crossed into Afghanistan. 'There goes SALT II!' he exclaimed.[5]

Carter was excoriated by the political right, who accused him of weakness and inaction. He had sought to reorient U.S. foreign policy: pledging to curtail defense spending, scale back military engagement, and reduce nuclear arms. He bemoaned the "inordinate fear of communism"

and exaggerations of the Soviet threat.[6] Such were the principles on which
Carter had campaigned as a Washington outsider. Now, one by one, these
were hastily dismantled. The Soviet invasion of Afghanistan, he said, was
"the most serious threat to world peace since the Second World War."[7]
A string of new hardline policies were adopted, many of them at odds with
the goals he previously espoused. Carter imposed a grain embargo against
the Soviet Union and ordered a U.S. withdrawal from the Moscow
Olympics. He promised to increase defense spending by 5 percent and
reinstated draft registration. He unveiled the "Carter Doctrine"—
extending the containment policy to the Persian Gulf and committing
U.S. forces to defend American interests in the region, if necessary by
military action. The U.S. ambassador to Moscow was recalled. A Rapid
Deployment Force was activated. Covert military aid was approved for
Afghan rebels and Pakistan. In July 1980, a year after signing the SALT II
Treaty, Carter issued PD-59—an aggressive strategy designed to give
U.S. presidents more flexibility in planning for and executing a nuclear
war.[8]

A new and more dangerous Cold War was in motion. This power
struggle would escalate into a confrontation so politically charged that
within three years U.S.–Soviet relations had reached their nadir. By then,
Ronald Reagan was embarking on the largest peacetime military buildup
in U.S. history, leading an administration with the most avowed anti-
communist agenda in at least two decades. A series of events in 1983 led to
the worst phase of the conflict in a generation. It was the year in which the
president denounced the Soviet Union as an "evil empire," having earlier
declared Marxism-Leninism destined for the "ash heap of history."
Reagan upped the military ante with Moscow by unveiling the Strategic
Defense Initiative—a proposal for a space-based missile defense system to
protect the United States from nuclear attack. In early September, Soviet
forces shot down a Korean airliner that had drifted into Russian airspace,
costing the lives of all 269 on board. Among the victims were sixty-two
Americans, including a member of Congress. In the following month,
U.S. forces invaded the Caribbean island of Grenada and ousted its pro-
Marxist government.

Worse was to follow. In early November, a NATO military exercise
spanning Western Europe was misinterpreted by Moscow as a possible
prelude to a U.S. nuclear strike. Soviet leaders prepared their forces for
a retaliatory attack. Oleg Gordievsky, the deputy KGB chief in London
(who doubled up as a spy for Britain's MI6), reported to Westminster and
Washington on the state of panic in the Kremlin.[9] Reagan was briefed by

his advisers on the Single Integrated Operational Plan (SIOP), which outlined the U.S. procedures to wage nuclear war. "It was," he recalled, "a scenario for a sequence of events that could lead to the end of civilization as we knew it."[10] Two weeks later, the first U.S. intermediate-range nuclear missiles were deployed in Western Europe; NATO's response to the Soviet SS-20 deployments. The Soviet Union withdrew from arms control talks. Reagan, like Carter, would enter election year amid an international crisis.

As the real 1984 loomed, journalists drew parallels with George Orwell's fictional world: a militarized culture, propaganda, and the specter of war. In the United States, bomb shelter sales were on the rise. The Federal Emergency Management Agency (FEMA) designed elaborate evacuation plans to help save communities from potential radiation sickness.[11] Doomsday scenarios were portrayed in print and film, illustrating the likely effects of nuclear catastrophe. Antinuclear activists took to the streets across America and Western Europe. Participants numbered in the hundreds of thousands, beseeching Reagan to halt the arms race. In the Soviet Union, signs indicating the location of air raid shelters were ubiquitous. Several times a day, Kremlin-approved broadcasts on the radio and television suggested the possibility of a U.S. nuclear attack.[12] Far from abating, the Cold War showed every sign of intensifying.

Yet abate it did. Like Carter, Reagan's foreign policy would be transformed during his fourth year in office. Within weeks of these events, Reagan used a televised address to announce a change in outlook. He depicted a fictional Ivan and Anya crossing paths with Jim and Sally, sheltering from a rainstorm and speaking in a common tongue. The theme was cooperation, not confrontation. "Together we can strengthen peace, reduce the level of arms," Reagan declared. "Let us begin now."[13] As 1984 progressed, Reagan—who had not met with a Soviet leader—pursued diplomatic exchanges and bilateral agreements as never before. In September, the president made his first direct contact with a top-ranking Soviet official (Foreign Minister Andrei Gromyko) during nearly four years in office. "For the sake of a peaceful world," Reagan said, "let us approach each other with ten-fold trust and thousand-fold affection."[14]

Few could have foreseen the events to follow. Within three years a major disarmament agreement was achieved. Two years further on, communist regimes in Eastern Europe collapsed, followed by the Berlin Wall. Decades of repressive rule were ended, families and friends were reunited. By the end of 1991 the USSR itself had ceased to exist. It was an astonishing transformation. The pace of change seemed to defy explanation. Even the protagonists were caught by surprise. "Did you ever expect this to happen?" a journalist asked Reagan, days after the Wall fell. Reagan shrugged. "Someday," he replied.[15]

How did the Cold War begin anew, and why did it escalate? Why did tensions start to recede? What led both presidents to adopt policies in their fourth year that were so at odds with the course they had earlier pursued, and on which they staked their reputation? These questions led me to examine the actions of American policymakers. I focus chiefly on what some historians call the "Second Cold War": the roughly six-year time frame between 1979 and 1985 which followed the era of détente.[16] This period witnessed the most serious challenges of the second half of the Cold War. The course of events was highly contingent (three Soviet leaders dying within three years), and it would not have taken an extraordinary stretch in circumstances to have produced a scenario in which U.S.–Soviet relations had deteriorated irretrievably, rendering a later breakthrough impossible. As fears of nuclear war were raised, so the domestic schisms deepened. The largest peacetime military buildup was challenged by the largest peacetime peace movement. The conflict began with the Soviet invasion of Afghanistan in late 1979. It concluded with the meeting of Reagan and Gorbachev in Geneva in late 1985—the first summit since Carter and Brezhnev had kissed cheeks in Vienna, six and a half years earlier.

THE DECLINE OF POLITICAL HISTORY

The end of the Cold War caught scholars by surprise. To explain the events, historians have assessed U.S.–Soviet relations at a state-to-state level, or within a wider global context.[17] More recently, the "transnational turn" has seen an emphasis on the role of non-state forces, such as human rights groups and peace movements. The prevailing argument today—though by no means a consensus—is that the Cold War ended because of the courageous efforts of citizens across Eastern Europe, and the reformist thinking of a new generation of Soviet leaders who took power in 1985. Led by Gorbachev, they saw that the arms race had placed an unsustainable burden on the Soviet economy, drained by the Afghan War and long-term structural problems. Reagan subsequently engaged, and their determination to reduce the nuclear threat was the catalyst for change.[18]

But what of the years *preceding* Gorbachev's arrival—one of the most fraught periods in East–West relations and the greater fraction of the late

Cold War? Studies on this era have been dwarfed by those on the Reagan–Gorbachev rapport. The trend is regrettable for several reasons. Firstly, the confrontation of the early 1980s offers important lessons for crisis management. U.S.–Soviet relations worsened to the point that a nuclear exchange appeared more likely than at any stage since the Cuban Missile Crisis. Why this did not materialize, and how tensions began to ease, are questions which warrant examination. The path which led to the events of 1986–89 was highly contingent. It was not preordained that the East–West crisis would be defused, or that war would be avoided. Secondly, the policy reversals of successive U.S. presidents merit far greater scrutiny. These symmetrical shifts had a huge bearing on the direction of the late Cold War, yet have rarely been explored. For most of Carter's presidency and most of Reagan's first term, both presidents pursued a course which seemed to reflect their convictions. Yet, in their fourth year in office, both adopted policies that bore little resemblance to what had gone before. Their turns—Carter to the right, Reagan to the center—helped lead to the rise and fall of the last great Cold War struggle. How and why they occurred are questions at the heart of this book. A third drawback has been the misconception that the change in U.S. policy and easing of tensions began only with the arrival of Gorbachev as Soviet leader. The "new thinking," combined with a greater readiness to reduce nuclear arms, led Reagan to believe that in Gorbachev the Soviets at last had someone with whom he could "do business." The conventional wisdom is that only then did Reagan reconsider his foreign policy approach.[19] It is demonstrated here that this was not so.

The lack of attention to these questions owes something to the decline of political history as a field of study.[20] The disorderly nature of politics is at odds with the academic ethos, which tends to reward neat, conceptual frameworks. (Hal Brands terms this "the elegance of theory versus the messiness of reality."[21]) In recent decades most historians have looked abroad to examine American foreign policy. Their work has focused on transnationalism, the role of non-state actors, and global interdependence.[22] The trend followed the rise of globalization. It breathed new life into the field, incentivizing scholars to pursue topical global issues. Many took the form of social or cultural studies at the expense of the political. The aim was to de-center the United States and engage with perspectives from around the world. To contend with a more interconnected, competitive academic market, younger historians were drawn toward research which could demonstrate transnational themes. A number of fine studies emerged, expanding our knowledge of how overseas actors influenced U.S. foreign policy.

But the "transnational turn" has come at a price. Lost in the discourse is the role of domestic politics. The result is a distorted portrayal of how decisions were reached. Presidents are cast less as politicians than global statesmen, whose rationale is based on strategic factors or an ideological hue. Only by examining the full landscape—international *and* domestic—can we truly grasp how the key figures operated: what influenced their risk calculus; why they chose certain policies and discarded others; or why they decided to change course at a given time. Long before Gorbachev's arrival, pressures closer to home presented constraints and incentives against which Carter and Reagan acted.

As Fredrik Logevall and Campbell Craig have argued, the trend toward internationalizing the study of American foreign relations is compounded by the fact that the United States, post-1945, was no ordinary actor. It was the sole superpower, with an unrivaled military, political, and economic reach. Studies which privilege the foreign over the domestic run the risk of becoming ahistorical, by ascribing greater importance to various overseas actors than they in fact warrant. Too much agency becomes assigned to the international sphere, without a corresponding examination of domestic forces, and the parameters they set for foreign policy. What is lost is the "intermestic" dimension of policy, where the international and domestic agendas become entwined.[23] If the Cold War ended largely because of events overseas, the fate of the six-year conflict which preceded it rested as much on how American decision-makers wielded power. Understanding why U.S. policy changed in 1980 and 1984, and with it the Cold War, is to understand that domestic variables—public opinion, election campaigns, congressional restraints, party politics, personal ambition—figured as much in their calculus as did proximate external factors.

The path of American foreign policy was not so linear as to follow global patterns. It was a more complex, messy process, subject to the push and pull of domestic pressures, prone to change for reasons distinct—though never independent—of international events. Foreign and defense issues frequently developed into partisan tug-of-wars: arms control; strategic defense; U.S.–Soviet relations; the Panama Canal treaties; intervention in Central America and Lebanon. In the post-Vietnam era, foreign affairs were matters of interest to an increasingly decentralized political constellation: Democratic and Republican Party hierarchies, members of Congress, interest groups, and labor unions, from the Committee on the Present Danger to the AFL-CIO. Added to this was the media and a public audience more attuned to events abroad than ever before. All presented pressures that shaped the context in which foreign policy was discussed.

For Carter and Reagan, success rested on their ability to master this international–domestic nexus. Managing the legislative demands, monitoring public opinion, and anticipating partisan challenges became as much a part of their thinking as did attitudes in the Kremlin.

None of which is to ignore the significance of external matters. It was precisely because of the purchase of globalization, and the expanding contours of U.S. policy, that domestic actors sought a more active engagement in foreign affairs. One example was human rights, where a complex of liberal and conservative humanitarian issues animated different constituencies.[24] Foreign policy decisions seldom have monocausal roots. This book by no means suggests that every position taken by Carter and Reagan was driven by partisan wrangling, electioneering, or personal ambition. Rather, it integrates discussion of domestic politics into an interpretative framework which also gives attention to geostrategy and ideology in explaining the course of the conflict.[25] Both presidents had profound ideas about how American power should be projected overseas. Both were strongly antinuclear, and targeted arms control agreements with Moscow using particular strategies. Some policies were the result of mainly external factors (Reagan's support for the Polish Solidarity movement, for example). But all major initiatives were taken only after the choices had been carefully measured against the consequences back home. Even the most strategic and ideological decisions, such as SDI or aid to the Contras ("Reagan's obsession"), were bound up with party politics, public opinion, and other domestic considerations. Not least the role of Congress, characterized by Reagan as a meddlesome "committee of 535."[26]

THE POLITICS OF FOREIGN POLICY

The notion that foreign policy is always a matter of domestic politics would be a truism for many nations.[27] In the United States, the foreign–domestic nexus is axiomatic. Nowhere among major Western democracies is a political system so decentralized, where national security or foreign trade impacts upon congressional districts across the country. Representatives and senators, career politicians, cater to the interest of their constituents as it pertains to foreign policy (e.g., an economic group, ethnic lobby, or industry), often with little regard for events overseas.[28] During the Cold War, regions dependent on military bases or weapons industries were typically prone to exploitation. But the openness of the U.S. system could also work in reverse. It ensured, for example, that the grassroots, antinuclear movement in Reagan's first term found easy access to political elites, with a freeze resolution adopted by the House in 1983.[29] Moreover, there are few (if any) nations in which the election cycle affects the foreign policy outlook of decision-makers as much as it does in the United States, where the campaigning never stops. Nor does any comparable nation have an executive branch whose external policies operate against such legislative oversight. Watchful units such as the Senate's Foreign Relations, Intelligence, and Armed Services committees are entrusted with vital tasks: blocking or passing treaties; monitoring aid and arms sales; authorizing foreign intervention and declaring war.[30]

A glance at America's Cold War should dispel any doubt about the weight of politics on the course of events. The two presidents who used tape recorders for the majority of their terms, Lyndon Johnson and Richard Nixon, revealed personal ambition, candid thinking, and a preoccupation with the domestic implications of foreign affairs.[31] Candidates, presidential and congressional, wrestled with the temptation to play politics with policy. With the Truman Doctrine of 1947, the East–West dichotomy was fertile ground for politicians looking to prove their anti-communist bona fides. Even during the "bipartisan age" of Senator Arthur Vandenberg, partisan wrangling shaped the treatment of foreign issues; politics never stopped at the "water's edge."[32]

The stances which proved risk averse with votes at stake were those which denounced communism, talked up the Soviet threat, or called for a greater military arsenal. In election season there were few drawbacks to creating alarmist impressions or labeling opponents weak. John F. Kennedy made the Republican handling of foreign policy the focal point of his campaign against Nixon in 1960. He charged the Eisenhower–Nixon administration with presiding over a decline in U.S. military power, and for allowing a "missile gap" to develop, with the Soviets "outproducing" America in nuclear weapons. "Never before have we experienced such arrogant treatment at the hands of our enemies," Kennedy declared, attacking Nixon's vice presidential leadership as one of "weakness, retreat, and defeat."[33]

America's costliest wars were among those issues most susceptible to political maneuvering. The Korean War, which stalemated as the battle lines held, coincided with the 1952 presidential campaign. Harry Truman, who faced criticism for not doing more to combat anti-communism at home, was under pressure to avoid appearing "soft" on Soviet expansionism. As election season neared, Republicans attacked the administration's military and diplomatic strategies, as well as the credentials of Democratic candidate Adlai Stevenson. Talk of negotiating an armistice was criticized as weakness and appeasement. Republicans called for a "rollback" of communism to replace the more cautious policy of containment. Dwight Eisenhower, the party candidate, claimed that Democrats were willing "to barter away freedom in order to appease the Russian rulers."[34] Democrats were blamed for the loss of China, for the Soviet atomic buildup, and for allowing the Communists time to regroup their forces in Korea. The weight of criticism led the Truman administration to conclude that the safer political option would be to "hang tough" in Korea, rather than compromise.[35]

The scope of America's commitment in Vietnam also became contingent on how decision-makers grappled with priorities at home. As the war effort foundered, successive presidents (Johnson and Nixon) contemplated how military realities would impact their electoral prospects. Johnson's decision to increase the U.S. role in 1964 owed much to his obsession with winning the election in November of that year. The subsequent "Americanization" of the war stemmed from concern that the administration's political credibility (and Johnson's personal credibility) would be irreparably damaged if the United States failed to sustain the military effort.[36] Nixon, as tape recordings reveal, sought to withhold an earlier exit from Vietnam in order to extract maximum benefit for the 1972 election. Between January and November his administration gradually modified its negotiating position. Troop withdrawals took place periodically, timed to remind the war-weary public that U.S. involvement was winding down, and to stifle criticism from Democrats. But a final settlement was delayed, so that any problems which resulted would occur too late to affect the election.[37] "Winning an election is terribly important," Nixon told Henry Kissinger, in August 1972. The national security adviser agreed. "We've got to find some formula that holds the thing together a year or two," he replied. "After a year, Mr. President, Vietnam will be a backwater. If we settle it this October, by January 1974 no one will give a damn."[38]

It was during the 1970s that the relationship between the executive and legislative was transformed. This was the symptom of a trauma. Conduct of the war in Vietnam, together with Watergate, produced a crisis of confidence in the government among Congress and the public. It ushered in legislative acts designed to restrict the executive's room for maneuver, ending the notion of an "imperial presidency." These changes had major consequences for foreign policy. The War Powers Act set limits on the ability of the president to send American armed forces into combat areas without congressional approval. The amendment to the Trade Reform Act made U.S. trade with other nations conditional on the right of citizens to free movement. Pressure from Congress to link foreign policy to human rights resulted in the formation of a bureau of human rights within the State Department.

The measures promised to bring accountability to the policymaking process. But other consequences emerged. With a more assertive Congress (and the proliferation of subcommittees), special interest groups began wielding greater power in domestic and foreign affairs. Senators and representatives capitalized on the new political landscape, often for their personal concerns. The number of moderates in both parties diminished. Harvard professor Samuel Beer described the trend as "a new and destructive pluralism," which disorganized public policy and set group against group.[39] Ideological schisms widened between liberals and conservatives. The Democratic Party was itself divided between the "neoconservative" wing that favored a large military buildup, and those of a liberal persuasion who advocated diplomacy, détente, and a freeze on nuclear weapons. As liberals campaigned for the reorientation of U.S. power, conservatives perceived a crisis, in which Soviet expansion was being met with retreat and submissiveness. By 1976, groups such as the Committee on the Present Danger were on the rise. They cast détente as weakness and appeasement that was "doomed to failure."[40] Notions of Soviet military supremacy were peddled, external threats were inflated, and American strength was consciously downplayed. Norman Podhoretz, the editor of *Commentary*, charged liberals with being so traumatized by Vietnam that they had turned into "isolationists." He decried the limits on presidential authority, which "damaged the main institutional capability for conducting an overt fight against the spread of Communist power."[41]

Carter's promise of U.S. military restraint met with a firm response. Interest groups mobilized to frustrate reform and campaign for new defense programs, anxious to protect long-existing policies and the military-industrial complex. To conservatives in both parties, Carter's pursuit of a SALT treaty with Moscow symbolized the way in which policymakers had throttled back power. Their lament would become the platform on which Reagan launched his presidential campaign. By 1980, many neoconservatives were switching party allegiance, with their convictions more aligned with the Republican candidate. Paul Nitze, Jeane Kirkpatrick, Eugene Rostow, Richard Pipes, and Elliott Abrams would all defect to hold key roles in the Reagan administration. As Carter took office, the distinction between politics and policy had already become blurred. It was against this backdrop that he and Reagan operated.

RISK, CREDIBILITY, AND TIMING

The "intermestic" concept was born in this era. Bayless Manning, the first president of the Council on Foreign Relations, was writing for *Foreign Affairs* in January 1977—just as Carter strode into the White House. He noted the decline in presidential prestige which made it easier for Congress to stymie the executive on certain matters. Special interests exerted increasing influence on foreign policy by applying pressure on their representatives. Manning stressed the growing interdependence between national economies, a trend which had more far-reaching effects than older examples such as tariffs. The Arab oil embargo of 1973 showed how quickly international events struck into the political and economic heart of domestic constituencies. U.S. industries, manufacturers, and farmers were immediately subject to any disruption of a supply of a commodity from overseas. "These new issues are simultaneously, profoundly, and inseparably both domestic and international," Manning argued. "These issues are intermestic."[42]

How did domestic politics shape U.S. policy in the late Cold War? Three interrelated themes—risk, credibility, and timing—pervade the narrative. The first is the way in which political pressures shaped risk perception. From the time they entered the Oval Office, Carter and Reagan were forced to weigh the domestic costs of their international agenda. Almost every issue with which they grappled became a tempestuous political struggle, from arms control and détente to Central America and strategic defense. Congressional powers, public opinion, and electoral considerations all weighed heavily, imposing restraints or incentives that would help shape the U.S. position.

Carter had to placate critics of the SALT I agreement, notably Henry Jackson, who had the potential to mobilize discontented, conservative Democrats and independents against a second SALT agreement, as well as Carter's bid for a second term. Carter began courting Jackson and acting on his advice in 1977 as he pursued negotiations with the Soviets. Reagan, too, acted on political considerations. He recognized the growing power of the nuclear freeze movement and the dangers it posed to his national security policies, particularly his buildup of military strength. The timing of his proposal for a Strategic Defense Initiative (Chapter 6) had everything to do with public opinion and the burgeoning strength of the freeze campaign. Reagan accepted the conclusions of the Scowcroft Commission in order to salvage support for his strategic program, promising to implement a more flexible approach to arms control, known as "build-down." As the presidents moved toward their fourth year the political stakes grew higher. Both administrations became as preoccupied about how their foreign policies would be perceived by *domestic* audiences as by Moscow: rival candidates, influential senators, the media, and the broad public. Identifying public attitudes, anticipating partisan challenges, and devising ways to reduce vulnerability became priorities.

For Carter, viewing the invasion of Afghanistan as a symptom of Soviet behavior, rather than an aberration or a defensive maneuver, was the risk-averse decision. Wider forces such as Afghan nationalism, radical Islam, and Soviet security interests were willfully downplayed. Instead, the key decision-makers saw Moscow's actions through the prism of the Cold War, as part of a "grand design" for global expansion. To have suggested otherwise would have exposed the president to further charges of softness and naivety. The consequences were profound. Carter's approval of a string of hardline countermeasures spanned the first half of 1980, ensuring that every facet of bilateral relations—economic, cultural, diplomatic, and military—became predicated on the Soviet presence in Afghanistan. With the closure of all political avenues, the structure upholding détente was firmly dismantled. Carter's new containment approach revived memories of the Truman and Eisenhower doctrines of the early Cold War. Soviet leaders, who made their fateful decision against the advice of diplomats and the military, were taken aback by the U.S. response.

For American presidents the risks are magnified in election season, which lends an urgency to the craft of foreign policy. It is not a coincidence that shifts often take place in the final year to eighteen months of a president's first term. One need not go back to Johnson and Nixon, or Carter and Reagan, for evidence. As Clinton's late intervention in the Balkans in 1995, and Bush's adjustments in Iraq in 2004 demonstrate, geostrategy is not the only rationale. "Anticipating that a bid for reelection will become a referendum on his record, an incumbent president has strong incentives to burnish his legacy by introducing course correctives that appear timely," notes author Michael Armacost.[43] By late 1983, Reagan's record in foreign affairs was anything but impressive. Three years of rearmament, sanctions, and tough rhetoric had failed to induce any positive change in Soviet policy. Bilateral relations were in disarray. For the first time in fifteen years strategic arms talks were off the agenda, increasing public fears about a nuclear war—the single greatest threat to Reagan's reelection. As 1983 progressed, Reagan's pragmatic advisers (Shultz, Baker, Matlock, and McFarlane) called for a more flexible approach with the Soviet Union. Terms such as "credibility," "timing," and "building a record" would increasingly seep through policy papers. "We must stress in public your call for dialogue and your desire to reduce tensions and solve problems," McFarlane warned Reagan in early 1984. "Tangible progress and a summit that produced positive results could be helpful if the Soviets decide to bite the bullet and adjust their policies sufficiently. But if they continue to resist negotiation, you must be in a position by late summer to make it clear that this was their fault, not yours."[44]

*

The second theme is credibility, which applied domestically and personally as much as internationally.[45] How to reconcile policy overseas with the quest for support at home became a prime consideration. Whereas political challengers are generally not judged on their foreign policy credentials, the records of first-term presidents are heavily scrutinized. Carter and Reagan grasped the importance of overseas accomplishments to bolster their credibility as commander-in-chief. Both understood that initiatives had to be adapted according to the domestic mood (e.g., Reagan's decision to withdraw U.S. forces from Lebanon in early 1984). In election year, more attention is devoted to the appeal of foreign policy positions at home rather than their efficacy abroad.[46]

In 1980, the need to demonstrate strength became the common denominator of almost every initiative taken by Carter and his national security adviser, Zbigniew Brzezinski. Within hours of the Soviet march into Afghanistan, Brzezinski warned Carter: "Our handling of Soviet affairs will be attacked by both the right and left [...] Soviet 'decisiveness' will be contrasted with our restraint, which will no longer be labeled as prudent but increasingly as timid."[47] The invasion, following the Iran hostage crisis, made it easy for Republicans to link the two events as examples of U.S. weakness. Reagan cited the Soviet action as proof that Carter's approach had been flawed all along. To outflank the political right, Carter would stake his credibility on a hawkish, alarmist response: authorizing new weapons systems, isolating the USSR diplomatically, and exaggerating the threat to national security. The credibility factor thwarted even the most tentative efforts to revive a dialogue with Moscow. When Vance proposed reopening talks with the Soviets in late February, Brzezinski

warned Carter of the "devastating political consequences" of being identified with the "soft side." "A further initiative could have the most fateful
domestic and international consequences [...] I shudder to think of the
impact this could have in Congress and in the mass media, and how it
would be used by our political opponents."[48]

The scale of Carter's opposition traversed party lines, making the
administration even more wary of its approach. Carter's pursuit of
SALT II was labeled "appeasement" by conservative Democrats such as
Jackson.[49] His overseas achievements—the Arab–Israeli accords; the
Panama Canal treaties; and the normalization of relations with China—
had reaped few political dividends at home. The external problems of Iran
and Afghanistan were joining long-existing internal ones: inflation,
unemployment, and a poor intraparty relationship. It left the president
exposed to attack from his Democratic rival, Sen. Ted Kennedy, who prior
to the hostage crisis led by thirty points in opinion polls.[50] The Afghan
crisis became a test of Carter's credibility on national security, a chance to
demonstrate decisiveness and blunt charges of weakness. "It represented
an opportunity for [Carter] to demonstrate his genuine toughness,"
recalled Brzezinski, whose own outlook was animated by strategy and
anti-communism as much as political expediency.[51] Brzezinski drew
Carter's attention to some dubious historical analogies, comparing the
power vacuum in the Persian Gulf to that of Europe in the late 1940s.[52]
The Soviets, he claimed, were capitalizing on an "arc of crisis," with
a strategic thrust toward the oil-rich Middle East and warm-water ports
of the Indian Ocean.[53] What emerged was a hasty, skewed analysis of the
Soviet motives for the invasion.[54]

Reagan was in a comparatively healthy position as he entered the final
stage of his first term. A glance at the 1984 election might tempt the
skeptical reader to conclude that domestic politics could have had little
to do with foreign policy adjustments. But that is to confuse cause and
effect. As Logevall notes, "what matters most is what candidates *think*
the importance of foreign policy in a given election will be or could be,
rather than what ex post facto analysis shows it to have been."[55] As
East–West relations sank to their lowest point, Reagan's handling of
foreign affairs—particularly nuclear arms talks—became the main area
of concern for his reelection campaign.

Public protests against U.S. policy had mushroomed from 1981, notably through a nuclear freeze movement. Congressional resistance duly
followed. Successive Boland amendments curbed U.S. efforts to assist the
Contras in Nicaragua; a nuclear freeze resolution was passed in the House

of Representatives; and to win support for his strategic defense program, Reagan accepted the recommendations of the bipartisan Scowcroft Commission. Democrats portrayed Reagan as the first president since Hoover who had not met with a Soviet leader, citing his opposition to arms control agreements reached by Kennedy, Johnson, Nixon, Ford, and Carter.[56] A poll in March 1983 gave Reagan a negative rating on his handling of nuclear arms talks by 64 to 29 percent.[57] Six months later, pollster Richard Wirthlin warned Reagan's chief of staff, James Baker, that "the handling of foreign policy and the fear of a possible unwanted war underlie public apprehension toward his reelection." The "sharpest issue" was opposition to the arms race.[58] The campaign plan of October 1983 (led by Baker and Wirthlin) made it clear where the accent for 1984 would be placed. "We must strongly position the President on the 'peace' side of the 'peace through strength' formula," they counseled. "We need to launch some foreign policy initiatives that dramatically symbolize 'peace'."[59]

The Cold War paradigm was inverted. In 1980 Reagan and Carter had sought to project military strength. Four years on, with public concern over nuclear war (and new defense programs in place), peace and diplomacy became the central themes. What Reagan sought was "a full, credible agenda on arms control," with "more flexible" positions on START and INF. He told policymakers to "build a record" of agreements with the Soviets, from MBFR and chemical weapons to missile tests and CDE, as well as a host of nonmilitary issues.[60] By mid-1984, Reagan was reversing most of the sanctions imposed by Carter in 1980, announcing sixteen initiatives under discussion with Moscow.[61] He invited Foreign Minister Andrei Gromyko to Washington for a White House meeting—instituting yet another change in U.S. policy. By early 1985 the arms talks had resumed. A thaw had developed in U.S.–Soviet relations, in which the sense of fear, paranoia, and distrust were eased. Orwellian scenarios did not come to pass.

*

The final theme is timing. Domestic politics intruded into foreign policy from the start of the Carter and Reagan presidencies, and became more prominent as their terms progressed. Both administrations calibrated policy: Carter and Brzezinski gradually forged a "middle ground" position, which was in place by 1979 (Chapter 2); Reagan and Shultz began reviewing the U.S. approach toward the Soviet Union during 1983 (Chapter 7). But the key policy changes were implemented at the same stage of their terms—in the first few months of their fourth year. The Reagan reversal was more modest, with the president able to effect his course corrective without conceding major ground on substantive issues. For Carter, whose political position was weaker, it marked a full-fledged turnaround from the course earlier pursued.

From the outset, Carter sought a new arms control agreement with Moscow. Soviet misbehavior prior to 1980—human rights abuses, adventurism in the Third World, the deployment of SS-20 missiles—did not dissuade him from pursuing this goal. He rejected criticism from conservatives who denounced his belief in détente and the SALT process. Only after the Soviet invasion rendered treaty ratification impossible, with domestic charges intensifying and electoral incentives at stake, did the administration change tack. It did so within days, and in a manner which obscured rational analysis of Soviet motives. The litany of punitive measures, defense procurements, and tough rhetoric which followed bore no resemblance to the principles outlined by Carter at Notre Dame in 1977. It culminated in the unveiling of PD-59, a targeting policy which flirted with the idea of "winning" a nuclear war.[62]

The Reagan administration resisted criticism during its first two years. The calls for a nuclear freeze and a more flexible negotiating position did not significantly alter U.S. policy. Only with domestic priorities at stake did the administration begin to effect changes. In 1983 Reagan became more wary of the political context, as his bid for a second term neared. He grew receptive to the idea of modifying the U.S. approach to arms control, opted for a restrained reaction to the KAL disaster, and displayed a newfound aversion to publicly attacking the Soviets. Reagan's own moderate instincts were gradually brought to bear. He began placing trust in pragmatists instead of hardliners. Secretary of State George Shultz was elevated to the top of the policymaking process, developing a framework to improve bilateral relations. Jack Matlock became NSC adviser on Soviet affairs in place of the hawkish Richard Pipes. And Robert McFarlane (rather than Jeane Kirkpatrick) succeeded William Clark as national security adviser. A different outlook became apparent before the *Able Archer* crisis—though it would not be developed or publicly articulated until 1984.

To be sure, there was more to this calibration than political maneuvering. Reagan became genuinely worried by the state of U.S.–Soviet relations. He was appalled by the military plans drawn up by the Pentagon, which toyed with the notion of waging "protracted" nuclear war.[63] The official policy rationale was tied to the military balance—that Moscow would not negotiate seriously until after the U.S. arms buildup. But by late 1983 the Soviets were not negotiating *at all*. With an election looming, Reagan was not waiting for the desired effect. In January 1984, he conveyed a new path for U.S.–Soviet relations in a major televised address. Despite objections from the hawks (such as Defense Secretary Caspar Weinberger), Reagan followed his pragmatic instincts. He sided with those who voiced support for a moderate, flexible approach, to "make moves that will demonstrate our interest in arms control, without prejudicing our substantive positions and without asking the Soviets to eat crow."[64]

NSDD-75 has been hailed by some as a "grand strategy" that wrought the collapse of the USSR. Scripted in January 1983, it stated that the administration was ready for improved relations "if the Soviet Union makes significant changes in policies of concern to it; the burden for any further deterioration in relations must fall squarely on Moscow." The United States, it warned, "must not yield to pressures to 'take the first step'."[65] Yet that is precisely what occurred in 1984. U.S. policy *did* move first, and it did so without any change in Soviet actions. The Reagan "turn" followed a long period of Soviet intransigence: the war in Afghanistan, human rights abuses, the attack on the Korean airliner, walkouts from arms talks, and violations of existing arms agreements. Reagan and Shultz had re-written the script. As author Louis Sell notes, NSDD-75 was "a dead letter" by 1985. "The United States had moved on in its relationship with the USSR."[66]

To explain the actions of American decision-makers is to consider a wide range of influences, external and internal. But they do not all carry the same force. The role of domestic politics ranks near the top of the causal hierarchy. Carter and Reagan made decisions on international issues based on political considerations throughout their presidencies. Both were pragmatic, subordinating ideology and principles when needed. Neither had the luxury of pursuing a consistent strategy, even had they wanted to. Foreign policy was always subject to the cut and thrust of domestic pressures. Congressional restraints; partisan politics; public opinion; interest group power; election campaigns; rival candidates; personal ambition: all were factors that helped lead both presidents to change course. As they began their fourth year, Carter and Reagan were pursuing very different approaches to the Soviet Union from those earlier proclaimed. What emerged was the rise and fall of the Second Cold War.

I

The Dwindling of Détente

"Going from total anonymity to being president of the United States in less than twelve months is unprecedented," recalled Carter's pollster Pat Caddell. "If it weren't for the country looking for something in 1976, Carter could never have gotten elected. He would never have been allowed out of the box. No one would have paid attention to him."[1] Caddell was not being flattering, but it is true that Jimmy Carter's ascent owed much to timing. Disenchantment with the Washington establishment was rife. Mishandling of the Vietnam War, rising unemployment, poverty, inflation, and Watergate all fostered distrust in the political elite.

Carter was assuredly not part of this category. Raised during the Great Depression in Plains, Georgia, his rise to power was a testament to hard graft. He graduated from the U.S. Naval Academy at Annapolis in 1946 and spent the next seven years in the navy, working as an engineer on the nuclear submarine program. When his father died of cancer in 1953, Carter returned to Plains to work on the family-owned peanut farm. Thereafter, he decided to enter politics. Carter served in the Georgia senate during the 1960s, before a successful run for governor in 1970. A tireless campaigner for civil rights, he built a record of social reforms through the legislature, irking officials by resisting attempts at compromise and coalition building.[2] Carter's message was grounded in his born-again Christian beliefs, and values such as honesty, integrity, and compassion. He was free of the lies and corruption that had sullied the reputation of those in government. In late 1972, when Nixon had coasted to reelection, Carter's adviser Hamilton Jordan urged him to look toward the top political prize. "Perhaps the strongest feeling in this country today is the general distrust of government and politicians at all levels," Jordan explained. "The desire and thrust for strong moral leadership was not satisfied with the election of Richard Nixon."[3]

The Watergate scandal forced Nixon's resignation in August 1974. With the support of a tightly knit group of advisers (dubbed the "Peanut Brigade"), Carter embarked on an unlikely bid for the presidency. He cultivated the role of outsider, campaigning without major sponsors and sleeping in the homes of volunteers. After Ted Kennedy declined to enter the 1976 race, Carter seized his moment to win the Democratic nomination. Promising to push through reform and restore trust in government, he received 40.2 percent of the primary vote, defeating California governor Jerry Brown and veterans such as Frank Church, Henry Jackson, and George Wallace.

Carter leaned heavily on moral principles in the presidential campaign. He used his obscurity to rail against the Watergate and CIA scandals, and spoke of his sincerity and faith. "I'll never tell a lie," he promised, in a television advert.[4] Carter's prospects were boosted by the problems besetting Gerald Ford. The Republican Party began distancing itself from the administration's foreign policies—particularly détente. Ronald Reagan (Ford's rival for the nomination) criticized the president for conceding too much ground in arms talks. Ford stopped using the term "détente" from March 1976 and began to harden his national security approach. But although he edged Reagan to win the party nomination, Ford's foreign policy remained a liability. The crowd jeered at Secretary of State Henry Kissinger when he appeared in the presidential box at the Republican national convention in Kansas City. Carter joined in the criticism. He rebuked Kissinger "for giving up too much and asking for too little" in negotiations with Moscow and promised to achieve deeper cuts in arms control—positions designed to appeal to the hawkish wing in his own party.[5]

But Carter's foreign policy agenda traversed both sides of the spectrum. He sought to placate liberals by targeting a defense budget cut of at least $5 billion and promising to reduce military commitments overseas. Invoking Wilsonian language and a sense of mission, he spoke of the need for a moral compass to guide America's outlook. Carter began to grasp the political utility of foreign affairs. By aligning a values-based platform with a vision for human rights abroad, he could attack the Ford administration for its support of dictatorial regimes (a grievance of liberals), while applying pressure on the Soviets to undertake internal reform (a stance favored by conservatives). Here was a strategy that appealed to both sides of the Democratic Party and a wider political audience. "It was seen politically as a no-lose issue," recalled Carter's speechwriter, Patrick Anderson. "Liberals liked human rights because it involved political freedom and getting liberals out of jail in dictatorships. Conservatives liked it because it involved criticisms of Russia."[6]

Though it would emerge as the centerpiece of his presidential (and postpresidential) legacy, Carter was a latecomer to global human rights.[7] He opposed the Helsinki Accords in 1975, excoriating the Final Act for facilitating "the Russian takeover of Europe."[8] Neither in his campaign memoir *Why Not the Best?* nor prior to the Democratic National Convention of July 1976 did Carter address the subject. Only in the final two months of the campaign did he champion the cause.[9] In the second presidential debate, Ford asserted that "there is no Soviet domination of Eastern Europe"—a blunder that allowed Carter to present himself as the candidate best equipped to confront the communist threat.[10] The promise of a humanitarian vision helped nudge Carter to victory: 50.1 percent of the popular vote and 297 electoral votes to Ford's 240. "Human rights was an issue with which you could bracket Kissinger and Ford on both sides," wrote Elizabeth Drew in the *New Yorker*. "It was a beautiful campaign issue, on which there was a real degree of public opinion hostile to the administration."[11] But addressing human rights on the global stage was a more complex task—one that would undermine Carter's efforts to reach agreements with Moscow.

THE BACKGROUND

Carter arrived in the White House against a background of worsening U.S.–Soviet relations. The Yom Kippur War of 1973 saw both powers back opposing sides in a Third World conflict, marking the most serious clash between Washington and Moscow since the Cuban Missile Crisis. Soviet military incursions into Africa and Southeast Asia were on the rise. And talks over a successor agreement to SALT I (on which so much of the relationship rested) had stalled as a powerful anti-détente faction mobilized on Capitol Hill.

The foundations for the Strategic Arms Limitation Talks (SALT) were laid during the 1960s. Fears evoked by the Cuban Missile Crisis and the Soviet nuclear arsenal prompted demands for arms control negotiations. The signing of the Test Ban Treaty (1963) provided the impetus for a summit between Lyndon Johnson and Alexei Kosygin in 1967. But the "spirit of Glassboro" was punctured by the Soviet invasion of Czechoslovakia a year later. The task of securing an arms control agreement was passed to Nixon and Kissinger, who sought to transform the relationship through a policy of détente. They established a secret backchannel of communications with the Soviet leadership (via Ambassador Anatoly Dobrynin), bypassing the State Department in the process. The primary goals remained the same: checking Soviet expansion and limiting Moscow's arms buildup. But Kissinger hoped to achieve this through diplomacy and mutual concessions, taking the ideological sting out of bilateral relations.[12]

The Nixinger approach was known as "linkage." They aimed to build a structure of relations in which the Soviets—should they cooperate on certain issues (e.g., strategic arms, regional problems)—would be offered economic rewards in return.[13] One aim was to secure Soviet assistance in confronting crises in the Third World. A second goal was to engage Moscow in economic ties that would make it difficult for Soviet leaders to adopt policies detrimental to Western interests.[14] It would also open new markets for American industries, manufacturers, and farmers. Having made the opening to China, the prospect of securing deals on arms control and trade were used as "a device to maximise Soviet dilemmas and reduce Soviet influence."[15] Although Kissinger invoked the "morality" of détente, his strategy did not apply to Soviet domestic affairs. The Nixon administration would come under attack for downplaying human rights violations in the USSR. For their part, Soviet leaders had a vested interest in securing agreements. General Secretary Leonid Brezhnev was anxious to boost the struggling Soviet economy, drained by years of disproportionate military spending. Support for détente in the Kremlin reflected an expectation that a U.S.–Soviet deal would reopen access to Western markets.[16]

The Moscow summit in May 1972 saw Nixon and Brezhnev finalize the Anti-Ballistic Missile (ABM) and SALT I treaties. The former restricted both sides to building two ABM fields of a hundred missiles each. Under the SALT I Treaty (which would last for five years), Washington and Moscow agreed to freeze the number of strategic weapons on each side.[17] But SALT I was not without problems. The treaty did not limit MIRVs (missiles with several warheads, capable of hitting multiple and dispersed targets), in which the United States held a 2:1 advantage. This negated the Soviet superiority in ICBMs, for a single U.S. submarine equipped with MIRVs could inflict 160 blasts on the scale of the Hiroshima bomb.[18] It was not long before the Soviets began testing their own MIRVs. The treaty also failed to control the Soviet deployment of new "heavy missiles" such as the SS-19 (the United States duly sought to develop the MX program). Although SALT I marked a new chapter in U.S.–Soviet relations, it did little to halt the arms race. In 1972, these problems mattered less to Brezhnev, eager to secure a deal, and to Nixon, focused on his reelection. Indeed, the Moscow summit had been carefully timed. In the words of Nixon's speechwriter William Safire: "Close enough to the 1972 election campaign to be effective, far enough away not to be blatantly political."[19]

Brezhnev and Nixon reveled in the agreement. In pursuing détente first with Western Europe and then the United States, the Soviet leader shored up his domestic support. The Kremlin used new economic and technological agreements as a way of circumventing the need for domestic reform.[20] Nixon's political stock also rose. His public approval rating soared to 61 percent after the successful visit to Moscow (the first ever by a U.S. president). Two foreign policy initiatives—détente with the Soviets, and the winding down of the Vietnam War—became the centerpieces of his bid for a second term.

The Moscow summit marked the high point of détente and, perhaps, the leaderships of Brezhnev and Nixon. The rapprochement declined amid U.S.–Soviet confrontation in the Yom Kippur War and over parts of Africa. But the role of domestic politics was also pivotal. The Vietnam War had shattered the Cold War consensus and provoked major questions about the conduct of foreign policy. Just how severe was the level of the communist threat? Was there political utility in applying military force overseas? If so, in what circumstances should it be used? The answers became sources of partisan and intraparty disagreement. Détente was subject to a barrage of criticism from Republicans and neoconservatives.

The neoconservatives emerged in the late 1960s when the liberal movement began to split. Conservative Democrats grew dismayed by radical politics (which followed protests over civil rights and Vietnam) and the failure of social reforms, believing the party had veered too far to the left. Foreign policy was a particular grievance. As liberals called for an end to the focus on anti-communism, neoconservatives warned of a Soviet arms buildup and expansion in the Third World. They urged U.S. policymakers to project military strength, denouncing SALT as "weakness" and "appeasement." Public intellectuals such as Norman Podhoretz, Nathan Glazer, and Irving Kristol took to the pages of *Commentary* to promote their views. They were joined by politicians such as Sen. Henry Jackson (D-Washington), who compared Soviet foreign policy to a burglar who walked down hotel corridors trying every lock.[21] In 1972, Jackson formed the Coalition for a Democratic Majority (CDM), a group of neoconservative politicians, bureaucrats, and intellectuals who campaigned for new military programs and a tougher stance against Moscow. While the "neocons" retained liberal views on many domestic issues, their views on foreign affairs closely aligned with Republicans. They criticized détente, warned of Soviet advances, and rejected the idea of negotiating verifiable arms agreements.[22]

On Capitol Hill the hawks were ahead of the game. With Nixon defenestrated, neoconservatives worked with Republicans to unravel his East–West policies. The anti-détente coalition grew as the imperial presidency gave way to a more assertive Congress. The War Powers Act (1973) was followed by the Jackson–Vanik amendment to the Trade Reform Act, which imposed conditions on the recent U.S.–Soviet trade agreement. The Soviet Union was required to relax its policies on Jewish emigration and guarantee the right of citizens to free movement in order to receive normal trade relations. Though Jackson championed human rights, his motives were as much political as ideological. Defeated in the Democratic primaries in 1972, he had identified Jewish voters as a key constituency in his bid for the 1976 presidential nomination. The connecting of U.S.–Soviet trade to the fate of Soviet Jews was a political winner for Jackson whatever the outcome. If the Kremlin acceded, the Jews would have their freedom. If they balked, détente would be further dented.[23]

The Jackson–Vanik bill was signed into law within weeks of the Ford–Brezhnev agreement at Vladivostok (November 1974), which set new (but moderate) limits on nuclear arms and a framework for SALT II. The Kremlin resented the anti-détente maneuvering, having sought new trade deals to ease their economic problems. For Soviet leaders, acceptance of the terms would mean acquiescing to U.S. interference in its internal affairs. "Perhaps no single question did more to sour the atmosphere of détente than the question of Jewish emigration from the Soviet Union," Dobrynin recalled.[24] U.S. credits to Moscow were limited to just $300 million over four years, while credits for developing oil and gas pipelines were prohibited—forcing the Soviets to turn to Western Europe. Soviet leaders responded by curtailing the number of Jews permitted to leave the USSR. They abandoned the pursuit of MFN status and stalled on repayments of the Lend–Lease debt, none of which helped the Ford–Kissinger efforts to engage with Moscow. "Jackson was about to launch his presidential campaign and was playing politics to the hilt," Ford complained. "He behaved like a swine."[25]

By 1976, "détente" had become a dirty word in conservative circles. The new legislative powers emboldened politicians to seize on foreign affairs, as the rise of special interest groups deepened the ideological wedge between the left and the right. As Ford and Kissinger had discovered, this complicated life for decision-makers. Within days of Carter's election, the Committee on the Present Danger (CPD) was formed—a coalition of Republicans, neoconservatives, and Democratic hawks with a similar foreign policy view. Carter would be as much a target of their criticism as Ford and Nixon before him.

CARTER: FORMING AN ADMINISTRATION

Aged 52, Carter entered office conscious of his inexperience in foreign affairs. His campaign pronouncements had seen contradictions and about-turns. In 1975, Carter declared his opposition to the Helsinki Accords and the Jackson–Vanik amendment (a cause adopted by human rights activists) on the grounds that it meant interfering in Soviet internal affairs. By late 1976, Carter had promoted global human rights to the front of his agenda, alongside the reduction of nuclear weapons. But there was a tension between these two goals. Carter's criticism of human rights suppressions in the USSR and its client states would hinder attempts to secure a SALT II Treaty. It raised questions for the new administration. To what extent should Carter apply pressure on the Soviets to undertake internal reform? Could he reconcile this goal with the effort to achieve agreements on deeper cuts in nuclear arms? And how would he manage relations with a more assertive, polarized Congress?

Carter's foreign policy appointees would reach diverging conclusions on these issues. For secretary of state, the president selected Cyrus Vance. Born into a politically connected family, Vance had served in the Navy during the Second World War, before emerging as a successful Wall Street lawyer. He operated in the Department of Defense during the Kennedy and Johnson administrations, resigning from the latter amid the escalation of the Vietnam War. Harold Brown, another veteran from the Johnson–McNamara years, took the reins as secretary of defense. But more controversial was the appointment of Zbigniew Brzezinski as national security adviser. Brzezinski was born in Warsaw but raised in Canada, where his father was posted as a diplomat in 1938. It was a period in which Polish fears of a Soviet invasion were palpable, and helped shape Brzezinski's lifelong antipathy toward Soviet communism. In 1958, he became a U.S. citizen. Brzezinski served as an adviser to the Kennedy and Johnson administrations, and as a professor of government at Columbia University. He developed a reputation as a staunch anti-communist and foreign policy hardliner.

Brzezinski had cofounded the Trilateral Commission—a think tank comprising academics, businessmen, and lawyers, designed to promote cooperation between industrialized nations. Carter met Brzezinski in 1973, soon after becoming a member, and the latter served as an adviser during his presidential campaign. Impressed by Brzezinski's grasp of geopolitics, Carter selected him for the key national security post. He did so despite warnings that "Zbig" was "aggressive" and "ambitious," someone who "might not be deferential to a secretary of state."[26] Campaign adviser Clark Clifford told Carter that Brzezinski's traits made him ill-suited for the position and incompatible with Vance.[27] But the president saw these as strengths, not deficiencies. "They were in accord with what I wanted," Carter argued. "The final decisions on basic foreign policy would be made by me in the Oval Office."[28]

Yet from the outset, it was Brzezinski to whom Carter looked to organize foreign policy. Power would lie not in the State Department but in the National Security Council. Presidential Directives (PDs) would be submitted by Brzezinski to Carter without being viewed by participants in the other committees: the SCC (Special Coordinating Committee) and the PRC (Policy Review Committee). Brzezinski was both "initiator" and "coordinator" of policy, not an intermediary. What emerged was a lopsided structure that did not facilitate a diversity of views. "The President often has to tell Brzezinski to shut up at meetings so he can listen to what others have to say," noted a Pentagon aide.[29] Vance resented the arrangement. He believed that the secretary of state should be the public spokesman on foreign affairs, with responsibility for policy coordination. But he did not issue Carter with an ultimatum.[30]

In style and substance, Brzezinski and Vance were not simpatico. Where Brzezinski was outspoken and abrupt, Vance was cool and mild-mannered. Brzezinski believed in the utility of military power to further U.S. diplomacy, whereas Vance felt it should be used sparingly or as a last resort. And while Brzezinski thought in geostrategic terms, Vance preferred to take an incremental, case-by-case approach. They also disagreed on Soviet policy. Brzezinski saw the USSR as a military power that would use every opportunity to expand its influence. He favored a more confrontational policy—if necessary, using American military might to restrain Soviet actions. Only from a position of strength, he reasoned, could the administration extract agreements from Moscow.[31] By contrast, Vance was an advocate of quiet diplomacy. He held less faith in the effectiveness of "linkage" and the idea of making agreements contingent on Soviet behavior. Vance rejected the notion that every crisis in the developing world was being orchestrated by the Kremlin. He cautioned against casting overseas conflicts in Cold War terms—arguing that political instability in newly emerging countries was often the result of indigenous nationalist movements that were independent of Moscow.[32]

Both men sought a better arrangement than SALT I and a reduction in tensions. But they disagreed on the aims and means. For Brzezinski, a SALT II accord would need to reverse the momentum of the Soviet military buildup. He feared that the Kremlin would "exploit Third World turbulence or impose its will in some political contest with the United States."[33] Vance's chief goals were more modest: to stabilize relations with Moscow and lower the prospect of nuclear war, while avoiding the sort of dangerous entanglements that had plagued past administrations. He preferred to focus on areas of mutual interest and cooperation, calling for patience in the pursuit of U.S. objectives. Unlike Brzezinski, Vance saw no Soviet design for global expansion, but rather the jostling for advantage to further its national interests. It was not long before the feuding began.[34]

Carter selected Paul Warnke (a senior Pentagon official in the Johnson administration) as director of the Arms Control and Disarmament Agency (ACDA) and his chief SALT negotiator. He too was a contentious appointment. The national security establishment had been divided post-Vietnam. On one side lay analysts such as Warnke, who criticized the quest for military power as a cynical formula for escalations in defense budgets and foreign interventions.[35] But others argued that the USSR could only be contained through a vast military buildup. Paul Nitze, Warnke's rival for the post, fell into this category.[36] Nitze warned that without increased defense spending, Soviet numerical superiority and advantage in missile throw-weight would make U.S. land-based missiles vulnerable to a first strike.[37] The notion of a "window of vulnerability" would become a key line of attack from conservatives.

If Carter's foreign policy selections were "establishment" figures, his domestic choices were anything but. The exception was his vice president, Minnesota senator Walter Mondale, who had withdrawn early from the 1976 race. A protégé of Hubert Humphrey, Mondale was well respected within Democratic ranks and shared Carter's commitment to civil rights. But other choices raised eyebrows. Aged 32, Hamilton Jordan, Carter's political adviser since 1970, would continue to serve as his chief aide. Jody Powell, 33, had met Carter as a student volunteer during his gubernatorial campaign in 1969, and was appointed press secretary. Jordan and Powell were so close to Carter, noted Brzezinski, "that they could have been his sons and had that kind of relationship with him."[38] They were but two of a string of appointees with connections to Carter during his stint as Georgia governor. Stuart Eizenstat was made domestic policy adviser; Griffin Bell became attorney general; Robert Lipshutz was appointed as White House counsel; Frank Moore headed the Office of Congressional Liaison; Jack Watson became cabinet secretary; and Bert Lance would serve as Carter's budget director. Andrew Young, the first black representative to serve Georgia in a century, was made ambassador to the United Nations. The "Georgia mafia" was largely unknown in Washington circles—an indication of Carter's intention to continue casting himself as a political outsider.

Perhaps his most fateful staffing decision, however, was the one left unfilled. The president did not appoint a chief of staff. Jordan was approached for the role but, aware of his inexperience, resisted the idea. Once he declined, Carter judged it "improper and inconsistent to bring an outsider in as a leader of all these people who had been with me since I was a young politician."[39] But the political reasoning was as important as the moral. Carter felt bound by a campaign mantra—made against the legacy of Watergate—which rejected the notion of an all-powerful chief of staff roaming around the White House. "'I'm going to be the President and I'm going to take decisions and run things' [...] that was a political reaction to the excesses of the Nixon administration," Jordan explained.[40] Carter opted for a spokes-in-the-wheel system, with cabinet members being granted equal access. But without a central figure overseeing the control of operations, prioritizing issues, and delegating responsibilities, it was a formula destined for problems. Bereft of such a presence, and with a cabinet lacking in diversity and executive experience, it was little wonder that the administration at times seemed incoherent. Not until mid-1979, after his "crisis of confidence" speech, did the president appoint Jordan as his chief of staff. By then, Carter was fighting for political survival.[41]

THE VIEW FROM MOSCOW

As a new broom arrived in Washington, a familiar one reigned in Moscow. In 1977 the Soviet Union was still led by Leonid Brezhnev. Now 70, Brezhnev was a shadow of the man who had succeeded Nikita Khrushchev in 1964. His health deteriorated following heart attacks in late 1974 and early 1976. Soviet doctors pronounced Brezhnev "clinically dead" after the second stroke, and his various illnesses (brain atherosclerosis, emphysema) worsened as the year progressed. Brezhnev was addicted to painkillers and sedatives, and frequently suffered from overdoses. He worked about two hours a day, with some Politburo meetings lasting just twenty minutes.[42] Public appearances became increasingly rare, and Brezhnev relied on the expertise of his troika of foreign policy advisers: KGB Chairman Yuri Andropov, Defense Minister Dmitry Ustinov, and above all Andrei Gromyko, who had served as foreign minister since 1957.

The son of Byelorussian peasants, Gromyko began his career at the Soviet embassy in Washington, where he was posted as chargé d'affaires in 1939. Since then he had witnessed most of the key diplomatic events firsthand. Gromyko accompanied Stalin to the Yalta Conference in 1945; sat next to Khrushchev when the Soviet leader banged his shoe on a desk in the UN; told John F. Kennedy that the Soviets had not stationed offensive missiles in Cuba (despite evidence to the contrary); and played an active role in Moscow's push for détente. Yet he remained inscrutable to most Americans. The stern brow and pouting lip betrayed a sense of humor so dry that it was rarely understood. At the UN, a diplomat once tried to break the ice by asking Gromyko if he had enjoyed breakfast. "Perhaps," answered Gromyko. Outwardly, he remained "Mr. *Nyet*," the dour, poker-faced statesman. "He was quite funny. It was the way he did things," Warnke recalled. "He looked like a Borscht Belt comic, a lot of funny faces and broad gestures." If his humor was lost on the public, however, Gromyko's reputation as a tough negotiator was well known. "Normally, Gromyko knew every shade of a subject," Kissinger noted. "It was suicidal to negotiate with him without mastering the record or the issues."[43]

Soviet leaders had failed to abide by the Helsinki Accords. Thousands of activists were jailed or exiled for expressing "unorthodox" views during the Brezhnev era. Some achieved international recognition. Aleksandr Solzhenitsyn, who won the 1970 Nobel Prize for literature, was allowed leave for West Germany after publishing the *The Gulag Archipelago*, a story about Stalinist terror. While several dissidents were allowed to move west, others were forced to remain in the USSR. They included large numbers of Soviet Jews, who were refused the right to emigrate. Among the most prominent was nuclear physicist Andrei Sakharov, whose crusade for civil liberties earned him the Nobel Peace Prize in 1975. In May 1976, the Moscow Helsinki Watch Group was formed to monitor human rights violations and report their findings to the foreign media. Similar watch groups were founded in Soviet republics such as Ukraine, Georgia, Lithuania, and Armenia. Human rights movements also gathered pace outside of the USSR. In January 1977, a group of dissident Czechoslovak intellectuals published a manifesto titled "Charter 77," which demanded that the Helsinki Accords be put into practice. As Carter took office, Soviet dissidents (relatively few in number) were calling for similar action.[44]

For Brezhnev, bilateral relations (e.g., trade, arms control) were more important than squabbles over human rights. The Soviet leader delivered a goodwill speech in Tula two days before Carter's inauguration. Its purpose was to publicly convey the Soviet foreign policy approach. He renounced the pursuit of military superiority, endorsed efforts to achieve a new SALT Treaty, and explained his views on détente. "Détente is above all an overcoming of the 'cold war,' a transition to normal, equal relations between states," Brezhnev declared. "Détente is a readiness to resolve differences and conflicts not by force, not by threats and saber-rattling, but by peaceful means, at the negotiating table. Détente is a certain trust and ability to take into account the legitimate interests of one another."[45]

But détente had not dissuaded Moscow from amassing larger stockpiles of nuclear weapons. Soviet leaders were pursuing two diverging policies at once: détente on the one hand; and a military buildup on the other. "During those years we were arming ourselves like addicts, without any apparent political need," recalled Georgy Arbatov, the Kremlin's chief adviser on American affairs.[46] In 1976 the Soviet Union began deploying a new intermediate-range missile system, known as the SS-20. Soviet officials argued that their missile forces required modernization—an explanation that was rejected on both sides of the Atlantic. NATO allies viewed the SS-20 deployment as a cynical attempt to decouple European security from America by presenting the former with a new nuclear threat. It was met with grave concern in West Germany, which (unlike Britain and France) had no "independent" nuclear deterrent. Chancellor Helmut Schmidt feared that the Carter administration might use U.S. cruise missiles as a bargaining chip in the SALT negotiations, whereby the Soviets would remove missiles targeting America but not those aimed at Europe.[47]

Brezhnev also faced internal opposition. The Secretariat of the Communist Party's central committee were elderly conservatives (the average age was 64) whose outlook had been shaped by the events of the Second World War.[48] Some Politburo hardliners felt that Brezhnev had conceded too much at Vladivostok and was overly eager to preserve détente. Yet the Vladivostok understanding suited most Soviet leaders. It targeted only a modest number of cuts, allowing Moscow to retain the vast majority of its heavy missile forces. Brezhnev also had a personal stake in the agreement, having suffered a heart seizure during the talks. To consolidate his position, Brezhnev would remove Politburo dissenter Nikolai Podgorny and replace him as president of the Supreme Soviet. With the arms race straining the Soviet economy and the SS-20 now in place, Brezhnev was ready for a SALT II deal.[49]

APPROACHING THE SOVIETS: SALT II

Rather than pursuing one or two foreign goals in the early months, Carter directed his administration to attack on all fronts. A range of difficult issues were confronted simultaneously. Mondale traveled to Europe to help revive transatlantic relations; Vance visited the Middle East to mediate in the Arab–Israeli dispute; Young toured southern Africa, a region torn with civil strife; Sol Linowitz worked on negotiating the transfer of the Panama Canal to Panama; and Patricia Derian (who led the newly formed Bureau of Human Rights) campaigned to use U.S. foreign aid as a lever for human rights across the globe.

But the most pressing matter was the Cold War. The administration had two issues to address ahead of Vance's trip to Moscow in late March 1977. One was the nature of the arms agreement to be negotiated. Should Carter make a deal along the lines of the Vladivostok accord reached by Ford and Brezhnev? Or should he seek a more ambitious agreement which could lead to deeper arms cuts? The former option was strongly favored by the Kremlin, but was denounced by conservatives at home for failing to remove the threat of a Soviet first strike. Conversely, the "deep cuts" formula was championed by Republicans and conservative Democrats, whose support Carter would need to ratify a SALT agreement. But deep cuts deviated sharply from Vladivostok, requiring the USSR to remove many of its land-based ICBMs, the backbone of its nuclear arsenal. The second issue concerned human rights. With the SALT I Treaty due to expire in October, Carter had to decide whether to marry his aim of achieving a SALT II accord with the goal of promoting civil liberties in Eastern Europe.

Carter was unknown to Soviet leaders, who expected to reach a deal along the lines of the Vladivostok understanding. In September 1976, Averell Harriman (a former U.S. ambassador in Moscow) was authorized to tell Brezhnev that Carter would sign a SALT II agreement based on Vladivostok if he were elected president. But Soviet doubts were raised toward the end of the election campaign, when Carter accused Ford of "giving too much up to the Russians."[50] As president-elect, Carter told Brezhnev (via Harriman) that he would act quickly to secure a SALT II agreement, but would not be bound by previous negotiations. Harriman indicated that Carter would seek deeper cuts, perhaps up to three hundred missiles. "Moscow was put on guard," recalled Anatoly Dobrynin, the long-serving Soviet ambassador in Washington.[51]

Once in office, Carter dithered over his SALT position. It did not help that his chief advisers were divided. Vance and Warnke (whose nomination was being contested) favored a pragmatic, gradual approach to arms control. In their view, the Vladivostok framework offered the best way of securing a SALT II Treaty and a stable basis for relations.[52] Brzezinski and Brown, who held less benign views of the Soviets, advocated a deep cuts formula. Their aim was to publicly test Soviet intentions: if Moscow responded favorably, a more comprehensive arms agreement would seek to "halt the momentum of the Soviet military buildup."[53]

Carter leaned toward Vance's logic early on. He indicated that the solution might be to work on the basis of Vladivostok, while deferring the two issues on which both sides were divided—the Soviet Backfire bomber and U.S. cruise missiles. Later, a SALT III deal could yield greater reductions and resolve the remaining differences. In his first press conference, Carter said he was willing to defer the contentious issues and reach "a quick agreement." He envisioned a two-stage process: the first would establish "firm limits"; the second would target "substantive reductions [...] to show the world that we are sincere." In a letter to Brezhnev on January 26, Carter called for "a SALT II agreement without delay."[54] The statements were well received in Moscow.[55]

But Carter (and some key advisers) did not feel obliged to abide by the Vladivostok terms. Before long, Carter was telling Dobrynin that he wanted "much deeper cuts" than those agreed at Vladivostok. He sought major reductions in strategic forces, cutting the number of missiles to perhaps several hundred (notably the Soviet heavy missiles). "There's no practical way to do it," Dobrynin responded. "We have just, with great difficulty, finished the Vladivostok agreement. It's better to finish what we have, and then go to these drastic reductions later." Dobrynin warned Carter that a deviation from Vladivostok would spell "serious problems" for the arms talks. "I think it's not enough," Carter replied. "We need to go further."[56]

Brzezinski urged Carter to pursue meaningful cuts in nuclear weapons. He warned that a "quick-fire" compromise would "not be politically

desirable," fueling criticism from conservatives that the agreement was
too narrow in scope.[57] Henry Jackson was publicly attacking Warnke,
calling his support for Vladivostok "disturbing" and accusing him
of targeting "irresponsible cuts" in the defense budget.[58] Aware of
Jackson's political sway, Carter began soliciting his views on SALT. On
February 4, Jackson arrived at the White House to tell Carter that he
would insist on much deeper cuts in the Soviets' ICBM and intermediate-
range ballistic missiles. To propitiate him, Carter designated General Ed
Rowny (Jackson's loyal confidant) as a "military observer" to the arms
talks. In so doing, Jackson would receive a regular flow of information
about the course of negotiations.[59] Carter wrote to Brezhnev the following week, explaining that he wanted to look at "drastic limitations on
nuclear weapons." Vladivostok was not mentioned. In his reply, Brezhnev
warned Carter against submitting "deliberately unacceptable" proposals
that departed from the 1974 agreement. The correspondence continued
into March, when Carter complained about Brezhnev's "harsh tone" and
lack of positive response. "The fact is that no final agreement was ever
reached at Vladivostok or in the subsequent negotiations," he told the
Soviet leader.[60]

Jackson pressed Carter to harden his position. On February 15, he
sent the president a twenty-three-page memo (co-written by Richard
Perle, his military aide), which set the criteria for an acceptable SALT
deal. The memo attacked the "Nixinger" approach, called for large
cuts in Soviet heavy missiles, and warned of the "vulnerability" of
U.S. strategic forces. Jackson likened the danger facing America to that
faced by European allies in the 1930s, with the nation "sliding into
a series of improvident risks [...] the cumulative result of which could
be irreversible." He told Carter that a "doubtful" agreement would be
"bad politics."[61] Carter took the advice seriously. The Jackson memo
was circulated to Vance, Brown, and other top advisers. Brzezinski and
Jackson met privately to help narrow the gap between their respective
positions.[62] "Your SALT memorandum is excellent, and of great help to
me," Carter assured Jackson.[63] Carter kept the memo in his private safe
near the Oval Office, referring back to it "to see if there were ways that
I could accommodate Scoop's very ambitious demands."[64] The irony
was inescapable. Just as Carter was defending Warnke in the Senate
confirmation vote—lobbying senators on his behalf—he was forming
an arms control approach based on the advice of Warnke's chief opponent in Congress. Warnke dismissed Jackson's memo as "a first class
polemic."[65]

Warnke's nomination was supported by liberal senators such as Hubert Humphrey (D-Minnesota), who deemed him "an excellent choice." It was opposed by hardliners in the Armed Services Committee, who felt that the dovish Warnke would offer too many concessions to Moscow. They included conservative Democrats such as Jackson, who said that he would "weaken Warnke as an international negotiator to the point of uselessness by holding the vote in his favor to 60 or less." CPD co-founder Paul Nitze testified against Warnke, charging him with disregarding the "clear and present danger" posed by the Soviet Union. The hawks got their wish. On March 9, Warnke was approved for the post, but only by a vote of 58–40. It was a margin well short of the two-thirds threshold needed to ratify any SALT Treaty that Carter might reach with the Soviets. The message was clear: Carter would have to toughen his SALT position in order to avoid a major defeat in the Senate.[66]

*

The politicking pushed Carter toward the "comprehensive" option. In the weeks following Jackson's memo, the proposals being discussed targeted deeper arms cuts. On February 25, two new formulas sought greater reductions in the permitted number of launchers: one called for cuts from 2,400 (the Vladivostok level) to 2,000; another proposed reductions to 1,500.[67] At a meeting on March 10, Brzezinski and Brown agreed on a compromise of 2,000 launchers. Warnke was skeptical about presenting the Soviets with a proposal that so differed from Vladivostok.[68] But his arguments were rejected. At a further meeting two days later, Carter expressed his desire for "real arms control." Brzezinski, Brown, and Mondale supported his decision. Vance did not, but reluctantly acquiesced. The secretary of state agreed to bring the deep cuts formula to Moscow, after being assured that he could also take a more modest proposal ("Vladivostok minus") as a fallback position.[69]

The proposal that Vance brought to Moscow aimed to change the SALT framework by lowering the strategic arms ceiling that was fixed at Vladivostok: ICBMs would be reduced from 2,400 to a level between 2,000 and 1,800; MIRVed ICBMs would be cut from 1,200 to 1,100; and Soviet heavy missile forces would be roughly halved from 308 to 150. The cuts excluded the U.S. cruise missiles, while the Soviet Backfire would not be counted as a strategic bomber—provided that Moscow adhered to a list of measures designed to inhibit its range. Although some U.S. programs would be affected (such as the MX), most were not yet under development. As author Strobe Talbott noted, "the U.S. was seeking substantial reductions in existing Soviet systems in exchange for marginal cuts in future American ones." In sum, the deep cuts formula targeted major cutbacks in land-based missiles (where the Soviets held an advantage), while containing few limits on submarines or air-launched weapons, areas in which the United States was superior.[70]

On March 18, Carter invited Kissinger, Brzezinski, and Vance for supper to discuss his SALT decision. The president asked Kissinger whether he thought the Soviets would accept his "ambitious" proposal. Kissinger rolled his eyes skyward and sighed. After a long pause, he replied, "Yes, I think they might accept it."[71] The Soviet ambassador was less bullish about the U.S. proposal after being briefed by Vance. Dobrynin warned that the deep cuts gambit would be rejected. He was baffled that the administration was publicizing its approach ahead of the meeting. As Vance departed for Moscow, Soviet leaders had already surmised that Carter's intentions were "not serious."[72]

HUMAN RIGHTS

The subplot to the arms debates was the humanitarian situation in Eastern Europe. Carter's dealings with the Soviets on human rights reflected a mixture of motives. His feelings on the subject mirrored his passion for civil rights in America. A deeply religious man, Carter was determined to project those same values overseas.[73] But the reasoning was not just morality. Brzezinski persuaded Carter to use human rights as an instrument to weaken Moscow ideologically and encourage opposition within Soviet society.[74] It was also an issue which had proved a domestic political winner, attracting the support of liberals, neoconservatives, and Republicans. "Of our numerous foreign policy initiatives, [human rights] is the only one that has a broad base of support among the American people and is not considered 'liberal'," Jordan explained to Carter.[75] The president was "convinced" that there was no contradiction between the pursuit of Soviet human rights and his quest for arms control. "He thought human rights was the general historical tendency in our time, and that the Soviet Union could not be immune to that process," recalled Brzezinski.[76] The national security adviser pressed Carter to pursue both goals at once. But the objectives were inconsistent. Simultaneously, Brzezinski sought to place the Kremlin "ideologically on the defensive" over human rights; promote a more "comprehensive and reciprocal" détente; and "move away from [...] our excessive preoccupation with the U.S.–Soviet relationship." As historian John Lewis Gaddis noted, the premise seemed to be that one could reform, negotiate with, and ignore the USSR all at the same time.[77]

Carter served early notice of his intentions. He raised human rights in his first letter to Brezhnev on January 26. At the same time, the State Department charged Czechoslovakia with human rights violations and of harassing those who campaigned for Charter 77. The next day the department praised Soviet dissident Andrei Sakharov and issued a warning against threats to intimidate him. But the KGB continued to clamp down on activists. The arrest of fellow dissidents Aleksandr Ginzburg and Yuri Orlov (founder of the Moscow Helsinki Watch Group) prompted more criticism from the administration.[78] On February 17, Carter sent Sakharov a letter of support, expressing his "firm commitment to promote respect for human rights."[79] Twelve days later Carter welcomed Soviet dissident Vladimir Bukovsky to the White House, and repeated his stance. "Our commitment to the concept of human rights is permanent," Carter declared. "I don't intend to be timid in my public statements and positions."[80]

Soviet leaders were furious. The new administration was not only "toppling the structure" built in Vladivostok, it was elevating human rights to the top of U.S.–Soviet relations. For Brezhnev, who had seen Kissinger downplay the subject for eight years, this was a personal affront.[81] Brezhnev told Carter that he would not brook "interference in our internal affairs, whatever pseudo-humanitarian slogans are used to present it." He rebuked Carter for corresponding with a "renegade [Sakharov] who proclaimed himself an enemy of the Soviet state."[82] Brzezinski tried to rationalize Brezhnev's response. Since the Soviets had issued "no direct public criticism" or "explicit threats," Carter's statements, he argued, were viewed as "non-events" by Moscow. He suggested that any Soviet concerns would be assuaged if Carter couched his human rights posture "more broadly [...] applicable to all nations—in other words, that this is not a matter of anti-Soviet tactics."[83]

Carter appeared similarly blasé. On March 22, he told a congressional group that his criticism of Soviet human rights violations would not destabilize relations. There was, Carter said, "no need to worry every time Brezhnev sneezes."[84] He did so despite a report from U.S. Ambassador Malcolm Toon, who described an "unusually tough" speech from Brezhnev to the trade unions. The Soviet leader charged the United States with a "campaign of slander," warning that "under no circumstances would interference in our internal affairs be tolerated." It was a reversal of the tone adopted by Brezhnev in Tula back in January.[85]

However well-intended, the administration had badly miscalculated. "Carter failed to realize that Soviet leaders would regard his position as a direct challenge to their internal political authority and even as an attempt to change their regime," recalled Dobrynin. "The telegram from the White House to Sakharov was very offensive. We considered this a departure from the normal diplomatic relations between two countries. Those were people Brezhnev very sincerely considered enemies. At that time, it stirred very strong emotions."[86]

WET RUG IN MOSCOW

What ensued in Moscow was a debacle. On March 28, Vance received a chilly welcome at the Kremlin. Brezhnev launched into a tirade against Carter's human rights campaign. It was followed by a long tribute to the Vladivostok accord, deemed by the Soviets as the only acceptable basis for a SALT II deal. Brezhnev called the U.S. proposal "unconstructive and one-sided," halving the number of Soviet heavy missiles in exchange for the deferral of some future American programs. He also raised the question of European-based nuclear missiles, which remained a threat to Moscow. Carter's position, he said, was "utterly unacceptable."[87] Gromyko told Vance: "The chief demand being made by the USA, namely that we destroy half our land-based ICBMs, is absurd. We are wholly opposed to tampering with the Vladivostok accords."[88] Vance arrived for the final day of talks expecting a Soviet counterproposal, with the aim of reaching some compromise. Instead, he found the opposition more irritable than before. Brezhnev noted the omission of U.S. cruise missiles, remarking that the Soviet SS-20 "can't hit [America] from anywhere, but you can drop thousands of missiles on us from Europe. It's my people who will be killed."[89]

Vance was whisked away without a Soviet counteroffer. "The problem that really arose was that when we put our proposals on the table, nobody would listen to them," he recalled. "Contrary to usual practice, nobody said, 'Well, let's sit down and talk about that and see if we can find a way to get around this thing.' We got a wet rug in the face, and were told to go home."[90] Vance defended the U.S. proposal before the press, euphemistically describing the talks as "businesslike." He refused to be drawn on the prospects for a SALT agreement.[91] Carter was less diplomatic: "Obviously, if we feel [...] that the Soviets are not acting in good faith, then I would be forced to consider a much more deep commitment to the development and deployment of additional weapons."[92] The statement was taken as an ultimatum by the Kremlin. Gromyko accused Carter of "seeking a public victory" and pursuing "deliberately unacceptable proposals." One Soviet official complained that Henry Jackson had so much influence in shaping the U.S. position that he possessed an "invisible chair" at the talks.[93]

Carter's attempts to engage Moscow had failed miserably. The bid to accommodate conservatives (to help carry a SALT deal) overrode concerns about Soviet sensibilities, already strained by the human rights issue. The basis of the anti-Warnke campaign had been to feed Carter's perceptions and preempt efforts to set a more modest course.[94] Already it had proved successful. The comprehensive proposal granted the anti-détente faction in Congress a valuable political tool. Carter's "deep cuts" stance now became the yardstick against which hardliners gauged the merits of a SALT II agreement.[95] Anything less would be attacked as weakness. Equally, the president's credibility would be undermined were he to retreat from his tough position. As the tactical errors dawned on the administration, new political actors mobilized in Washington.

THE COMMITTEE ON THE PRESENT DANGER

Carter was not alone in benefiting from the political disorientation of the Vietnam–Watergate era. A more decentralized power structure allowed other actors (e.g., interest groups, lobbyists, public intellectuals) to capitalize on the new landscape. Few did so with as much success as the Committee on the Present Danger, a foreign policy interest group revived when neoconservatives joined forces with Republicans. Comprising establishment politicians, bureaucrats, and intellectuals, the CPD's raison d'être was to rail against détente while campaigning for a vast U.S. military buildup. The committee was a reincarnation of the group formed back in 1950 to promote the policies of NSC-68. It, too, owed its ascent to election-year politics.

During the Republican primaries in 1976, Ford's foreign policy approach was derided by rival candidate Ronald Reagan, who accused intelligence agencies of underestimating Soviet military strength. Pressured by hawks to produce a new analysis of Soviet capabilities, Ford authorized CIA director George Bush to commission an external group of "experts" (Team B) to appraise the intelligence data available. But Team B proved less than objective. Four of the seven members were future CPD founders, including historian Richard Pipes and the veteran diplomat, Paul Nitze. The result was an alarmist report that attacked

U.S. intelligence for underestimating the Soviet military buildup. It warned of a Soviet Union outproducing the United States in strategic and conventional weaponry, and developing a superior first-strike capability. Team B's aim was to reinstate containment militarism as the cornerstone of U.S. foreign policy—a return to the pre-Vietnam, early Cold War doctrine of NSC-68.[96] Their claims about Soviet capabilities were later debunked. But at the time Team B's views went unchallenged.[97]

Nitze detected a "public complacency" about the Soviet threat. He called on a vast network of establishment friends to form the CPD, one of the most effective citizen-lobbying groups of the Cold War.[98] Created three days after Carter's election, the committee lived up to its name. "Soviet expansionism threatens to destroy the world balance of forces on which the survival of freedom depends," read its founding statement. "If we continue to drift, we shall become second best to the Soviet Union in overall military strength. Our national survival itself would be in peril."[99]

Nitze had served as an adviser and diplomat for five presidents dating back to Franklin Roosevelt. White-haired and deeply lined, he was approaching 70 and in the twilight of his career. He resigned, disillusioned, as Ford's SALT negotiator in 1974, and began attacking the Vladivostok agreement. He appeared on television and in Congress, articulating his views on the "Vietnam Syndrome" or the Soviet threat. As a conservative Democrat, Nitze sided with Carter in the presidential race only after Jackson was out of contention. But when invited by Carter to brief him on national security, Nitze made a poor impression, haranguing the candidate instead of engaging in a friendly exchange of views. His "arrogant" style irritated Carter. "Nitze was a typical know-it-all," Carter recalled. "He didn't seem to listen to others and he had a doomsday approach."[100] Nitze was duly shunned in favor of Warnke—his rival and one-time colleague—with whom he held opposite views on arms control.

Bitter at being overlooked for the position of SALT negotiator, Nitze did everything to block Warnke's appointment. He telephoned friends in Congress and sent a letter to John Sparkman, chairman of the Senate Foreign Relations Committee, explaining that Warnke "may not be a qualified student or competent judge of military affairs." "I cannot bring myself to believe that the Senate would be well advised to give its consent," he wrote.[101] After being invited to testify at the confirmation hearings, Nitze got personal. He called Warnke's views "absolutely asinine [...] screwball, arbitrary, and fictitious." And when asked by liberal New Hampshire senator Thomas McIntyre if he thought he was a "better

American" than Warnke, Nitze replied, "I really do." Even Jackson, who endorsed Nitze's views, watched uneasily.[102]

Warnke's appointment did not discourage Nitze's CPD. Of the 141 founding members, many were influential, establishment figures. They included Douglas Dillon and Henry Fowler (former secretaries of the treasury); William Casey (president of the Import-Export Bank); General Andrew Goodpaster (former NATO Supreme Allied Commander); Lane Kirkland (secretary-treasurer of the AFL-CIO); Norman Podhoretz (editor of *Commentary*); and Dean Rusk (former secretary of state).[103] The board was bipartisan: 60 percent of the members were Democrats and 40 percent were Republicans.[104] The committee was incorporated as a nonprofit, research, and educational organization. It received exempt status from the Internal Revenue Service, and was mainly financed by voluntary donations from individuals.[105] While the CPD seized on numerous issues, it was arms control and the Soviet Union that generated the most political capital. Alliances were formed with military-industrial lobbyists, members of Congress, and interest groups such as the Coalition for a Democratic Majority. Disillusioned with the direction of the Democratic Party, many of the CDM's leading lights would join the CPD. Among them were Richard Pipes, Eugene Rostow, Norman Podhoretz, and Jeane Kirkpatrick. Over the next four years, this panoply of forces strove to mould public opinion about the threat posed by the Soviet Union.[106]

The administration's setback in Moscow had been a useful start for the CPD. It allowed Nitze and others to cast the Soviets as intransigent and untrustworthy. Within days the committee published its first pamphlet, "What is the Soviet Union up to?" which was distributed to politicians, newspapers, and editorialists.[107] It portrayed a militarily superior power, whose designs were "global," "expansionist," and "uniquely dangerous."[108] Of the Soviet deficiencies—qualitatively inferior stockpiles, economic and technological decline, social problems, and ethnic unrest—there was no mention.

MAKING A COMPROMISE

The failure of the Vance mission prompted a rethink. In a bid to revive the arms talks, the Carter administration implemented two key changes. One was the conduct of U.S. diplomacy; the other was the nature of the SALT proposal. Humiliated in Moscow, Vance insisted that the negotiations could no longer take place in public. He called for a return to secret diplomacy via Anatoly Dobrynin, Soviet ambassador since 1962. In April,

Dobrynin met privately with Carter's top advisers, warning that the state of relations was the "most unsatisfactory in the last ten years." Carter and Brezhnev traded words in public, expressing their desire to revive talks. The president said he was "very eager to change" any terms that the Soviets could prove were inequitable. Moscow took the statement as a sign of flexibility.[109] Dobrynin recalled: "It looked like the administration was looking for a way out of a blind alley into which it had driven—at least that was how Vance saw it."[110]

Carter knew he had overreached by pushing the deep cuts proposal.[111] Liberals in Congress complained of inadequate consultation, and the president was urged to widen his base of support. "Everyone agrees that we should not allow Senator Jackson to monopolize Senate commentary on our SALT positions," wrote political aide Landon Butler, after speaking with Brzezinski. "By broadening the base of support, the President can help ensure that he has the trust of the public and the Senate when he presents the agreement for ratification." The State Department began holding SALT briefings for senators selected by Democratic Party whip Alan Cranston (D-California).[112] Conscious of the degree to which he had placated the Jackson wing, Carter told his SALT team to "repackage" the deal offered to the Soviets. Vance and Warnke began synthesizing the three arms control formulas (the deep cuts proposal; Vladivostok-minus; and Kissinger's compromise).[113] To avoid antagonizing the Soviets, Carter ordered his negotiators not to raise the issue of human rights.[114]

The changes had the desired effect. In late April, Vance struck an agreement with Dobrynin for a new three-part SALT framework which would run until 1985. The first part would reduce the Vladivostok weapons ceilings; the second was an interim agreement for three years on issues such as cruise missiles; and the third was a commitment to negotiate deeper cuts in a future SALT III deal.[115] The revised package was approved by Vance and Gromyko in Geneva on May 21. It targeted a modest reduction from the Vladivostok ceiling of 2,400 ICBMs, while the United States agreed to ban the deployment of its long-range land and sea-based cruise missiles for a period of three years. Although the gap had been narrowed, the finer details remained unresolved. Gromyko was still rejecting the U.S. efforts to reduce Soviet heavy missiles (the U.S. proposal this time was to cut the number from 308 to 190).[116]

Neoconservatives were furious with the decision to jettison the deep cuts proposal. On May 12, Jackson's CDM had written to Carter, urging him to "hang tough" and ignore liberal critics: "You have set off on a long, challenging course. But it is the right course. We promise to do all we can to rally the public support that will enable you to pursue it."[117] However, the Jackson–Carter rapprochement ended after details of the new SALT proposal became public. The senator sent Carter a private letter, expressing his anger at the concessions.[118] But the Committee on the Present Danger were more open in their criticism. Unlike the CDM, it opposed the deep cuts formula back in March, and found the new position even less palatable. Brzezinski was besieged by letters from founding member Eugene Rostow, who sent copies of Team B reports.[119] On July 6, the committee published a paper titled "Where We Stand on SALT." It attacked the administration for a "prompt and substantial retreat." "The Soviets evidently believe [. . .] that the United States is so eager to achieve an agreement, that they merely have to say 'no' to our proposals, and we will come forward with modifications more advantageous to their side."[120]

Brzezinski accepted some of the criticism. He told Jordan: "There is a tendency on our side to want an agreement so badly that we begin changing our proposals until the point is reached that the Russians are prepared to consider it." To shore up the domestic side, both agreed on the need for a "tougher position."[121] Brzezinski pointed out that the geopolitics favored America. The Soviets faced hostility on two fronts—from the West and China—while a CIA report pointed to growing economic concerns in Moscow. Hard currency debt was already $14 billion, and the expected decline in Soviet oil production would exacerbate their problem. (Oil exports to the West accounted for 40 percent of Soviet hard currency.) The power of the United States to "greatly aggravate the Soviet dilemma," Brzezinski wrote, "will bring Brezhnev back to a foreign policy of moderation."[122]

Brzezinski was therefore uneasy with Carter's repeated efforts to arrange a meeting with the Soviet leader. On four occasions in mid-1977, the administration made proposals for a summit. All were rejected by Moscow. In one letter Carter suggested hosting a summit in Alaska, reasoning that its remoteness was similar to that of Vladivostok. Brezhnev declined, stating that the differences on SALT had to be settled before a summit could take place.[123] After further Carter enquiries, Brzezinski insisted that efforts to arrange a meeting be drafted as proposals by Harriman rather than the president. 'I told Carter that he ought to stop proposing the meeting,' Brzezinski recalled. 'I developed the sense that at their end it was becoming bargaining leverage against us.'[124]

*

As Carter approached Brezhnev, he was also making efforts to contain the CPD. Harold Brown told the committee of Carter's displeasure with their statements. But in a tacit admission of their influence, Brown invited a committee delegation to the White House. Carter's aim was to persuade the CPD to establish a line of private communication, rather than going public. The invitation was not official. A White House press release announced only that the president was to meet "a group of leaders from a private industry."[125] Nitze, Rostow, and six other CPD members (Democrats and Republicans) arrived on August 4. The meeting was torturous. After patiently listening to their arguments, Carter defended his SALT position. He said that "defense spending cannot go up because public opinion is against it." "No, no, no!" Nitze interrupted, as Carter was speaking. "Paul," he complained, "would you please let me finish?" The mood was one of "exasperation" according to a *Washington Post* report, and the meeting lasted for two hours—twice its allotted time. Carter vented anger at their attacks. "I am the President trying to do his best and achieve goals we all agree on. Why don't you support me instead of picking on me?" Pointing to their bipartisan committee, Henry Fowler asked Carter not to be so touchy.[126] Rostow described the meeting as "a farce," which signaled the point of departure between the administration and neoconservatives. "We listened to Carter, but did not know what to make of it. The President was so disconnected. We suddenly realized that he was not really interested in our views but was asking us to support him."[127]

CARTER MEETS GROMYKO

In September 1977, Carter held his first meeting with a top-ranking Soviet official, when Andrei Gromyko arrived in Washington. The aim was to build on the SALT II framework agreed in May. Gromyko momentarily shed his dour image, telling stories about the Second World War and lavishing praise on Averell Harriman. But he soon reverted to type. The foreign minister showed no flexibility, and refused to compromise over the Soviet heavy missiles.[128] His mood was not improved when Carter raised the issue of human rights. The president cited the imprisonment of Soviet Jews, including the dissident Anatoly Shcharansky. Gromyko played dumb. "Who is Shcharansky?" he asked. Carter was baffled. "Haven't you heard about Shcharansky?" "No," said Gromyko. After an awkward silence, he added: "Nobody knows him. These questions have minute significance [...] The question of emigration from the Soviet Union of any nationality is our domestic problem, to be resolved internally."[129]

Despite the altercation, progress was made on arms control. Vance and Gromyko agreed on a basic framework which would form the outline of a new SALT Treaty. Gromyko accepted an overall limit of 2,250 missile launchers (down from 2,400 at Vladivostok), of which 1,250 could contain multiple warheads, with a ceiling of 820 for MIRVed ICBMs. Since the SALT I Treaty was due to expire in October, both sides agreed to honor the terms until SALT II could take effect. Carter also spoke of new possibilities for U.S.–Soviet trade. "I inherited the [Jackson–Vanik] law, which links trade with other questions," he told Gromyko. "I would like to see this problem solved. I hope that together we can influence our common 'friend', Senator Jackson, to annul the trade limitations adopted on his initiative."[130]

There was little warmth between the two men. Gromyko thought that Carter was "not overburdened with foreign policy expertise."[131] Carter considered Gromyko "obstinate" and "uncooperative [...] much more charming to my wife than he was to the rest of us." In a bid to lighten the mood, Carter said that while Gromyko had the greater diplomatic experience ("maybe 500 more months"), both knew that peace was what the American and Soviet people wanted most.[132] Before they parted, Carter left Gromyko with a surprise gift; a wooden model set displaying all Soviet and American missiles lined up side by side. The Soviet missiles, painted black, outnumbered the pristine white U.S. ICBMs. Placing the set on the table, Carter drew Gromyko's attention to the largest Soviet missiles. "These are the ones we are most afraid of," he explained. Gromyko was unimpressed. When Carter left, he handed the set to Dobrynin, saying that he did not "play with toys." The Soviet ambassador kept the gift.[133]

On Capitol Hill, Henry Jackson was on the warpath. He attacked Carter for having abandoned the proposals made in March, and for continuing the provisions of SALT I after its expiry.[134] Jackson said that the existing formula gave the Soviets enough heavy weaponry to destroy the entire U.S. ICBM fleet. Moscow's military "superiority," he claimed, would inhibit America's ability to launch retaliatory attacks on Soviet cities in the event of a first strike. "It's high time that we stopped the dangerous practice of entering into unequal deals with Moscow in the misguided notion that Soviet leaders would reward our generosity with restraint in international affairs."[135] Vance was summoned to appear before the Senate Armed Services Committee on October 15, to explain the compromises that were made. Carter wrote to Jackson five days later, explaining that his requests would be met "as well as possible." He provided the senator with a copy of the SALT draft text, but rejected Jackson's demand to view the instructions given to the U.S. delegation.[136]

Yet Jackson remained the key figure in the battles over SALT ratification and U.S.–Soviet trade legislation. In another effort to woo the senator, Carter asked Dobrynin to invite Jackson to Moscow for a meeting with Brezhnev. Dobrynin obliged in mid-November, arriving for dinner at Jackson's home to discuss the details. But the Jackson–Brezhnev meeting (projected for March 1978) never materialized. Jackson's adviser, Richard Perle, insisted that the Kremlin permit the senator to meet with leading dissidents (including Sakharov) as a condition of his visit. Jackson knew that it would annoy Brezhnev, but refused to relent on the demand. The Soviets responded by canceling his visit.[137]

SALT II was back on track after the Carter–Gromyko meeting. But there were various obstacles to a final agreement. Technical issues such as the Backfire bomber, verification procedures, and the use of encryption meant that talks dragged on for more than a year. Carter's launch of a new diplomatic opening with China in 1978 would further delay the completion of a treaty until mid-1979.

DEFENSE DECISIONS

Carter's problems with the neoconservatives were aggravated by his decision to cancel the B-1 bomber program in June. Anti-SALT hardliners accused the president of being "soft" on defense. It was a refrain that continued until November 1980. Vance agreed in principle with Carter's decision (based on ideological and economic grounds), but regretted the lack of political consideration. The seeking of some Soviet concession in return for canceling the B-1 might have assuaged conservative fears. But Carter deemed the program "a gross waste of money."[138] The cancellation angered figures on both sides of the political aisle, including Sen. Sam Nunn (D-Georgia) – described by Brzezinski as "the most crucial senator in the SALT ratification battle."[139] The opposition to Carter's decision would linger when the SALT II Treaty came up for consideration in Congress. Vance recalled that the B-1 cancellation "became a millstone around the administration's neck."[140]

It was a measure of the partisan divisions that the B-1 debates took place before an almost empty chamber: senators merely delivered prepared remarks before departing. Senate Minority Leader Howard Baker (R-Tennessee) said that it had ceased to be a forum for meaningful debate.[141] Carter's decision to spurn the B-1 reignited interest in a new missile system called MX (or Missile Experimental). It was originally conceived as a weapon which could be used in a "limited" nuclear war against Soviet strategic forces. For example, 300 MXs (each equipped with ten or more warheads) would be capable of targeting the Soviets' 300 newly deployed SS-18 ballistic missiles.[142] Critics of Carter's defense posture now argued for the deployment of such a weapon. But with the Pentagon estimating costs of some \$33 billion, Carter resisted their pleas.[143]

Carter's decision to halt production of the ERW (or neutron bomb) brought him further political grief. The initial plan was to equip U.S. artillery units in Europe with an enhanced radiation weapon (ERW). The ERW was so called because it killed enemy forces with a surge of radiation, while reducing damage to property by suppressing the heat and damage from the blast. (The Soviets called it the "capitalist bomb.") Its purpose was to reassure allies of the U.S. commitment to deter Soviet aggression, following Moscow's production of the SS-20 missiles. In the event of a Soviet invasion the bomb could be used against tanks and troops, while lessening the danger of "collateral damage." West Germany, home to most of America's nuclear weapons in Europe, was the intended location.[144] The secret plan predated Carter's arrival, but became headline news after it was reported by the *Washington Post* in June 1977.[145] Most Republicans and conservative Democrats (e.g., senators John Stennis and Sam Nunn) urged Carter to press ahead with the ERW. So did Brown and Brzezinski, who saw it as a way of deterring Soviet force and a bargaining chip: Carter could offer to defer deployment of the neutron bomb in return for the Soviet non-deployment of the SS-20s.[146] But liberals argued that the ERW was morally repugnant, and increased the chance of war by implying the ability to fight, win, and recover from a nuclear attack. Opposed to the ERW on these grounds, Sen. Ted Kennedy (D-Massachusetts) and moderate Republican Sen. Mark Hatfield (Oregon) tried to veto the funding, but lost both votes.[147]

Carter vacillated in the face of pressure from the left and right. An NSC memo in November warned: "If we decide to go ahead, we will be heavily criticized for opening a new round of the arms race in a horrible way. No amount of public education will mute this criticism. On the other hand, a decision to forego production will be criticized as a sign of weakness in the face of political pressure. Following the B-1 and recent SALT furore, a negative decision would reinforce the President's problems with the hawks, which could well be greatest on the Hill."[148] Morally and politically Carter was uncomfortable with the neutron bomb. He told

Vance and Brzezinski that he would "press the Europeans to show greater interest in having the bomb and therefore a willingness to absorb some of the political flak." Carter pledged to move ahead only if the Western Europeans demanded it.[149] But there were no takers. Public protests against neutron warheads took place in various European capitals, and West German Chancellor Helmut Schmidt had his own domestic concerns. Many in the SPD were opposed to the bomb, with his party forming part of a coalition government that supported détente with the Soviets and closer relations with East Germany. Schmidt favored the ERW deployment to help counter the Soviet SS-20s. But since his political base was weak, the chancellor had no intention of publicly taking a position.[150]

A NATO statement was cobbled together in early 1978, pledging to support the ERW deployment. But before it was finalized, Carter balked. The terms of the agreement linked the ERW to arms control talks, and left Carter complaining that the European commitment was "too vague," placing all of the political responsibility on him. "I wish I'd never heard of this weapon," he told advisers.[151] Despite Brzezinski's protests, Carter agreed only to "defer," rather than cancel, a final decision.[152] The ERW deferral angered some European leaders and damaged Carter's public image. Schmidt, already frustrated by Carter's handling of SALT and human rights, accused him of "disengaging from Europe."[153] Domestic criticism was no less intense. Carter's opponents charged him with pursuing unilateral disarmament. "First we give away the B-1 bomber, and now we're giving away the neutron bomb," bemoaned Howard Baker, calling it "another in a long line of national defense mistakes by the President."[154]

*

Carter's rejection of the B-1, MX, and neutron bomb conformed to his early agenda, outlined in a major speech in May 1977. At the University of Notre Dame, Carter reaffirmed the commitment to human rights as a "fundamental tenet" of American foreign policy. He pledged to reduce the volume of arms sales to foreign states and restrict the transfer of advanced weapons. He also stressed the need to reduce the nuclear threat: "The arms race is not only dangerous, it's morally deplorable. We must put an end to it. We desire a freeze on further modernization and production of weapons, and a continuing, substantial reduction of strategic nuclear weapons." In a jibe at Cold War alarmists, Carter declared that America was "now free of that inordinate fear of communism." The "unifying threat" from Moscow had become "less intensive." It was time, he said, to move beyond the outdated policy of containment and embrace a new approach. While expressing his support for détente, Carter added: "We hope to persuade the Soviet Union that one country cannot impose its system of society upon another, either through direct military intervention or through the use of a client state's military force."[155]

But Carter's bold approach had already hit stumbling blocks. As Leslie Gelb (assistant secretary of state) recalled, the administration was caught between "two rising conservative tides: one in the United States; the other in the Soviet Union."[156] Both were becoming more entrenched in their position, and concessions to one party adversely affected Carter's relations with the other. The consensus in Washington was that the Soviets were now "more muscular." Over the summer, Brzezinski and his military assistant, William Odom, convinced Carter to toughen up the U.S. posture.[157] On August 24, Presidential Directive 18 was issued. It called for enhanced U.S. military capabilities and a more assertive, flexible posture overseas. PD-18 committed the United States to increase defense spending by three percent each year in real terms (contradicting Carter's campaign pledge); to improve the combat ability of American forces in Europe and the Middle East; and to review the "targeting policy" for a hypothetical nuclear war with the Soviet Union. It was a reflection of Carter's efforts to strike a balance between the hawks and doves, and of Brzezinski's ascendancy. The directive stated: "It is clear that in the foreseeable future, U.S.–Soviet relations will continue to be characterized by both competition and cooperation, with the attendant risk of conflict as well as the opportunity for stabilizing relations."[158]

THE HORN OF AFRICA

Cooperation gave way to competition in early 1978. Brzezinski urged Carter to "convey toughness" following Soviet military support for Ethiopia against Somalia. The two Soviet client states were at war over the Ogaden, a desert in eastern Ethiopia largely populated by ethnic Somalis. The region had strategic importance: Somalia bordered the Red Sea, the Gulf of Aden, and the Indian Ocean. Although traditionally a U.S. ally, Ethiopia was led by the ruthless Mengistu Haile Mariam, who had pledged allegiance to the USSR. The Kremlin tried to dissuade the Somali president, Mohamed Siad Barre, from pursuing his territorial claims on the Ogaden. But Siad Barre refused to negotiate a settlement. A Somali offensive in July 1977 (via 40,000 troops) prompted the Soviets increase their military aid to Ethiopia. The Somalis responded by

renouncing their treaty arrangements with Moscow, expelling Soviet
diplomats and military advisers. By September 1977, Somali forces controlled almost all of the Ogaden. In November, the Soviet Union and Cuba
began a military buildup in a bid to remove the invading troops. By
January 1978, 12,000 Cuban soldiers had been airlifted into Ethiopia,
joined by Soviet advisers, tanks, and ammunition.[159]

At an SCC meeting, Brzezinski proposed sending a naval task force to
the Red Sea as a show of U.S. military might. The regional powers, he said,
had to see that America was not "passive in the face of Soviet and Cuban
intervention." Brzezinski told Carter that failing to act would make the
administration look "weak," and would be "exploited by political opponents with considerable effect." Vance viewed the situation differently. He
argued that the Ogaden War was a local conflict which had to be dealt
with regionally—not as a Cold War struggle between Washington and
Moscow. The Soviets had moved to preserve their influence, and little else.
"We are getting sucked in," Vance protested. "The Somalis brought this
on themselves. They are no great friends of ours."[160] Since Somalia was
the prime aggressor, Brown and the Joint Chiefs also rejected the idea of
sending a task force. Carter decided against taking military action. But on
March 2 he publicly criticized the Soviet actions, warning that interference
in the Horn of Africa would affect the SALT process.[161]

By March 15 the Ogaden War was over. Soviet–Cuban efforts had
forced the withdrawal of Somali troops from the region. But détente
continued to weaken. In one report after another, Brzezinski pressed
Carter to toughen his rhetoric. He warned that "the state of public
opinion" did not give the president the luxury of confining U.S.-Soviet
talks to "a bargaining exercise on the specifics of SALT."[162] "Once
concluded SALT II will be a target for attack," Brzezinski wrote. "That
attack will be sustained, and I have reason to believe that Ford, Kissinger,
Baker, and Scoop [Jackson] will oppose the likely agreement." To ease the
domestic hurdles, he advised Carter to "take some decision that conveys
your toughness in dealing with the Russians."[163] In set-piece speeches,
Carter began denouncing the Soviet behavior in Africa, their "excessive"
military buildup, and the "totalitarian and repressive" Soviet system.
During an address at his alma mater in June, Carter declared: "The
Soviet Union can choose either confrontation or cooperation. The
United States is adequately prepared to meet either choice."[164] His decision to up the rhetorical ante did nothing to improve domestic perceptions
of the Soviets. By casting the Ogaden War in Cold War terms and riling
public opinion against Moscow, the administration was undermining

support needed to ratify a SALT Treaty. "We were shooting ourselves in the foot," Vance recalled.[165]

PLAYING THE CHINA CARD

A sign of the tougher U.S. posture in 1978 was the decision to pursue full diplomatic relations with China. The Sino–American rapprochement had been initiated in 1972, when Nixon visited China to sign the Shanghai Communique (paralleling the push for détente with the Soviets). For Beijing and Washington, the aim was to enhance their political leverage over Moscow. But subsequent events curtailed progress. Vietnam and Watergate consumed the remainder of Nixon's presidency, while his successor Gerald Ford refused to support normalization. Ford's reluctance was twofold. He was under pressure from a strong Taiwan lobby in Congress—which opposed the Beijing government's legitimacy—and wary that an approach to China might impair the SALT process with Moscow.

Sino–Soviet relations had been deteriorating since the 1960s. Mao Zedong's "Great Proletariat Cultural Revolution" fueled nationalist sentiment and opposition to Soviet "revisionism." The relationship worsened in 1969, when a long-simmering territorial dispute escalated into armed clashes along the Sino–Soviet border. By then, the economic effects of isolationism led Mao to reorient Chinese foreign policy and cast aside ideological constraints. He sought an opening with the United States, with potential access to Western technology and new opportunities for trade. Although Sino–American normalization did not result, relations between Moscow and Beijing remained tense, with border disputes continuing to emerge. After Mao's death in 1976, Deng Xiaoping moved to consolidate power by pursuing economic reform, modernization, and closer ties to the West. Soviet leaders grew suspicious of Deng's motives, concerned about the implications of a new Sino–American rapprochement.[166]

The opening of diplomatic relations with China had been a goal from the start of Carter's presidency. The main question was the timing. In early 1977, the administration exercised caution. Chinese Ambassador Huang Zhen told Carter that under the Shanghai Communique, normalization would require the abrogation of the U.S.–Taiwan defense treaty.[167] China's stance posed political difficulties. Since Carter had prioritized the Panama Canal treaties, an early approach to Beijing would scupper his chances of securing congressional ratification. "I didn't want to make a public move on China until after the Panama Canal issue was resolved,"

Carter recalled. "Senator Barry Goldwater and other members of the Taiwan lobby were undecided about the Panama treaties, and any move away from Taiwan would have driven them against us on the treaty votes."[168] China was placed "on the back burner" until early 1978, when Brzezinski pressed Carter to begin the normalization process. Brzezinski saw the issue through the lens of the Cold War: closer U.S.–China security cooperation would give the administration geopolitical leverage over the Soviets, which could be used to pressure Moscow into making concessions on SALT. Brzezinski asked Carter to send him to China "to engage in quiet consultations [...] thereby sending a signal to the Soviets which might prove helpful on the African Horn and SALT." "Domestically," he added, "it would be viewed as a hard-nosed act," softening the Senate opposition to a SALT II Treaty.[169]

Carter relented in March 1978. He told Mondale and Vance (who opposed Brzezinski's trip) that an opening with China could be used to apply pressure on the Soviets. It would strengthen the administration's credibility at home, helping to win support from reluctant senators in the SALT ratification bid.[170] The economic, strategic, and political benefits outweighed concerns over human rights. China's dismal record was noted by the U.S. ambassador to Hong Kong, Thomas Shoesmith, who reported that the number of executions in 1977 was as high as 20,000.[171] In spite of this, Carter sent Brzezinski to Beijing in May to advance diplomatic relations and brief Chinese leaders on SALT. "The strong consensus was that we ought to move ahead as quickly as possible to normalize relations with China," Gelb recalled. "While this would cause complications in concluding the SALT II agreement, it would substantially improve our position domestically. It would show doubters in Congress that this was an administration that could play hardball and do power politics, and when the time came to ratify the SALT II Treaty, we would be in a better position to do so."[172]

Brzezinski relished the chance to emulate Kissinger. "Last one to get the top gets to fight the Russians in Ethiopia," he joked on a visit to the Great Wall. Brzezinski struck up a rapport with Chinese Vice Premier (and de facto leader) Deng Xiaoping, giving him a list of suggestions on how China could improve the attitude of the U.S. public toward Beijing. He spoke publicly of "aggressive" Soviet designs and called for "more tangible cooperation between China and the U.S." A path for normalization was put in place. The administration agreed to meet the Chinese conditions: diplomatic and military relations with Taiwan would be terminated, and U.S. personnel would be withdrawn. The United States would retain the right to export defensive arms to Taiwan, a measure which Carter hoped would placate the Taiwan lobby on Capitol Hill.[173] Liberals and conservatives expressed unease about the change to U.S.–Taiwanese relations. Sen. Jesse Helms (R-North Carolina) accused Carter of threatening to "sell Taiwan down the river." As a compromise, Congress passed the Taiwan Relations Act, with the United States continuing to supply arms to Taiwan to defend itself from the mainland. Although unhappy about the bill, Chinese leaders did not allow it to undermine normalization.[174]

U.S. and Chinese officials finalized terms over the next six months. On December 15, Carter and Hua Guofeng (the Chinese Communist Party leader) issued a joint statement announcing the normalization of diplomatic relations. A visit by Deng Xiaoping to Washington was scheduled for January. The news broke just days before Vance was to meet Gromyko for a "final" round of SALT talks. Carter wrote to Brezhnev, explaining that the U.S.–China agreement had "no other purpose but to promote the cause of world peace."[175] In the circumstances, the Soviet reaction was restrained. Brezhnev raised no public objections, and would wait to see how the process was carried out.[176] But the completion of SALT II was now delayed. Brezhnev wanted to avoid a scenario whereby a U.S.–Soviet summit was directly preceded by one between Carter and Deng. Dobrynin recalled that the U.S.–China declaration produced "more irritation than fear" in Moscow, creating "a situation which spoiled our negotiations." Soviet leaders were frustrated that China had been given priority at the expense of arms control.[177] The Vance–Gromyko meeting in December had been expected to lead to a Carter–Brezhnev summit at which a SALT II Treaty would be signed. The politically vulnerable document would not be finalized until June 1979—six months closer to election season. The venue: Vienna, scene of the Kennedy–Khrushchev encounter eighteen years earlier.

CARTER, CONGRESS, AND THE PANAMA CANAL

Carter's difficulties were not confined to the Soviet Union. Just as worrying was the administration's sour relationship with Congress and the Democratic Party. To be sure, the changed power structure of the 1970s would have posed challenges for any new president. Congress was more assertive, partisan, and fragmented—a climate exacerbated by the proliferation of subcommittees (many of which were themselves divided) and interest groups. Carter later admitted to being surprised by the sheer number of committees and subcommittees which had to be navigated to achieve legislative packages.[178] Despite boasting a majority in both chambers, the Democratic Party remained splintered. There was, recalled Butler, "no unifying consensus, no program, no set of principles on which a majority of Democrats agreed."[179]

But the administration was also culpable. The quest to build support and bridge divides on Capitol Hill required organization, leadership, and persuasion. For reasons of principle and inexperience, the team assembled by Carter struggled in these areas. Carter was an antiestablishment politician, an evangelical Christian, whose moral compass helped to guide his convictions (though not always his decisions). He secured the Democratic nomination in 1976 without the help of most of the party hierarchy, and disliked the extravagant aspects of the presidency. Carter told the Marine Corps to stop playing "Hail to the Chief" whenever he entered a room; sold the presidential yacht, *The Sequoia*; and held town meetings around the country.[180] He hosted dinners with senators and lawmakers to outline his initiatives. But often there was as much confrontation as compromise. Carter loathed the give-and-take of politics and had little time for convention. He was forthright and disinclined to stroke egos. "It has never been my nature to be a hail fellow well met, or to be a part of a societal, cocktail party circuit," he explained. "It's just not me."[181] Carter clashed with congressional Democrats over a string of legislative issues, from federal water projects to public works packages. He endured a difficult relationship with Senate Majority Leader Robert Byrd, who complained of Carter's tendency to vacillate, for the "leadership vacuum" that existed, and about having to lecture him on how Congress functioned. Byrd warned that the administration's "them against us" approach was damaging relations between the White House and Capitol Hill.[182]

The young figures entrusted with managing this task, Frank Moore and Hamilton Jordan, incurred the wrath of senators and representatives. Both earned a reputation for not responding to phone calls. Tip O'Neill became so exasperated by Jordan that he began referring to him as "Hannibal Jerkin" to friends on the Hill.[183] Moore (congressional liaison) was "just plain dumb," according to the House Speaker. While their appointments were meant to signal the end of White House pandering to special interests, many in Congress interpreted it as Carter's contempt for political Washington.[184] O'Neill believed there was a divide between Democrats from the north-east and those in the south. Carter's Georgian team, O'Neill said, "just didn't understand Irish or Jewish politicians, or the nuances of city politics."[185]

Congressional complaints were manifold: a poor organizational structure, communication problems (such as the lack of advance consultation on decisions), and a failure to devise a coherent legislative program. Jordan suggested that Carter appoint a "staff coordinator," responsible for convening bi-weekly meetings of domestic and foreign policy officials. Jordan fancied the job. "This person should be me," he wrote. "Not only am I the best person to do this, but I am also the only person on the staff with the flexibility and perspective to perform such a function." Carter approved him for the role.[186] Moore acknowledged that the administration had "not paid enough attention to the needs of individual members of Congress."[187] Recognition of the need for more effective coordination was put into focus by the Panama Canal treaties—one of Carter's major international goals.

*

The United States had exercised control of the Panama Canal Zone since the Hay–Bunau–Varilla Treaty of 1903. For decades, Panamanians viewed the arrangement as an affront to their national sovereignty. Protests were held against the American zone which divided their country. Following an outbreak of violence in 1964, Lyndon Johnson agreed to begin talks that would lead to the return of the canal to Panama. But the issue became bound up in domestic politics. In the 1976 Republican primaries, Ronald Reagan attacked President Ford for his willingness to cede the canal. "When it comes to the canal, we bought it, we paid for it— it's ours," Reagan declared.[188] Carter treaded carefully, saying that he would continue the negotiations, but would not give up possession of the canal.[189] But once elected he changed tack. Eager to project a moral approach to foreign affairs, Carter placed the Panama Canal near the top of his agenda. In September 1977, he and General Omar Torrijos signed a treaty that would abrogate the 1903 agreement and transfer control of the canal to Panama by 2000. Meanwhile, a neutrality treaty was signed to keep the canal open and neutral once Panama assumed sovereignty.

What followed the agreement was a bitter, partisan struggle. Liberals supported the canal transfer, while the majority of conservatives opposed it. The Panama saga became entwined with SALT II and the congressional elections. Brzezinski told Carter that ratification of the Panama treaties "will clear the way for SALT [. . .] Failure, on the other hand, will severely undermine your ability to ratify future agreements."[190] Conservatives viewed the Panama Canal Treaty as a "dry run for SALT," giving anti-disarmament forces the opportunity to link the two issues and label the administration "soft" on national security.[191] With a host of senators standing in the midterm elections, the Panama issue provided Republicans with added incentive to embarrass a Democratic president. "There's no basic constituency in favor of the treaty," Jordan lamented. "The only people who give a damn are the ones who oppose it."[192] Early public opinion polls ran two to one against the treaties.[193]

As with SALT, conservatives went on the public offensive. A coalition of twenty interest groups mobilized, including the American Conservative Union, the Conservative Caucus, and the Council for National Defense.[194] An umbrella group, "The Emergency Committee to Save the Panama Canal," organized a "Truth Squad." Leading conservatives such as Reagan and Sen. Paul Laxalt (R-Nevada) toured the states represented by undecided senators. They argued that foreign powers would view the ceding of the canal as an "act of weakness" by the United States.[195] "This is the best political issue that could be handed to a party in recent years," Laxalt beamed. "It's a natural issue to galvanize our people for fundraising and to gear up the troops." Howard Philips, chairman of the Conservative Caucus, added: "I can't think of any other issue that better unites grassroots conservatives than the canal."[196] A multimillion dollar campaign was unleashed by lobbyists, using direct mail, paid television adverts, and grassroots activism. Early initiatives proved effective. Sen. Gaylord Nelson (D-Wisconsin) told Mondale that he was inundated with mail campaigning against the U.S.–Panama talks. The Senate minority leader, Howard Baker (R-Tennessee), had received 22,000 anti-treaty letters, with only 500 in support.[197]

But the Carter administration responded well. Jordan devised a plan for a public outreach effort and a focused political campaign. A Citizens Committee was formed to counter the "Truth Squad," with high-profile conservatives solicited to express support for the Panama treaties. They included Henry Kissinger, David Rockefeller, Dean Rusk, George Shultz, Maxwell Taylor, John Wayne, Elmo Zumwalt, and William F. Buckley, who debated Reagan in a live national broadcast. Carter met with a range of interest groups, organizations, and individuals: the U.S. Chamber of Commerce, National Association of Manufacturers, AFL-CIO, NAACP, multinational executives, religious leaders, governors, mayors, and party chairmen.[198] The political campaign targeted undecided senators in ten key states. With midterm elections looming, Carter's task was to create an atmosphere that would enable the senators to vote for the canal treaties.[199] He invited Torrijos to Washington to make a joint statement clarifying the neutrality agreement. It stated that the United States retained the right to defend the canal against any threat to its continued neutral service, but did not have the right to interfere in Panamanian internal affairs. Carter urged members of Congress to visit Panama and meet with U.S. military officials stationed there to help sway their votes. By the spring of 1978, some forty-five senators had made the trip.[200]

The lobbying yielded results, including the endorsement of both Senate leaders, Robert Byrd and Howard Baker, in January 1978. By the time the floor debates began in February, a Gallup poll showed that Americans favored the treaty by 45–42 percent.[201] Many Republicans remained fiercely opposed. Sen. Orrin Hatch (R-Utah) suggested that America was "going the way of Rome," with the Panama treaties reflecting "that pattern of surrender and appeasement that has cost us so much all over the world."[202] But the administration secured the clinching Senate votes by agreeing to a reservation, which asserted the U.S. right to station troops in Panama after 2000. The canal transfer treaty—as with the neutrality treaty—passed by 68–32 on April 18, narrowly meeting the two-thirds majority threshold. For months thereafter, House members bickered over the implementation details. Carter recalled hosting representatives "ad nauseum" in an effort to garner support, an experience he described as "horrible."[203]

The Panama treaties rank among Carter's finest achievements in foreign affairs. But the political price was high. Officials had erred in assuming that a victory would provide "a momentum useful to SALT." In fact, the quest to secure the treaties would hurt Carter for the rest of his presidency. In asking reluctant senators to risk office for an unpopular cause, the administration had expended enormous political goodwill. The 1978 midterm election results bore this out. Of the twenty senators who had voted to ratify the Panama treaties and were up for reelection, six decided not to run and a further seven lost their seats. And by pointing to Panama as an example of their bipartisan support, moderate Republicans such as Howard Baker would now find it easier to oppose SALT II on its merits.

A second consequence of the treaties was that the canal "giveaway" was viewed by the political right as more evidence that Carter was weak on national security. Notwithstanding his rethink over military spending, the result of decisions made in 1977–78 was a perception that the administration was soft on defense: the ditching of the deep cuts proposal; the cancellation of the B-1 bomber; the deferral of the neutron bomb deployment. By mid-1978, Carter's advisers were concerned at the administration's lack of credibility on national security. "Each of these [policies] can be justified, but together they contribute to an impression that we are "retreating" from a position of strength around the world, and that we are not being 'tough' with the communists," warned Richard Moe (Mondale's chief of staff). "I can think of nothing more damaging to the President, both domestically and internationally, than to suffer a Senate defeat on SALT. It would be an unmitigated disaster."[204]

Carter was under no illusions about his opposition. "When I was approaching the end of the Panama Canal vote, the Republican leaders were telling me very frankly that they would never support SALT II, no matter what was in it," he recalled. "I was told this by Ford, Kissinger, and Baker. They said they had gone as far as they could as a Republican Party in supporting my positions, as they had endorsed Panama."[205] It was but one of several foreign policies entailing domestic costs. SALT II, the normalization of relations with China, and the Camp David accords drew criticism from hawks, anti-communists, and Taiwanese and Jewish lobby groups, respectively. "All of these things that we engaged were political losers," Jordan admitted.[206]

*

In his speech at Annapolis (June 1978), Carter posed the essential issue: America and the Soviet Union had to choose between détente and confrontation.[207] By the end of the year the latter course appeared more likely. U.S.–Soviet relations—affected by disputes over strategic arms, human rights, and Third World competition—now rested almost entirely on SALT. Carter's decision to prioritize closer ties with China over the completion of a major agreement with the USSR was symptomatic of the tensions between Washington and Moscow.

But there was more to the dwindling of détente than geostrategy or ideology. Political considerations affected every major issue with which Carter grappled—from SALT and the neutron bomb to China and the Panama Canal. On arms control, Carter adjusted policy to straddle the demands of his conservative critics (who called for a tougher posture toward Moscow) and the need to maintain a functional relationship with the Kremlin. The efforts to strike a balance between international goals and domestic needs were at times mishandled, with the administration appearing indecisive, contradictory, or both. "The political realities in the United States started to impose a linkage on our freedom to make compromises and concessions," Brzezinski recalled. "We had to start asking ourselves, 'What will happen in the ratification process?' And I think it did start constraining our SALT negotiating position—or, alternatively, getting us to do things which otherwise we might not have done in regards to the strategic equation: for example, the MX decision [June 1979]."[208]

Carter tried to resist the political intrusions. He rejected calls for a withdrawal from SALT. He refused to succumb to demands for a more aggressive military posture—canceling the B-1 bomber program, halting production of the neutron bomb, and defying requests to develop the MX. In August 1978, Carter vetoed a defense authorization bill (sponsored by Jackson and Nunn) that included $2 billion in funding for a nuclear aircraft carrier, deeming it an unnecessary expense.[209] Moreover, some of his most acclaimed achievements—the Panama Canal treaties, the Camp David accords, and the opening to China—had aroused as much political flak as support. But the cracks were appearing. Carter had reneged on his campaign pledge to reduce defense spending. He began to toughen his rhetoric, denouncing Soviet behavior domestically and overseas. He sanctioned an approach to Beijing despite the Chinese record on human rights—giving the United States strategic leverage over the USSR and boosting the prospects for SALT ratification at home. This firmer posture was adopted to meet political pressures as much as concerns over Soviet expansionism, reflecting the mutual give-and-take process that Carter so disliked. Yet the greatest challenges lay ahead. Problems at home and abroad were brought sharply into focus in 1979.

2

"It's All Political Now"

As his third year began, Carter could have been forgiven for reflecting on his global accomplishments. The Arab–Israeli peace accords, the diplomatic opening with China, and the Panama Canal treaties appeared to bode well. Meanwhile, the quest to achieve a SALT II agreement with the Soviets was nearly secured. "Administration credibility is high after Camp David," beamed Hamilton Jordan.[1] But problems lay ahead. Domestic troubles would spiral in the first six months of 1979. An economic recession, mounting inflation (resulting from a new oil crisis), and intraparty disagreements all undermined support for the president. Together they conjured images of an administration in turmoil. As the year progressed, the idea of "national weakness" was invoked by opponents of Carter's foreign policies.

The sense of political crisis struck at the very moment that Carter began looking toward the 1980 election. The auguries were not good. In early January, Carter's public approval rating stood at 50 percent. But as economic woes deepened his credibility rapidly diminished. By the end of June, Carter's approval rating had slumped to just 28 percent.[2] In terms of political resources and popular prestige, Carter was, noted Richard Neustadt, "worse off than any other elected president of modern times."[3] In 1979, Carter came under greater pressure to align foreign policy with his domestic needs. His decision to authorize production of the MX program appeared perverse in light of everything that preceded it. Here was a notable policy departure, veering beyond the sort of compromise or rhetorical device that Carter had deployed earlier in his term. Soon after, the bungled U.S. response to the "discovery" of a Soviet brigade in Cuba undermined relations with Moscow, just weeks after the Vienna summit.

This politically manufactured crisis would jeopardize support for the SALT II Treaty—and the quest for Senate ratification.

BRZEZINSKI AND THE "ARC OF CRISIS"

International success could not disguise Carter's grim domestic predicament. Conflicts with Congress, Democratic leaders, and interest groups plagued his first two years. At a midterm party conference in Memphis, Carter outlined his federal budget proposals for 1980, which were cast in terms of economic austerity. His pledge to limit the deficit to $29 billion ($12 billion less than in 1979)—from which a 3 percent increase in defense spending was still to come—drew criticism from liberals such as Tip O'Neill, who targeted areas such as jobs, healthcare, education, and housing. The 1980 election was very much on Carter's mind. At the conference, he and Jordan geared their efforts toward winning support from the broadest possible spectrum rather than the liberal wing. The move provided an opening to the party's refulgent star, Massachusetts senator Ted Kennedy, who appealed to the traditional Democratic base. Kennedy attacked Carter's austerity measures as "seriously defective" and gave a rousing speech on healthcare reform. Jordan turned to Pat Caddell, Carter's pollster, and said, "That's it. He's running."[4] Kennedy was touted as a likely opponent to Carter, though publicly he pledged support for the president. Carter knew better. "Kennedy's laying the groundwork for a campaign," he wrote in his diary. "Every day he takes some tiny thing out of the budget and issues a press release condemning me, which is getting tiresome."[5] Carter's concerns were vindicated: a *Los Angeles Times* poll in January 1979 put Kennedy 23 points ahead of the president in a national election.[6] That month the effects of the energy crisis (emanating from the Iranian revolution) began to undercut the administration's efforts to curb inflation. The consequences would be devastating.

Foreign policy was now being viewed through the prism of the election. "The question as we approach 1980 is what we can do for an encore," Brzezinski explained to Carter. "The achievement of a SALT summit will evolve into a long, bitter, and potentially inconclusive ratification debate. It is hard to believe it will provide much political momentum for the campaign of 1980, especially if the Soviets do something that generates further public concern about their motives." Spinning the globe, Brzezinski was downbeat. Problems in the Middle East were mounting (notably in Iran), while the American–Jewish community harbored a "deep suspicion" of the administration. A success in Southern Africa, such as Rhodesia, would have no real public impact in the United States. More broadly, Brzezinski worried about the perception that the administration was in "disarray." "We have not dispelled the notion that we are amateurish and disorganized, and that our policies are uncertain and irresolute," he told Carter. "Abroad and increasingly at home the United States is seen as indecisive, vacillating, and pursuing a policy of acquiescence." To boost the president's credibility, Brzezinski called for "tough-minded consultations" with the Soviets, and for a foreign policy speech on American power.[7]

Brzezinski also told Carter about Moscow's strategy of creating new spheres of influence in the Third World. In December 1978, he introduced his "arc of crisis" theory, based on the notion of Soviet expansionism. Brzezinski claimed that America was in a situation similar to that faced by Truman over Europe in the 1940s. "If you draw an arc on the globe, stretching from Chittagong through Islamabad to Aden, you will be pointing to the area of our greatest vulnerability," he told Carter. "Fragile social and political structures in a region of vital importance to us are threatened with fragmentation. The resulting political vacuum may well be filled by elements more sympathetic to the Soviet Union."[8] By April 1979, Brzezinski was urging Carter to harden the tone of his foreign policy. "It is very important for you to counter the impression that American leadership is not firm. The answer is more deliberate emphasis on strength and resolve in your public statements. You should not hesitate to stress the need to forcefully counter Soviet ambitions." With a SALT treaty at stake, senators required assurances that the president was "tough, resolute, and *determined* not to let the Soviets gain a politically exploitable advantage."[9]

CHINA PLAYS THE AMERICAN CARD

With SALT II delayed, the administration turned its attention to two other summits early in the New Year. First, Carter headed to the Caribbean, where he met the leaders of America's key NATO allies. The Guadeloupe summit marked a new Western effort to commit to détente and form a more united defense. European leaders had complained that their security concerns were not being addressed in the SALT process. The Soviet deployment of SS-20 missiles in Eastern Europe had raised fears of a possible "limited" nuclear war arising in the continent. In Guadeloupe, Carter was joined by West German Chancellor Helmut Schmidt, British Prime Minister James Callaghan, and French President Valéry Giscard d'Estaing. The four leaders agreed on a "dual-track" response to counter the Soviet SS-20s. The United States would prepare to deploy new Pershing II intermediate-range ballistic missiles and ground-launched cruise missiles in 1983—spanning West Germany, Britain, Italy, Belgium, and the Netherlands. Concurrently, Washington would engage Moscow in talks in a bid to limit the intermediate-range nuclear weapons on both sides. If an agreement was reached, the U.S. deployment would be forestalled.

Later in January, Deng Xiaoping arrived for a nine-day tour of the United States, where the new Sino-American relationship was formalized. His visit received top billing. The vice premier had just been crowned *Time Magazine*'s "Man of the Year," cast as "visionary of the new China."[10] A string of lavish events were held, including a White House dinner and a gala at the Kennedy Center, where Deng charmed senators and the Harlem Globetrotters. Deng visited Martin Luther King Jr.'s grave, the Ford Motor Company plant, and attended a rodeo in Houston.[11] He concluded his trip with a visit to Seattle, where he and Henry Jackson held private talks. The Washington senator delivered a keynote address for a dinner held in Deng's honor, before escorting him on a tour of the Boeing aircraft plant.[12]

Deng's most pressing concern was to ensure that the United States remained quiet in the event of a Chinese move against Soviet-allied Vietnam. On January 30, he told Carter and Brzezinski of the Chinese plans to launch an invasion. Despite being forewarned, neither was willing to try to dissuade Beijing. Nor was Carter moved to press Deng on China's human rights record—something which did not escape the attention of Moscow. (In 1979, Brezhnev permitted 50,000 Jews to leave the USSR.) The issue of Taiwan was barely touched upon. Deng had achieved his goals. The previous night's "delightful dinner partner" was now a "tough Communist leader, determined that his nation not appear soft." Carter's impression was that "Vietnam would be punished."[13] Less than three weeks later Vietnam was invaded, with fourteen Chinese divisions (totaling 170,000 troops) stationed in the northern part of the country. China had played the American card.

In his State of the Union address, Carter said that the new relationship with China was not intended for use against the Soviets. He expressed a desire to welcome Brezhnev to America "in the near future."[14] But Deng's visit and the Chinese action in Vietnam raised concern in Moscow about an anti-Soviet alignment. To dispel any notions of U.S. involvement, Carter wrote to Brezhnev on February 17—just after Chinese troops had crossed the Vietnamese border.[15] He urged the Soviet leader to "exercise restraint" and avoid taking any military action. Brezhnev was unimpressed. "The Soviet Union cannot remain indifferent," he replied, trying to distinguish China's behavior from that of Vietnam against Kampuchea. Brezhnev pointed to the proximity between Deng's U.S. visit and the Chinese invasion. "Is this a simple coincidence?" he asked.[16] Gromkyo castigated America's use of the "China card," and warned the Beijing government to leave Vietnam "before it's too late."[17] When Chinese forces quickly withdrew (as Deng had indicated they would), Carter relayed his appreciation for Brezhnev's restraint.[18] A U.S.–Soviet crisis was averted and plans for a summit remained intact.

SELLING SALT

Planning for SALT II ratification began in October 1978. The expectation then had been that the treaty details would be in place by the end of the year. But with the Sino–American rapprochement, a Carter–Brezhnev summit was postponed until mid-1979. A SALT Working Group was established to help broaden domestic support. In October, a report indicated "overwhelming" public support (71 percent) for cooperation with the Soviets in arms control. However, a large segment remained "deeply mistrustful" of Soviet intentions: an NBC poll in August 1978 suggested that more than one-fifth of the public were resolutely against any SALT agreement.[19]

Congressional support was another matter. The Panama treaties had been a good barometer of the scale of the task facing Carter. But the administration was entering uncharted territory. When Nixon and Brezhnev signed the SALT I Treaty in 1972, all of Congress (and most of the executive branch) were unaware of the details of the accord. Only later were senators fully briefed and in a position to make informed criticisms as to its perceived weaknesses. Much had now changed. The political winds of the mid-70s altered the conduct of foreign policy, not least the domestic parameters facing decision-makers. Executive-legislative talks on SALT II had been very different. Influential figures such as Henry Jackson were regularly briefed on developments. The administration co-opted the Democratic Whip, Alan Cranston, to lead a series of meetings to educate fellow senators on SALT. But many were unprepared to make the case to their constituents, and susceptible to Jackson's argument that the SALT agreement was weak.[20] Senate Majority Leader Robert Byrd (D-West Virginia) was "deeply distrustful" of the Soviets, and unlikely to campaign for SALT II.[21] Minority Leader

Howard Baker, having supported the Panama treaties, could ill afford to champion another Carter cause without winning major concessions. All of which left Cranston as the only senator in a leadership position who was wholly committed to SALT.

In February 1979, the SALT task force was expanded. It was led by Jordan and included the likes of David Aaron (Brzezinski's deputy at the NSC) and figures from the Office of Congressional Liaison. By May, seventy-five senators had met privately with Vance, Brzezinski, Brown, or Gelb. Anne Weyler directed a broader outreach effort from the Public Liaison Office. Hundreds of thousands of SALT brochures were distributed. Publications were mailed to 6,000 editors, columnists, and broadcasters. A public speakers bureau was formed, with State and ACDA officials presenting the administration's case on television, radio, and in print.[22]

MISSILE EXPERIMENTAL

Carter came under renewed pressure to toughen his defense posture as the SALT treaty neared completion. He was warned of the ratification battles ahead, and the skepticism of senators who had their own campaigns to fight in 1980. Brzezinski told Carter:

Given the domestic time pressures, you will need to discriminate very carefully between the things you *must* do in order to maintain momentum in foreign policy; the things that you *should* do because of their potentially positive impact on foreign policy and domestic politics; and the things that you *should not* do because they either detract from your foreign policy accomplishments, or because they would complicate your domestic political situation.[23]

For the rest of his presidency Carter would follow this logic.

Anti-SALT interest groups mobilized in early 1979. In March, the CPD produced two more publications denouncing Carter's approach and pointing to new Soviet military capabilities.[24] Moscow's recent testing of the SS-18 and SS-19 missiles caused concern among hawks in the national security bureaucracy. Paul Nitze criticized the supposed disparity between U.S. and Soviet forces, citing the Soviet advantages in heavy weapons.[25] The Soviet military advances (though again overestimated) were said to have made the American Minuteman III vulnerable to a first strike. As such, conservatives demanded that Carter approve production of the MX mobile ICBM system (known as "Missile Experimental").[26] Brzezinski sent Carter a full analysis of the military, political, economic, and technological capabilities of the United States and the Soviet Union. He concluded that while America led the way in technological aspects, "the trends in the military components of national power all favor the Soviet Union." To win the support of conservatives for the SALT II Treaty, Brzezinski urged Carter to authorize the MX program before his summit with Brezhnev.[27]

The MX was controversial for environmental, economic, and political reasons. It weighed 100 tons, measured 70 feet, and was almost eight feet long in diameter.[28] Finding a basing plan was therefore difficult. Military planners recommended moving the missiles on vehicle launchers to widely spaced concrete shelters in remote parts of Nevada and Utah. Numerous alternatives were devised. But whatever the proposal, it met with objections on Capitol Hill. The MX contained ten 5.5-foot-long nuclear warheads, each of which was seventeen times more powerful than the atomic bomb that had leveled Hiroshima.[29] While many in Congress backed the idea, there were few volunteers to host the MX. "Congress did not oppose the idea of a new heavy missile in principle, but rather feared public opposition to their deployment," explained diplomat Jack Matlock, later to serve as U.S. ambassador in Moscow. "Nobody wanted them in his backyard. If they were in fixed locations, they would be vulnerable to a surprise attack; if they were mobile, an accident could have disastrous consequences for the people in the vicinity."[30] There were also financial objections. While the Pentagon judged the cost of the system to be $33 billion, the Congressional Budget Office's estimate was $60 billion.[31]

Conservative demands for the MX drew a loud response from liberal senators—whose support Carter also needed in the SALT ratification debates. On March 2, Mark Hatfield (R-Oregon), George McGovern (D-South Dakota), and William Proxmire (D-Wisconsin) told Carter that a SALT treaty would be "very difficult, if not impossible to support" if the MX proceeded. It was, they argued, "too high a price" to pay.[32] But the MX and SALT became entwined in the weeks leading up to Vienna. Sen. Sam Nunn (D-Georgia), a conservative Democrat, called for a 5 percent increase in defense spending as his price for backing the treaty. He stated that the bulk of this money should be used to develop the MX.[33] Additionally, Pat Caddell told Carter that there was now a strong plurality among the American public for an increase in military spending. Nearly two-thirds (62 percent) believed that the U.S. position in the world was becoming weaker rather than stronger. Caddell warned of "the general spirit of unhappiness," and the "great dissatisfaction with the way [Carter] is doing the job."[34]

Carter finally succumbed to the pressure. He accepted that the MX would have to be approved if SALT II was to pass through Congress. The credibility of the agreement (and of Carter himself) would rest on convincing his domestic audience that he would redress the "adverse trends" in the U.S.–Soviet military balance. The MX decision veered against Carter's principles. At an NSC meeting on June 4, the president complained to Brzezinski that he was "jamming a decision" down his throat.[35] In his diary entry for that day, Carter wrote of his "disappointment with the memo on MX mobile basing. It was a nauseating prospect to confront, with the gross waste of money going into nuclear weapons of all kinds."[36] Nauseating or not, the decision was made. Jimmy Carter in 1977 would hardly have given the MX plan much of a glance. Except, perhaps, a derisory one. In the fall of 1978, he assured Warnke that he would never sanction the MX.[37] But political pragmatism had forced a rethink. As Brzezinski recalled: "The MX decision was heavily driven, in addition to its strategic merits, by the thought that this would ensure a higher degree of probability for SALT ratification, which otherwise was very problematic."[38]

CARTER AND BREZHNEV: THE VIENNA SUMMIT

Final details of the SALT II agreement were completed by Vance and Dobrynin in May 1979. Carter suggested Washington as the venue for the meeting, given that the previous summit was in Vladivostok. Brezhnev, on his doctors' orders, proposed Moscow. But Carter ruled this out: senators would accuse him of granting another concession to the Soviets, further complicating ratification efforts. As a compromise, Carter and Brezhnev settled on Vienna (June 15–18).[39]

The Soviet leader's ill-health dictated the pace of events. "Brezhnev's physical condition will severely limit what he can do," Vance told Carter. "Two hours is about the maximum he can spend in a negotiating session, and he will require long rests."[40] The *Washington Post* predicted it would be among "the most choreographed summits in history."[41] Meetings would indeed be short, and Brezhnev relied heavily on close advisers such as Gromyko, Defense Minister Dmitry Ustinov, and Politburo member Konstantin Chernenko. "He is old, human, and emotional," warned Averell Harriman. "Brezhnev looks on this meeting as one of the great events of his life [...] His deepest commitment is to keep war away from his own people."[42] Harriman advised Carter to adopt a warm, personal style. Carter obliged and there were few signs of acrimony, save for

Brezhnev's complaint that the dinner menu at the U.S. embassy was only printed in English.[43]

Brezhnev's dotage was apparent throughout the summit. Gromyko whispered instructions and turned pages for the Soviet leader. After the formalities in the Austrian president's office, Carter and Brezhnev spoke privately. Brezhnev placed his hand on Carter's shoulder and said, "If we do not succeed, God will not forgive us." Moments later, as they walked down the steps to leave the building, Brezhnev kept his hand on Carter's arm to steady himself. For Carter, "this simple and apparently natural gesture bridged the gap between us more effectively than any official talk." The night before the signing ceremony, both men attended the Vienna State Opera for a gala performance of Mozart's *The Abduction from the Seraglio*. The next day, much to his surprise, Carter found himself embracing Brezhnev and kissing cheeks "in the Soviet fashion." Brezhnev told his associates that Carter was "quite a nice guy after all."[44]

After twenty-seven months of complex negotiations the SALT II agreement was completed. The treaty set a ceiling of 2,400 units for strategic nuclear delivery vehicles, to be reduced to 2,240 by January 1981, which would remain in effect until 1985. A ceiling of 1,200 MIRVed intercontinental and submarine-launched missiles was agreed upon, with the overall number of land, sea, and air missiles not to exceed 1,320. There were also limits on the number of "heavy" ICBMs, and on the deployment of new ICBMs. Brezhnev gave a written assurance that the Soviet "Backfire" would not be used as an intercontinental bomber, with annual production limited to thirty aircraft per year.[45] But amid these modest achievements there was regret on both sides. Carter was "disappointed at our inability to have made even more progress," while Brzezinski recalled a "sober" meeting, with little discussion of strategic problems.[46] Dobrynin pointed to the delay in holding the summit, which had come "too late" for personal diplomacy: "During those two or three years Brezhnev had grown physically and mentally more decrepit—he dozed off in the Vienna Opera. Besides, there was no way of knowing what Carter's political fortunes would be in the following year's presidential election."[47]

In fact, the summit coincided with a dramatic slump in Carter's public approval rating, which now stood at just 28 percent.[48] Don Oberdorfer wrote in the *Washington Post*: "His popularity is at an all-time low in public opinion polls, his policies are under constant attack, and his chances for success in the approaching presidential election year seem increasingly doubtful."[49] Carter was feeling the strain from Democrats as much as Republicans. Jackson denounced SALT II as "appeasement in its purest form." He likened Carter's summit with Brezhnev to the Chamberlain–Hitler meeting at Munich in 1938. So sensitive was Carter to this analogy that he refused to use an umbrella (Chamberlain's trademark accessory) during a rainstorm when disembarking from the plane in Vienna. "I'd rather drown than carry an umbrella," Carter commented, soaking wet.[50] The day after returning to Washington, he attended a congressional leadership breakfast. When a liberal member asked him what he would do if Ted Kennedy ran for president, Carter snapped, "I'll whip his ass!" His staff thought it was the best thing for morale since the Willie Nelson concert of July 1978, when Carter joined onstage to sing *Georgia on My Mind*.[51]

DOMESTIC CRISIS

The Vienna summit provided only a brief respite for Carter. Domestic problems came in droves. Their chief root was rising inflation emanating from the world energy crisis. The Iranian revolution earlier in the year had cut that nation's oil production by 90 percent. In June, OPEC announced its fourth and largest price surge since January. Queues at those gas stations still providing fuel began to lengthen, and the price of gasoline doubled from $18 to $36 a barrel. Carter's advisers pointed out that the blame for these troubles was being placed largely on the president.[52]

Carter canceled a planned vacation in Hawaii. For the next ten days he was ensconced at Camp David (a venue which evoked happier memories) to work on addressing the sources of discontent. Caddell advised him to confront the "crisis of spirit" in America, which he believed to be the most pressing issue. Walter Mondale dissented, arguing that the main cause of public dismay was the economic problems.[53] Carter conflated the two schools of thought. On July 15, he delivered a self-critical (and ill-advised) speech to a national television audience. Carter spoke of "a crisis of confidence [...] that strikes at the very heart, soul and spirit of our national will. We can see this crisis in the growing doubt about the meaning of our own lives and in the loss of a unity of purpose for our nation."[54] He outlined measures to ensure a more energy-independent America and spoke of his own shortcomings. Carter admitted that his efforts to fulfill campaign promises had met with only "mixed success," citing a complaint from a southern governor who accused him of "managing the government" rather than leading the nation. The president tried to address the criticism: "I do not promise a quick way out of our nation's problems—when the truth is that the only way out is an all-out effort. What I do promise you is that I will lead our fight. I will enforce fairness in our struggle. I will ensure honesty and, above all, I will act." Although grim and subsequently derided, the address (dubbed the "malaise speech") was initially well received.[55] Carter, without the stentorianism of Roosevelt or the charisma of JFK, had spoken in direct terms.

As if to underline his desire to act, Carter elevated Jordan to chief of staff and began purging his cabinet. The process was carried out in bizarre fashion. Carter asked all cabinet members to submit their offers of resignation; he would then decide which of those to accept or reject. Among the four victims were Treasury Secretary Michael Blumenthal and Energy Secretary James Schlesinger. The strange and sudden manner infuriated Democrats on Capitol Hill. "The way he went about it was inexcusable," recalled Tip O'Neill. "To make matters worse, he engineered the entire arrangement without even informing me."[56]

SALT II AND THE SENATE

"There has been virtually no political question over the past three months on which the administration has tried to overcome congressional opposition without playing the anti-Soviet trump card," complained Frank Church in 1978. "Clouds are gathering in the Senate over the SALT agreement." The Democratic senator for Idaho said that arguments against SALT II rested on the "hackneyed claim of Soviet expansionism."[57] Church was a firm supporter of SALT from the start of Carter's presidency, countering the Jackson–Nitze criticisms in the Warnke appointment debate. In the fall of 1978, he published a long article on behalf of the Arms Control Association, passionately supporting a new treaty. "Arms control is the only realistic alternative to a senseless nuclear arms race which neither side can win," Church argued. "We have already assembled a nuclear arsenal of such staggering proportions that the United States could destroy the Soviet Union several times over, even after enduring an attack on itself."[58] As the new chairman of the Senate Foreign Relations Committee, Church would be central to the congressional hearings on SALT. Mondale referred to him as "the most important man in America regarding the fate of the treaty."[59] Since Church was a liberal, the Carter administration welcomed his elevation, hoping it would offset the hawkish voices in the Armed Services Committee led by Henry Jackson.[60]

Church opened the SALT II hearings on July 9, 1979. Though eight other Democrats were on the Foreign Relations Committee, three anti-SALT Republicans—Jesse Helms (North Carolina), Richard Lugar (Indiana), and Samuel Ichiye Hayakawa (California)—had joined after the 1978 elections, to link up with three other Republicans, including Senate Minority Leader Howard Baker. All provided stiff opposition to the administration's chief witnesses: Vance, Brown, Stansfield Turner (CIA Director), George Seignious (who succeeded Warnke as ACDA director), and General David Jones, chairman of the Joint Chiefs of Staff. The anti-treaty case was bolstered by testimony from CPD members such as Paul Nitze, who judged SALT II to be "8 to 1 in favor of the Soviets."[61] The administration faced an even tougher task in the hearings of the Armed Services and Intelligence Committees, where Sam Nunn demanded a 5 percent rise in defense spending (rather than Carter's 3 percent) as his price for supporting ratification.[62]

The domestic intrusions were far greater than those which appeared during the SALT I process. In 1972 the hearings held by the Foreign Relations Committee had lasted only seven days. By contrast, the schedule proposed for SALT II would be twenty days of hearings, with a further four days for the markup (for rewriting or amendments), and a target date of September 25 for submission of the report to the Senate. When the hearings were concluded, the record filled five volumes of 2,266 pages with evidence provided by eighty-eight witnesses, and a further thirteen executive sessions.[63] But the target date was never reached—the result of domestic politics and one of the most farcical episodes of the late Cold War.

THE SOVIET BRIGADE IN CUBA

By August 30, 1979, Frank Church was under pressure. The liberal senator had returned to Idaho in a bid to revive his flagging election campaign. At a hastily convened press conference, he announced the existence of a Soviet "combat brigade" operating in Cuba. "The United States cannot permit the island to become a Russian military base 90 miles from our shores," Church told startled reporters. He insisted that Carter demand its "immediate withdrawal."[64] So began a political episode known as the "Soviet brigade crisis."[65] The administration's handling of the affair would further erode public confidence in Carter's management of foreign policy. It would deal a devastating setback to his efforts to ratify the SALT II Treaty. And arriving just ten weeks after Vienna, it undermined any newfound U.S.–Soviet trust, raising doubts as to whether détente could still be salvaged.

The history can be traced to the events of 1962. Four armed Soviet regiments were dispatched to Cuba in September as part of an expeditionary force, along with the nuclear missiles which hastened the October crisis. After nuclear Armageddon was averted, Fidel Castro pleaded with the Kremlin to keep the four brigades in Cuba—demonstrating to Washington that the Soviet commitment to defending the island remained intact. In May 1963, the Soviets reluctantly agreed to keep one brigade in situ, a small force of between 2,000 and 3,000 men. The brigade had no more than symbolic importance. It did not pose any threat to the United States or neighboring countries, nor did it violate the agreements of 1962 and 1970 regarding the stationing of Soviet weapons or nuclear-powered submarines in Cuba. But as the years passed the presence of the small brigade was forgotten. The intensity of intelligence reports waned. The military advisers who remained in Cuba were thought by U.S. intelligence to be the only Soviet forces on the island.[66]

In March 1979, Brzezinski asked CIA Director Stansfield Turner to monitor events in Cuba. Any sign of Soviet violations could be raised at the Vienna summit, rather than in Congress, which might doom SALT ratification. (Cuba tends to evoke emotion in the Senate.) The request was made against the backdrop of Soviet–Cuban military cooperation in Africa, and Moscow's export of Soviet MiG aircraft to the island. But these measures were found not to be in violation of the 1962 agreements. At the Vienna summit, Carter merely told Brezhnev that a Soviet military buildup in Cuba would damage U.S.–Soviet relations.[67] In mid-June the National Security Agency (NSA) finalized an intelligence report. It revealed pictures of troop encampments which matched those designed for Soviet (rather than Cuban) deployments. Moreover, it discovered Russian-language use of the word "*brigada*" in reference to a Soviet unit southwest of Havana. Some NSA officials suspected the unit to be a "combat brigade." However, the Defense Intelligence Agency Director (Lt. General Eugene Tighe), the State Department's Bureau of Intelligence, and CIA Director Turner all disagreed with the NSA assessment. A further report on July 12 stated that the Soviet unit was probably distinct from the advisory group, but did not specify its size, content, or purpose. The unit was believed to have been in Cuba for years, and use of the word "combat" was consciously avoided.[68]

On July 17, Sen. Richard Stone (D-Florida) ambled in to the Armed Services Committee hearings on SALT, when a staff member tugged at his sleeve. The aide told Stone that he had overheard a conversation among administration officials, who mentioned a Soviet "combat brigade" in Cuba. Stone was facing a tough election in Florida, a swing state home to a large Cuban émigré population. He had voted for the Panama Canal treaties in 1978 and was under pressure from conservatives to oppose SALT II. After the hearings opened, Stone raised the question of Soviet troops in Cuba. Harold Brown, caught off guard, said that he was unaware of a change in Soviet activities. When pressed, Brown authorized the committee to make a statement (issued in the name of Frank Church) which said that aside from an advisory group, "our intelligence does not warrant the conclusion that there are other significant Soviet military forces in Cuba."[69] But Stone was dissatisfied, calling it "an equivocal answer." He met with John Carbaugh, an aide to Sen. Jesse Helms (R-North Carolina)—himself a staunch opponent of SALT II. Within hours Carbaugh broke the story to ABC television. The next day, ABC's Ted Koppel reported that "a brigade of Soviet troops, possibly as many as 6,000 combat-ready men, has been moved into Cuba within recent weeks."[70]

With no evidence emerging, the episode appeared to have died down. But on August 23, Carter was told of new intelligence showing satellite photos of Soviet forces equipped with tents, tanks, and artillery. The CIA's National Foreign Assessment Center judged the structure to be a Soviet "combat brigade." The word "combat" set off alarm bells in Washington.[71] Four days later, the news was reported in the *National Intelligence Daily* (NID), a classified report with a circulation to those in government. On August 29, the NID report was leaked by an intelligence official to *Aviation Week & Space Technology*, an influential journal whose stories were often seized on by the media. *Aviation Week* called on the State Department to confirm the story. With senior officials away on holiday, David Newsom (undersecretary of state) told Vance that the new brigade intelligence was about to go public. It left the administration in the awkward position of having the information appear in the press before Congress learned of the details. Vance therefore briefed members of the three relevant committees on events in Cuba. Most senators agreed that the story should not be exaggerated. Most, but not all.[72]

Frank Church, who had served four terms in the Senate, was stumbling in his quest for reelection. The weak U.S. economy had taken its toll on his home state of Idaho, particularly its timber industry. Central and northern Idaho faced growing unemployment. Church was on the campaign trail in Boise when Newsom told him of the latest intelligence—the Soviet "combat brigade" in Cuba. "That will sink SALT!" Church exclaimed over the phone.[73] Church had voted for the Panama Canal treaties and was (like Richard Stone) viewed by conservatives as vulnerable in the 1980 elections. The main line of attack was that Church was "soft" on the communists. An anti-Church commercial was broadcast on local television, showing footage of the senator smoking cigars with Fidel Castro on a recent trip to Havana.[74] Weeks earlier, Church had signed a Senate statement, giving an assurance that there had been no change in Soviet activities in Cuba. He now sensed a dreadful déjà vu. In 1962, Church had assured Idahoans that there was no Soviet military threat in Cuba. The subsequent missile crisis almost cost him political office. In 1979, Church's reassurance again had the appearance of looking foolish. "They just can't let this leak!" he fumed.[75]

Church beseeched the administration to announce the news, rather than have the information leak without context. He asked Vance over the phone whether he or the president would make an official statement. "No," Vance replied. The senator then asked what would happen if he made the statement. Vance told Church that it would be "harmful," but did not try to dissuade him. His expectation was that Church would keep quiet.[76] But Vance was wrong. After failing to contact Carter (who was unavailable), Church organized a press conference in his living room. He told the local media of "new developments" in Cuba, and demanded that the Soviets remove the brigade immediately. He warned that unless the Soviets withdrew their troops, the SALT II Treaty would not pass the Senate. On September 4, Church canceled the SALT hearings and held an inquiry into the Soviet presence in Cuba.

The administration panicked. Despite knowing that the brigade was neither new nor a threat, Vance told the press that the administration "would not be satisfied with the status quo in Cuba." He suggested that SALT II would be delayed until the Soviet Union addressed their concerns.[77] Carter exacerbated matters with his own public statement on September 7. He called the presence of the Soviet brigade a "very serious matter," and declared that the status quo was "not acceptable." "We have the right to insist that the Soviet Union respect our interests and our concerns," Carter added. "Otherwise, relations between our two countries will inevitably be adversely affected."[78] By the end of his statement, the president's appeal for calm had morphed into a direct warning for Moscow.

Carter's response was counterproductive. It provided political ammunition for the anti-détente faction on Capitol Hill, who could now point (however speciously) to the inability of the administration to monitor developments in Cuba, as well as Soviet bad faith. Both spelled ominous repercussions for Carter's SALT ratification hopes. On September 9, Church again postponed the SALT II hearings. The troops in Cuba, he claimed, had placed the entire U.S.–Soviet relationship at stake.[79] "It's all political now," a senior intelligence official told the *New York Times* with a thin smile. "We've done our job."[80]

THE SOVIET REACTION

Soviet officials were baffled. To the Kremlin, this was no more than a manufactured political crisis. The more suspicious officials surmised, wrongly, that Carter was seeking a pretext to extricate himself from SALT II and spark a confrontation for 1980.[81] Their initial response, outlined by Vladilen Vasev (the chargé d'affaires), was that the Soviets were maintaining a "training center" that had been in Cuba since 1962. He denied the presence of "organized Soviet combat units."[82] Anatoly Dobrynin, a veteran of the Cuban Missile Crisis, had particular reason to be irritated. He had just returned to Moscow, where his parents were dying. But Vance, under pressure to clarify matters, had requested his return. After burying his father, Dobrynin left his mother's deathbed (missing her funeral) to tell Vance in Washington: "Cy, it's still the old stuff. Nothing has changed from 1962. It's the same situation as during the Kennedy, Johnson, Nixon, and Ford administrations." Vance agreed. "This is my understanding too. Then what is this all about?" Dobrynin replied, "I should ask *you* the same question!"[83]

Gromyko mocked the idea that a brigade was sent to threaten U.S. security. "Are you addicted to mystery stories?" he asked Vance in September.[84] Carter and Brezhnev even exchanged letters, so long had the episode dragged on. The president claimed that the presence of Soviet troops with a combat capability was of "genuine and deep concern" to Americans. Brezhnev's response was forthright. "My advice to you: discard the story. We have a military training center in Cuba that has existed there for more than 17 years. It fulfills its training function [...] it does nothing more." He criticized the administration for the "artificially contrived" affair.[85] Vance, who publicly declared the status quo "unacceptable," began appealing to Dobrynin in private. "Can't you get them to move some ships around—or move some troops a little bit— so that we could say it was now acceptable?" he asked. Dobrynin replied: "After the Cuban Missile Crisis, there is no way we are going to do that sort of thing. It would be too humiliating."[86] This was history repeating as farce.

ENDING THE "CRISIS"

Carter sought to end the crisis without damaging prospects for SALT ratification. He consulted with a range of officials during September, including his national security adviser. Brzezinski told Carter of the "direct political benefits" at stake. "A cosmetic outcome will not wash," he warned. "The country will see through it. SALT will be jeopardized and you will be seen as zigzagging ('the status quo is not acceptable'). A gradual toughening up in our policy is therefore the preferable alternative." The tough posture would include a further increase in defense spending, the strengthening of U.S. forces at Guantanamo, the declaration of a "Carter Doctrine" for the Caribbean, an expansion in trade with China, and public statements condemning Soviet intervention in the Third World. Brzezinski claimed that these hardline measures would give Carter the edge over campaign rival Ted Kennedy. "By toughening up our posture vis-à-vis the Soviets, you will either force Kennedy to back you, or to oppose you [...] If he backs you, he is backing an assertive and tough President; if he opposes you, he can easily be stamped as a latter day McGovernite."[87]

Carter was unconvinced. At the suggestion of White House Counsel Lloyd Cutler, he conferred with sixteen "wise men"—a bipartisan group of statesmen led by Clark Clifford. The alumni included Dean Rusk, McGeorge Bundy, and Henry Kissinger. Together, their service spanned every presidency from FDR to Gerald Ford.[88] The consensus of the wise men was that "the whole commotion was unnecessary." Of the participants only David Packard, a former deputy secretary of defense, showed concern.[89] (Packard was a member of the CPD.) In a scathing memo on September 26, Bundy told Carter:

The present crisis over a Soviet infantry brigade in Cuba is the product of internal accident and error in the United States. It should be ended mainly by American good sense and only secondarily by an effort to get clarifications or concessions from the Russians [...] It is not the brigade that has stirred us up: it is the sudden and embarrassing overreaction to a minor intelligence error [...] The very worst response to this kind of trouble is to huff and puff and then have nothing serious to do. Those senators for whom the SALT treaty is the enemy will be unrelenting.[90]

Vance, Mondale, and Byrd agreed that the brigade issue should be treated in isolation, so as to avoid dooming SALT ratification.[91] The

Senate majority leader urged Carter to "cool the rhetoric," telling him that the matter was "peripheral and unrelated" to SALT.[92] Carter decided to give an address to the nation to reflect this advice. On October 1, he explained that the brigade in Cuba was minor, presented no threat to America, and listed assurances given by Moscow. References to Soviet expansionism were omitted. But Carter used the moment to press home the theme of U.S. military strength. "Our national defenses are stronger tonight than they were two years ago; and they will be stronger two years from now," he declared. "Our strategic nuclear forces are powerful enough to destroy any potential adversary many times over, and the invulnerability of those forces will soon be further assured by a new system of powerful mobile missiles [the MX]." This was the very rhetoric that Carter had waged against in 1976, and avoided in the earlier phases of his presidency.[93]

The brigade issue diminished over the next few weeks. But its after-effects remained. On September 18, the Senate adopted a resolution by fifty-five votes to forty-two permitting 5 percent annual increases (after inflation) in the 1981 and 1982 defense budgets. "Without Cuba, that vote never would have happened," an administration official told the *Washington Post*. Sam Nunn again called on Carter to announce a 5 percent increase in defense spending. "We in this country have gone to sleep on the assumption that we could end the arms race by slumbering it away," he declared. "Today, there is only one country running in the race, and that happens to be the Soviet Union."[94] The SALT II hearings were delayed, and the Senate passed another resolution stating that there would be no agreement unless Carter gave the assurance that the brigade in Cuba had no combat role. Public and congressional trust in the Soviets plummeted, and further questions arose about Carter's handling of foreign affairs. Hopes for an improved U.S.–Soviet relationship had been undermined so soon after Vienna.

*

The Second Cold War was not yet underway, but détente was looking less secure. Brzezinski recalled that the Cuban "crisis" had shaken public confidence, heightened hostility toward the Soviets, and "deprived us of momentum in the SALT ratification process."[95] CIA official Robert Gates was as critical about Carter's response to the leak as the "politically motivated and excessive reaction by the Congress." "This chain reaction of blundering jeopardized the fate of SALT II well before the Soviets invaded Afghanistan," Gates argued. "It was all a self-inflicted wound."[96] Carter's collapse from heat exhaustion, while running a six-mile race in the Catoctin Mountains, put the seal on a dire few months for the administration.[97]

In January 1978, Anthony Lake (director of policy planning in the State Department) wrote that "the human rights policy may be the best thing this Administration has going for it."[98] By mid-1979 that belief may still have held good. But the public and political mood had changed. Although as important as ever in principle, human rights as an issue was no longer the campaign winner of 1976. A survey led by the Chicago Council on Foreign Relations found that while 67 percent of the public favored human rights promotion, only 50 percent believed that Soviet treatment of minorities was a U.S. concern. Just 1 percent placed human rights among the three most important international issues. Meanwhile, 62 percent of the public felt that America's position in the world was becoming weaker.[99] Caddell told Carter that although the American public believed SALT II would mark progress toward a more peaceful world, they felt that he was "not tough enough" with the Soviet Union.[100] Polls conducted by NBC and Roper in July indicated that support for SALT II was slipping, while demands for increased defense spending were rising, despite the economic crisis.[101] "The anti-defense stigma of the Vietnam era is fading," advised officials from the Office of Congressional Liaison. "A defense spending increase that seeks to strengthen what we already have will not be automatically dismissed by liberals as a bone tossed to the military-industrial complex."[102]

The pressure led Carter to adopt a "middle ground" position— pledging to increase defense spending by 3 percent and authorizing the MX program. But this policy carried risks. "The political risk is that the middle ground position will find itself an orphan, abandoned by both left and right," explained Landon Butler, the deputy chief of staff.[103] Jordan was also downbeat. He told Carter:

Few senators or their staffs think we will win SALT ratification. The pessimism comes from the appearance of formidable opponents like Jackson attacking SALT, and the lack of any conservative or moderate Senate support [...] Although the concept of SALT is popular, distrust of the Russians and the perception of the administration as weak on defense will make this agreement an unpopular political issue.[104]

By October, Carter's third year had already marked sacrifices and policy departures. The viability of his "middle ground" position would soon be under threat.

3

To the Right

The torrid days of summer did not prevent Carter from visiting an unlikely ally. In May he called into the UCLA Medical Center, where John Wayne was receiving treatment for cancer. Although a staunch Republican, Wayne had supported Carter's quest to ratify the canal treaties (his first wife was a native of Panama). In so doing, he accused Ronald Reagan of "misinforming people."[1] "He was in good spirits, appreciated my coming," wrote Carter in his diary. The veteran actor had kind words for the president's new hairstyle, which now swept to the right rather than the left. "He said the left-hand part of my hair had improved the shape of my head," Carter added. "He was a professional and recognized things like that."[2]

Wayne was dead by the time Soviet forces invaded Afghanistan. The administration's "middle ground" also ended. In 1980, Carter's response to Soviet actions would mirror his new coiffure. He imposed a grain embargo against the USSR and led a Western boycott of the Moscow Olympics. The bilateral cultural agreement was not renewed, nor were plans to open consulates in Kiev and New York. The U.S. ambassador to Moscow, Thomas Watson, was recalled. Carter pledged to increase defense spending by 5 percent for the next five years, reinstated draft registration, and activated a Rapid Deployment Force. He unveiled the "Carter Doctrine"—extending the containment policy to the Persian Gulf and committing U.S. forces to defend American interests in the region, if necessary by military action. Covert military aid was approved for Afghan rebels and Pakistan, as well as for Egypt, Israel, and Saudi Arabia. Later, Carter would announce Presidential Directive 59—an aggressive strategy designed to give U.S. presidents more flexibility in planning for and executing a nuclear war.

Seldom had American foreign policy been transformed so dramatically. Carter's stated objectives of nuclear disarmament, limited overseas intervention, and a restrained military budget were cast aside. The course pursued in 1980 marked a departure from the three years which preceded it, and the vision outlined at Notre Dame. Although U.S.–Soviet relations had deteriorated during this time, the purpose of the negotiations had not. From January 1980, however, the structure upholding détente was dismantled. The fate of bilateral relations became contingent on nothing less than a Soviet withdrawal from Afghanistan.[3] Where Carter had previously been open to patience and compromise, he now adopted an approach which offered little, if any, room for maneuver. Where earlier moves to the right had been intermittent and modest in scope, or made with reluctance, the new course was relentlessly pursued. The string of hardline, anti-Soviet measures would span the first seven months of the year and with it, the Democratic primaries.

The Soviet military intervention was a watershed moment in the late Cold War. It brought détente to a final, shuddering halt. The long quest for an arms control agreement was killed off. The invasion, together with the U.S. response (the force of which would surprise Moscow), marked the beginning of a "second" Cold War. It was a conflict that grew more tense, dangerous, and unpredictable over the next four years. Afghanistan followed on the heels of one of the most humiliating episodes in modern American history. The hostage crisis in Iran became headline news on television, radio, and in print. Though lacking the strategic importance of the Soviet invasion, it struck an emotional chord with the American public in a manner rarely seen. That the two events occurred when they did—at the end of Carter's third year—meant that foreign policy became bound up in electoral politics. Together, Iran and Afghanistan played into the hands of Carter's critics, who accused him of "weakness." The president, they argued, could neither stem the tide of Soviet expansionism nor bring home the captive Americans. The setbacks allowed political opponents such as Ronald Reagan to declare that the pursuit of SALT had been misguided all along. That Carter was uncertain of becoming the Democratic nominee made him even more susceptible to the logic of the intermestic. Here were two overseas crises that, while undesired, presented an opportunity to display resolve and leadership. With criticism mounting, Carter would stake his credibility on a vigorous, alarmist response to the Soviet invasion. It was, he claimed, "the most serious threat to world peace since the Second World War."[4]

THE CANDIDATES

In the fall of 1979, the administration continued to press the case for
SALT II, which remained tied up in Congress. But there were other
concerns now at hand. The problems besetting Carter—an energy crisis,
inflation, and the fallout from his "malaise speech"—had given Ted
Kennedy the final incentive to run for president.[5] In September, the
Massachusetts senator turned to an old friend. He arrived at Tip
O'Neill's Capitol office to sound out the House Speaker about his decision. "I'm going to win," Kennedy said. "I've got him beat two to one in
the polls." "Forget the polls," replied O'Neill. "You can't beat an incumbent president. Besides, you've got a morality issue."[6] But O'Neill's
reference to Chappaquiddick did not deter Kennedy, buoyed by polls in
late August which showed him with a lead over Carter of 62–24 percent
among Democrats.[7]

Carter was painfully aware of the figures. On the same day that the
senator met with O'Neill, Carter discussed "the Kennedy challenge" with
Mondale. "The weekend newspapers were unbelievable," he grumbled,
"practically anointing Kennedy as the president and claiming the 1980
election is already over."[8] Carter also courted the House Speaker. In
October, he invited O'Neill to attend the seventh game of the World
Series in Baltimore, where the president would throw out the first pitch.
While O'Neill marked his scorecard, Carter talked politics. Aware of
O'Neill's friendship with Kennedy, he asked the Speaker to chair the
1980 Convention in New York—a position which required neutrality in
the Democratic race. O'Neill agreed.[9]

The Republican contest also took shape. George Bush (former CIA
director) and Rep. John Anderson (Illinois) were among the pretenders.
But the favorite was Ronald Reagan, who had served as California governor for eight years before an unsuccessful run for the GOP nomination
in 1976. Reagan's disdain for communism dated back to his acting days,
and he remained a staunch critic of Soviet policies. On public platforms he
described the Soviet Union in blunt, unflattering terms. He lamented
Roosevelt's signing of the Yalta agreement in 1945, which had sealed
the fate of the "captive nations" in Eastern Europe.[10] Nor did Reagan
approve of the policies pursued by more recent presidents. "Détente—
isn't that what a farmer has with his turkey—until Thanksgiving Day?" he
quipped over the airwaves.[11] Reagan's policy instincts differed from those
of Carter. He called for large increases in defense spending, championing
the B-1 bomber, the MX, and the neutron bomb. He also opposed the

Panama Canal and SALT treaties. "We are negotiating the SALT II Treaty from a position of weakness," Reagan declared in July. "Without doubt that agreement will be flawed and not in our best interest." He called on the United States to "go forward with a military buildup of our own."[12] Reagan appealed to conservatives disenchanted by what they saw as "appeasement" of the Soviets, and of a U.S. retreat post-Vietnam—a war which he had proclaimed "a noble cause."[13]

Carter faced serious challenges from the left and right. A *New York Times–CBS* poll in October showed the president trailing Kennedy by 54–20 percent. Even more disconcerting were figures that gave Carter an approval rating of just 30 percent, with 50 percent disapproval and the balance undecided. Other polls were less gloomy. But two days after the Iran hostage crisis began, Pat Caddell delivered another forthright report. "I would guess that the margin is about 52 percent to 32 percent with a sizable number undecided," he told Carter. "Kennedy dominates *all* the leadership questions—more knowledgeable, more experienced, strong, effective, even in handling a crisis. Indeed, you are viewed as less of a leader by great margins when compared to all the other candidates." Caddell added: "We are hostage to *real* events and to the *appearance* of how we respond. People make that judgment every day—*that events dominate us; that we react to, not lead events.*" He implored Carter to "personally take action."[14]

THE IRAN HOSTAGE CRISIS

The American interest in Iran dated back to 1946, when Joseph Stalin refused to withdraw Soviet forces from occupied Iranian territory. Although the Red Army eventually disengaged, the region remained a geopolitical flashpoint. Prime Minister Mohammad Mossadeq, locked in a political struggle with Shah Mohammad Reza Pahlavi, was overthrown by a CIA-led coup d'état in 1953. Applying the logic of Cold War containment (Iran bordered the USSR), President Dwight Eisenhower approved Operation Ajax. The outcome allowed the Shah to consolidate his grip on power, and suited Washington, dependent on good relations with Iran to help control the price of oil and to use the territory as an intelligence post to monitor Soviet affairs. But the Shah's control weakened during the mid-70s. Efforts to modernize Iran, restrict the influence of Islam, and develop industrial programs clashed with the beliefs of Islamic traditionalists, who resented the change in customs. Resistance to the Shah's reforms increased after the violent repression of political opponents, while unemployment and inflation spiraled.[15]

Carter did not endear himself to the masses in early 1978, paying tribute to the "respect, admiration, and love" in which the Iranian people held their leader. By then the Shah was in failing health, diagnosed with cancer that affected his judgment. The political crisis escalated in September, when the Shah proclaimed martial law and authorized the military to fire on protestors. Three months later, Carter ditched the (Brzezinski-led) policy of standing by the monarch. He agreed with Vance that the Shah would have to be replaced by a civilian government. Islamist radicals, led by Ayatollah Ruhollah Khomeini, seized power in early 1979. The Shah was granted refuge in Egypt and then Mexico, before seeking medical treatment in the United States. In October, after his condition worsened, Carter agreed to his request.[16]

Carter's compassion sparked outrage in Tehran. But his decision was not apolitical. The Shah had American friends in high places. An influential network (including David Rockefeller, Henry Kissinger, and Richard Nixon) had been lobbying intensively for his admission. Carter initially resisted their pleas. "I don't have any feelings that the Shah or we would be better off with him playing tennis several hours a day in California instead of in Acapulco," he wrote in July.[17] For Carter, the sword was double-edged. If he allowed the Shah to enter the United States, he would be criticized by the left for welcoming a "murderous despot." If he stood firm, the right would attack him for refusing to come to the aid of a longtime international ally. In the fall of 1979, the latter scenario was of more concern. Political advisers stressed the importance of Kissinger's support for SALT ratification. Jordan told Carter: "If the Shah dies in Mexico, can you imagine the field day Kissinger will have with that? He'll say first that you caused the Shah's downfall and now you've killed him."[18] Carter accepted that pressure from the political right had influenced his decision to admit the Shah. "I can't deny that that may have been a factor," he later admitted. "It probably was."[19]

Khomeini proclaimed himself the leader of Shia Iran and the entire Muslim world, and used the Shah's admission to rally Islam against the United States. On November 1, over two million people marched through the streets of Tehran in protest. Three days later, 3,000 anti-Shah demonstrators converged upon the U.S. embassy. A group of revolutionary students stormed the building and took sixty-six American citizens hostage. Although thirteen were soon released (and later, a fourteenth), fifty-two would remain captive. The rebel militants, backed by Khomeini, demanded that Carter return the Shah to Iran to face trial. The hostage crisis became an all-consuming emergency for the administration and the news story of the year. Television network ABC launched *The Iran Crisis: America Held Hostage*, which aired every weeknight, displaying the number of days that had elapsed since the embassy was held. Few expected the figure to reach 444. During that time the show was retitled *Nightline*, hosted by Ted Koppel. The crisis was afforded more media coverage than any other event since the Second World War, including the Vietnam War.[20] "The first week of November 1979 marked the beginning of the most difficult period of my life," Carter recalled.[21]

He was not short of counsel. Domestic policy adviser Stuart Eizenstat advocated punitive measures such as refusing to purchase oil from Iran, and freezing the assets of Iranian students illegally in the United States. As a symbolic gesture, he recommended closing the Iranian embassy and expelling those attached to it. Alonzo McDonald (the White House staff director) cautioned against imposing a food embargo for trade and electoral reasons. But he urged Carter to act quickly, to avoid appearing "wishy-washy and indecisive." The most pressing analysis arrived from the chief of staff. "I do not believe that SALT II will be ratified unless we have a politically satisfactory resolution of this crisis," Jordan told Carter.

It is taking a toll on your presidency and your ability to lead. A protracted crisis will prevent you from doing the very minimal things that you need to do to win the Democratic nomination [...] We have to do something that is measured and reasonable to meet domestic political pressures. This is absolutely essential to your own reelection and to America's image in the world.[22]

Carter heeded the advice. On November 6, the administration discounted a rescue operation as "impractical or unlikely to succeed without considerable loss on both sides."[23] With military options limited, Carter sought diplomatic channels to help secure the hostages' release, including appeals to the UN and the International Court of Justice. He decided to retain diplomatic relations with Iran, on the basis that avenues of communication would need to remain open. But Carter also displayed firmness. Oil would no longer be purchased from Iran. Iranian assets in U.S. banks (estimated at $6 billion) were frozen. Carter instructed Attorney General Benjamin Civiletti to begin deportation proceedings against Iranian students illegally in the United States. He also told Brzezinski to expedite plans for an unofficial economic embargo (though food was considered distinct from other trade commodities).[24]

The U.S. public approved of Carter's measured response. As anti-American sentiment grew in Iran, the nation rallied behind the president. The support was reflected in a Gallup Poll on December 4, which placed

Carter's approval rating at 54 percent—a surge from the precrisis figure of
31 percent.[25] Carter thought the figures were "surprisingly good."[26]
Privately, he could take heart from the problems besetting Ted Kennedy.
On the same day that the hostage crisis had stunned the world, CBS
broadcasted an interview between the senator and correspondent Roger
Mudd, entitled "Teddy." But Kennedy stumbled. When asked why he
wanted to run for president, the senator froze. His answers to questions
about policy, Carter, and Chappaquiddick were halting and incoherent.
Kennedy would announce his candidacy a few days later, which made his
disposition all the more baffling.[27] Carter described the interview as
"devastating."[28] Jordan was even less restrained. "I could hardly contain
my pleasure," he wrote. "The public opinion polls were turning back in
Carter's favor, and the Mudd interview would be reverberating throughout
the political community. We all snickered."[29] Kennedy compounded matters on December 3. In response to a reporter's question on the hostage
crisis, he rebuked Carter for admitting the Shah, "with his umpteen billions
of dollars that he'd stolen from Iran." Kennedy's tone allowed the president
to take the moral high ground. "I don't give a damn whether or not you like
the Shah. I don't care whether you think he's a thief or not," Carter told
congressional leaders. "I don't care whether you think I was wise or was not
wise in accepting the Shah as one of our allies. The issue is that American
hostages, 50 of them, are being held by kidnappers."[30]

But the political gains were ephemeral. An ABC–Harris survey released
on January 7, 1980, gave a better indication of Carter's predicament. Asked
if the president's policy on Iran should be judged a failure if the hostages
were still captive in three weeks' time, 53 percent agreed and only 27 percent
disagreed.[31] Public patience eroded as the months passed and diplomatic
efforts failed. The hostage crisis became a major political burden.[32]
Brzezinski grew anxious to explore military options over Iran, "to give us
more direct bargaining leverage."[33] Carter remained calm. On
December 13, he told the press: "I think we've learned from the Vietnam
War that to become unnecessarily involved in the internal affairs of another
country when our own security is not directly threatened is a serious
mistake."[34] Hours earlier in Moscow, unbeknownst to Carter, Soviet
leaders had frantically debated the same issue. A fateful decision was made.

AFGHANISTAN: THE SOVIET DECISION TO INVADE

The Kremlin watched events in Iran with unease. The rise of the Shia
Islamist radicals threatened Afghanistan, a predominantly Sunni Muslim

state with a large Shia minority. Afghanistan bordered not only Iran, but also the large Soviet republics of Turkmenistan, Uzbekistan, and Tajikistan. They, too, were territories home to large Islamic populations. For geopolitical reasons, Soviet leaders had long sought the cooperation of the government in Kabul. But regional instability stirred by the Iranian revolution in 1978–79 prompted Moscow to devote further attention to its southern frontier.

Afghanistan had experienced its own political turmoil. In 1978 the Saur (April) revolution, led by the leftist PDPA, resulted in the overthrow of the secular, modernist government of President Mohammed Daoud Khan. The coup had little to do with the Kremlin, which expressed misgivings about the new communist rulers: Prime Minister Nur Muhammad Taraki, his deputy Babrak Karmal, and Foreign Minister Hafizullah Amin. They hailed from the Khalq wing of the PDPA, and began purging political opponents, including the rival Parcham faction of the party. Still, Moscow held back. From March 1979, Soviet leaders rejected calls from Taraki to send in troops, even after a major uprising in Herat against Khalqi forces (in which Soviet advisers were killed). But the Kremlin, fearful of events in Iran spilling across the border, opted to increase their links with the Khalqi regime. Soviet–Afghan contacts expanded through the defense ministry, foreign ministry, and the KGB, while Soviet military aid increased. Soviet advisers (political and military) toured the country, frustrated by Taraki and Amin, whose ruthless measures had seen the violence escalate.

At Brezhnev's behest, Taraki visited Moscow in September 1979. The Soviet leader urged him to ease the tensions by bringing members of the Parcham wing back in to government fold. Brezhnev also warned Taraki that Foreign Minister Amin (who had just purged several of Taraki's cabinet) was plotting to overthrow him. The Soviet leadership wanted Amin removed. Taraki's bodyguard duly tried to assassinate Amin, but ended up firing on his security chief, who had obscured the target. Amin suspected that Taraki had acted on Soviet instructions. He ordered his own forces to arrest Taraki, and declared himself the leader of Afghanistan on September 14. Within weeks Taraki was killed.[35]

Moscow chose to back Amin, but the new Afghan president was proving implacable. "We are not pleased by all of Amin's methods and actions," Brezhnev told the East German leader, Erich Honecker, in early October. "He is very power driven, repeatedly revealed disproportionate harshness."[36] Afghanistan's civil war worsened, despite Soviet military aid for Amin's forces. Soviet leaders also grew anxious that Amin's foreign policy was shifting. On October 29, Brezhnev's advisers reported that Amin aimed "to conduct a more balanced policy" in relation to the Western powers: "It is known that representatives of the USA, on the basis of their contacts with the Afghans, are coming to a conclusion about the possibility of a change in the political line of Afghanistan—in a direction which is pleasing to Washington."[37] The hostage crisis a week later increased Moscow's concern that having "lost" Iran, the United States would look to Afghanistan as an alternative staging post to monitor Soviet affairs. Aware of Amin's background (he had studied at Columbia University in the early 60s), the Soviets suspected that closer Afghan–American ties would emerge. On the other hand, if Amin lost power, the Kremlin felt that he would likely be succeeded by an anti-Soviet, religious fundamentalist regime. Either of these scenarios could grant the United States and China opportunities to establish a foothold on the Soviet southern border. To Soviet hardliners, the danger of inaction seemed as great as the risk of action.[38] "We were concerned that if the United States were forced from Iran, they would move their bases to Pakistan and grab Afghanistan. That was our logic at that time," recalled Valentin Varennikov, deputy chief of the General Staff. "We thought that they would try to put their intelligence centers in the north of Afghanistan, from where they would be able to monitor the grounds where we tested our most important weapons."[39]

In March 1979, Gromyko expressed concern about deploying troops to Afghanistan. He told the Politburo that détente and arms control were at stake:

We would be largely throwing away everything we achieved with such difficulty, particularly détente, the SALT II negotiations would fly by the wayside, there would be no signing of an agreement—and that is for us the greatest political priority. There would be no meeting of [Brezhnev] with Carter [...] and our relations with Western countries, particularly the FRG, would be spoiled.

KGB Chairman Yuri Andropov seemed to agree. "To deploy our troops would mean to wage war against the people, to crush the people, to shoot at the people," he told Politburo members. "We will look like aggressors, and we cannot permit that to occur."[40]

But Soviet attitudes hardened after Amin's arrival and the escalation in violence. The deputy foreign minister, Georgy Korniyenko, recalled that Gromyko became "locked in" to the arguments of Andropov and Ustinov, who gradually favored military action.[41] The die was cast in early December. Having failed to remove Amin, Brezhnev's "troika" pressed for intervention. But the military brass led by Nikolai Ogarkov (chief of the General Staff) remained opposed. Ogarkov said that an influx of troops would be "reckless" and unite Muslims against the Soviet Union. Ustinov rebuked the marshal for talking politics and told him to focus on achieving military goals.[42] Aware that senior figures such as Alexei Kosygin were also skeptical, Andropov and Ustinov bypassed the Politburo and went to the source of action. They obtained the support of Brezhnev's closest allies (personal assistant Andrei Aleksandrov-Agentov and chief ideologist Mikhail Suslov), while writing alarmist letters to the Soviet leader. "We have been receiving information about Amin's behind-the-scenes activities which might mean his political reorientation to the West," Andropov told Brezhnev. "He keeps his contacts with the American chargé d'affaires secret from us."[43]

The politicking was effective, facilitated by Brezhnev's illness and a hyper-centralized decision-making structure. On December 10, the Andropov–Gromyko–Ustinov troika told Ogarkov of their plan to deploy 80,000 troops in Afghanistan. Two days later in the Kremlin, Ogarkov made a final plea against intervention. He cited the logistical problems and said that suspicions about the United States were "purely hypothetical."[44] Again his arguments were dismissed. But the decision was already a fait accompli: key figures who opposed the invasion, such as Kosygin, did not bother to attend the meeting. Others against intervention acceded under pressure. A frail Brezhnev, on the periphery for some of the crucial debates, signed the directive to introduce Soviet troops. The expectation that this would be a brief war, won within two months, made it easier for Brezhnev to reconcile himself with the decision. "Do not worry," he told Dobrynin in January. "We will end this war in three or four weeks."[45] So began an avoidable, ill-conceived, and largely undesired conflict.

AFGHANISTAN: THE INTERNATIONAL CONTEXT

Soviet actions were deplorable and spelled consequences: the end for SALT II and any hopes of preserving détente. But it was not preordained that the entire foundation of U.S.–Soviet relations would unravel. The Carter administration would adopt a string of hardline measures, leaving it without scope for political maneuver, either with Moscow or its domestic audience: Ted Kennedy, Ronald Reagan, Republicans, conservative Democrats, and a public anxious about events in Iran. Geostrategy was part of Carter's decision calculus. But timing, risk, and credibility—domestic and personal as much as foreign—were the lenses through which policy options were assessed. The decisions of Moscow and Washington had major ramifications. East–West relations would descend into a state of peril from which it did not escape until the second half of the 1980s. While the Soviet invasion was the direct and immediate cause, it was not the only factor. The force of the American response (which misjudged the context of the Soviet action) took Moscow by surprise. It led to the subsequent hardening of the Soviet posture, with respect to Afghanistan and wider international affairs. For these reasons the U.S. deliberations are of much importance.

The Carter administration was not privy to all the debates in Moscow. But three questions are pertinent. Firstly, given the administration's knowledge of events in Afghanistan, and of Soviet sensitivities about its southern frontier, why did officials make scant effort to convey the seriousness of the U.S. position on intervention in advance, or at any prior stage of the civil war? Secondly, why did decision-makers choose to pursue such a vigorous, sustained reaction, one which they knew would place an adversarial U.S.–Soviet relationship (with all its concomitant threats of nuclear attack) into a state of disrepair? That in turn raises a third question. Beyond the desire to confront or "punish" the Soviets, what were the strategic objectives behind the countermeasures—and how were they to be achieved?

American attitudes to Afghanistan were pragmatic and cautious— before and after the revolution of April 1978. U.S. involvement was confined to supplying a modest program of economic aid. As such, the coup which brought the Marxist PDPA to power evoked little reaction in Washington beyond that of disappointment. The administration broadly accepted that Afghanistan lay in the Soviet, and not American, sphere of influence. "The United States had few resources in the area and we held the view that our vital interests were not involved there," Vance noted.[46] Gary Sick, one of the NSC's Middle East specialists, recalled: "The United States had lost interest in Afghanistan many years before. It had pretty much decided that it was in the Soviet sphere of influence. We wanted to maintain a position there, but we were not going to go in and fight, or do anything, for that matter, to stir up trouble."[47] Carter exercised restraint throughout the Afghan civil war. There was no official protest when Taraki took power, or when a Soviet–Afghan "treaty of friendship" was concluded in December 1978. The administration rejected requests from the Iranian Shah for America to take greater interest in Afghanistan, such as increased covert operations. "We turned our back on that," recalled CIA Director Stansfield Turner. "In the

context of 1978 and early 1979, Afghanistan was not very high on the
American foreign policy agenda. We had lots of other things that were of
much greater concern to us. There were very few Americans who had
been to Afghanistan. It is not an area in our proximity, or in our sphere of
influence."[48]

Brzezinski viewed the geopolitics in a different light, alerting Carter to
the increased Soviet interest in November 1978 and his "arc of crisis"
theory.[49] The national security adviser believed that Soviet actions—
whether in Africa, Kabul, or the oil-rich Middle East—were part of
a global effort by the Kremlin to spread communism and create new
spheres of influence. The Afghan crisis was raised, fleetingly, at the
Vienna summit in June. Carter told Brezhnev that "the United States has
not interfered in the internal affairs" of Iran and Afghanistan and that "we
expect the Soviet Union to do the same."[50] But there were no sustained
talks between Washington and Moscow on events in Kabul. Afghanistan
received limited attention at top-level meetings and in Brzezinski's reports
to Carter.

After the instability wrought by the Iranian Revolution (the loss of
U.S. intelligence facilities and increased dependence on imported oil),
Brzezinski suggested an improved military presence in the region.[51] On
October 1, Carter announced plans to create a Rapid Deployment Force
(later to become CENTCOM). But the RDF proposal won little support
from high-level policymakers.[52] The State and Defense Departments
opposed the idea, and Carter did not push for a decision.[53] Not until
1980, after the Soviet invasion and with the administration under attack,
was the RDF formed under the aegis of a "Carter Doctrine." "Efforts
had been made to create a Rapid Deployment Force from early on in the
Carter administration and people had mostly given it lip service," Sick
recalled. "Some things had been done, but not very much. With this
event [the Soviet invasion], suddenly everyone got serious. The movement of Soviet forces into Afghanistan marked the real birth of the Rapid
Deployment Force."[54] The case for an alarmed American position pre-
1980 rests on claims made by Brzezinski in his memoirs. He recalled
having warned Carter about "Russia's traditional push to the south,"
briefing him on "Molotov's proposal to Hitler in 1940 that the Nazis
recognize the Soviet claim to pre-eminence" in the region. In fact, this ill-
conceived memo was dated March 28, 1980—more than three months
after the Soviet invasion.[55] Weighed against Carter's actions in 1980, the
sum total of U.S. engagement with Afghanistan beforehand appears
meager.

That is not to suggest that the administration was naive about Afghanistan. Economic aid was curtailed after the murder of U.S. Ambassador Adolph Dubs, amid the revolt against Taraki's efforts to centralize political control. Dubs had been taken hostage by anti-Taraki rebels on February 14. He was killed five days later in the police attempt to secure his release.[56] After the Herat uprising in March, officials debated covert U.S. action and a potential Soviet response. The national intelligence officer, Arnold Horelick, recommended covert action—raising the costs for the Soviets and inflaming Muslim opinion against Moscow. The consensus was that "non-lethal assistance" should be provided for the Mujahideen, the Afghan resistance groups. The CIA's "finding" was passed to Brzezinski's NSC, yet languished for nearly three months until a meeting was held on July 3. There, Carter signed the first finding to help the Mujahideen.[57] But the covert actions were impotent. Support was restricted to aiding insurgent propaganda, establishing radio access for Afghans, and the provision of cash and medical supplies. "Our covert activities in Afghanistan until December 1979 were limited to rather insipid actions intended to give some kind of support to the insurgents; they really were of a very limited nature," Turner recalled. "Congress would have been very concerned about our moving into any kind of undercover military activity in a country about which there was not any great concern at that time. Afghanistan was not in the newspapers; people in the Congress were not upset about it, and so on."[58]

The dispassionate attitude continued in the months prior to the Soviet invasion, when the political violence had escalated. "The United States is opposed to any intervention in Afghanistan's affairs," declared the State Department, days after Amin had deposed Taraki. There is no evidence that the administration attempted to intervene directly in the Afghan crisis or sway Amin away from the Kremlin.[59] Notwithstanding the fact that U.S. intelligence doubted the prospect of a full-scale invasion, Carter took a pragmatic view of events. With rare exception, Afghanistan was seen as an issue which lay in the Soviet sphere and one of little interest to America. A high-level dialogue with the Soviets was notable by its absence. Mark Garrison, the deputy ambassador in Moscow, called it "the dog that did not bark in Washington."[60] A meeting between Brzezinski and Dobrynin on December 6—less than three weeks before the invasion—contained no mention of Afghanistan.[61] In sum, Carter's hawkish response in 1980 was out of sync with the policies and postures of the previous three years. To understand the discrepancy is to understand the political pressures closer to home.

THE DOMESTIC CONTEXT

From a domestic viewpoint there was no good moment for a Soviet invasion. But for Carter, the move could scarcely have arrived at a worse time. In December, the administration held a string of meetings on SALT II with vulnerable senators who were up for election. A week before Soviet forces mobilized, nineteen undecided senators told Carter of their concern about Soviet heavy missiles, limitations on MX basing modes, and lack of restrictions on the Backfire bomber. The Foreign Relations Committee voted to recommend ratification of the treaty to the full Senate (by nine to six), but this was conditional on changes to the terms. The Armed Services Committee denounced SALT II as "not in the national security interests of the United States." Its highly critical report was adopted (by a vote of ten to seven) on December 20—four days before Soviet troops crossed the Afghan border. Authored by Henry Jackson, it labeled Carter's planned defense spending increase "inadequate," cited Soviet advantages in throw-weight missiles, and the failure to address verification procedures and the Backfire bomber.[62] The committee's anti-SALT majority called the treaty "advantageous to the Soviets," granting them "a license for a massive buildup in strategic arms." Jackson said that the treaty did not have the sixty-seven Senate votes it would need for approval. When asked if SALT II was dead, he replied, "It's in a state of repose."[63]

Senate resistance to SALT was the culmination of a relentless campaign led by the New Right, a grassroots conservative coalition which grew during the 1970s to counter the liberal movement. In 1979, the Committee on the Present Danger accelerated its efforts to discredit Carter's pursuit of arms control. Board members testified before the Senate on seventeen separate occasions. Leading figures appeared on nearly 500 television and radio programs, public debates, and press conferences. More than 200,000 copies of CPD reports were distributed, reciting complaints that the military balance favored the USSR. As with the Panama debates, the conservative cause was boosted by support from about fifty affiliated lobby groups, many of which had financial clout. The Coalition for Peace Through Strength (boasting 191 members of Congress) was particularly influential, with lobbying expenditures exceeding $2.5 million. The outlay for the American Security Council's anti-SALT campaign reached $3 million in 1979 alone. With elections on the horizon, the New Right had left nothing to chance.[64]

Carter viewed the SALT II Treaty as a cornerstone of his election campaign. The Panama Canal treaties and the Arab–Israeli peace accords had not yielded much political capital. If the Senate vote prior to Christmas was a setback for SALT ratification, the Soviet invasion of Afghanistan sealed its fate. "I've never seen Jimmy more upset than he was the afternoon the Russian invasion was confirmed," recalled his wife, Rosalynn.[65] Carter later described the failure to secure SALT ratification as "the most profound disappointment" of his presidency.[66] But SALT was only part of the foreign–domestic nexus. It is difficult to overstate the shadow that the Iran hostage crisis had cast over his administration. The incarceration of Americans in Tehran was draining public faith in Carter's ability to lead the nation. The boost in support after the initial trauma had evaporated. On December 18, Carter's political advisers reported on the rise in public criticism which centered on two questions: "Who lost Iran?" and "Why was the Shah admitted for medical care?" The prospect of congressional investigations loomed. "The issue could become poisonously politicized," they warned.[67]

Carter's handling of foreign affairs was also under attack from within the Democratic Party. The Coalition for a Democratic Majority remained a powerful obstacle to his agenda. Neoconservatives such as Jackson and Sen. Daniel Patrick Moynihan (D-New York) raised alarm at U.S. "passivity." Moynihan expressed anger at politicians "who have decided that [America] has no capacity to resist the advance of totalitarianism, and that the best thing to do is accommodate and appease."[68] The monthly *Commentary* magazine, edited by Norman Podhoretz, was a useful public forum for neoconservatives. One contributor was Georgetown University professor Jeane Kirkpatrick, a member of the CPD and CDM. In November 1979, Kirkpatrick published a withering attack on Carter's foreign policies. "The failure [...] is now clear to everyone except its architects," Kirkpatrick wrote. "In the thirty-odd months since the inauguration of Jimmy Carter there has occurred a dramatic Soviet military buildup, matched by the stagnation of American armed forces, and a dramatic extension of Soviet influence in the Horn of Africa, Afghanistan, Southern Africa, and the Caribbean, matched by a declining American position in all these areas."[69]

Kirkpatrick claimed that the U.S. was "passive" in the face of communist expansionism. She charged Carter with having "actively collaborated in the replacement of modern autocrats friendly to American interests with less friendly autocrats of extremist persuasion." Kirkpatrick's premise was that right-wing autocrats (such as Pahlavi and Somoza) were more compatible with U.S. interests than Marxist totalitarian dictators, and that Carter had failed to make that distinction. The former, she argued, tended to leave existing social institutions in place and did not disturb the habitual rhythms of daily life, such as work and leisure, places of residence, and the practice of religion. The latter "claimed jurisdiction over the whole life and society," and tolerated no interference in state power. Kirkpatrick thus believed the administration exercised a "double standard" when dealing with dictators.[70] The article, "Dictatorships and Double Standards," was a landmark moment in conservative thinking. Here was an argument that chimed with a broad range of conservative intellectuals and politicians, Republican and Democrat. As historian John Ehrman noted, it showed just how conservative the neoconservatives' view of American foreign policy had become. By the time Soviet forces invaded Afghanistan, many "neocons" began switching party allegiance. Increasingly, they abandoned hope of reforming the Democratic Party, and found a more sympathetic ear among Republicans.[71]

None more so than Ronald Reagan, who was deeply impressed with Kirkpatrick's thesis. During 1979 he made public charges of weakness and appeasement, likening a Carter speech to "the sorry tapping of Neville Chamberlain's umbrella on the cobblestones of Munich."[72] Reagan announced his candidacy on November 13 in a nationally televised address. He spoke of the perception that America was now "weak and fearful." "During a time when the Soviet Union may enjoy nuclear superiority over this country [. . .] we must be clear voiced in our resolve to resist any unpeaceful act wherever it may occur. Negotiations with the Soviet Union must never become appeasement. Our unease can almost be called bewilderment at how our defense strength has deteriorated." Reagan spoke in an optimistic tone, despite his alarmism, referring to America's "greatness" and its obligations to the "free peoples of the world."[73] His arguments conformed to those of many conservative Democrats. Within weeks, Reagan co-opted Kirkpatrick to serve as his foreign policy adviser for the 1980 campaign.

In sum, the scale of Carter's opposition traversed the political spectrum: from Republicans, to disillusioned neoconservatives, to Kennedy liberals. When Soviet forces invaded Afghanistan, his critics began linking the two events in Southwest Asia. Carter was castigated for presiding over an administration unable to assert itself, and for failing to modernize U.S. military forces. Both, so it was argued, had encouraged the Soviets to steal a march on America. The Soviet invasion allowed Reagan to underscore his argument that Carter's approach to détente and arms control had been flawed from the start. As the hostage crisis lingered, Carter's advisers worried that the president lacked credibility on national security. "The hostage crisis symbolizes our impotence," Caddell warned. "Ronald Reagan's message is 'Elect me and you won't have to take that anymore'."[74] Carter decided to jettison his approach once the Soviet invasion spelled the end of SALT II. Against a tide of conservative criticism, the notion of a "middle ground" policy no longer made sense to the president or some of his top advisers. To outflank the political right, Carter would stake his credibility on a hawkish, alarmist response to the Soviet action.

THE CARTER ADMINISTRATION RESPONDS

Brzezinski wasted no time in directing the countermeasures. "Pull out all the work you have done on punitive sanctions and things we can do," he told William Odom, his military assistant.[75] In Brzezinski's view, America's loss of influence in Iran had led to the collapse in the balance of power across Southwest Asia. Afghanistan marked the first step in a Soviet quest to expand its power in the region, and establish a presence deep into the Middle East. "If the U.S. is perceived as passive in the face of this blatant transgression of civilized norms, our international credibility and prestige will be seriously eroded," he told Carter. Moreover, Brzezinski warned of the "grave" domestic political concerns. "Our handling of Soviet affairs will be attacked by both the right and left [...] Soviet 'decisiveness' will be contrasted with our restraint, which will no longer be labeled as prudent but increasingly as timid."[76] The prospects for SALT ratification were now minimal. Brzezinski advised Carter to defer bringing the treaty to a vote on the Senate floor. "Placing the blame on Soviet aggression in Afghanistan will make it less of a political setback for us," he explained.[77] Brzezinski called for money and arms to be provided to the Afghan rebels; for a review of U.S. policy toward Pakistan; for Chinese help with the resistance effort; and for Carter to issue direct warnings to the Kremlin about the damage to U.S.–Soviet relations.[78] To Brzezinski, this "represented an opportunity for [Carter] to demonstrate his genuine toughness." A swift, decisive response was needed to project strength to Moscow and the American public.[79]

Privately, Carter was gloomy. "This is deliberate aggression that calls into question détente and the way we have been doing business with the Soviets for the past decade," he told Jordan over the phone.[80] Carter wrote to Brezhnev, claiming that the invasion marked "an unsettling, dangerous, and new stage in your use of military force." He criticized the Soviet leader for approving a decision that "flouts all the accepted norms of international conduct." "Unless you draw back from your present course of action," Carter warned, "this will jeopardize the course of U.S.–Soviet relations throughout the world." Brezhnev's reply was disingenuous. The Soviet intervention, he argued, was in response to a direct request from the Afghan government. Its purpose was "to provide assistance in repulsing acts of external aggression." Brezhnev offered no information as to who posed this external threat. He told Carter that the Soviet troops would be withdrawn once the objective was achieved, and criticized the president's "immoderate tone." "Would it not be better to evaluate the situation more calmly?" he asked.[81]

But the atmosphere in the White House was one of "pure pandemonium," according to Odom.[82] What emerged was broad support for immediate punitive actions. Brzezinski claimed that there was a consensus on the need to "condemn the Soviets."[83] Yet the need for a condemnation was not really in doubt. The critical question surely centered on the nature and extent of the response, and how it would affect U.S.–Soviet relations. That could only be addressed by deducing why Moscow had chosen to intervene in the first place.

Two arguments were invoked: one local, the other global. Vance believed that Soviet objectives were "primarily local, and related directly to perceived threats to its national security." Fearing that Afghanistan would succumb to Islamic fundamentalism (as in Iran), Moscow had acted to protect its political interests on its southern border.[84] Brzezinski saw the invasion through his "arc of crisis" theory. According to this logic, the Soviets had embarked on a major strategic thrust toward the oil-rich Middle East and the warm-water ports of the Indian Ocean. "If the Soviets succeed in Afghanistan, and Pakistan acquiesces, the age-long dream of Moscow to have direct access to the Indian Ocean will have been fulfilled [...] It could produce a Soviet presence right down on the edge of the Arabian and Oman Gulfs."[85] Brzezinski was concerned that Carter might side with Vance, viewing Afghanistan as an isolated problem rather than a strategic one.[86] On January 2, he told the president: "I believe it is important, for both domestic and international reasons, to follow your strong comments with a packet of actions, to be announced all at once for maximum effect."[87] Brzezinski need not have worried. In 1980, Carter swung unreservedly toward his hardline views.

Far from giving themselves time to weigh policy and strategy, decision-makers rushed to judgment. Conclusions on the actions to be taken were reached within days. On January 2, 1980, twenty-six countermeasures were approved from a list compiled by Brzezinski. The SALT II Treaty was left on the Senate calendar; no efforts would be made to bring it to a vote. Ambassador Thomas Watson was recalled from Moscow—an action not taken when the Soviets had intervened in Hungary in 1956 or in Czechoslovakia in 1968. The Soviet diplomatic staff in the U.S. were reduced to the American level in the USSR. Travel restrictions were placed on Soviet political and media officials. The administration suspended plans to open consulates in Kiev and New York, and the negotiations on a bilateral exchange agreement. The U.S. control of exports to the USSR was tightened. And the administration reached out to allies in a bid to convince them to deny the Soviets further credit.[88]

Carter's turn to the right was outlined in interviews and two major speeches, in which he announced further anti-Soviet policies. The first was a televised address to the nation on January 4. The president imposed a grain embargo against the USSR, and a ban on high-technology exports to the Soviets. Military aid would be granted to the Afghan rebels and Pakistan. Carter also threatened a U.S. boycott of the summer Olympics in Moscow. "The response of the international community to the Soviet attempt to crush Afghanistan must match the gravity of the Soviet action," he declared. "This invasion is an extremely serious threat to peace because of the threat of further Soviet expansion [...] A Soviet-occupied Afghanistan threatens both Iran and Pakistan and is a stepping-stone to possible control over much of the world's oil supplies."[89] In an interview, Carter accused Brezhnev of lying about the reasons for the invasion. "The tone of [Brezhnev's] message was completely inadequate and misleading," he told ABC's Frank Reynolds. "The action of the Soviets has made a more dramatic change in my opinion of what the Soviets' ultimate goals are than anything they've done in the previous time that I've been in office."[90] Advisers told Carter that the statement left him exposed to charges of naivety.[91] Republican candidates seized the moment. Reagan criticized Carter for making a "shambles" of U.S. defense, and being "totally oblivious to the Soviet drive for world domination."[92]

Carter also went on the rhetorical offensive. "This in my opinion is the most serious threat to world peace since the Second World War," he told NBC's *Meet the Press* on January 20. "It's an unprecedented act on the part of the Soviet Union. I am still committed to peace, but peace through strength, and letting the Soviets know in a clear way that they cannot invade an innocent country with impunity; they must suffer the consequences." Carter said he was steering clear of party politics, opting out of campaigning in Iowa to focus on Iran and Afghanistan. NBC anchor David Broder was unimpressed. Taking up the crisis theme, he asked Carter: "With all due respect, we still have 5.8 percent unemployment. Inflation has risen from 4.8 percent to 13 percent. We still don't have a viable energy policy. Russian troops are in Cuba and Afghanistan. The dollar is falling. Gold is rising. And the hostages, after 78 days, are still in Tehran. Just what have you done, sir, to deserve re-nomination?"[93]

The president made his case three days later in his State of the Union address. Carter pointed to some landmark achievements, such as the Arab–Israeli peace accords and the normalization of relations with China (for political reasons, he omitted the Panama Canal treaties). He said that SALT remained "in the best interests of both countries," and would not be abandoned.[94] But Carter made the Soviet challenge the main subject of his speech. He talked of a resurgence in Soviet power, of the need for a large U.S. arms buildup, and for greater military engagement abroad. These were the very policies that Carter had scorned earlier in his presidency, couched in the sort of alarmist language that he abhorred. In 1980, some of the goals outlined at Notre Dame in 1977 were not so much discarded as they were inverted.

Carter warned of the "steady growth and increased projection of Soviet military power beyond its own borders." The invasion of Afghanistan was a "radical and aggressive new step [...] a grave threat to the free movement of Middle East oil." It could, he said, "pose the most serious threat to peace since the Second World War." (Pointing to Berlin, Korea, and Cuba, his advisers had now urged use of the conditional tense.[95]) Carter repeated the list of measures already taken against the Soviets, and expressed his intention to withdraw the United States from the Moscow Olympics. He also unveiled a new five-year defense program with a large increase in military spending. "It's imperative that Congress approve this strong defense budget for 1981, encompassing a 5 percent real growth in authorizations without any reduction," Carter declared.[96]

The theme was military might, not human rights. Carter spoke of deploying modern, intermediate-range nuclear forces to meet the "increased threat" from Moscow. The U.S. naval presence in the Indian Ocean would be strengthened, along with military bases in Northeast Africa and the Persian Gulf. Carter announced that he would reinstate draft registration, claiming that the time had come to "revitalize" the Selective Service System. Finally, he unveiled the coup de grâce: a new regional "cooperative security framework" (which the press labeled the "Carter Doctrine"). Carter declared: "An attempt by any outside force to gain control of the Persian Gulf region will be regarded as an assault on the vital interests of the United States of America, and such an assault will be repelled by any means necessary, including military force."[97] The commitment was modeled on the Truman Doctrine of 1947, which had then been launched to contain the Soviet threat to Greece and Turkey. With the Soviet invasion of Afghanistan, and an apparent power vacuum, Brzezinski compared the situation in the Persian Gulf to that of Europe in the late 1940s. "You have the opportunity to do what President Truman did on Greece and Turkey," he told Carter. "I believe this is desirable for both domestic and international reasons. The country will respond to a firm call for sustained action."[98] The new framework was accompanied by the activation of a Rapid Deployment Force. Carter approved the policy on January 9, but demurred from calling it the "Carter Doctrine."

*

Rarely had U.S. foreign policy swung so dramatically and so quickly. Carter's policies had gradually hardened during his first three years as president. At its core, however, remained a basic commitment to operate within the framework of détente, and to work to reduce the nuclear threat. The Soviet invasion placed these foundations in jeopardy. With the hasty, exorbitant U.S. response, they were finally shattered. The countermeasures ensured that every facet of bilateral relations—economic, cultural, diplomatic, and military—became predicated on the Soviet presence in Afghanistan. Wider forces such as Afghan nationalism, radical Islam, and Soviet security interests were willfully downplayed. Instead, Moscow's actions were viewed through the prism of the Cold War, as part of a "grand design" for global expansion. To have suggested otherwise in 1980 would have exposed Carter to further charges of softness and naivety.

The strategic objectives behind the U.S. response are difficult to discern. On December 31, 1979, the State Department outlined three aims: "The first is punitive: we want them [Soviets] to pay a price for infringing fundamental principles of international behavior. The second is coercive: we want them to withdraw their troops and allow Afghanistan to return to a semblance of sovereignty and neutrality. The third is deterrent: we want to prevent the Soviets from crossing further thresholds." Carter commented that the first and third objectives were "interrelated," while the second was "unlikely."[99] But quite how the U.S. actions would facilitate these objectives was unclear, and remained so for the rest of Carter's term. If the aim really was to coerce the Soviets into a withdrawal, or even a gradual shift in posture, the U.S. reaction proved counterproductive. The absence of political and diplomatic avenues with Moscow would not advance American interests. And for all the logistical problems facing the Red Army, the costs associated with a humiliating retreat had now been raised in the eyes of Soviet leaders. Instead, their resolve was stiffened. To the Kremlin, the U.S. measures (particularly the "Carter Doctrine") merely reinforced the notion that securing Afghanistan was a strategic necessity.[100]

Together, politics and strategy guided Carter's response. The most revealing oral testimony was provided by Marshall Shulman, his chief adviser on Soviet affairs. Pressed on why the administration chose to interpret Soviet actions from a global, rather than local perspective, Shulman explained:

Because of the emotional climate. Because, in this conservative tide, the prevailing view about the Soviet Union was to attribute to it a rather unlimited strategic ambition in that area. The election of Ronald Reagan that was to come in 1980 had cast its shadow ahead of it, and profoundly affected the second half of the Carter administration. It was very much influenced by pressures from the Right. That had particular relevance for policy toward the Soviet Union, because efforts at negotiating on arms control, cultural exchanges, trade, and mutual accommodation became subject to attack in the political scene as being 'soft', and inadequately assertive of the American interest.[101]

SOVIET REACTIONS

The Soviets were taken aback by the hardline response. "From all my experience of anti-Soviet campaigns in the United States, I had never encountered anything like the intensity and scale of this one," recalled Dobrynin, whose ambassadorship spanned twenty-four years and six presidents. Gromyko accused Carter of acting "like an elephant in a china shop."[102] The level of surprise owed something to the hyper-centralized Soviet system. Only a handful of senior figures were privy to the invasion plans, with diplomats effectively omitted from proceedings. As a result, no contingency list anticipating Western reactions was compiled. The Soviet surprise can also be attributed to the lack of prior notification from Washington. A meeting between Brzezinski and Dobrynin on December 6 (eighteen days prior to the invasion) contained no mention of Afghanistan, despite the political turmoil.[103] And when asked by the House Foreign Affairs Committee if the administration had warned the Soviets about the consequences of a military move, Shulman bluntly replied, "No."[104] "There was a general understanding at the top level that there would be a bad reaction," Dobrynin explained. "There would be propaganda, and so on. But nobody at the Politburo discussed what concrete actions the West might take. The Soviet leaders did not foresee any specific Western reaction; just a negative one."[105] As noted, however, Gromyko expressed concerns about the damage that Soviet intervention might inflict on détente and SALT II.[106] Moreover, East–West tensions were raised by NATO's final "dual-track" decision on the deployment of theater nuclear forces in Europe on December 12. The announcement was made just as Soviet leaders were reaching their fatal decision on Afghanistan.[107]

On January 6, TASS criticized the "lack of balance" in the American measures. The Soviet news agency said it showed a "disregard for the fundamental long-term interests of peace and the constructive development of U.S.–Soviet relations." In *Pravda*, Brezhnev claimed that Washington had "embarked on a course hostile to the cause of détente, spiraling towards the arms race." The United States, he added, was "a completely unreliable partner [...] capable at any moment of violating international agreements." The Soviet leadership also engaged in hyperbole, calling the Carter Doctrine "an overt U.S. claim to world domination," which marked "a course toward confrontation and a renunciation of the achievements of détente."[108]

In late January, Vance told Dobrynin of his aim to protect bilateral relations against "extremists" in Washington. The timing of the invasion "could not have been worse," Vance said, because it was an election year. He explained that Carter was ready to continue talks, but only privately and without publicity. Dobrynin replied that the U.S. sanctions and rhetoric went "beyond any reasonable limit." He was baffled when Vance asked if the Soviets were planning to invade Iran, Pakistan, or Yugoslavia (in case of Tito's death), and suspected that the question was driven by Brzezinski's "arc of crisis" theory.[109] "There was no discussion in the Kremlin about any 'grand design'," Dobrynin recalled. "I spoke privately with Brezhnev, Gromyko, and Andropov, and there was never a single word about it. On the contrary, in one of the Politburo meetings, Brezhnev asked me: 'Anatoly, where is the Arc of Crisis that Brzezinski was talking about. What is this about?'"[110]

"THE COLD WAR HAS RESUMED"

On January 30 (prior to his recall to Washington), Ambassador Thomas Watson was embroiled in a heated argument with Gromyko. Watson criticized Soviet motives in Afghanistan, pointing to the assassination of Amin (on December 27) and his replacement by Babrak Karmal, who arrived in Kabul on a Soviet plane. Upon hearing this, Gromyko leapt from his chair and began shouting at Watson.[111] He charged the administration with having sought to damage U.S.–Soviet relations before the invasion, citing the decision to deploy new medium-range missiles in Western Europe, and the handling of the brigade "crisis" in Cuba. On SALT, Gromyko accused the administration of "negotiating for the sake of negotiating, without any intention of reaching agreement." Watson did not refute the charges. (Privately, he was "surprised at how vehemently Carter reacted" to the invasion.) But he walked away from the meeting telling Gromyko that "the Cold War has resumed."[112]

Carter spurned a suggestion from Vance that he should write to Brezhnev. Instead, Vance (with Carter's assent) wrote to Gromyko on February 8. Vance raised concern about the Soviet desire "to conquer and subjugate the Afghan people," and the possibility of military action against Iran and Pakistan. He told Gromyko that the United States would defend its interests, and that "unrestrained actions" would affect bilateral relations.[113] Gromyko criticized American efforts to reduce everything down to Afghanistan, listing prior decisions taken by Carter that had worsened the situation: the development of the MX, the "artificially created mini-crisis in Cuba," and the decision to deploy theater nuclear forces in Europe. "Can these be seen in any way other than a departure from the principle of equal security which was reconfirmed in Vienna?" he asked.[114]

In late February, Brezhnev declared that the Soviets were willing to withdraw their troops "as soon as all forms of outside interference directed against Afghanistan" were ended, and after certain guarantees were obtained.[115] Carter responded by arranging an Oval Office meeting on February 28 (with Brzezinski, Vance, Shulman, and Mondale) to discuss the possibility of renewing a dialogue. There had been indirect communication from Moscow, suggesting that the Soviets might consider a withdrawal from Afghanistan if the United States reconsidered its position on sanctions and the Olympic boycott. Vance told Carter that Boris Ponomarev (Communist Party secretary) and Nikolai Patolichev (minister of foreign trade) had called the Soviet invasion a mistake. The Politburo was thought to be divided on the intervention. As such, Vance proposed that Shulman speak with Brezhnev as a "special emissary" to explore the possibilities for a diplomatic solution. If the response was positive, Vance would meet with Gromyko. Brzezinski was "appalled" at the idea.

He warned against projecting an "image of uncertainty." A meeting with the Soviet foreign minister, he said, "would be politically devastating at home."[116]

Carter felt that there was nothing to lose. He emerged from the Oval Office in favor of Vance's proposal that Shulman go to Moscow to meet with Brezhnev (with a Vance–Gromyko meeting in reserve).[117] But the next day Brzezinski sent Carter a stern memo, warning that a further initiative with the Soviets "could have the most fateful domestic and international consequences." "If the messenger [Shulman or Vance] is identified in the simple-minded public perception with the 'soft' side, it will have devastating political consequences for you. I shudder to think of the impact this could have in Congress, and in the mass media, and how it would be used by our political opponents." Brzezinski dismissed the possibility of Soviet leaders considering a climb-down from Afghanistan. "They are pursuing the 'fight and talk' strategy—consolidating their position while diluting external criticism," he told Carter. "We have to be very careful not to play into their hands."[118] After reading the memo, Carter dropped the Vance–Shulman initiative. His draft letter to Brezhnev, giving assurances of U.S. support for "a neutral, non-aligned Afghanistan [...] and non-interference in its internal affairs"— conditional on a full Soviet withdrawal—was never sent.[119] Instead, Carter said that the U.S. position on Afghanistan would stick, and that this should be communicated to the Soviets.[120] On March 13, Carter publicly called for a boycott of the Moscow Olympics, a decision that was made official the following week. The prospects for averting a confrontation vanished.

*

With Vance sidelined, Brzezinski was in firm control of foreign policy. On March 17, he told Dobrynin of his own ideas for a neutral Afghanistan and for other areas of the "arc of crisis." Dobrynin called the approach "rather queer," given the litany of anti-Soviet measures and public actions that Brzezinski had been directing for the past three months. Moscow, deeply distrustful of Brzezinski, rebuffed his proposal.[121]

"All of these decisions were being made in a highly charged atmosphere," Brzezinski recalled. "The President's political stock was low, and he was irritated by the Kennedy challenge and frustrated by our inability to break through on the Iran hostage issue." Brzezinski claimed that Mondale's judgment was "more and more colored by domestic-political interests."[122] The irony was rich. Brzezinski drew Carter's attention to the foreign–domestic nexus perhaps more than any other adviser. Domestic politics had influenced the administration's response to the Soviet invasion, and its decision to abandon high-level talks. Serious attempts to revive a dialogue fizzled out, and Vance's position was further undermined. U.S.–Soviet relations remained in a state of disrepair for the rest of Carter's presidency.

DOMESTIC REACTIONS

Carter's turn to the right was set against a troubled time for the Democratic Party. On foreign policy it remained divided between the conservative wing that favored a large military buildup (e.g., the CDM), and those of a more liberal persuasion who advocated diplomacy, détente, and a freeze on nuclear weapons. Carter's opponent for the Democratic nomination, Ted Kennedy, fell into the latter category. By contrast, the Republicans in 1980 had no such divisions. Carter was well aware that in Ronald Reagan, the party boasted a candidate who was placing the Soviet threat at the heart of his campaign.

Carter's reaction to the invasion helped to offset the Kennedy challenge. In the Iowa caucuses, he received 59 percent of the delegates to Kennedy's 31 percent. The senator tried to revive his campaign in a speech at Georgetown University in late January, seizing on Carter's new focus on strength and military acquisition. Kennedy attacked the 5 percent increase in the defense budget as "excessive spending on irrelevant strategic systems."[123] He condemned the grain embargo, which he said would mainly hurt U.S. farmers. And Kennedy mocked Carter's comment that the Soviet invasion marked "the most serious threat to world peace since the Second World War." "Is it a graver threat than the Berlin blockade, the Korean War, the Soviet march into Hungary and Czechoslovakia, the Berlin Wall, the Cuban Missile Crisis, or Vietnam?" he asked. Kennedy criticized Carter for being "surprised" by the Soviet invasion, for failing to respond to the Afghan coup in 1978, and for missing the warning signs. He also blamed the administration for over-hyping the episode. "Exaggerated dangers and empty symbols will not resolve a foreign crisis. It is less than a year since the Vienna summit, when President Carter kissed President Brezhnev on the cheek. We cannot afford a foreign policy based on the pangs of unrequited love."[124]

Spokesmen for Carter dismissed the speech as "opportunistic and irresponsible." They said that Kennedy's opposition to the grain embargo and draft registration smacked of "appeasement."[125] Carter achieved victory in Maine and New Hampshire—states in which Kennedy had been expected to win. The senator triumphed in his home state of Massachusetts, but this was to prove only a fleeting setback for Carter. Despite Kennedy victories in Connecticut, New York, Washington D.C., and California, the president maintained a healthy lead in the primaries, eventually securing 51 percent of the vote.

But if Carter's new approach helped to win the support of some moderate Democrats, it was not enough to satisfy the conservative wing. On January 10, Moynihan made a foreign policy statement that was, noted Madeleine Albright, "generally supportive in a backhanded way: i.e., the President has finally seen the light."[126] In late January, Carter made a final effort to court the neoconservatives. He invited leading CDM members (including Podhoretz, Kirkpatrick, and Elliott Abrams) to the White House. But the president failed to win them over. "Carter indicated that, in fact, he had learned nothing from Afghanistan," bemoaned Abrams. "The universal reaction after the meeting was that this guy was hopeless."[127] Kirkpatrick switched party allegiance to join the Reagan campaign as foreign policy adviser. Abrams, too, would cast his support for the Republican front-runner. Within a year both would be serving in a Reagan administration. The CDM's filial ally, the Committee on the Present Danger, was also discontented. Paul Nitze said that there were "grounds for serious doubt" about the U.S. response to Afghanistan. He was not convinced by the new defense plans, claiming that Carter was underestimating the Soviet threat to Southwest Asia. "He has not proposed an increase in defense budgets of programs beyond those agreed with Senator Nunn before the invasion," Nitze argued. "There is a material question as to whether the program he proposes is adequate to support the very firm policy declaration he has made."[128] The CPD endorsed Reagan, charging Carter with having done too little, too late. Nitze, a conservative Democrat, would also join Reagan in 1981, heading the U.S. delegation to the INF talks.

Reagan, for all his anti-Soviet rhetoric, treaded cautiously on the SALT debate. While continually criticizing details of the treaty, he stopped short of rejecting it out of hand. Polls indicated that some found Reagan too hawkish, while the agreement retained large public support. As such, Richard Allen, his foreign policy adviser, urged restraint. "Everyone expected Reagan to be against SALT II, so he would gain nothing by shooting too early," Allen recalled. "The mood of the country would harden and he could ride that wave." Prior to the

Soviet invasion, Reagan therefore argued that the treaty should be "shelved," rather than rejected. In mid-September, 1979, he stated: "The Senate should declare that this treaty, fatally flawed as it is, should be shelved, and that the negotiators should go back to the table and come up with a treaty which fairly and genuinely reduces the number of strategic nuclear weapons."[129]

In the spring of 1980, Reagan went on the offensive. On March 17, he delivered an address to the Chicago Council on Foreign Relations. "The Carter Administration and the Democratic-controlled Congress have neglected our military strength and have cut back our defense programs," Reagan declared. "For nearly two decades the Russians have been building theirs to an extent never before witnessed by the world. Only now, since the Soviet invasion of Afghanistan, and the President's discovery that the Soviets can't be trusted, has he indicated that he recognizes the importance of a strong defense. But his actions do not match his new rhetoric [...] it leaves us totally unable to match the Soviet buildup." Reagan outlined his plan to achieve "peace through strength"—based on a massive arms buildup—before returning to criticize Carter. "The humiliations and symbols of weakness add up. The unwillingness of the Carter Administration to make our case is pervasive. We apologize, compromise, withdraw and retreat; we fall silent when insulted and pay ransom when we are victimized." Citing a popular conservative grievance, Reagan called on Americans to "rid ourselves of the 'Vietnam Syndrome.' It has dominated our thinking for too long."[130]

Reagan was less assured in his handling of the Olympic boycott issue. On March 26, he admitted to being conflicted on Carter's decision. "It's a tough one," Reagan said. "You'll just have to let me stew about that one for a while." Soon afterward he changed tack, arguing that the decision should be left with the athletes. "I don't believe the government should be in the position of saying you can't have a visa, you can't leave the country." But Reagan's stance drew criticism, with campaign manager William Casey conceding that the issue had caught him unprepared. After monitoring public opinion, Reagan again altered his position. "We should boycott the Moscow Olympics," he declared, claiming it was "hypocritical" that the games should be held in a nation engaged in aggression.[131] Reagan's confusion on the Olympics did not deter the voters. He cantered to victory in the primaries, seeing off Bush and Anderson (who dropped out of the Republican race to run as an independent) by winning forty-four of the fifty-one contests.

PRESIDENTIAL DIRECTIVE 59

Carter shifted his attention from Kennedy to Reagan and the November election. But the conservative criticism mounted. For all the hardline rhetoric, sanctions, and defense plans, the president could not escape charges of "weakness." In 1980 there was, it seemed, nothing that he could say or do to shirk such accusations. The Iran hostage crisis remained top of the agenda. Round-the-clock media attention and partisan attacks would influence his decision to launch a rescue attempt to free the U.S. hostages. The rescue mission was urged by Jordan, among others, who called for action "to snatch our people up [...] to prove to the columnists and political opponents that Carter was not an ineffective Chief Executive who was afraid to act."[132] Carter told his advisers: "I've got to give expression to the anger of the American people [...] If they perceive me as firm and tough in voicing their rage, maybe we'll be able to control this thing."[133] But on April 24, a U.S. helicopter collided with a C-130 aircraft, resulting in the death of eight American soldiers. Carter promptly aborted the rescue mission. For Cyrus Vance, who had opposed the operation, this was the final straw. He resigned in protest, with Carter appointing Maine senator Edmund Muskie as the new secretary of state.

Republicans denounced Carter for canceling or deferring defense programs (such as the Minuteman missile, the B-1 bomber, and the neutron bomb), and for the delay in production of cruise missiles and the MX. Reagan's Chicago address provoked debate among Carter's top advisers. Within days, Brzezinski wrote to Carter calling for a "unifying theme" on foreign policy and a new presidential statement. "The theme we propose is that the Soviet invasion of Afghanistan must focus our attention on a major new order of politico-economic-military threat to non-communist world security," he explained. "Aggressive Soviet behavior, against the backdrop of constantly growing Soviet military power, betokens a grave and imminent threat to the entire world to which it must respond."[134]

It was in this political climate that Carter issued Presidential Directive 59 (PD-59), one of the most controversial nuclear policy statements of the Cold War. Its purpose was to grant the U.S. president more flexibility in planning for, and executing, a nuclear war. PD-59 sought nuclear capabilities that ensured "a higher degree of flexibility, enduring survivability, and adequate performance in the face of enemy actions." If deterrence failed, the United States "must be capable of fighting successfully so that the adversary would not achieve his war aims and would suffer costs that

were unacceptable." PD-59 planned for nuclear targeting against categor-
ies such as strategic and theater nuclear forces, command-and-control
posts, stationary and mobile military forces, weapons storage, and military-
industrial facilities. Carter signed the directive on July 25.[135]

Harold Brown told the press that PD-59 was "not a radical departure
from U.S. strategic policy over the past decade or so." But this was only
true in the sense that talks on planning for a nuclear war, and what might
constitute Mutual Assured Destruction (MAD), were an ongoing
process.[136] Debates on nuclear strategy had taken place intermittently
since 1977, when PD-18 was issued. Yet PD-59 was a far more aggressive
policy statement, introducing an explicit option for striking directly at the
Soviet command structure ("nuclear decapitation").[137] As historian Betty
Glad notes, PD-59 marked a departure from the traditional concept of
MAD—and the beliefs which Carter held prior to 1980.[138] At the Vienna
summit in June 1979, Carter told Brezhnev and Ustinov that he favored
a nuclear balance in which both nations would have invulnerabilities for
a small number of weapons, allowing either side to survive a first strike
and retaliate. One example, Carter said, was the designation of "safe
havens for missile submarines." He believed this would help to nullify
the most destabilizing threat of all: "the ability of either nation to first
destroy the retaliatory forces of the other, and still have enough weapons
remaining to launch a follow-up attack with relative impunity."[139]

PD-59 veered from this logic. By quickly targeting command structures
and tank divisions, rather than firing a first "warning" strike, Soviet
leaders would be denied control over their military forces once a war
had begun. The action would inflict casualties and rule out any possibility
of the Soviets achieving a military victory. The acquisition of new capabilities, targeting the Soviet leadership, would be a strong inducement for
Moscow not to start a nuclear war. In sum, PD-59 signaled a more
aggressive national security posture, which flirted with the idea that
a limited nuclear exchange could be controlled, or even "won."[140]
Critics compared PD-59 with NSC-68, the early Cold War doctrine
which called for the expansion of American military power to meet the
Soviet threat.[141] Paul Warnke, Carter's former arms control guru, called
PD-59 "apocalyptic nonsense."[142]

While meetings on strategic defense were held in 1979, it was not until
March 1980 that the quest for a directive on nuclear targeting really
emerged. On March 22, Odom sent Brzezinski a draft version of PD-59—
five days after Reagan's attack on Carter in Chicago, when he called for
a "clear capability" to destroy Soviet military targets.[143] Further drafts

were devised between the NSC and the Defense Department in April and May.[144] Brzezinski was the prime architect, with Brown having been "dragged along" on PD-59. As he prepared Brzezinski for his briefing with Carter, Odom explained: "You should know that the Republican platform includes a lot of nuclear war-fighting doctrine. The issue may or may not come up in the campaign, but from a national security and foreign policy viewpoint, the PD is needed to clarify our policy and leave no room for confusion."[145]

Brzezinski, wary of press criticism, emphasized the "incremental" nature of PD-59. He feared that Richard Burt (of the *New York Times*) would hype the issue, and told his NSC staff to decline to speak. Instead, Brzezinski asked the Defense Department to give Burt "a balanced briefing, stressing the evolutionary character of the doctrine."[146] But watchful reporters knew better. The *Washington Post*'s Michael Getler noted: "The timing of the new directive would seem to have a political target in this country—Ronald Reagan—with the administration seeking to show it is moving to improve U.S. defense, even though it came to office claiming that it would cut defense spending."[147] Carter's liberal opponents criticized the doctrine, with the president accused of attempting to "out-Republican the Republicans." Kennedy argued that it would make nuclear war more likely, providing incentives for parties to launch preemptive strikes.[148] Tellingly, while the State Department had been involved in earlier discussion of nuclear policy, it was deliberately cut from planning in 1980. Brzezinski told Carter that it was far too sensitive for "diplomatists" and should not be "reviewed or discussed by those not required to deal with it."[149] Muskie learned about PD-59 from reading the newspapers.[150]

EUROPEAN ATTITUDES

Carter's relations with European allies remained problematic. He had called for a firm Western stance on both Iran and the Soviet Union. But West German Chancellor Helmut Schmidt and French President Valery Giscard d'Estaing were also facing elections. Neither was prepared to sacrifice his domestic political interests. British Prime Minister Margaret Thatcher faced no such preoccupations. Following the Iran hostage crisis, Thatcher promised her "full backing."[151] But with British commercial interests at stake—its monthly trade with Iran exceeded $40 million—her support fell short of what Carter had hoped for. Giscard and Schmidt promised only to issue supportive statements condemning Iranian actions. On March 26, Carter again pressed European leaders to support the

U.S. sanctions against Tehran. When they resisted, he severed diplomatic relations with Iran and imposed full-scale sanctions.[152] Carter recalled: "It soon became apparent that even our closest allies in Europe were not going to expose themselves to potential oil boycotts or endanger their diplomatic arrangements."[153]

Transatlantic relations after the invasion of Afghanistan were, in their own way, just as difficult. Giscard held a low opinion of Carter and felt that he was being unnecessarily provocative with Moscow. Carter, for his part, grew weary of the "rapidly changing" French position. "I don't know what's going on in France," he admitted on February 9.[154] Franco–American relations worsened as the year progressed. Far from severing diplomatic ties with the Soviets, Giscard met privately with Brezhnev in Warsaw on May 19. Muskie was furious, and rebuked the French government for arranging the meeting without consulting fellow allies.[155]

The British position on Afghanistan was more favorable. Thatcher, despite her political reservations about Carter, strengthened relations with China, Turkey, and Pakistan, while expanding the British military presence in the Indian Ocean. She agreed that a boycott of the Moscow Olympics would be a fine way of denting Soviet prestige. However, opposition from the British Olympic Committee meant that Thatcher was unable to deliver a boycott.[156] Britain would send more athletes to Moscow than any other Western nation. British diplomats raised eyebrows at the scale of the U.S. response to the Soviet invasion. But they understood the political logic. After Carter's early triumphs in the primaries, the Foreign Office reported: "President Carter experienced a falling of the scales from the eyes after Afghanistan. This, as well as the hostage episode, put far more pep into him than had ever existed before. Now that he has found that his response matches the mood of Americans and is electorally useful, he will no doubt continue to stick to the hawkish policies which he has been pursuing post-Afghanistan."[157]

The most hostile relationship remained that of Carter and Schmidt. Like Giscard, the West German chancellor wanted to maintain a dialogue with the Soviets and, if possible, salvage détente. Although he supported the Olympic boycott, Schmidt resisted Carter's pleas to apply sanctions against Iran and the USSR. He criticized the president for failing to conceive of a long-term strategy for East–West relations. "We saw clearly that there was no logical and self-containing strategy for managing the crisis," Schmidt recalled. "I had to ask myself whether Carter was sincere in his efforts to achieve a Soviet retreat from Afghanistan. By the beginning of 1980, I realized that Jimmy Carter was profoundly worried about his chances of reelection that November. His foreign policy was increasingly being shaped by short-term considerations of the effect it would have at home."[158]

Schmidt did not hide his feelings about Carter's motives (or his own) during a meeting with Vance on February 20. The chancellor said that he and Giscard also had their domestic problems. He understood that "much of what the President says and does has something to do with the domestic situation in the United States and with the political campaign." Schmidt explained that for political reasons West Germany had to build up exchanges with the Soviets. "FRG trade with the Soviets is five times more important to the FRG than U.S. trade with the USSR," he told Vance. Schmidt would not risk a rise in West German unemployment because of sanctions against the Soviets.[159] Robert Blackwill (NSC director of Western European affairs) told Brzezinski: "Punishing actions against the Soviets would sharply alienate the left-wing of the SPD. Most party activists come from this group and Schmidt needs them badly in the election campaign." Blackwill explained that after the neutron bomb postponement in 1978, "Schmidt lost his confidence in Jimmy Carter [...] He knows that a public row with the U.S. in the next few months is just about the only thing that could derail his reelection hopes."[160] In November 1980 Schmidt was reelected.

CARTER VERSUS REAGAN, POLAND, AND THE POPE

Carter's reelection prospects were dwindling. His turn to the right seemed to vindicate the foreign policy criticisms leveled against him prior to 1980. Opposition candidates focused chiefly on those first three years. An unsparing report from Caddell conveyed the enormity of the task. The Reagan challenge from the right was crowding the center, while Anderson's decision to run as an independent was raiding Carter's unhappy left base and the industrial belt. Inflation, unemployment, and rising energy costs blotted the president's record domestically. Internationally, things looked little better. Carter's achievements (the Arab–Israeli accords, the Panama Canal treaties, and the normalization of relations with China) had yielded little profit in the polls. "To the public, American foreign policy appears in disarray," Caddell explained. "The hostages are still captive, the Russians are on the move, and a sense of political and military decline pervades the public mood. The public is anxious, confused, hostile, and sour [...] By and large the American people do not like Jimmy Carter."[161]

Carter's popularity among American farmers had suffered. In imposing a grain embargo he had rejected the advice of Mondale and Eizenstat, who argued against taking the measure for political and moral reasons.[162] In June, Brzezinski told Carter that the embargo was "doing serious political damage" to the administration. But he felt that ending it would damage Carter's credibility by confirming that it was a failure and a mistake to begin with. It would also leave the president open to the charge of "giving in" to the Soviets for narrow political reasons. Weighing up the risks, Brzezinski advised Carter not to remove the embargo against the USSR. "To do so in this context would prove more damaging politically, even with the farmers, than any conceivable political gain," he wrote.[163]

In August, Brzezinski told Carter that his handling of foreign policy had the potential to "significantly influence" the outcome of the election: "Despite the constraints on Presidential power, foreign affairs is the area in which you have the greatest discretion and the most opportunity for demonstrating effective leadership, taking dramatic action, and mobilizing national support." Republicans were concerned about a possible "October surprise" from the administration, in order to wrestle attention away from the grim economic climate. But no such opportunity was on the horizon. "Unfortunately, the present international situation simply does not lend itself to some sudden and dramatic stroke—unless we are confronted with a crisis," wrote Brzezinski. "In that event, a very strong and firm response, involving a military action, is likely to be quite popular. But something like Eisenhower's 'I would go to Korea' doesn't seem to be available."[164]

At the presidential debate in Cleveland, Reagan framed the election as a referendum on Carter's record. "Are you better off than you were four years ago?" he asked voters. "Is America as respected throughout the world as it was? Do you feel that our security is as safe, that we're as strong as we were four years ago?"[165] The Soviet leadership had reached its verdict on the election. "Fed up with Carter and uneasy about Reagan, it decided to stay on the fence," Dobrynin recalled.[166] Bilateral relations hit a new low in September, when Gromkyo traveled to New York for the UN General Assembly. On the instruction of state governors, the special plane carrying the foreign minister was refused permission to land at Kennedy and Newark airports. A "very angry" Gromyko was instead forced to disembark at a remote military airport.[167] Ahead of the election, Brezhnev remarked: "Even the devil himself could not tell who is better—Carter or Reagan."[168] The American public decided on November 4. Reagan achieved a landslide victory, securing 489 electoral votes (across forty-four states) to Carter's forty-nine. Moments after Reagan was sworn in, the fifty-two hostages in Tehran were released into U.S. custody.

Ironically, the foreign crisis for which Brzezinski had hoped occurred in his native Poland, and too late to influence the election. On August 14, 1980, 17,000 Polish workers went on strike at a shipyard in Gdansk in protest at rising food prices. An electrician named Lech Walesa (fired from his job in 1976) formed a trade union named Solidarity, which became the platform for a wider Polish movement. The crisis escalated in late November. Although the Gdansk workers were granted a pay rise, they remained on strike, and the Solidarity campaign continued. Similar strikes spread throughout the country, crippling the Polish economy and presenting the communist rulers (and Moscow) with a decision: to intervene militarily or accept more of the workers' demands.

Brezhnev pressured Stanislaw Kania (Polish first secretary) and General Wojciech Jaruzelski (head of the Polish armed forces) to stand firm against Solidarity.[169] CIA reports of military exercises by Warsaw Pact armies near the Polish border raised fears of a Soviet invasion. On December 3, Brzezinski, Brown, and Muskie held a meeting to discuss contingency plans and a possible public warning to Moscow. "Wouldn't it be odd if Governor Reagan and Richard Allen appeared to make the stronger statements?" Brzezinski mused.[170] Later that day, Carter warned Brezhnev against resorting to military action. In a brief letter, he explained that U.S.–Soviet relations "would be most adversely affected if force was used to impose a solution upon the Polish nation."[171] After an NSC meeting on December 7, the administration told NATO allies that a Soviet invasion could be imminent. With Carter's approval, Brzezinski telephoned the Vatican to speak with (Polish-born) Pope John Paul II, whose status helped to embolden the Solidarity movement.[172] But by late 1980 there was little appetite in Moscow to launch another military operation. KGB Chairman Yuri Andropov, who had supported the Soviet invasions of Hungary, Czechoslovakia, as well as Afghanistan, commented: "The quota of interventions abroad has been exhausted."[173] The Soviets did not intervene by force of arms.

*

"The arms race is not only dangerous, it's morally deplorable. We must put an end to it," Carter declared at Notre Dame in 1977. "We desire a freeze on further modernization and production of weapons, and a continuing, substantial reduction of strategic nuclear weapons." He spoke of America being free from its "inordinate fear of communism."[174] Candidate Carter called for a cut of at least $5 billion in the "bloated" defense budget, and for a measured level of military engagement.[175] In 1980, Carter's foreign policies bore little resemblance to these goals. He described the Soviet invasion of Afghanistan as "the most serious threat to world peace since the Second World War."[176] He announced a 5 percent increase in the defense budget, and extended the containment doctrine to the Persian Gulf. A Rapid Deployment Force was activated, and covert military aid was approved for Afghan rebels and Pakistan. Carter unveiled a new directive on nuclear targeting, reinstated draft registration, having earlier authorized the production of the MX missile.

If the world had changed during those three years, so too had the American mood. Memories of Vietnam were still vivid, but they no longer carried the same emotional resonance that had helped sweep Carter to victory in 1976. Public opinion favored a more vigorous foreign policy and increased defense spending, despite the economic hardships and the support for a SALT treaty. By 1979, notes historian Gaddis Smith, Carter was "changing his approach, emphasizing American strength more than human values."[177] The pressure to do so increased after the Iran hostage crisis, which haunted Carter's campaign. In the eyes of many voters, the crisis symbolized America's domestic problems and a loss of international prestige. "To the public, Iran became a metaphor for everything," recalled Gerald Rafshoon, Carter's director of communications.[178]

To be sure, Carter's stance had gradually hardened, as his administration succumbed to the cut and thrust of party politics, a splintered Democratic coalition, and a more assertive Congress. But not until 1980 did the shift to the right truly take shape. Carter's State of the Union address was devoted almost entirely to military strength. The need to dispel charges of weakness became a priority after the Soviet invasion. "It is far too easy, in an election year, to let what may seem smart politics produce bad policies," Vance warned in a speech at Harvard University in June.[179] Domestic factors had colored perceptions of the Kremlin's motives, and of the countermeasures that were necessary. In the political climate of 1980, viewing the invasion as a symptom of Soviet behavior, rather than an aberration or a defensive maneuver, was the most risk-averse option. The U.S. response increased the bilateral tensions, contributing to the rise of a "second" Cold War.

"There were lots of reasons why progress occurred and why it didn't occur," recalled Leslie Gelb, Carter's assistant secretary of state. "Cy Vance pointed to a very useful corrective: namely, domestic politics. We can put a lot of theories on our behavior. But in truth, much of what we did or didn't do had to do with political considerations, and what individuals in positions of power felt their strengths and weaknesses were at a particular time."[180] David Aaron, the deputy national security adviser, would put it more simply: "When you are the president, *everything* is political."[181]

4

Confrontation

On November 4, 1980, Ronald Reagan became the oldest candidate to be elected president in American history. Carter, by contrast, was the first incumbent to lose a reelection since 1932, when Franklin D. Roosevelt (Reagan's early idol[1]) had walloped Herbert Hoover. The elevation of a new president reflects its time, and 1980 was no different. Reagan ran on a platform which promised to end the sense of gloom that pervaded the Carter years, and much of the period preceding it. The images were depressing: Vietnam, Watergate, interest group pandering, credibility shortages, gas shortages, inflation, unemployment, hostages. Carter detected a "crisis of confidence," but offered the public neither assurances nor remedies. Each of Reagan's predecessors dating back to Johnson had, in some way, contributed to that deficit.[2] America's fortieth president, inaugurated prior to his seventieth birthday, was tasked with restoring morale and public faith in government.

For Reagan, foreign policy was the perfect political tonic. In the downbeat climate of the late 70s, he made the Cold War a focal point of his quest for office. The notion of a "philosophy" may be hyperbole (Reagan was not an introspective man), but there were several tenets to which he adhered. The first was his anti-communism, which dated back to Reagan's acting days when 1930s Hollywood flirted with Marxist ideals. In 1963, the year of the Test Ban Treaty, he charged the "liberal establishment" with pursuing "a policy of accommodation with the Soviet Union."[3] After making the transition to politics, Reagan campaigned as a vigorous anti-communist, accusing Soviet leaders of trapping their own citizens in a "backwash of history." "We have seen nothing like it since the age of feudalism," he declared in a foreign policy speech.[4] He took to the

114

airwaves, denouncing communism as a "disease" or "sickness" afflicting society. "Communism is neither an economic nor a political system," Reagan argued. "It is a form of insanity—a temporary aberration which will one day disappear from the earth because it is contrary to human nature."[5]

The latter point reflected one of Reagan's inherent beliefs: his optimism in the ability of mankind—above all, the United States—to outlast the Soviet system. For Reagan, America *was* exceptional, "a shining city upon a hill, whose beacon light guides freedom-loving people everywhere."[6] He spoke, too, of the burdens which accompanied this role. "We cannot escape our destiny, nor should we try to do so. The leadership of the free world was thrust upon us two centuries ago," Reagan proclaimed. "We are today the last best hope of man on earth."[7] Reagan's faith in American ideals, and the capacity of U.S. power to resolve world problems, appealed to disillusioned voters. He made sure that criticism of the Soviet Union was accompanied by references to the superiority of the United States. "Our foreign policy should be to show by example the greatness of our system and the strength of American ideals," he argued in a 1980 campaign address.[8] Foreign leaders were struck by these convictions. Recalling his meetings with the president, Helmut Schmidt wrote of Reagan's "unshakeable belief" in the elements which had made America great—capitalism and free enterprise, optimism, moral idealism, and a readiness to use strength when other means of achieving justice were impossible.[9]

Yet Reagan's idealism belies another, somewhat paradoxical, trait. Pragmatism was a feature of his professional life. Seven terms as president of the Screen Actors Guild saw him develop the art of nuance, compromise, and negotiation. Viewed by the right as too liberal and the left as too woolly, he forged a middle ground when testifying to the House of Un-American Activities (then investigating communist influence in the movie industry).[10] While governor of California, Reagan's conservative rhetoric did not deter him from signing one of America's most liberal abortion laws.[11] Nor did it prevent him from implementing the largest tax increase in Californian history—worth $1 billion—to confront a mounting deficit.[12] The struggle between Reagan the ideologue and Reagan the pragmatist also surfaced in the 1980 presidential campaign. When required, he had no hesitation in playing the latter role. Reagan, for all his anti-Soviet rhetoric and criticism of détente, treaded carefully on the SALT II issue. Conscious of public support for the treaty, he stopped short of rejecting it out of hand, arguing only that it should be "shelved" until a better deal could be achieved.[13] On the Moscow Olympics, too, Reagan was happy to abandon his convictions. Having earlier denounced Carter's decision to boycott the games, Reagan performed a U-turn after monitoring public opinion polls, which indicated strong support for the administration's position.[14] As historian Kyle Longley notes, "[Reagan] was a pragmatic politician with significant flaws, who often subordinated ideology and principles for politics."[15]

For much of his first three years as president, Reagan the ideologue seemed to prevail. Living up to conservative expectations, his administration embarked upon the most hardline, anti-communist agenda in at least two decades. As year four neared, however, the pragmatist reemerged. Like Carter before him, Reagan's Cold War approach would undergo a significant change, as foreign policy became entwined with domestic imperatives. His was no conventional presidency. But as with any good politician (or actor), Reagan understood what played well with his audience and what did not.

MILITARY BUILDUP

The White House was a long way from Tampico, Illinois, where Reagan was born, and nearby Dixon, where he grew up. His optimistic demeanor was shaped by his mother Nelle, whose religious beliefs instilled a sense of faith and perspective.[16] Reagan was less close to his father, Jack, who was of Irish ancestry and an alcoholic for most of his adult life. Remarking that he looked like "a fat little Dutchman," Jack nicknamed his son "Dutch"; a moniker that was reinforced by his pageboy haircut.[17] Reagan graduated from Eureka College in 1932 at the depth of the Great Depression, and began a career as a sports broadcaster. When that proved unsatisfying, he used a trip to California to schedule a screen test for the Warner Brothers studio. After winning a contract, Reagan forged a solid reputation in Hollywood, starring in a series of B movies in the late 1930s. But over the next decade his career stuttered, as did his marriage (to actress Jane Wyman). It was a period in which communist involvement in the movie industry came under scrutiny, and left an indelible mark on Reagan. He recalled: "More than anything else, it was the Communists' attempted takeover of Hollywood [...] that led me to accept the nomination as president of the Screen Actors Guild and, indirectly at least, set me on the road that would lead me into politics."[18]

The 1950s was a time of change in Reagan's life. In 1952, he married another actress, Nancy Davis, and soon afterward began hosting General

Electric Theatre, a weekly television drama series. Reagan's political views were also in transition. Once a New Deal Democrat (voting for FDR on four occasions), he gradually eschewed his liberal leanings. He became an opponent of government regulation and progressive income tax, which he believed was undermining free enterprise and individual initiative. Eight years as national spokesman for General Electric (one of America's largest corporations) was an ideal forum for Reagan to air his increasingly conservative views, on television and in speaking engagements across the country.[19] "By 1960, I had completed the process of self-conversion," he recalled. "I realized the real enemy wasn't big business. It was big government."[20] After registering as a Republican, Reagan campaigned for Barry Goldwater in his presidential race against Lyndon Johnson. On October 27, 1964, he delivered one of his most famous speeches: "A Time for Choosing." Goldwater was soundly beaten. But Reagan received national exposure for his oratory skills, and was propelled to the front of the Republican Party. During Johnson's "Great Society," Reagan positioned himself as a leading critic of big government, and began his own run for office. Two terms as governor of California followed (1967–75), a period blighted by division over taxes and spending cuts, and which saw student protests across major public universities.[21] While willing to compromise on certain issues, he instituted a variety of conservative programs and staunchly defended the Vietnam War. Following a narrow defeat to Ford in the battle for the 1976 Republican nomination, Reagan honed his message in time for the 1980 campaign.

"Let's not delude ourselves," he told an interviewer in June 1980. "The Soviet Union underlies all the unrest that is going on. If they weren't engaged in this game of dominoes, there wouldn't be any hot spots in the world."[22] Reagan had spent much of the past four years talking up Soviet military advances, while criticizing American decision-makers for granting "unilateral concessions." He invoked the putative "window of vulnerability" in land-based missiles, which left the United States exposed to a first strike. Soon, Reagan said, that window would be open so wide "the Russians could just take us with a phone call."[23] But he also saw weakness. Reagan argued that the Soviet system was ideologically bankrupt, with economic problems which could not sustain an arms race. He reasoned that if the United States was willing to outspend the Soviets militarily, Moscow would be forced to negotiate seriously on arms control. Only through a position of military strength could America set the terms of negotiations and bring the Soviets to heel. In the interim, it was hoped that the acquisition of expensive new defense programs would discourage Moscow from embarking on further adventurism in the Third World.[24] All told, it represented a more hardline approach. Gone was Nixon's elaborate détente and Carter's emphasis on human rights. To be sure, Reagan would champion the cause of freedom in Eastern Europe (though he was skeptical about the utility of the CSCE).[25] But the broad effect was to abandon Carter's policies. Rather than pressuring pro-American dictatorships to improve their human rights records, his administration would demonstrate a willingness to cooperate with them in order to oppose communist advances.[26]

Reagan sought to win support for the arms buildup by insisting that America was no longer the world's foremost military power. "In military strength we are already second to one; namely, the Soviet Union," he claimed.[27] He did so despite being briefed on the nuclear balance by departing CIA Director Stansfield Turner, who said that "according to CIA estimates, the USSR has no advantage over the United States." Turner commissioned the study in 1980, with the aim of achieving the official estimate of the nuclear balance. "We worked from the assumption that the Soviet Union would launch a surprise first strike, optimized to destroy our nuclear forces, and we would do nothing," Turner recalled. "And it came out that the nuclear balance was such that we could still destroy the Soviet Union twice over, and the Soviet Union could destroy us at least one more time." Even in the event of a Soviet first strike, CIA data indicated that the United States would have enough strategic nuclear weapons to destroy all Soviet cities with populations of over 100,000. But Reagan's apathetic response left Turner in doubt about how he wished to proceed.[28] Privately, some of the president's advisers dismissed the notion of Soviet parity, let alone supremacy. "Under all circumstances, U.S. foreign policy must be predicated on the fact that while there are two nuclear superpowers, the United States is the only truly global power," wrote Richard Beal, special assistant to the president.[29]

Reagan's "appeasement" charge and call for a military buildup were politically appealing messages. "Peace through strength" was a slogan which found favor with conservatives in both parties. But there was little evidence of a strategy to complement the buildup to achieve that goal. It would be more than a year before Reagan himself offered a comprehensive statement on policy toward the Soviet Union. Nor was it an immediate priority. In contrast to his predecessor, Reagan began his presidency by placing domestic reform at the top of the agenda. The passage through Congress of a program of major tax and budget cuts (the Economic Recovery Tax Act and the Omnibus

Budget Reconciliation Act) was the chief focus of his administration. Dubbed "Reaganomics," a supply-side economic plan was implemented in 1981, with the top tax rate falling initially from 70 to 50 percent.

The tax cuts would be accompanied by a massive increase in defense spending. Reagan intensified the program of military acquisition initiated by Carter. But whereas Carter had lurched to the right almost in desperation, Reagan pursued his policies with conviction. Before long, it would evolve into the largest peacetime military buildup in American history. Between 1980 and 1985, defense spending doubled from $150 billion to almost $300 billion a year, eventually reaching 6.4 percent of GDP.[30] Funds were allocated for the development of the B-2 Stealth bomber, the resumption of the B-1 bomber, and expensive weapons systems such as the Pershing II and Trident II missiles. Plans for a new basing mode for the MX missile were accelerated. There were also significant initiatives in conventional weaponry. Citing the growing Soviet blue-water naval force, the Reagan administration began the development of a 600-ship navy, a considerable expansion from the 479 ships bequeathed by Carter. Reagan's outlay of well over $1 trillion in his first five years would nearly equal the total expenditure of Nixon, Ford, and Carter in their combined twelve years in office.[31] With the accent placed on strength, not peace, there was little energy expended on diplomacy in the first half of Reagan's first term.

But the Reagan administration would not have things all their own way. In the realm of foreign policy, this was not a conservative mandate. True, Reagan's triumph over Carter had been a resounding one. His political ascent helped to sway key Senate elections, enabling Republicans to wrestle back control of the upper chamber for the first time since 1954 (Democrats retained the whip hand in the House). But the break in the Cold War consensus remained wide. As in the 1970s, the early 80s would be rife with partisan divisions over national security. Nuclear policy; East–West relations; defense procurement; overseas intervention: all were issues on which the two parties continued to clash. The composition of the Senate Foreign Relations Committee had changed markedly after the 1980 elections. Veterans such as Frank Church (D-Idaho) and Jacob Javits (R-New York) had been defeated, and their departure cleared the way for ideologues such as Jesse Helms (R-North Carolina) to push their agenda. Judith Miller of the *New York Times* reported of the deepening "ideological divisions, legislative disarray, and political floundering" in the committee. This internal dissent would see the Senate Armed Services Committee increasingly intrude into foreign affairs terrain during the early 1980s.[32]

Divisions in Congress reflected a divided public where it concerned national security. Support for strengthening the U.S. military was high among Republicans and Democrats. But the liberal, anti-war cause of the past decade had not diminished. Vietnam continued to cast a long shadow over American life. While Reagan spoke of banishing "the Vietnam Syndrome" (a grievance of many conservatives), he was conscious of the lack of appetite among the public for further military entanglements. The new authority wielded by Congress at the expense of the executive (such as the War Powers Act), and the public attitudes underpinning it, would limit the scope of what his administration could accomplish. As with the Carter years, domestic variables would set the parameters for U.S. foreign policy as much as developments abroad.[33]

REAGAN: FORMING AN ADMINISTRATION

Reagan brought to office a unique blend of assets and deficiencies. He was a master of public performance, as adept in front of the camera as any politician of his time. He excelled as a communicator, with the ability to simplify messages and engage audiences in set-piece speeches (skills honed over decades as an actor, public spokesman, and politician). In formal meetings, he disarmed interlocutors with jokes and anecdotes. Reagan's bonhomie and cool demeanor enabled him to form relationships with Republicans and Democrats, as well as with the press. "He handles the media better than anybody since Franklin Roosevelt, even Jack Kennedy," conceded House Speaker Tip O'Neill.[34]

Reagan had less success in grasping the substance of policy, whether domestic or foreign. He was often inattentive to details. David Gergen, Reagan's director of communications, felt that he had less curiosity about public policy than any president since the 1920s.[35] The House majority leader, Jim Wright (D-Texas), voiced a similar complaint. "The President is a very affable, charming individual. He enjoys telling a story and tells one well. But I'd like to see more substance. I've only been in two meetings so far. One was inconclusive and the talk in the other was superficial."[36] Reagan was highly dependent on his staff for expertise. He would let his advisers deal with the cut and thrust of the daily issues, preferring to take a backseat until the moment for decision was at hand. "You fellas work it out," was a familiar line at cabinet meetings. "He made no demands, and gave almost no instructions," recalled Martin Anderson, a longtime friend and economic adviser. "Essentially, he just responded to whatever was brought to his attention and said yes or no, or I'll think about it."[37] But Reagan was less passive than commonly depicted. He held strong, independent views and was prepared to air them publicly where he saw fit. As author Richard Reeves observed, Reagan was staff-dependent, but not staff-driven. Unlike Carter, he focused on a small number of issues: the federal budget, a military buildup, defeating communism. Reagan would be a president of "big things." He possessed good political instincts—an awareness of the broad landscape and the issues that mattered most to Americans.[38]

As presidential styles go, Reagan's was the gentle approach. He was happy to deliver speeches, tell anecdotes, and write letters, but did not allow the burdens of office to overwhelm him. He arrived at the Oval Office after nine and was usually back at his residence by half past five. Unless confronted by a crisis, he scheduled two to three hours of "personal staff time," and often returned to his California ranch for a "working vacation." Where Carter labored on policy papers into the late hours, Reagan preferred to watch movies. Secure in the approach that had proved successful, and happy to rely on his staff for advice, Reagan refused to bend to the demands of office. It was, wrote biographer Lou Cannon, "his most appealing quality and his greatest defect as president."[39]

To help bring clarity to his "peace through strength" goal, Reagan assembled his foreign policy team. For secretary of state he selected Alexander Haig, a retired four-star general who had worked under four U.S. presidents. Haig had served in Korea and Vietnam, before being appointed military assistant to Kissinger in the Nixon administration. When the Watergate scandal escalated, Haig replaced Haldeman as chief of staff, and played a key role in easing the transition from Nixon to Ford. Thereafter, he became NATO supreme allied commander, before retiring from service in 1979—a decision hastened by ill-health. Reagan's decision to appoint Haig was influenced by Nixon's personal endorsement, and Haig's reputation as a staunch anti-communist. His military background and no-nonsense approach to foreign affairs would send a clear signal of intent to Moscow. At the Republican National Convention in July 1980, Haig warned that the primary task ahead would be "the management of global Soviet power." He criticized détente and the failure to check Soviet "illegal interventions" in the Third World.[40] Like Brzezinski, he viewed Soviet objectives as expansionist, with its military power "a global phenomenon [...] used to establish, not merely preserve, Communist rule."[41]

But if these sentiments endeared him to Reagan, Haig's personal ambition and proclivity for arguments were far less appealing. From the outset he saw himself as the "vicar" of foreign policy, and sought to establish control of this field.[42] Haig soon became embroiled in disputes with senior figures. The bureaucratic feuding steadily worsened, often between hardline conservatives and pragmatic moderates. Ideological differences, personal rivalries, and leaks to the press would plague the administration. William Clark (Reagan's chief of staff while California governor) was selected as Haig's deputy. His appointment followed a tough confirmation hearing, at which Clark confessed to knowing little about foreign nations or their leaders.[43] It all contributed to a lack of direction in foreign policy initiatives.

Caspar Weinberger, another ally from Reagan's days as California governor, was appointed secretary of defense. Educated at Harvard in the late 1930s and early 40s, Weinberger served in the army during the Second World War. Thereafter, he entered private law practice in San Francisco, and became active in state politics. As vice-chair of the California GOP in the 1960s, he recruited Reagan to speak on conservative issues, before making the switch to Washington.[44] Weinberger became chairman of the Federal Trade Commission, and in 1972 was appointed director of the Office of Management and Budget. With his penchant for budget cutting, Weinberger was dubbed "Cap the Knife." In his subsequent role as secretary of health, education, and welfare, he did little to dispel that nickname. Above all, Weinberger was fiercely anticommunist. Like Reagan, he believed in the need for a military buildup in order to dictate terms to the Soviet Union. His self-proclaimed mission was "to rearm America."[45] At the Pentagon, Weinberger's aim was to spend rather than save money. He gained authorization to add a total of $32.6 billion to Carter's 1981 budget and the proposed FY 1982 budget. It represented a 12.5 percent real growth in military budget authority for 1981, and 12 percent for 1982.[46]

Abrasive in style, Weinberger and Haig soon developed a personal rivalry. This stemmed from their quest for control over policy rather than differences in ideology, although Weinberger favored a more hawkish approach.[47] The defense secretary stressed the threat from Moscow in his first major statement, citing "clear evidence of aggressive Soviet activity around the world." He bemoaned America's "descent from a position of clear strategic superiority to the present perilous situation."[48] The aim, Weinberger declared, was to expand America's military capacity "for deterring or prosecuting a global war with the Soviet Union."[49]

These alarmist views were shared by many in the new administration. In a further nod to the hawks, Reagan appointed Richard Allen (a founding member of the Committee on the Present Danger) as his national security adviser. Allen was part of the inner circle which helped guide Reagan to power, serving as his foreign policy adviser from 1977 to 1980. As one of the leading voices in the CPD, he played a key role in persuading conservative Democrats to join forces with the Republicans. The thrust of Allen's approach was familiar: increased defense spending and a firm stance toward the Soviet Union. But his influence on foreign policy would be curtailed, with Reagan having pledged to limit the role of the National Security Council. Nonetheless, Allen ensured that the CPD achieved maximum representation in the national security bureaucracy. Some fifty committee members were appointed to senior positions in the first year of the administration. William Casey was named CIA director; Fred Iklé was unveiled as undersecretary of defense; Jeane Kirkpatrick became ambassador to the UN; Richard Perle was selected as assistant secretary of defense; and Richard Pipes, a Harvard professor of Russian history, was made NSC adviser on Soviet affairs. Paul Nitze and Eugene Rostow, Cold War hardliners par excellence, would serve as Reagan's top arms control diplomats: the former as chief negotiator for theater nuclear forces; the latter as director of the Arms Control and Disarmament Agency.[50]

But none of these officials could gain access to Reagan without encountering at least one of the president's three main advisers: Chief of Staff James Baker, Deputy Chief of Staff Michael Deaver, and Counselor Edwin Meese. Reagan was a strong believer in cabinet government, and all three would play a central role. Deaver and Meese were Californians, whose association with Reagan dated back to his gubernatorial victory in 1966. They were also an integral part of the 1980 campaign, and ranked among his most trusted advisers. While Deaver was personally closest to Reagan (and the First Lady), Meese, a lawyer by trade, was highly regarded. But Meese was upset at being overlooked for the position of chief of staff— adding to the competitive atmosphere in the White House. That role fell to another lawyer, James Baker, a Texan and former Democrat who previously led the unsuccessful Senate campaign of George Bush—now Reagan's vice president. Although Baker entered politics at a late stage, he was adept at campaign management, and helped engineer Reagan's victory over Carter in 1980. An arch-pragmatist with strong political acumen, Baker would prove a sound choice for chief of staff, formulating the president's early agenda.

Aware of Reagan's credulity and lack of policy chops, the troika concluded that at least one of them should be present whenever the president held a meeting. Baker, Meese, and Deaver adopted a protective approach, fearful that Reagan would base his decisions on what he was told by whomever was the last to see him. Meese, for example, told the national security adviser to report directly to him rather than the president. In so doing, Reagan was distanced from the policymaking process. This did not please loyalists such as political aide Lyn Nofziger, who wanted to "let Reagan be Reagan." Nor did it sit well with Haig or Allen, who found the structure intolerable. Allen described Meese as "a 400-pound obstacle," while Haig labeled Baker a "guerrilla in the White House."[51] Neither would last long in their respective roles.

THE LEGISLATIVE STRATEGY GROUP

The brains trust of the administration was the Legislative Strategy Group. Established by Richard Darman (assistant to the president), it would prove the key to the sweeping legislative successes of Reagan's first two years. Although the LSG was initially conceived to coordinate passage of the economic program, it quickly became the nerve center of the White House, reconciling policy with politics on a range of issues. The LSG expanded the troika (Baker, Deaver, Meese) to include other players central to the policy agenda. Alongside Darman was Elizabeth Dole (public liaison), Kenneth Duberstein (congressional liaison), Craig Fuller (cabinet secretary), David Gergen (director of communications), Don Regan (treasury secretary), Larry Speakes (press secretary), and David Stockman (OMB director).[52]

The LSG met every day (sometimes by the hour), discussing tactics around the mahogany table in Baker's office. Conscious of the problems with had dogged the Carter administration, the group sought to cover all areas in order to pass legislation on Capitol Hill.[53] Decisions were usually taken by consensus, which meant that the interests of the administration, Congress, and Reagan's various constituencies had to be weighed. Flexibility was the watchword. Baker argued: "Some claim it's better to fight and lose than to give 10 percent and get 90 percent. Well, they're wrong." His cautious pragmatism, which guided policy toward the center, drew much criticism from the New Right. Howard Philips, chairman of the Conservative Caucus, complained: "Baker only understands negotiating and compromise. What he is doing is destroying Reagan's reputation for integrity and principle."[54] Darman also came under attack from right-wing politicians, who saw him as "the dark prince of centrism."[55] The tension between hard-shell, ideological conservatives and the pragmatic moderates would be a feature of Reagan's first term, and gave the administration's policies a distinctive right-center orientation. "The Reagan presidency was like a coalition government," Meese recalled. "Albeit a coalition among different varieties of Republicans."[56] As such, the LSG had to carefully measure which issues to confront. "We're not a policymaking group," Gergen explained. "But we marry policy and politics every day as we set strategy. We're action-oriented."[57]

Their actions proved successful. In 1981–82, the LSG's record was near-flawless. It helped navigate Reagan's tax and budget cuts through Congress, secured passage of contentious proposals to sell AWACS planes to Saudi Arabia, and achieved a spending resolution which passed the Democrat-controlled House by thirteen votes.[58] But the toughest tests were yet to come. It was in the realm of foreign policy that the group's record would come to grief. Reagan's approach to arms control, in particular, would meet with mounting domestic opposition as his term progressed.

CONFRONTING THE SOVIETS

The administration served early notice of its tough posture. At his first news conference on January 29, 1981, Reagan described détente as "a one way street that the Soviet Union has used to pursue its own aims," with the Soviet goal being "the promotion of world revolution and a one-world Communist state." He charged Soviet leaders with having "openly and publicly declared that the only morality they recognize is what will further their cause [...] that they reserve unto themselves the right to commit any crime, to lie, to cheat, in order to attain that."[59] The speech provoked some gasps, including that of Haig. Afterward, Reagan turned to Richard Allen, and said: "Say, Dick, they do lie and cheat, don't they?" "Yes, sir," Allen replied.[60]

Following Reagan's remarks, Dobrynin arrived at the State Department to discover that the private entrance—which he had used for the past decade—was no longer being made available. The limousine carrying the Soviet ambassador was forced to reverse onto the street, where he battled his way past the media en route to the front door. Dobrynin cited Reagan's hostile press statement, accusing the administration of "looking for a pretext for public confrontation."[61] Haig warned against Soviet moves into Poland, questioned the military aid to insurgents in Central America, and criticized Soviet actions in Afghanistan—views which he also conveyed to Gromyko in a letter.[62] In response, Gromyko told Haig of the pessimism in Moscow about the new administration, pointing to Reagan's "anti-Soviet statements."[63] Dobrynin recalled that the U.S. rhetoric prompted the opposite reaction from the one intended. "It strengthened those in the Politburo, the Central Committee, and the security apparatus who had been pressing for a mirror-image of Reagan's own policy. Ronald Reagan managed to create a solid front of hostility among our leaders. Nobody trusted him."[64]

By the end of the second Haig–Dobrynin encounter a week later, any thoughts of a summit had subsided. Haig said that there could be "no business as usual" because of Soviet international conduct. He invoked the notion of "reciprocity," drawing a parallel between Moscow's concern with Poland and Washington's worries about Central America. The Soviet Union would have to "demonstrate goodwill" before a serious dialogue could take place. Arms control talks were not on Reagan's agenda.[65] The first high-level U.S.–Soviet meeting (between Haig and Gromyko) would not take place until late August 1981. "I think the problem is not communication," Haig told ABC News. "The problem is that the Soviet leadership, thus far, has not liked what they have heard from this administration." Reagan would not deem it necessary to send a new ambassador to Moscow for nine months. Not until October 26 did Arthur Hartman arrive to present his credentials.[66] Haig recalled: "At this early stage there was nothing substantive to talk about, nothing to negotiate, until the USSR began to demonstrate its willingness to behave like a responsible power. That was the basis of our early policy toward Moscow."[67] In the spirit of reciprocity, the State Department refused to extend the visa of Georgy Arbatov, the Kremlin's top specialist on U.S. affairs and a frequent guest on American television. "We're under pressure from the White House to flex our muscles every time we can," a State official told the *Washington Post*.[68]

Soviet leaders deliberated over how to proceed. Some felt that détente could still be resuscitated. But hopes of a more forthcoming approach from Reagan (even parallels with Nixon) soon disappeared. The Politburo was united in its skepticism about the new administration. "Angry and emotional" members denounced Reagan for his rhetoric at a meeting on February 11.[69] At the Communist Party Congress three weeks later, Brezhnev attacked the "openly belligerent statements" of the new U.S. leadership, "deliberately calculated to the poison the atmosphere of relations." He declared the need for talks to address the arms race. "We are ready for a dialogue," Brezhnev said. "The decisive link is meetings at the highest level."[70]

To this end, Brezhnev sent Reagan a long letter on March 6. Its tone was formal, though he avoided referencing the president's public remarks. The most provocative part (lifted from his CPSU speech) was his reiteration that the Soviet Union would not permit Washington to attain a position of military superiority. "Such attempts, as well as attempts to talk to us from a position of strength, are absolutely futile," Brezhnev wrote. He proposed various avenues of cooperation, such as the Helsinki Conference and nuclear arms reductions. Some of Brezhnev's ideas were unfeasible in the political climate of early 1981. He suggested, for example, that both sides agree to an immediate moratorium on the deployment of new medium-range missiles in Europe, and a freeze on their existing nuclear capacities. But he repeated his wish for a personal exchange with the president, referring to the "special significance" of summit meetings.[71]

Brezhnev's letter went unanswered for a month. When a message from Reagan finally arrived, it focused solely on Poland and warned of the consequences of Soviet military action. The letter was sent on April 3, four days after an assassination attempt on Reagan which had left him wounded. It drew a forthright response from Brezhnev, who accused the United States of applying "crude pressure" on Polish internal affairs.[72] But after leaving the hospital, Reagan reconsidered Brezhnev's initial message. He decided to write an informal letter. "I thought I'd try to convince him that, contrary to Soviet propaganda, America wasn't an 'imperialist' nation and we had no designs on any part of the world," Reagan recalled.[73] He invoked their first meeting in California nine years earlier, when they had clasped hands after the summit with Nixon. "Never had peace and goodwill among men seemed closer at hand," Reagan wrote. "Is it possible that we have permitted ideology, political, and economic philosophies, and governmental policies to keep us from considering the very real, everyday problems of our peoples? [...] Should we not be concerned with eliminating the obstacles which prevent our people—those we represent—from achieving their most cherished goals?"[74]

But the personal tone of Reagan's handwritten letter was accompanied by a confrontational typed letter. Concerned that an end to the grain embargo (see later) would send the "wrong signal" to Brezhnev, Haig drafted a second letter stating that the United States did not accept the Soviet presence in Afghanistan.[75] Reagan opted to send both letters, with the formal message "putting him on notice that we weren't going to accept any longer the so-called 'Brezhnev Doctrine'."[76] He referred to Moscow's "unremitting and comprehensive military buildup [...] pursuit of unilateral advantage in various parts of the globe, and its repeated resort to the direct and indirect use of force." The actions raised "serious questions about the Soviet Union's commitment to peace." Reagan rejected Brezhnev's moratorium proposal, claiming it would "perpetuate Soviet superiority" in long-range theater nuclear forces. He also rebuffed the suggestion of a personal meeting, stating that the necessary conditions did not exist. A puzzled Brezhnev received both letters on April 25. In a reply full of angry banalities, he blamed Washington for the state of tension, charging it with having pursued a postwar policy of "Pax Americana."[77] "So much for my first attempt at personal diplomacy," Reagan mused, presumably referring to his handwritten message.[78]

Reagan's relationship with the Soviet leader was not the only one in a state of difficulty. His understanding with the secretary of state had been damaged by Haig's remarks about the presidential line of succession, after the attempt on Reagan's life. "Constitutionally, you have the president, the vice president, and the secretary of state in that order," Haig told the press, as Reagan lay in the operating room. "As of now I am in control here in the White House, pending the return of the vice president." As an afterthought, Haig added: "If something came up, I would check with him."[79] Haig's remarks were viewed as another attempt to seize power. The secretary of state was not third in line for the presidency; the House Speaker and president pro tempore of the Senate preceded him.[80] Haig remained in his post but became isolated within the administration.

If Reagan's hawkish approach raised concern among liberals, his grace under pressure after being wounded won universal admiration. "Honey, I forgot to duck," he told his wife, Nancy, as he was wheeled into surgery. When he was eased on to the operating table, Reagan eyed his doctors and said, "Please tell me you're all Republicans."[81] *Newsweek* likened him to the Sundance Kid "grinning into the face of death," and to "the Duke [John Wayne] defending the Alamo."[82] House Speaker Tip O'Neill stopped by the hospital to bring Reagan a book of Irish jokes. "Because of the attempted assassination, the President has become a hero," he said. "We can't argue with a man as popular as he is." Within a week of the attack, Reagan's public approval rating had surged by ten points, and would continue to rise. "Just when the honeymoon might ordinarily have been expected to fade, it was deepened and extended," Darman noted.[83]

AFGHANISTAN AND CENTRAL AMERICA

It was not only the military buildup, rhetoric, or symbolic measures which upset Moscow. From the outset, the administration moved to combat communism across the globe. In Afghanistan, where Soviet forces were struggling to make progress, Reagan continued Carter's policy of providing covert assistance to the Mujahideen, the collective Afghan resistance group. By mid-1981, more than $100 million had been supplied to the Afghans, while China, Pakistan, Egypt, and Saudi Arabia all joined the anti-Soviet coalition, financing and arming the effort against the Red Army. Meanwhile, to reinforce the economic pressure on the Soviets, the administration lobbied Saudi Arabia and OPEC countries to reduce oil prices.[84]

While Reagan received broad domestic support over Afghanistan, his policies toward Central America proved far more divisive. In Nicaragua, the leftist Sandinistas (who toppled the dictatorship of Anastasio Somoza in 1979) consolidated their grip on power by signing arms deals with Moscow, canceling elections, and supplying rebels fighting to overthrow El Salvador's military government. The Carter administration had provided the Sandinistas with $125 million in economic assistance, but the latter failed to carry out political reform. Conservatives attacked Carter for abandoning friendly right-wing regimes in favor of radical insurgents. Upon taking office, Reagan reversed this policy. He issued a secret presidential finding which instituted a covert action plan to prevent the supply of arms from Nicaragua to El Salvador. In November 1981, Kirkpatrick's thesis was put into practice, as Reagan authorized the CIA to train and equip the Nicaraguan rebels (the Contras) in their fight against the Sandinistas. The Contras, a motley crew of anti-Sandinista thugs (including many of Somoza's national guardsmen), were supplied with $1 billion worth of aid over a two-year period, as well as bases in Honduras from which to launch their attacks. The administration also sought to assist the right-wing government in El Salvador in its efforts to defeat the communist rebels.[85]

The hardliners struck an alarmist tone. William Clark (national security adviser from early 1982) compared the danger to that posed by Nazi Germany in the late 1930s. "We are now at a watershed in U.S. foreign policy," Clark told a meeting of the NSC. "The threat to the Caribbean is unprecedented in severity *and* proximity *and* complexity." Cuba and the Soviet Union were the "chief instigators."[86] The level of U.S. aid to the Contras dwarfed that of Soviet support for the Sandinistas. The USSR made it known that they could not offer military protection or major economic aid to the Nicaraguan government. Soviet military aid totaled just $12 million in 1979–80, a figure which would rise to $45 million in 1981—after the U.S. decision to fund exile groups. Military aid from Soviet bloc nations would peak at $250 million in 1984, while economic assistance would reach $253 million in 1982, before steadily declining. The Sandinistas received more aid from Western Europe and Latin America than from the Soviets and their client states.[87]

Reagan's decision to supply the Contras soon developed into a partisan struggle. The president won the support of Republicans and neoconservatives, who pointed to Cuba and saw the need to roll back Soviet-led communism in the Western hemisphere. They cited Carter's "soft" approach toward Nicaragua as evidence that diplomacy would not suffice, and that regime change through force was necessary. Reagan used the language of human rights and spoke of moral legitimacy in a bid to increase domestic support for his position. He described the Contras as "freedom fighters," and "the moral equivalent of the Founding Fathers," despite wide reports of terrorist acts, torture, and the murder of civilians.[88]

The policy of assisting anti-communist guerrillas who waged war on leftist governments (and helping conservative regimes fight off leftist attacks) would later be labeled the "Reagan Doctrine" by neoconservative writer Charles Krauthammer.[89] From Afghanistan to Angola, Cambodia to Central America, it was designed to "roll back" communism in the developing world. Reagan's views were uncomplicated: communists and their sympathizers were bad; anti-communists and their supporters were good.[90] But policy had to be crafted in the knowledge that neither the American public nor Congress had the appetite for direct military involvement, or the resultant casualties. Advisers such as James Baker and Michael Deaver felt that U.S. intervention would be "a sure-fire political loser." Baker feared that a military success by the communist rebels in El Salvador would prompt demands from conservatives for increased U.S. force against Nicaragua, dragging the nation into a war it did not want.[91]

In March 1982, Richard Wirthlin (Reagan's pollster) warned that intervention in Central America would add to the perception that the president was a "warmonger," alienating swathes of the electorate. "The biggest fear expressed by the American people is that involvement would lead to another Vietnam," he told Baker. "Over two-thirds of the public feel that giving aid would precipitate involvement similar to that experienced by the U.S. in Southeast Asia."[92] Reagan was sensitive to images and symbols. He knew that war had a knack of toppling presidents. Korea had turned public opinion against Truman, while Vietnam proved to be Johnson's undoing. Reagan would attempt to walk the political tightrope: uphold a vigorous stance against communism—satisfying the demands of conservatives—while avoiding the prospect of flag-draped coffins returning home.

Democrats invoked the ghost of Vietnam. Backed by public opinion, Tip O'Neill and his cohort in Congress were opposed to any large-scale operation in Central America. O'Neill was influenced in his thinking by left-leaning Jesuit priests and missionaries based in the region, who were fiercely critical of the right-wing forces being backed by the Reagan administration. "I have a lot of friends in the Maryknoll Order, and they keep me highly informed," O'Neill told reporters. "They look at it like Vietnam."[93] Democrats called for diplomatic solutions and sought to restrict U.S. military support, particularly to the Contras. In November 1982, O'Neill's interest was piqued by major stories in *Newsweek* and the *Boston Globe*, which revealed details of CIA efforts to overthrow the Sandinista regime. The Speaker worked with Rep. Edward Boland (D-Massachusetts)—chairman of the House Intelligence Committee—to push through legislation prohibiting the use of U.S. funds to help the Contras overthrow the Nicaraguan government. The Boland Amendment, enacted in December, reflected the domestic intrusions into foreign policy.[94]

ENDING THE GRAIN EMBARGO

Perhaps the one issue on which the administration took a position favorable to Moscow was that of the grain embargo, imposed by Carter on the Soviet Union in early 1980. In late April, 1981, Reagan announced that he would lift the embargo. Although Reagan framed this as a gesture of goodwill in his letter to Brezhnev, it was a decision which stemmed purely from domestic politics. Throughout 1980 Reagan had denounced Carter for adopting the measure, and pledged to reverse it were he to become president. In so doing, the Republican candidate carried strong support from farm belt states.

Reagan lived up to his campaign promise. For all the anti-Soviet rhetoric and talk of reciprocity, it was clear that domestic political interests would not be sacrificed. Within weeks of taking office, reports emerged of "extreme Hill pressure" from a dozen Republican senators, who lobbied for the grain embargo to be suspended immediately—regardless of the diplomatic exchanges.[95] It was not the ideal scenario

for Reagan, who wanted the Soviets to "understand the signals" before
he lifted the embargo.[96] Reporting on his talks with the senators,
Congressional Liaison Max Friedersdorf warned: "The grain embargo
meeting was a disaster from the President's standpoint. All it accomplished was a forum for the senators and the congressmen to dump, both
in the meeting and on camera later."[97] Reagan decided to act after
further pressure was applied on Secretary of Agriculture John Block,
who was seeking to achieve a new four-year farm bill. On April 24,
Reagan announced that the grain embargo against the Soviet Union was
to be lifted. Just three months into his presidency, the most economically
effective of Carter's 1980 sanctions was removed for domestic purposes.

While pragmatists in the administration supported the move, the secretary of state was opposed. "It was an issue fed by farm belt legislators
and commodity interests to relieve the plight of their constituents," Haig
bemoaned. "I argued that the issue could be explained to farmers in such
a way that they would accept a delay in lifting the embargo in the national
interest."[98] But Reagan and his troika disagreed. A White House memo
warned that the American farm sector had experienced "serious economic
hardships" due to an overabundance of grain supplies, high interest rates,
and a cost/price squeeze. Negotiations on a new U.S.–Soviet grain agreement would "guarantee U.S. farmers higher minimum sales," and be
viewed as "a demonstration of the Administration's commitment to the
agricultural sector."[99]

Grain sales talks began in June, and by the end of September the Soviets
had agreed to purchase 6 million tons. In August 1981 another deal was
reached with Moscow. The long-term grain agreement, which had run from
1976 to 1981, was extended by a further year. In mid-1982, as the midterm
elections approached, the grain agreement was again extended, with Reagan
renewing his pledge to farmers.[100] On October 15, 1982, the president made
a final push for Midwestern votes. He approached the Soviet Union with an
offer to buy up to twenty-three million tons of grain. The Soviet leadership,
with Brezhnev gravely ill, snubbed the U.S. proposal.[101] The irony of the
grain embargo decision was soon magnified. Within months, Reagan would
criticize Western European leaders for putting their domestic interests first
by negotiating a gas pipeline deal with Moscow.

POLAND

By 1981, the USSR faced serious politico-economic problems. The cost of
assisting or maintaining sixty-nine Soviet satellites and clients around the

world entailed disproportionate military spending. From the mid-1960s, more than a quarter of Soviet GDP had been spent each year on financing the arms race. Added to these economic burdens were the oil crises of the 1970s (which saw oil prices quadruple), and the occupation of Afghanistan—which prompted sanctions from the West. The cumulative effect was devastating, leading to shortages in food and agricultural output. The troubles extended well beyond the Soviet border. At a meeting in February 1980, party secretaries of Warsaw Pact nations told their counterparts in the Kremlin that they could no longer afford to limit trade with the West. Otherwise, shortcomings in their economies would have to be financed entirely by Moscow.[102]

The Soviet dilemma was brought into focus by the crisis in Poland, which by 1980 was saddled with a $20 billion external debt. As the economy plummeted, the movement led by Solidarity (a noncommunist labor union) had gathered momentum. Brezhnev was perturbed by the authorities' failure to suppress the protests, and replaced Polish First Secretary Kania with General Jaruzelski. But with financial resources stretched, and U.S. warnings about further sanctions, Soviet decision-makers opted against an invasion. "We do not intend to introduce troops into Poland," declared KGB Chairman Yuri Andropov, pointing to the "very burdensome" prospect of Western sanctions.[103] Soviet leaders instead pressured Jaruzelski to impose martial law—a decision that was announced on December 13.

For years Reagan had championed the cause of "freedom-loving people," while castigating the Soviets for suppressing the rights of citizens in Eastern Europe. He backed Carter's tough rhetoric over Poland in late 1980, and sounded warnings against Soviet intervention in his first year as president. "We must take on the problem of what to do or if to do something to help the Polish people," he wrote in his diary in July. "Here is the first major break in the Red dike—Poland's disenchantment with Soviet communism."[104] The crackdown by Polish military leaders five months later (a curfew, communications restrictions, and the arrests of thousands) was, notes author Seth Jones, "a defining moment for Reagan [...] by late 1981, his interest in Poland had become deeply personal and emotional."[105] Reagan demanded a forceful response, heartened by Solidarity's democratic principles. The "shining city on a hill" would not stand idly by. "This is the first time in 60 years that we have had this kind of opportunity. There may not be another in our lifetime," Reagan said at an NSC meeting. "Can we afford not to go all out? I'm talking about a total quarantine on the Soviet Union. No détente! We know—and the world knows—that they are behind this."[106]

The internal debates focused on the question of sanctions against Moscow. But any response was complicated by the recent gas pipeline deal between the Soviets and Western Europe—which had caused a rift in U.S.–European relations. Following the oil crises of the 1970s, West Germany and France negotiated a multi-billion dollar deal to help the Soviets build a 6,000 km pipeline that would transport natural gas from Siberia to six European nations. It would serve as both an investment project and a way of helping Western Europe meet its energy needs. However, the pipe-laying machines used for its construction were made by *Caterpillar*, an American firm. Other essential components were manufactured by subsidiaries of U.S. corporations in Europe, or by companies operating under a U.S. license.[107]

Reagan's chief advisers were angered by the pipeline agreement. Weinberger bemoaned the prospect of European dependency on Soviet resources, noting that valuable hard currency for Moscow would be devoted toward its arms buildup. He urged Reagan to place oil and gas technology and equipment under national security controls, while trying to persuade European leaders to withdraw from the deal.[108] For the hawks, it resembled a Soviet–European détente which could reduce U.S. leverage over NATO allies in the nuclear arms talks. By contrast, Haig (while favoring sanctions) pleaded with Reagan to avoid taking measures which might damage the Western alliance. "If Defense has its way, we'll have the United States in a war scare and the Europeans off the bridge," he warned.[109] Haig told Reagan that his credibility was at stake, given the U.S. decision to place its own domestic needs first. "We have just lifted the grain embargo. Three-quarters of U.S. trade with the Soviet Union has been decontrolled. We must be careful that we do not follow inconsistent policies."[110]

But Reagan sided with Weinberger's approach. He wondered if "those chicken littles in Europe" would follow suit. "Remember, everyone, stock up on vodka!" he joked.[111] A letter to Brezhnev was accompanied by robust public statements on either side of Christmas. Reagan denounced the policies of the Polish government and their Soviet backers. "If the outrages in Poland do not cease, we cannot and will not conduct 'business as usual' with the perpetrators and those who aid and abet them," he warned. "The Soviet Union bears a heavy and direct responsibility for the repression in Poland." Reagan offered the carrot of economic aid, should the Polish government rescind martial law and release those arrested. But the emphasis was on the stick of sanctions. Shipments of agricultural products to the Polish government were suspended, landing rights for

Polish planes at U.S. airports were canceled, and Polish ships were denied fishing privileges in American waters.[112] On December 28, Reagan announced new measures to be taken against the USSR. Talks over a long-term U.S.–Soviet grain agreement were suspended, as were negotiations on new maritime arrangements. The bilateral scientific exchange agreement would not be renewed. Most significantly, Reagan suspended the sale of U.S. oil and gas technology, and the issuance of export licenses for high technology—sanctions which placed the gas pipeline deal in jeopardy and infuriated European allies.[113] All the while, the shipment of U.S. grain to Moscow continued. Schmidt, Mitterrand, and Thatcher all pointed to the contradiction. "There will be dire consequences for the Western Alliance if you proceed," Thatcher told Reagan. "Whatever the perception in America, the cost of sanctions are greater to Europe than the United States." Haig retorted: "The perception in the U.S. is that the allies have not done nearly enough."[114] A rift developed within the alliance.

*

Reagan's response to the Polish crisis was driven by a sense of moral duty, his antipathy toward communism, and the need to constrain Soviet aggression. But there were domestic elements exerting pressure behind the scenes. AFL-CIO President Lane Kirkland, a Cold War liberal, was publicly demanding a tougher response to the clampdown in Poland.[115] The labor unions were Solidarity's largest source of U.S. support prior to martial law, with $160,000 having been raised for their cause even before Reagan took office. By mid-January 1982, the AFL-CIO had organized major rallies in fourteen cities, convincing House Speaker Tip O'Neill and Senate Majority Leader Howard Baker (R-Tennessee) to participate in worldwide satellite telecasts.[116] Kirkland (a Democrat) was a founding member of the CPD and a fervent anti-communist. Having succeeded George Meany as president in 1979, he expanded the AFL-CIO's vast foreign operations across the globe. Kirkland passionately supported Solidarity's movement, and threatened to create a de facto embargo through labor action after the introduction of martial law. It raised fears among Reagan's advisers, who noted that "the costs to the domestic economy would be as great as if we had instituted a de jure embargo."[117] Kirkland was invited to the White House to discuss the Polish crisis on December 15. He called the administration's response "inadequate," and urged Reagan to impose "the toughest possible sanctions."[118] Kirkland warned Reagan that the labor unions might refuse to load U.S. ships. Reagan took the threat seriously. At an NSC meeting, he mused: "How will we look if we say yes [let U.S. exports to the Soviets proceed], while our unions—our own Solidarity—won't load the ships?"[119]

Reagan's initial round of sanctions failed to placate neoconservatives or the AFL-CIO. Kirkland fumed at what he viewed as merely symbolic measures. Although sharing Reagan's anti-communism, support for freedom, and belief in strong defense, Kirkland opposed most of his domestic policies. Their personal relationship was nonexistent. In a break with tradition, Reagan ignored Kirkland during the cabinet selection process for a new labor secretary, remarking that union leaders were "no longer close to the rank and file." Kirkland retorted that Reagan was "out of touch with the lives of ordinary Americans." He was fiercely critical of "Reaganomics," claiming that the military buildup was being paid for by the working classes. The AFL-CIO thus formed an independent defense committee in February 1982. Their resolution declared that "labor's long-standing support for a strong national defense does not oblige it to support a defense budget that is unfairly balanced." It denounced Reagan's response to events in Poland as "too slow and insufficiently confrontational with the Soviets."[120]

As the Polish crisis worsened, NSC officials warned of the "considerable domestic pressure to move forward with more energetic measures."[121] But the question of extending sanctions against Moscow was double-edged. On the one hand, it served Reagan's goal of applying pressure on the Soviets while showing support for the citizens of Eastern Europe. It would also avert a confrontation with the American labor unions. On the other hand, further sanctions would deepen the wedge between the United States and its European allies, who had clear economic interests at stake (notably Britain and France, where component parts of the gas pipeline were manufactured). Reagan explained the dilemma at an NSC meeting on February 26:

It seems to me that if we do it at all, we should figure out whether we want to throw a block at the Soviet Union. If we are not prepared to do that, there will be a split between us and American labor. Labor will refuse to load ships. The question is: can we avoid going all the way? Can we avoid telling Europe that our sanctions apply to [foreign] subsidiaries and licensees [of U.S. corporations]?[122]

Reagan decided to send James Buckley (undersecretary of state for international security affairs) on a mission to Europe to win support for the U.S. position. The "Buckley mission" aimed to convince the allies of the need for "significant restraints on credits" to Moscow, while encouraging their governments to limit their energy dependence on the Soviets. But European governments had their own national interests, and each found the American goals "unworkable."[123] At an NSC meeting on March 25, Buckley told Reagan of his frustration with European attitudes: "The purpose of the mission was to show the idiocy of subsidizing the Soviet arms buildup through credits [...] we wanted to accomplish a moratorium on further credits. We failed in the objective." The West German government put up the most resistance, criticizing U.S. policy as "hostile." But Reagan was prepared to extend the sanctions against the Soviets even without allied support. "They are still in Afghanistan, they are still supplying Cuba, they are still preventing Jews and Christians from emigrating," he argued. "Is there a right time for the West to cooperate? The Europeans do not understand."[124]

All of these debates took place amid criticism from hawkish conservatives. Already dismayed at the lifting of the grain embargo, commentators attacked Reagan for not translating rhetoric into policy. The president had again failed to pursue the hardline position of a full economic embargo against Moscow.[125] Norman Podhoretz wrote in the *New York Times*: "What President Reagan's response to the Polish crisis reveals is that he has in practice been following a strategy of helping the Soviet Union stabilize its empire, rather than a strategy aimed at encouraging the breakdown of that empire from within."[126] At a Conservative Political Action Conference (CPAC), Reagan's reaction to the Polish crisis was labeled "half-hearted and inadequate" by Midge Decter, a political commentator (and wife of Podhoretz). "Accommodation to the Soviet Union's power remains the operative policy of the United States government," she charged.[127]

But as the Polish situation deteriorated, the administration adopted more forceful measures. In May 1982, a broad national security strategy (NSDD-32) was signed into law with the aim of "containing and reversing the expansion of Soviet control and military presence throughout the world." In early September, Reagan signed NSDD-54, titled "United States Policy Toward Eastern Europe." A prime objective was to differentiate U.S. policy to the USSR from that of Warsaw Pact nations. To do so, the United States would encourage liberal trends in Eastern Europe, pursue the cause of human rights, reinforce the "pro-Western orientation" of their peoples, loosen their economic and political dependence on Moscow, and encourage "private, market-oriented development" of their economies.[128]

On September 29, a working group discussed the options for supporting Solidarity, such as financial aid and the dissemination of propaganda. It concluded that CIA action would enable the movement to continue. In early October, CIA Director William Casey told Reagan that countering the Soviets with covert action through local forces was preferable to a direct, visible U.S. presence, which could escalate into a nuclear war. After a further meeting on November 4, Reagan authorized Casey to begin a covert program of financial assistance. He signed into law a presidential finding to provide money and nonlethal equipment to Polish opposition groups through "surrogate third parties."[129] At its peak, some $8 million annually would be transferred to the movement. The aid program consisted of printed material, communications equipment, and office supplies—allowing Solidarity to continue its underground campaign. The administration also increased its support for Radio Free Europe, which became the chief media outlet for Solidarity, broadcasting news throughout the Eastern European satellite states.[130] In a symbolic event at the Vatican in June, Reagan discussed the crisis with Pope John Paul II (who had also survived a recent assassination attempt). For the rest of the decade they worked together, with the aim of bringing an end to the Soviet dominance of Eastern Europe.[131]

THE ZERO OPTION

Reagan's Cold War approach alarmed Soviet leaders, who feared that the development of new weapons systems would give Washington a first-strike capability. Hardliners in the Kremlin hyped the military threat. In May 1981, KGB Chairman Yuri Andropov told Soviet intelligence officials that the Reagan administration was "actively preparing for nuclear war." There was, he declared, "now the possibility of a nuclear first strike by the United States."[132] At Andropov's prompting, the KGB put its Western stations on the alert. A global intelligence operation, codenamed RYAN, was developed to gather information on the U.S. nuclear threat. Agents in America, Britain, and other NATO countries were tasked with identifying signs of preparations being made to launch a nuclear strike.[133]

A dialogue of sorts resumed in September 1981. Haig met with Gromyko at the UN, while Reagan wrote to Brezhnev, expressing his interest in peace and "a more constructive and stable relationship." But he also listed events in Poland, Afghanistan, Kampuchea, and Central America, while criticizing Moscow's "unremitting and comprehensive military buildup." "I believe that a great deal of the present tension in the world is due to actions by the Soviet government," Reagan wrote. Brezhnev responded by pointing to the American military buildup and the lack of clarity regarding its position on arms talks.[134] However, one avenue that emerged was a U.S. willingness to begin talks on limiting intermediate-range nuclear forces (INF) before the end of the year. This was the product of growing public concern across Western Europe and, increasingly, in the United States.

In 1979, NATO had agreed on a "dual-track" response to counter the Soviet missile deployments (SS-20s): the U.S. would prepare to deploy new Pershing II intermediate-range ballistic missiles and ground-launched cruise missiles in 1983 (spanning West Germany, Britain, Italy, Belgium, and the Netherlands), while simultaneously negotiating the limitation of these forces with Moscow. Worried by the prospect of the "Euromissiles," hundreds of thousands of Western Europeans took to the streets in protest. Public opinion in West Germany was particularly sensitive, since it bordered the GDR and (unlike Britain and France) had no "independent" nuclear deterrent. Peace activists on both sides of the Atlantic argued that the U.S. deployment would intensify the arms race. From late 1979, therefore, West German Chancellor Helmut Schmidt had been proposing a "zero option," whereby the removal of Soviet missiles would make the U.S. deployments unnecessary.[135]

Most of Reagan's foreign policy advisers treated the zero option with contempt, linking it to a climate of appeasement. During a CPAC speech in March 1981, Allen declared that only "pacifist" elements "believe that we can bargain the reduction of a deployed Soviet weapons system for a promise not to deploy our own offsetting system."[136] But by October, public opinion had hardened to such a degree that the administration decided to change tack. Chief advocate of the zero option was none other than Richard Perle, the hawkish deputy defense secretary (and longtime adviser to Henry Jackson). Perle had opposed almost every arms control initiative over the past decade. But he saw political advantages in the zero option, and persuaded Weinberger of its utility.

Presenting it as a novel idea, Weinberger outlined the zero option to Reagan at an NSC meeting in mid-October. As with the plan pushed by Schmidt for the past year, it entailed the removal of Soviet SS-20s in return for a U.S. agreement not to deploy the Pershing and cruise missiles. Weinberger said that the Soviets would "certainly reject" the proposal. It was nigh inconceivable that Brezhnev would agree to dismantle Soviet weapons in return for an American pledge not to deploy. But the zero option was deemed politically safe, and therein lay its appeal. If somehow successful, it would serve Reagan's goal of achieving genuine arms reductions. If it was rejected, the blame would be placed squarely on Moscow, and European allies would have little choice but to proceed with TNF modernization. Above all, the proposal would help to offset public criticism on both sides of the Atlantic. "We would be left in good shape and would be shown as the White Hats," Weinberger told Reagan. He urged the president to consider this "bold plan, sweeping in nature, to capture world opinion." Weinberger said that Reagan might even win the Nobel Peace Prize. For maximum public effect, he recommended that the zero option be unveiled in a "spectacular presidential announcement."[137]

This cynical ploy was resisted by Haig and Richard Burt, director of politico-military affairs in the State Department. They criticized the "take-it-or-leave-it" nature of the zero option which they felt would "trivialize" the negotiating process.[138] Haig believed it would fuel suspicion that America was only interested in "a frivolous propaganda exercise [...] disingenuously engaging in arms negotiations simply as a cover for a desire to build up its nuclear arsenal." State officials also felt that the zero option risked decoupling the U.S. nuclear deterrent from the defense of Western Europe, straining relations with the allies. "We wouldn't want it even if we could have it," Haig argued.[139] The matter came to a head at an NSC meeting on November 12. Vice President George Bush cautioned Reagan of the perception "that the President does not want to negotiate anywhere at any time." The zero option "would do a lot for public opinion." Despite Haig's protestations, Reagan sided with the hardliners.[140] The president felt that a more flexible proposal (e.g., "zero-plus") would undermine the U.S. negotiating position. "I'd learned as a union negotiator that it's never smart to show your hole card in advance," he recalled.[141]

But Reagan was well aware of the zero option's political benefits. It was easy to understand and would, theoretically, be more attractive to the public at home and in Europe. It was less likely to invite criticism from hawkish conservatives, who were querying the strength of his early initiatives. On November 18, Reagan delivered the "spectacular announcement." He outlined the zero option as the basis for INF talks in a nationally televised address. The president read out passages from his handwritten letter to Brezhnev in April (but not from his typed letter). Reagan's speech contained twenty-four references to "peace," and cited the "increasingly overwhelming advantage" enjoyed by the Soviets in INF forces. On the strategic arms talks (or lack thereof), he called for proposals that could achieve arms reductions, rather than limitations, and conveyed these points to Brezhnev in a letter.[142]

Two weeks later, Perle explained the zero option to the Senate Armed Services Committee. "We have gone to Geneva with a proposal we can defend, and defend it we will," he told senators. Perle pointedly quoted the rueful memoirs of Samuel Hoare, the British diplomat associated with Chamberlain's appeasement at Munich in 1938.[143] INF negotiator Paul Nitze would become exasperated at the lack of U.S. flexibility. So too would Brezhnev. He responded to Reagan's letter by accusing the president of "double bookkeeping," overstating the number of Soviet arms while downplaying the American figures. He refused to consider a proposal which did not include the strategic arsenals of Britain and France. "Mere statements, no matter how good they sound, are not enough to achieve progress," Brezhnev told Reagan. "What is required are realistic positions and practical proposals [...] not just an attempt to score a propaganda point."[144]

The zero option did nothing to quell public disquiet about the nuclear arms race. As 1982 began, the administration had still not crafted a strategic arms control proposal or a meaningful policy statement. Although diplomatic contact continued, U.S.–Soviet relations would remain virtually nonexistent throughout the year.[145] Opposition to Reagan's approach gathered momentum—in Europe and America.

5

The Nuclear Freeze Movement

By the end of year one, the administration's foreign affairs record made for grim reading. Reagan's policies had raised tensions with Moscow, upset NATO allies, alienated swathes of Congress, and generated mass antinuclear movements in Western Europe—protests which would soon appear across America. Remarks by Thomas Jones (deputy undersecretary of defense for strategic forces) portrayed an administration with a cavalier attitude to nuclear war. "If there are enough shovels to go around, everybody's going to make it," he told the *Los Angeles Times*. "With enough shovels, everyone could dig a hole in the ground, cover themselves with two or three feet of dirt, and survive the nuclear holocaust."[1] When asked if he feared nuclear war, Eugene Rostow (ACDA director) replied that Japan had survived a nuclear attack and flourished.[2] Reagan's domestic predicament was little better. By July 1981, the economy had plunged into recession, and public support began to wane. Reagan's approval rating had fallen to 48 percent by December, and the slide would continue throughout 1982.[3]

Democrats seized the initiative. On October 20, 1981, Walter Mondale admonished Reagan for "dividing" the Western alliance by refusing to negotiate with Moscow. "This administration has put us in the astounding position of appearing that it is we, and not the Soviet Union, which is unwilling to talk," he told the Foreign Policy Association in New York. Mondale criticized Reagan for "abandoning the cause of human rights" around the world, and "surrendering the high ground of moral leadership to the Soviet Union."[4] But the political counterattack was not confined to elites in Washington. Just as conservatives had coalesced over foreign policy in the late 70s, so the liberal left mobilized in 1981 to confront the nuclear arms race. A grassroots antinuclear campaign took off in Reagan's first year, winning the support of churches, university groups, scientists, environmentalists, pacifist groups, and women's organizations. It soon morphed into the largest peacetime peace movement in American history. The sheer magnitude of the campaign would make arms control—and foreign policy in general—the political liability of the Reagan administration. It was not long before leftist demands for a "freeze" on nuclear weapons began to elicit support from the Democratic establishment. The nuclear freeze campaign, and a broader "peace movement," became the Democrats' most potent political weapon against Reagan's conservative revolution.[5]

THE NUCLEAR FREEZE CAMPAIGN

The roots of the freeze campaign can be traced to the latter part of the Carter administration. Liberals and peace activists grew disturbed by the rightward drift of national politics, as détente gave way to confrontation. Carter's embrace of new defense programs and hawkish rhetoric in 1980 aroused concern among liberal sections of the public and media. Democrats began absorbing the lessons of Reagan's ascent, which was made possible by a united conservative coalition. The New Right had pushed for the abandonment of SALT II, increased military procurement, and a hardline posture overseas—attracting support from Republicans and neoconservatives. By contrast, the Democratic Party was splintered. It struggled to find common ground on many issues, not least in foreign affairs, in which many to the right of center were alienated by the liberal, new internationalist agenda post-Vietnam. But with many "neocons" having defected, the nuclear freeze idea served as a unifying theme.

Randall Forsberg, a 38-year-old defense analyst/peace activist was the driving force behind the movement. In 1979, she outlined the "Call to Halt the Nuclear Arms Race," which demanded that the United States and the Soviet Union adopt "an immediate, mutual freeze on all further testing, production and deployment of nuclear weapons."[6] During 1980, a range of groups (antinuclear, pacifist, religious, civic) joined forces to rally behind the call for a nuclear freeze. Most had no affiliation with the Democratic Party, with freeze leaders arguing that their campaign should be bipartisan. But Forsberg was eager to push the movement from the margins toward the political mainstream, working "within the system rather than alienating it from the system."[7] The freeze campaign expanded in 1981. Groups such as the religious American Friends Service

Committee, the pacifist Fellowship of Reconciliation, and public interest organizations such as SANE, grew in numbers and attracted generous donations. The Council for a Liveable World (an arms control lobby group and Senate PAC) quintupled from 12,000 members to more than 60,000 between 1980 and 1984—success which prompted a PAC for the House in 1982. Membership of SANE (founded back in 1957 in response to Eisenhower's policies) quadrupled from 20,000 to 80,000 in the same period.[8]

The momentum reflected a change in public opinion. Although Reagan had won office with support for rearmament, there were growing demands for a freeze on arms production and cuts in the arsenals of the world's two major nuclear powers. In March 1982, a poll led by NBC News and the Associated Press found that 74 percent of Americans supported a freeze on the production of nuclear weapons in the United States and USSR, with only 18 percent opposed.[9] By November 1982, just 16 percent believed that the administration was spending too little on defense, while 41 percent said too much.[10] Freeze leaders criticized Reagan's reluctance to pursue serious arms talks and meet with Brezhnev. Their campaign soon won the backing of the liberal wing of the Democratic Party. Among those to recognize the potency of the issue were Sen. Ted Kennedy and Rep. Ed Markey, both representing Massachusetts. In March 1982, Markey introduced a resolution with 115 cosponsors, which called on the administration to negotiate a freeze on the production, testing, and deployment of nuclear weapons. Kennedy ridiculed Reagan's policies as "voodoo arms control."[11] He teamed up with dovish Republican Mark Hatfield (Oregon) to bring a joint freeze resolution to the Senate, accelerating the movement's schedule.

While the freeze campaign thrived on the East Coast, activists were keen to strengthen support across the nation. To expand the movement and emphasize its grassroots nature, freeze leaders based their headquarters in St. Louis, Missouri, the symbolic center of the country. It was run by Randy Kehler, a Vietnam-era activist and draft resister who led the freeze referendum campaign in western Massachusetts.[12] To persuade voters in California, the most populous state, Kennedy wrote in the *Los Angeles Times*. "Instead of worrying about a theoretical and exaggerated 'window of vulnerability', we should focus on this window of opportunity for arms control," he argued. "A freeze can ensure that nuclear reductions negotiated in the future will not be made meaningless by the development of new and destabilizing weapons."[13] Tip O'Neill wrote to Harold Willens (chairman of Californians for a Bilateral Nuclear Weapons

Freeze), imploring activists to reach out to as many voters as possible: "It's up to the people of California to send a clear message to the Congress, and President Reagan. We must stop this nuclear madness before it's too late."[14] The campaign was boosted by support from within the Reagan family. Both of the president's daughters publicly signed petitions to place the nuclear freeze referendum on the California ballot. One daughter, actress Patti Davis, spoke at rallies in opposition to her father's policies, symbolizing the political divisions across the nation.[15] By June 1982, the campaign had taken root in 75 percent of congressional districts.[16]

Freeze leaders were taken aback by the speed with which Democrats pressed for resolutions. The momentum on Capitol Hill exceeded their expectations, which had been low. "We never canvassed the House or Senate. We've had no mailings," Forsberg remarked. "The history of the last ten years demonstrated that direct lobbying efforts were fruitless if you didn't have a movement."[17] Freeze activists wanted to ensure that there was sufficient time to gain bipartisan support before a vote was held. With Republicans controlling the Senate, and a large conservative contingent in the House, both resolutions would face stiff opposition. Moreover, key moderate Democrats voiced concern about the freeze initiative. Rep. Les Aspin (D-Wisconsin), a member of the Armed Services Committee, argued that it would grant the Soviets a permanent strategic advantage in long-range, land-based missiles. Aspin refused to endorse the resolution, along with three other House Democrats: Tom Foley (Washington), Richard Gephardt (Missouri), and Al Gore (Tennessee).[18]

But all four congressmen would duly change course. In mid-April, the freeze movement achieved national prominence, when a massive educational exercise ("Ground Zero Week") was launched. It was led by Dr. Roger Molander, whose service in the ACDA, Pentagon, and NSC (under Nixon, Ford, and Carter) lent legitimacy to the campaign. Ground Zero Week involved the participation of 150 major metropolitan areas, 330 college campuses, and more than 1,000 high schools, reaching over a million Americans. A plethora of antinuclear books emerged in 1982. Molander published an updated edition of his book, *Nuclear War: What's in it for you?*, while Jonathan Schell's influential work, *The Fate of the Earth*, portrayed the devastating effects of nuclear war.[19] Peace groups persuaded European movement leaders to engage in speaking tours across the United States. The freeze coalition broadened to include new groups involving lawyers, educators, scientists, nurses, and businessmen. The Physicians for Social Responsibility, a group composed primarily of doctors, toured the country to describe the consequences of a nuclear attack.[20] On June 12, the campaign reached its apotheosis, when 750,000 people turned out in Central Park, New York, in protest against the arms race. It was larger than any of the anti-Vietnam demonstrations which had taken place in the city, and thought to be the single biggest political rally in U.S. history. Some establishment figures such as George Kennan embraced the idea of a nuclear freeze, while many celebrities (among them Martin Sheen, Bruce Springsteen, and Meryl Streep) gave their public endorsement.[21]

The political effect was swift. By mid-1982, over 400 town meetings, more than 200 city councils, and nine state legislatures had voted in favor of a nuclear freeze.[22] An increasing number of Democrats, and even some moderate Republicans, expressed their support. The House Resolution acquired 176 cosponsors, securing a 26–11 vote in the Foreign Affairs Committee on June 23. Seven of the committee's sixteen Republicans sided with the resolution. When asked why so many Republicans voted in favor of the freeze, Rep. Stephen Solarz (R-New York) replied: "Fear not of the bomb, but of their voters."[23]

THE REAGAN ADMINISTRATION RESPONDS

The strength of the freeze movement caught the administration by surprise. Much of the criticism centered on Reagan's refusal to proceed with arms control negotiations. More than a year into his term, "the great communicator" had yet to offer a meaningful policy statement on the issue. Advisers urged him to make a personal commitment to peace. Richard Beal, special assistant to the president, identified foreign affairs as Reagan's most vulnerable area. "The president must increase domestic support for the 'peace' component of his 'peace through strength' foreign policy," he warned Chief of Staff James Baker.[24] Wirthlin told Baker of the Democratic efforts "to generate political gain" out of the freeze movement, and stressed the need to co-opt the peace marchers' positions.[25] Opinion polls showed that 70 percent of the public favored the Kennedy–Hatfield freeze proposal, while a survey by the Foreign Policy Association revealed that only 17 percent supported another sharp increase in defense spending.[26] Reagan was now losing the support of moderate Democrats who had earlier endorsed his arms buildup. "The defense consensus of last year has been frittered away," Aspin told the *New York Times*. "The consensus has been hurt by the administration's casual talk about limited nuclear war, which really worried people. It has also been hurt by too much greed, trying to put everything into the Pentagon budget, and by poor articulation of what we are getting with the money." At the same time, conservatives were criticizing Reagan for failing to come up with a long-term basing plan for the MX missile, which remained in limbo from the Carter era. The view of the Senate Armed Services Committee was that the military buildup lacked direction.[27]

In a press statement on behalf of the administration, Richard Burt criticized the Kennedy–Hatfield freeze resolution of March 10. He argued that such a policy would put the United States in a position of "dangerous vulnerability."[28] The objections focused on two main problems. Firstly, the freeze idea did not go far enough; it was instead necessary to seek a *reduction* in nuclear arms levels. Secondly, the proposal would "freeze" the United States into a position of military disadvantage—legitimizing the Soviet advantage in strategic forces (e.g., intermediate-range missiles), while removing any incentive for Moscow to negotiate in good faith.[29] "*Nuclear Freeze* had a nice-sounding emotional appeal," Reagan recalled. "But the Russians had such a huge advantage over the United States in land-based missiles with multiple warheads that if we agreed to one, we'd have to meet them at the arms talks as second class citizens [...] Well-meaning or not, the nuclear freeze movement had an agenda that could have been written in Moscow."[30]

Reagan's first effort to cool domestic criticism was to endorse another "freeze proposal," devised by Republicans and conservative Democrats. In response to the Kennedy–Hatfield resolution, they formed a bipartisan initiative sponsored by senators Henry Jackson (D-Washington) and John Warner (R-Virginia). A key phrase was inserted, calling for a "long-term, mutual, and verifiable nuclear forces freeze at equal and sharply reduced levels." The change was worded to accommodate Reagan's forthcoming START proposal. The word "forces" would nullify the freeze's impact on the testing and production of nuclear weapons, allowing Reagan to continue the military buildup. "Equal and sharply reduced" would ensure that any arms reduction agreement with the Soviets would *precede* a mutual nuclear freeze—a policy of "build now, freeze later."[31] The administration lobbied intensively behind the scenes.[32] Reagan met with Jackson and Warner, who aimed to address public concern about the arms race "in a way that is consistent with the President's objectives."[33] On March 30, Reagan endorsed the Jackson–Warner resolution, calling it "an impressive initiative for world peace and stability."[34] It was backed by a Senate majority, with fifty-six of their colleagues expressing support—including Minority Leader Robert Byrd (D-West Virginia) and his deputy, Alan Cranston (D-California), who sponsored both resolutions.

START

The second part of Reagan's counterattack against the freeze movement was to expedite the first arms control proposal of his presidency. In its first year, the administration had done almost nothing about the issue, except to state that it would target arms reductions rather than limitations: Strategic Arms Reduction Talks (START) instead of SALT. Since then the president had replaced National Security Adviser Richard Allen with William Clark (Reagan's longtime friend), and named Robert McFarlane as his deputy. Reagan had won office promising to seek an agreement better than SALT II. His arms negotiator, Ed Rowny, told the Senate in his confirmation hearing that a proposal would be ready by March 1982. The freeze movement was coalescing, with leading political, academic, and religious figures querying Reagan's policies. Congress was growing impatient, as an increasing number of Democratic senators considered resolutions supporting a nuclear freeze. Rostow urged the White House to "combine the decision about starting START with the problem of the freeze resolutions." In late February, Clark and McFarlane issued an NSC directive giving the executive branch two months to finalize a START proposal.[35]

The START Interagency Group struggled to agree on an approach. The Defense Department (led by Weinberger and Perle) and ACDA (led by Rostow) called for a proposal that "departs clearly from the SALT agreements," with sharp reductions to a low and equal level of warheads and missile throw-weight. Their aim was to force the Soviets to dismantle over half of their ICBM forces. But the State Department advocated a more moderate proposal. Richard Burt lobbied Chief of Staff James Baker, the leading pragmatist in the White House. They were far more conscious of public attitudes: "It is imperative that our proposal elicits broad support in the U.S. and with our allies, enhancing the credibility of our arms control policy and strengthening the President's position. This is clear in view of the political challenges of the freeze movement in the U.S. and the peace movement in Europe."[36] Haig appealed for a "realistic" START position. "To achieve and sustain public and Allied support for our START proposals we need to choose an approach which the public will find comprehensible, fair, and reasonable," he told Reagan.[37]

But the hardliners held sway at an NSC meeting on April 21. Weinberger told Reagan: "We should not hesitate to ask the Soviets to reduce more than we do, since to do otherwise would be to freeze their superiority." Rostow added: "The antinuclear movement is important. But perhaps more troubling is what I sense to be a return to isolationism. There are more people now who, in the face of the Soviet buildup, want to pull U.S. troops out of Europe and to fold the U.S. inward. I think we really need to restore our credibility." Reagan contributed little to the debate, doodling a horse on his notepad. He said that the proposal had to be based on deep arms reductions. START had to be different from the "lousy" SALT II.[38] (Although the treaty was unratified, Reagan had agreed to observe the numerical limits of SALT II since becoming president.) Over the next two weeks, Burt whittled down some of Weinberger's demands. But the START proposal still aimed to strike a hard bargain. The Soviets would be asked to reduce their ICBM warheads from the 6,000 allowed under SALT II to only 2,500, and their total launchers from more than 2,300 to 850.[39]

On May 9, in a speech at his alma mater (Eureka College), Reagan unveiled the START proposal. "The focus of our efforts will be to reduce significantly the most destabilizing systems, the ballistic missiles, the number of warheads they carry, and their overall destructive potential," he explained. Reagan would target a ceiling of 5,000 warheads on ballistic missiles, with a maximum of 2,500 permitted on ICBMs. The proposal entailed a reduction in missile warheads (of which the U.S. and Soviets each deployed about 7,500) by roughly one-third.[40]

To Soviet leaders, START was as unpalatable as the zero option, and just as one-sided. The proposal required substantial cuts in the numbers of U.S. ballistic missiles and warheads, but placed few constraints on future programs such as MX. It also called for much larger reductions in the Soviet ICBM forces. The Soviets would need to dispense with their greatest strategic weapons—the SS-17s, 18s, and 19s—while the United States could retain most of its Minutemen, proceed with MX and cruise missile deployments, and the modernization of its submarine and bomber fleets.[41] Although Leslie Gelb hailed START as "sweeping and dramatic" in the *New York Times*, it became clear that the proposal was anything but. Reagan, noted author John Newhouse, "was not changing course."[42] Brezhnev's response was predictably negative. In a letter to Reagan, he questioned the president's "seriousness of intentions," arguing that the substantial reductions would apply only to the Soviets. "Mr. President, this is not a realistic position, not the path toward an agreement,"

Brezhnev wrote. "Besides, as you know, we are not the only ones who hold such a view," he added, in reference to the freeze movement. The Soviet leader called for both sides to agree to a quantitative freeze on strategic weapons, and for a limit on modernization (proposals which suited Moscow). "He's a barrel of laughs," Reagan wrote in the margin of the letter.[43] Despite their objections, the Soviets accepted a U.S. proposal to begin negotiations in late June.

NSDD-32

The START proposal did not satisfy hardline conservatives, who were still awaiting an articulation of a national security strategy.[44] In the *New York Times*, Podhoretz attacked Reagan for failing to deliver on his pledge vis-à-vis the Soviets, and wrote of the "anguish" felt by conservative groups.

Judging by the discrepancy between the stated objectives of the Reagan administration in foreign policy and the actions it has so far taken, I am driven to one of two conclusions. Either this administration does not in fact know what it wishes to do, or what it wishes to do does not correspond to what the President himself has said [...] The President has even said that he welcomes the signs of an impending breakup of the Soviet empire from within and he has looked forward to a time when Communism itself will disappear. Yet presented with an enormous opportunity to further that process, what has President Reagan done? Astonishingly, he has turned the opportunity down.[45]

The Committee on the Present Danger warned of the "highly adverse" U.S.–Soviet military balance, with America facing choices between defeat and submission. With Reagan's "modest" defense spending, the nation was now "second best."[46]

On February 5, Reagan ordered a review of national security strategy. It was crafted by Richard Pipes (NSC adviser on Soviet affairs), William Clark (national security adviser), and Thomas Reed, a former secretary of the air force who had spearheaded Reagan's gubernatorial campaigns. All were hardliners, who sought to confront the Soviet Union—through a vast military buildup, through the spread of ideas in Eastern Europe, and on the "battlegrounds of the Third World."[47] Their arguments were sealed with alarmist rhetoric. Reed told the NSC on April 16: "The threats we face and the nature of our objectives are such that we are at a time of the greatest danger to our national security since World War II."[48] A national security strategy directive (NSDD-32) was finally issued on May 20. It aimed "to reverse the expansion of Soviet control and military presence throughout the world, and to increase the costs of Soviet support and use

of proxy, terrorist, and subversive forces." The administration sought
"to foster [...] restraint in Soviet military spending, discourage Soviet
adventurism, weaken the Soviet alliance system by forcing the USSR to
bear the brunt of its economic shortcomings, and to encourage long-term
liberalizing and nationalist tendencies within the Soviet Union and allied
countries."[49] Quite how these sweeping objectives would be achieved
was unclear, but the emphasis was placed on straining Soviet economic
resources. After a briefing on March 26, Reagan noted: "They're in very
bad shape and if we can cut off their credit they'll have to yell 'Uncle' or
starve."[50]

The directive was more confirmation that the hawks remained in
control of U.S. policy. NSDD-32 was partly based on a 132-page
Defense Guidance drawn up in the Pentagon, which was leaked to the
press on May 30. It contained a startling plan to develop the capability
to fight a "protracted" nuclear war. The Defense Guidance advocated
a nuclear war strategy known as "decapitation"—strikes at the Soviet
political and military leadership and communications lines. "Should
deterrence fail and strategic nuclear war with the USSR occur, the
United States must prevail and be able to force the Soviet Union to seek
the earliest termination of hostilities on terms favorable to the U.S."[51] The
notion of "prevailing" in a nuclear war drew much attention. Weinberger
denied that the administration had adopted the view that a nuclear war
could be won. But he did not distinguish between "prevailing" and
"winning."[52] The objectives seemed to surpass those of Carter's hawkish
PD-59. So appalled was General David Jones (outgoing chairman of the
Joint Chiefs of Staff), that he broke with protocol by likening the defense
plans to throwing money down a "bottomless bit." "I don't see much
chance of a nuclear war being limited or protracted," he remarked.[53]

NSDD-32 furthered the perception that Reagan was more concerned
about besting the Soviets militarily than seeking a negotiated solution.[54]
He was a peripheral figure at the NSC meeting discussing the directive,
and appeared ill at ease in the more technical debates.[55] "Ronald Reagan
totally lost, out of his depth, uncomfortable," noted Pipes after an NSC
meeting. "After making some nonsensical remarks he didn't speak for
45 minutes. He chewed vigorously on his jelly beans, which I suppose are
his equivalent of cigarettes. He didn't listen attentively [...] He has not
enough knowledge or decisiveness to cut through the contradictory advice
that is being offered to him." But Pipes felt that Reagan understood the big
issues "intuitively rather than intellectually."[56] While the technical detail
and military jargon may have been beyond him, Reagan possessed good

political instincts and a keen grasp of public perceptions. He was more pragmatic than most of the officials offering advice at NSC meetings. Above all, Reagan had no desire to incite a conflict with Moscow. The hallmarks of his gubernatorial career, flexibility and compromise, would in time become a feature of his foreign policy. But in 1982 these traits could not possibly have been apparent to Soviet leaders.[57]

THE "ANTI-FREEZE" CAMPAIGN

The third element in Reagan's fightback against the freeze movement was to launch a public affairs campaign, which aimed to regain control of the nuclear arms debate. "The nuclear freeze movement is growing," McFarlane warned the president. "Unless the Executive Branch attempts to understand the movement and refute its fallacies, the end result could have grave consequences for your programs. It could impact on the defense budget, arms control, and allied relationships."[58] Baker and Clark devised a campaign to align the public and political strategies. The administration would avoid attacking the freeze movement and instead focus on generating enthusiasm for START. "We should welcome the public's concern about this issue [the prospect of nuclear war] as it parallels our own," wrote Clark. "But we must convince the public that *our* policies are the best for dealing with their newfound concerns." On April 22, Clark outlined a strategy to be implemented prior to the midterm elections. Among his suggestions was an enhanced communication effort to convey Reagan's "philosophy" on arms control: public speeches, television appearances, media interviews, and group meetings. A foreign policy speech in May would capture the "boldness" of the START initiative, and give the president "genuine national support" as he prepared for his tour of Europe.[59]

To coordinate the "anti-freeze" campaign, the administration formed a new interagency committee, known as the Nuclear Arms Control Information Policy Group (NACIPG). From May 1982, meetings were cochaired by the NSC's Robert "Bud" McFarlane on the policy side, and David Gergen (director of communications) on the public side.[60] The NACIPG worked from the premise that "negotiating nuclear questions with the Soviet Union is a domestic issue as well as a foreign policy issue." It aimed to rally public support for START, while undermining the Kennedy–Hatfield freeze proposal. The NACIPG focused on national and regional coverage, media markets, and sought platforms before professional organizations, television shows, and radio programs.[61]

"We have let this issue get in front of us," warned Joanna Bistany, special assistant for communications. "Looking at the polls, it is obvious that the general public feels a great deal of emotion and concern. Ronald Reagan should be out front in the role of peacemaker."[62]

Reagan followed the advice. He delivered a radio address to the nation at Camp David. Although criticizing Soviet belligerence in Afghanistan and Poland, the accent was on peace. "I know there are a great many people who are pointing to the unimaginable horror of nuclear war. I welcome that concern," Reagan said. "So, to those who protest against nuclear war, I can only say I'm with you. Like my predecessors, it is now my responsibility to do my utmost to prevent such a war. Nobody feels more than I the need for peace."[63]

But the European tour in June saw Reagan deliver another robust, anti-Soviet speech. The day after meeting the Pope, Reagan told the British Parliament: "It is the Soviet Union which runs against the tide of history by denying freedom and human dignity to its citizens. It is also in deep economic difficulty [...] a country which employs one-fifth of its population in agriculture is unable to feed its own people." The "march of freedom and democracy," Reagan said, would "leave Marxism-Leninism on the ash heap of history."[64] The mixed reactions in Westminster mirrored the divisions in America. Margaret Thatcher and fellow Conservatives applauded lustily, but only a handful of Labour Party MPs followed suit. Labour leader Michael Foot (a founding member of the UK Campaign for Nuclear Disarmament) was an outspoken critic of the U.S. military buildup. After the address, his party issued a statement denouncing Reagan's policies on arms control, as well as his approach toward apartheid South Africa.[65]

As the NACIPG targeted the broad public, the Office of Public Liaison tried to mobilize the conservative coalition that had backed Reagan two years earlier. Elizabeth Dole led the efforts to engage the cluster of pro-defense, limited government, religious-political activist groups, collectively known as the New Right. In liaising with the Republican base, the tenor of their message differed from those of Baker and Gergen. Morton Blackwell, who coordinated between conservative groups and the White House, advocated a hawkish tone ahead of the midterm elections. "You cannot fight Soviet oppression and have the oppressors in the Kremlin think you are a nice guy," he wrote. "For your militant foes to think you are a nice guy, you have to be weak. Being weak ravages your base of active supporters who expected you to be a leader. Political victories, even more than military victories, are won more by offense than by defense."[66] The sentiments appealed to Reagan, whose memo paper was decorated with a cartoon character and the words "No More Mr Nice Guy." "I find that it helps a little with some of the memos I scratch out," he joked to the White House press.[67]

SHULTZ FOR HAIG

Al Haig's reign as secretary of state ended on June 25, when Reagan accepted a previously submitted letter of resignation. His swansong was a fractious meeting with Gromyko in New York. Although a range of subjects were discussed, no progress was achieved. "The general impression is one of wasted effort," Pipes told Clark. "Gromyko restated in *all* cases the standard Soviet positions and would not budge an inch from them. His tone throughout was condescending, sometimes snide, and downright rude. Much of the time he lied through his teeth." According to Pipes, Haig was subjected to a "verbal humiliation."[68] Haig's resignation the following week was not unexpected. Weinberger's grip on foreign policy had been buttressed by Clark's arrival as national security adviser at the start of the year. Isolated and unloved, Haig complained about what he saw as interference in his arena. Reagan, who hated personal disputes, decided to make a change. He had grown weary of the "jealousies and turf battles," describing Haig as "utterly paranoid."[69] "[Haig] didn't even want me as the president to be involved in setting foreign policy," Reagan recalled. "He regarded it as his turf."[70]

Haig was succeeded by 61-year-old George Shultz, whose career spanned the academic, government, and business sectors. Shultz graduated from Princeton University in 1942 with a degree in economics, and soon after joined the Marines, serving in the Pacific theater during the Second World War. He later earned a Ph.D. from MIT in industrial economics and became a professor at the University of Chicago in 1957. Within five years he was appointed dean of the business school. After the 1968 presidential election, Nixon appointed Shultz as secretary of labor. It was a position he held until 1970, when he switched to become the first director of the Office of Management and Budget (with Weinberger serving as his deputy). In 1972, Shultz became the first economist to be appointed secretary of the treasury, and left Washington two years later with his reputation enhanced. Thereafter, he became president of the Bechel Corporation in San Francisco, and a professor at Stanford University.[71]

In character and approach, Shultz differed from his predecessor. While Haig was often rash or outspoken, Shultz was usually calm and cautious.

Haig's foreign policy views were strongly anti-Soviet, whereas Shultz offered a more nuanced outlook. He believed that patient dialogue could yield results. "From my time in the Nixon administration, I had learned something of the human dimension to the Soviet Union," he recalled. "I also learned that the Soviets were tough negotiators but that you could negotiate successfully with them." Shultz felt that the Soviet readiness to engage would depend on how they perceived their interests. He believed that such a time would arrive only when American strength was accompanied by a willingness to make agreements that were mutually advantageous.[72] In 1982, that moment had not yet arrived. Burly and granite-faced, Shultz was known as "the Sphinx" for his low-key, guarded demeanor. Over time he would become the pragmatic voice on foreign affairs in the administration. His practical, ratiocinative approach would put him at odds with the hardliners: Casey, Clark, Kirkpatrick, and above all, Weinberger, his former deputy in the budget bureau.

But Shultz's arrival did not bring about a change in U.S. policy anytime soon. Reagan's START proposal was formed prior to Haig's departure, and remained the U.S. position for the strategic arms talks, which began at the end of June.[73] It was promptly rejected by the Soviet delegation in Geneva. Meetings between Shultz and Gromyko in late September followed a familiar pattern. The secretary of state blamed the Soviets for the deterioration of relations, and raised Moscow's failure to comply with the Helsinki agreements on human rights. He invoked the plight of Soviet Jewry, including Anatoly Shcharansky, a prominent dissident who remained in detention. Gromyko replied: "Is it so important that Mr. or Mrs. so and so can or cannot leave such and such a country? I would call it a tenth-rate question."[74]

NITZE'S WALK IN THE WOODS

Having campaigned against détente and worked his way back into power, Paul Nitze's views were shifting. The INF negotiator appealed for greater flexibility in the hardline position ("zero option") that had been pushed by Perle and Weinberger. This sort of about-turn was a feature of Nitze's career. Long before his Team B and CPD were formed, Nitze tailored his approach to suit the politics of the day. When out of office during the late 1950s, for example, he denounced Eisenhower for allowing the Soviets to surpass the U.S. in strategic weapons, citing a "missile gap" between Moscow and Washington. By the time he was serving in the Kennedy administration, however, Nitze had modified his views.[75] As Reagan's presidency progressed, Nitze would adopt a more moderate approach to arms control, advocating continued compliance with the terms of SALT II ("interim restraint")—the same agreement that he had long criticized Carter for pursuing.[76]

The INF talks in Geneva had remained deadlocked since their inception in November 1981. Nitze, now 75, chose to take matters into his own hands. Working outside of formal diplomatic channels, he proposed a deal to his Soviet counterpart, Yuli Kvitsinsky. On July 16, the pair went for a walk in the woodlands near the Jura Mountains. Resting upon a log, Nitze made a suggestion to address the primary concern of each side. A ceiling would be placed at 225 INF aircraft and missiles in Europe for both nations, with a limit of seventy-five INF missile launchers. The United States would agree to deploy only cruise missiles and relinquish its Pershing II ballistic missiles. In return, the Soviets would agree to destroy their older midrange missile systems and deploy no more than seventy-five SS-20s.

Nitze's formula was less a final proposal than a starting point from which both sides could negotiate. When leaked, the idea met with approval in Western Europe, for it committed the USSR to dispense with 80 percent of its midrange systems that targeted the allied nations.[77] But the reaction in Washington was very different. Perle and Weinberger argued that the initiative was one-sided. It was, they said, misguided to allow Moscow to maintain SS-20s in Europe and Asia while the United States relinquished the right to deploy its Pershing IIs.[78] The State Department, even with Shultz's arrival, was also cool on the idea. So too was the president. When Nitze warned that the Soviets would find the existing U.S. position unworkable, Reagan replied: "Well, Paul, you just tell the Soviets that you're working for one tough son of a bitch."[79] In any event, the reaction in the Kremlin was also negative.

ANDROPOV FOR BREZHNEV

By the time of Nitze's proposal, Leonid Brezhnev (also 75) was in failing health. On November 10, he died in his sleep. Command was assumed by 68-year-old Yuri Andropov, Second Secretary of the Communist Party. Andropov was a renowned hardliner who had served as KGB Chairman for fifteen years. As ambassador to Hungary, he had overseen the Soviet military intervention in 1956, a role for which he was dubbed the "Butcher of Budapest."[80] As head of the KGB he had helped to instigate the invasions of Czechoslovakia in 1968 and Afghanistan in late 1979. The rising

East–West tensions were seen as a factor in his ascent, as was the support of Gromyko and Ustinov—the other two members of Brezhnev's troika.[81] But Andropov, too, was in ill-health. The *New York Times* reported of his "pallor complexion" and "hesitant gait," while rumors persisted that he had already suffered at least one heart attack.[82]

Unlike Brezhnev, Andropov accepted the need to wring changes in the Soviet economy, however modest. He publicly acknowledged the existing problems. Two younger members of the Central Committee Secretariat, Mikhail Gorbachev and Nikolai Ryzhkov, were ordered to begin work on a program of cautious reform.[83] But in foreign affairs there was little sign of a new Soviet outlook. According to Dobrynin, Andropov's views were similar to those of Gromyko and most of the Politburo. The general secretary struck an aggressive tone in his first public remarks: "We know very well that peace cannot be obtained from the imperialists by begging for it. It can be upheld only by relying on the invincible might of the Soviet armed forces."[84] After Brezhnev's funeral, Andropov met with Shultz and Bush, and blamed Washington for the poor state of relations. Without using the words "human rights," he made it clear that he would not tolerate interference in Soviet internal affairs. "Andropov had covered in twenty minutes what I and Gromyko had spent seven and a half hours discussing in New York," Shultz recalled. "I put him down as a formidable adversary."[85]

Within days of Brezhnev's death (and after the midterm elections), Reagan announced the lifting of the pipeline sanctions. An agreement was reached with European allies on economic strategy toward the Soviet bloc. U.S. officials quickly denied that the move was a gesture toward the new leadership in Moscow.[86] The impetus for change was led by Shultz, who saw that the sanctions were counterproductive—causing a rift in the alliance, while doing little to prevent the Soviets from building the gas pipeline. As his predecessor Al Haig noted: "It was supremely ironic that when the hammer of American economic power finally smashed down, it did not strike the Russians or the military government of Poland, as the hardliners had wanted, but instead battered our friends and allies."[87]

THE NUCLEAR FREEZE AND THE MIDTERM ELECTIONS

The Reagan administration faced problems ahead of November. Its chief concern was the struggling U.S. economy. The 1981 tax cuts did not produce a supply-side success, with annual budget deficits leading to huge increases in the national debt. Unemployment was approaching

ten percent, with more than 9 million Americans out of work. By
January 1983, that figure would climb to 11.5 million. Democrats seized
on the "Reagan recession" as the midterm elections neared. But foreign
affairs were also important. With a prolonged impasse on arms control,
Reagan was criticized for a reckless approach to nuclear weapons, and
relations with the Soviet Union in general.[88]

While a U.S.–Soviet dialogue struggled to yield anything in 1982, the
nuclear freeze campaign continued in earnest. On July 12, the Republican-
led Senate Foreign Relations Committee rejected the Kennedy–Hatfield freeze
resolution by a vote of twelve to five—backing instead the Jackson–Warner
resolution (and Reagan's START proposal). But the debates in the House,
where Democrats held the majority, were closely fought. Clement Zablocki
(D-Wisconsin), chairman of the House Foreign Affairs Committee, brought
a freeze resolution to the floor on August 5. The Zablocki resolution called for
an "immediate freeze," but was diluted by various amendments (e.g., clauses,
reductions, and verification requests). Conservatives proposed an alternative
resolution, based on the Jackson–Warner bill, led by William Broomfield
(R-Michigan) and Samuel Stratton (D-New York). The Broomfield amendment endorsed Reagan's START proposal, calling for negotiated arms reductions to be followed later by a nuclear freeze.[89] Conservatives argued that an
immediate nuclear freeze would undermine the U.S. negotiating position with
the Soviets. By the tightest of margins (204 votes to 202), Broomfield's
resolution defeated Zablocki's "immediate freeze" proposal.[90]

The narrow defeat pointed to deficiencies in the freeze campaign. It
tended to say little of the Soviet Union, a major nuclear power about which
public attitudes were generally distrustful. And while criticizing Reagan's
START proposal, proponents struggled to make the case that a nuclear
freeze was a better alternative than other means of arms control.[91] At
a political level, there were competing visions of what a freeze would
entail, and of the adequacy of the U.S. nuclear arsenal. Though all but
one of the Democratic presidential candidates would endorse the freeze in
late 1983, each had their own ideas of what it should constitute.

*

The wafer-thin success of the Broomfield resolution gave Reagan more
food for thought. A Gallup poll found that 79 percent of the public
supported the idea of a nuclear freeze: 58 percent favoring an immediate
freeze; with 21 percent backing Reagan's position of a freeze only after the
completion of the military buildup.[92] With freeze resolutions on the ballot
in nine states, the NACIPG continued to wage a vigorous "anti-freeze"

campaign. ACDA and Defense speakers appeared on television, radio, and in newspaper editorials. An outreach program targeted religious, ethnic, veterans, and women's interest groups. An information campaign was particularly aimed at Catholic voters, of whom a large number expressed support for a nuclear freeze.

However, the "anti-freeze" campaign struggled to make an impact. McFarlane told Clark that the events were neither broad nor visible, and involved appearances by "second and third-level officials." The exercise, he warned, had become one of damage limitation.[93] Senior figures sought to press home the administration's case against the nuclear freeze. Rowny was sent to Wisconsin owing to his rapport with the Catholic and Polish segments. Weinberger delivered speeches in California, where he retained strong political connections. Clark reached out to the Veterans of Foreign Wars in Los Angeles.[94] And in a bid to woo Catholic voters, Reagan addressed a crowd of 7,000 in the Civic Center Coliseum in Hartford, Connecticut—an event which marked the centennial meeting of the Supreme Council of the Knights of Columbus.[95] Interest groups such as the American Conservative Union began linking the peace movement to Soviet foreign policy designs.[96] Reagan echoed the theme in a speech to military veterans in Columbus, Ohio. He declared that the freeze campaign was "inspired not by the sincere, honest people who want peace, but by some who want the weakening of America."[97] According to Tom Wicker of the *New York Times*, Reagan's charge was "McCarthyism, low-road politics, and disinformation—all delivered in the familiar aw-shucks style."[98]

But the efforts were for nought. On November 2, freeze referenda passed by wide margins in eight of the nine states. Only in Arizona was it defeated. Democrats gained twenty-six seats in the House, all but ensuring the passage of a freeze resolution in the lower chamber in 1983 (Democrats also gained one seat in the Senate). A further setback for Reagan followed in December, when Congress voted to deny funds for the MX program. The administration's "Dense Pack" basing plan was deemed unacceptable. The results confirmed Reagan's poor political standing. A Lou Harris poll at the turn of the year found that 66 percent of the U.S. public disapproved of his handling of arms control.[99] Only 41 percent of Americans now approved of Reagan's governance, a lower figure than his four elected predecessors had received by the midpoint of their presidencies.[100]

*

Reagan had entered office at a difficult juncture, and East–West relations deteriorated in the first two years of his presidency. The administration's approach was generally unconstructive, yielding few (if any) tangible results. While Reagan could take heart from the confidence borne of a military buildup, the cumulative effect of U.S. policies was negative. Jack Matlock, who would soon become Reagan's chief adviser on Soviet affairs, recalled that the president "was not eager to take up serious negotiation."[101] "It was clear to me that the Reagan administration did not have a clear policy in regard to arms control, other than an antipathy to SALT II," he added.[102] Prospects for bilateral talks were stymied by U.S. sanctions, some of which were detrimental to American interests (notably the absence of a consulate in Kiev). With diplomatic contact minimal, the administration wielded many sticks but few carrots. Talk of summitry had been quickly scotched. Instead, through tough rhetoric and selective sanctions, Reagan challenged the Kremlin to change its way of thinking. The vigorous, anti-Soviet posture which helped lead Reagan to office showed little sign of abating. At NSC meetings, where arms control decisions were crafted, the president continued to side with the hardliners.

The confrontational approach deepened Soviet distrust. The cautious, sclerotic leadership gave no indication of altering its own uncooperative positions, whether on arms control or its behavior overseas.[103] Nor had Reagan's policies prompted any positive change in the Soviet approach to human rights. Feeling "besieged" from the West, conservative hardliners escalated their repression of humanitarian groups. The Moscow Helsinki Watch Group was dissolved by September 1982, with most of its members either imprisoned or in exile.[104] Yet diplomacy was a two-way street. Soviet leaders themselves displayed little interest in pursuing agreements, and frequently engaged in provocative rhetoric. A dangerous stalemate resulted. As Shultz recalled: "Relations between the two superpowers were not simply bad; they were virtually non-existent.'[105]

U.S.–European relations were also strained, owing to disputes over the Siberian gas pipeline, sanctions against Moscow, and the lumbering INF talks. Mass antinuclear demonstrations emerged throughout Western Europe in protest at Reagan's policies. Domestically, the administration's approach to arms control had galvanized its political opposition. The antinuclear protests in Europe were replicated in America, where the largest peacetime military buildup was challenged by the largest peacetime peace movement. The pressure hastened the arrival of Reagan's START proposal, but had not altered his basic position. Yet the momentum of the freeze campaign had shifted the views of moderates in Congress, who increasingly withdrew their support for rearmament. Bitter divisions over the MX program would bear this out. In sum, the broad approval for "peace through strength" with which Reagan began his term had dwindled by late 1982. Democrats portrayed a president with a negligent attitude to foreign affairs. Pressure for a change in approach would mount in the New Year—at home and abroad. What followed was the most dangerous phase of the Cold War since the Cuban Missile Crisis of 1962.

6

Star Wars and the Evil Empire

For all his optimism, the winter of 1982 was a miserable time for Reagan. The figures told a grim tale. The president's approval rating had dropped from 67 to 29 percent "positive" over the past twelve months. At the turn of the year his overall approval stood at just 41 percent. The chief root of public distress was the economic recession, which Reagan blamed on Jimmy Carter and Democratic Congresses. Unemployment was approaching 11 percent, having entered double digits for the first time since 1940. The gross national product, which the White House had predicted would rise 4.2 percent, in fact declined by 1.8 percent. A deficit projection of $91.5 billion over the next three years was countered by projections from the Congressional Budget Office, which stood at $650 billion.[1] On foreign affairs Reagan fared little better. More than 70 percent of Americans now favored a bilateral, verifiable freeze on the testing, production, and deployment of nuclear weapons.[2] Freeze referenda passed easily in eight (out of nine) states during November. And with the Democrats gaining twenty-six seats in the House, the passage of a resolution in 1983 was all but ensured. The midterm elections demonstrated that the military buildup was losing public and political appeal. To counter the freeze movement and revive domestic support, Reagan would unveil a dramatic proposal for a space-based missile defense system. The Strategic Defense Initiative (or, to its critics, "Star Wars") emerged as a major development in the story of the end of the Cold War.

DOMESTIC CRISIS

Reagan came under attack from across the political spectrum. George Stigler, winner of the Nobel Prize for Economics (and a conservative), declared that the nation was now in a "depression," calling supply-side economics "a gimmick," and "a slogan."[3] In his *Washington Post* column, David Broder was more critical: "What we are witnessing this January is not the midpoint in the Reagan presidency, but its phase-out. Reaganism, it is becoming increasingly clear, was a one-year phenomenon [...] What has been occurring ever since is an accelerating retreat from Reaganism, a process in which he is more spectator than leader." Walter Mondale, who was delivering speeches across the nation, called Reagan's fiscal policy "one of the biggest mistakes in modern economic history."[4] A Gallup poll in early January showed Reagan trailing prominent Democrats. Mondale held a 52–40 percent lead, while Sen. John Glenn (Ohio) had a 54–39 advantage.[5] The statistics had worsened by the end of the month. "I've some bad news for you," Wirthlin told Reagan. "Your approval rating is down to 35 percent, the lowest ever." Patting his pollster's arm, Reagan quipped: "I know what I can do about that. I'll go out and get shot again."[6]

Reagan had not lost his sense of humor. But he was losing support for his handling of foreign affairs. The issue affected Reagan personally; his daughter Patti was a vocal supporter of the freeze movement. At her request, Reagan met with Dr Helen Caldicott, an outspoken freeze activist who founded Women's Action for Nuclear Disarmament. But their conversation on December 6 was fruitless. Both maintained their strong views on the merits of a nuclear freeze. "[Caldicott] seems like a nice, caring person, but is all steamed up and knows an awful lot of things that aren't true," Reagan wrote. "I tried but couldn't get through her fixation. For that matter, I couldn't get through to Patti. I'm afraid our daughter has been taken over by that whole damn gang."[7]

Four days later, Reagan repeated his charge that the Soviet Union was manipulating the freeze campaign. He declared that the movement originated with a Soviet front called the "World Peace Council." When asked to support the claim, Reagan said that he had verified "several rather well-documented articles." They included two pieces in *Reader's Digest* and a classified report from the House Intelligence Committee. But when the report was declassified, Chairman Edward Boland (D-Massachusetts) said that it contained "no evidence that the Soviets direct, manage, or manipulate the nuclear freeze movement." Freeze campaign officials took umbrage at being cast as offspring of the World Peace Council, arguing that it was only one of many groups that supported the freeze proposal. "Individuals in the council may support the freeze, but individuals in the Republican Party support it too," remarked Barbara Roche, co-director of the campaign headquarters in St. Louis.[8]

Reagan faced a political crisis in January 1983. Economic woes, diminishing public support, the poor state of arms talks—all undermined prospects for his strategic defense program. A *Washington Post–ABC* poll showed that 59 percent of the public approved of cuts in the defense budget to help reduce the deficit; a figure which easily surpassed other avenues such as social programs.[9] The bipartisan National Conference of State Legislatures voted to endorse the freeze, calling on Reagan to apply to civilian purposes the money he could save from the arms race.[10] Reagan's military buildup suffered a huge setback in December, when Congress voted to deny funds for the MX program (central to his "peace through strength" strategy). Democrats criticized the president for spending lavishly on defense while social programs were being starved. "In America we now see the shameful inequality of the hungry lining up at soup kitchens, and the homeless sleeping outside in the cold," declared Ted Kennedy, a freeze advocate who had joined the Senate Armed Services Committee. "And every time one of those people dies on a sidewalk or a grate, a little bit of America dies, too."[11]

A bitter exchange between Reagan and O'Neill at the Oval Office in January reflected the political divide. The Speaker refused to support Reagan's request for a $770 billion budget, which called for defense outlays of $238 billion, citing unemployment and poverty levels. O'Neill, who backed the freeze campaign (though not all that passionately), warned that his party would make every effort to amend a "Beverly Hills budget." His criticisms infuriated the president. "God damn it, Tip, we do care about those people!" Reagan said. "It's easy to say that you care," replied O'Neill, "but you aren't willing to do anything about it." House Majority Leader Jim Wright (D-Texas), who attended the meeting, called it "the toughest going-over I've ever heard a President subjected to."[12] Reagan bemoaned the "drumbeat of criticism" that was eroding public support for the arms buildup.[13] A White House analysis was gloomy: "It will be a brand new ball game; one in which we are not now prepared to play [...] going on bended knee to Tip O'Neill for his support on issue after issue."[14]

The implications of these political obstacles became clear to Reagan and his advisers. If the arms buildup was to be saved, Reagan would need to persuade a skeptical Congress that he was willing to compromise on the most contentious military program (the MX), and make a concerted effort in talks with Moscow. The issue was brought into focus over the Christmas holidays, when Reagan decided to run for a second term.[15] James Baker warned that the legislative and public affairs aspects of the defense budget, arms control, and nuclear freeze movement had a "major domestic impact on the President's constituency." To confront the challenges, he and Clark began cochairing a small group of White House, NSC, and State Department officials, to monitor the communications, legislative, and political sides of foreign policy.[16] Darman led the Outreach Strategy Group, modeled on the LSG, to help coordinate the lobbying of Reagan's core constituencies ahead of the 1984 election.[17] Stuart Spencer, a key strategist in 1980, was brought back into the fold after the poor returns in November, and began devising a campaign plan.[18]

THE SCOWCROFT COMMISSION

Of all the nuclear weapons systems pursued by the administration, few provoked as much domestic opposition as that of the MX. A legacy of Carter's drift to the right in 1979–80, the expensive program had come to symbolize Reagan's military buildup, and what Democrats deemed Pentagon excess. Because of its theoretical first-strike capability, it emerged as the bane of the nuclear freeze movement. As noted in Chapter 2, conservatives argued that a "window of vulnerability" in U.S. strategic forces necessitated the development of a new "superweapon," named MX (or Missile Experimental). They claimed that without such a weapon, a Soviet first strike would obliterate nearly all of the U.S. missiles that lay in their silos. Moreover, the program would demonstrate American resolve to outspend the Soviets in strategic arms. But finding a basing scheme for the missiles had proved impossible, provoking much opposition on Capitol Hill. Carter had proposed deploying the missiles on multiple, widely spaced concrete shelters in remote parts of Nevada and Utah. But the plan was attacked by liberals and conservatives: the former on the grounds of peace and finance (projected costs were more than $30 billion); the latter because of the local environmental effects. Indeed, two of Reagan's closest allies, senators Paul Laxalt (R-Nevada) and Jake Garn (R-Utah), campaigned against the plan alongside farmers and pacifists.[19]

"We're going to have trouble," Reagan admitted. "The Dems will try to cancel out the whole system. It will take a full court press to get it. If we don't, I shudder to think what it will do to our arms reduction negotiations in Geneva."[20] After considering thirty-four different basing options, the administration unveiled its "Dense Pack" formula in November 1982. It proposed to bunch 100 missiles as tightly as possible in fixed silos at a remote site in Wyoming. The dubious reasoning was that any incoming Soviet missiles would commit "fratricide"—exploding each other rather than hitting the intended target.[21] The administration launched a lobbying campaign in a bid to win support for the MX. Reagan renamed it "The Peacekeeper," and made a nationally televised appeal on November 22.[22] He urged members of the House Appropriations Committee to resist an amendment sponsored by Rep. Joseph Addabbo (D-New York), designed to prevent the MX from proceeding. Weinberger told members of Congress that a rejection of the MX would "send the wrong signal" to the Kremlin.[23] The administration teamed up with an informal business coalition named "MX Associates," which was established to support the president's position. The group included Reagan's former employer, General Electric, and declared that the MX project would generate more than 15,000 jobs across 41 states and 128 congressional districts.[24] But these efforts were unavailing. The "Dense Pack" was ridiculed as the "Dunce Pack," and was openly criticized by the Joint Chiefs of Staff. On December 7, the House overwhelmingly voted to reject funding the MX. Reagan was warned that no further funds would be provided, unless a suitable solution to the basing problem was found.[25]

The administration moved to save the program. Robert "Bud" McFarlane, the deputy national security adviser, reached out to senators early in 1983. "Your problem is your witness," explained Sam Nunn, a conservative Democrat from Georgia and a key figure on the Armed Services Committee. He told McFarlane that much of the congressional opposition centered on their distrust of Weinberger, who lacked credibility on defense issues. Across the political aisle, Sen. William Cohen (R-Maine) echoed the advice: "You had better put together a bipartisan team of respected analysts to study this issue in the next two months. If the new plan is sent up here in March by Cap Weinberger, it will definitely fail."[26] McFarlane relayed the news to his boss, William Clark. Although allied with Weinberger on most issues, Clark felt that if the MX was to be salvaged they would need to compromise by forming a bipartisan commission of experts. Reagan agreed. On McFarlane's recommendation, he named Brent Scowcroft (NSC adviser under Ford) as chairman of the commission.[27]

The Scowcroft Commission was bipartisan, boasting two ex-secretaries of state (Haig and Kissinger), four ex-secretaries of defense (including Harold Brown and Donald Rumsfeld), and former CIA directors Richard Helms and John McCone. Its purpose was political: to produce a compromise on nuclear policy which would enable the MX to pass through Congress. On April 6, after three months of haggling, the commission released a three-pronged report. To placate the administration, it recommended that a fixed-silo approach be used for 100 MX missiles. To satisfy congressional hawks, it suggested the development of a single-warhead missile, the "Midgetman." And to allay the fears of moderates, the commission requested changes to Reagan's START position to target the reduction of nuclear warheads.[28]

Scowcroft's report did little to solve the oft-invoked "window of vulnerability." Indeed, his commission downplayed the threat: "The vulnerability of such silos [...] is not a sufficiently dominant part of the overall problem of ICBM modernization to warrant other immediate steps."[29] Senator Nunn and Rep. Les Aspin (D-Wisconsin) tried to persuade fellow Democrats to vote for the MX on the basis of the report. Aspin had served on Scowcroft's panel and helped enforce the Midgetman idea. He promised to help implement a more flexible approach to arms control (known as "build-down") to reflect Scowcroft's conclusions. "Build-down" proposed that the United States and the Soviets remove more than one older nuclear weapon for each new one they add to their arsenals. Additionally, it called for the destruction of two older warheads for every new warhead deployed. This would allow for strategic modernization while also achieving reductions. With the commission demanding the "vigorous pursuit of arms control," Reagan promised to comply with the report.[30]

Aspin's politicking did the trick. Moderate Democrats acquiesced, assured that Reagan would now engage more readily in talks with Moscow. The AFL-CIO "defense committee" also gave its approval. (Kirkland's deputy, John Lyons, served on Scowcroft's panel.) While calling for increased defense spending, Kirkland's committee said that it "should be fully financed by a progressive surtax on income." The AFL-CIO cited cuts in social programs and "tax breaks for the wealthy," attacking Reagan for having "damaged the consensus for a strong national defense which it enjoyed on assuming office."[31] For others, the politics was local. Tip O'Neill, who had called the MX "a waste of money," opted to endorse Aspin's efforts.[32] O'Neill worried that his party would be labeled "soft" on defense, and was aware that the MX project promised to bring money and jobs into Boston.[33] With this support the MX deal passed the Senate on May 24 (by 59 votes to 39) and the Democrat-led House (by 239 votes to 186). It was a setback for the nuclear freeze campaign, whose resolution (albeit a diluted one) had sailed through the House on May 4 by 278 votes to 149.[34] The MX vote had been timed to follow that of the nuclear freeze. The logic was simple.

Having already demonstrated their support for arms control to liberals, House Democrats would then find it easier to vote for the MX and balance the disparities in public opinion.[35]

A DIALOGUE BEGINS

It was in this political context that the administration began to calibrate its approach. Back in August 1982, Reagan had formed an interagency group to examine U.S. policy toward the Soviet Union.[36] On January 17, 1983—two years into his presidency—the administration finally crafted a statement of policy. Circulated for internal use only, it was known as National Security Decision Directive 75 (NSDD-75): "U.S. Relations with the USSR." It was largely written by Richard Pipes and outlined three main tasks: (1) To contain and reverse Soviet expansionism; (2) to promote a change toward a more pluralistic political and economic system in the USSR; (3) to engage in negotiations that enhance U.S. interests.[37]

Few national security directives have been more misconstrued. The nine-page document is still invoked by Cold War triumphalists as "evidence" of a carefully conceived plan which would bring down the Soviet Union.[38] In fact, most of the stated objectives had already been outlined in NSDD-32. Many of the aims were broad and long-standing, resembling those declared by past administrations.[39] Following NSDD-32, the moderates (mainly from the State Department) had called for more flexibility in the U.S. position to help meet the public pressures. NSDD-75 thus amounted to a marginally less rigid statement. It concluded: "The U.S. must demonstrate credibly that its policy is not a blueprint for an open-ended, sterile confrontation with Moscow, but a serious search for a stable and constructive long-term basis for U.S.–Soviet relations."[40] But as a policy guidance, NSDD-75 was ambiguous. On the one hand, it reaffirmed containment and the continuation of a confrontational approach. On the other hand, it expressed support for negotiation, yet offered little detail: decisions on whether, when, and what to negotiate remained unresolved.[41] McFarlane recalled "a very ideological statement," that offered "no basis for believing that a framework for stability exists." Instead, the aim was "to stress the [Soviet] system as best we can."[42]

The directive made it clear that prospects for better relations would be contingent on the Soviets initiating a shift in course. The U.S. would remain ready for improved relations "if the Soviet Union makes significant changes in policies of concern to it; the burden for any further deterioration in relations must fall squarely on Moscow." The United States, it warned, "must not yield to pressures to 'take the first step'."[43] As will be seen, Reagan and his chief advisers would rewrite the script in 1984. Louis Sell (head of the U.S.–Soviet bilateral relations office) recalls that by 1985, NSDD-75 was already "a dead letter [...] the United States had moved on in its relationship with the USSR."[44]

Far more important was the initiative of Shultz and Reagan. Since his arrival in mid-1982, Shultz had been frustrated by the internal wrangling which beset the White House. He resented the leverage enjoyed by Clark (NSC) and Weinberger (Defense), whose policy instincts veered against those of the State Department.[45] Shultz and Weinberger shared a mutual hostility which dated back to their time in the OMB under Nixon. Their rivalry was institutional and ideological.[46] Weinberger treated any diplomatic approach as a concession, a return to détente which could imperil the arms buildup. His office wall was adorned with a framed quotation from his idol, Winston Churchill: "Never give in, never give in, never, never, never, never; in nothing, great or small, large or petty, never give in."[47] Weinberger's philosophy was at odds with that of Shultz, a pragmatist who was keen to pursue avenues with Moscow. Reagan's first two years had seen the hardliners in control of foreign policy. The trend looked set to continue in January, when Eugene Rostow was eased aside as arms control negotiator. Rostow's crime was to express support for Nitze's "Walk in the Woods" proposal, which aimed to reach a compromise with the Soviets. In so doing he had diverged from the "zero option" pushed by Weinberger, and became alienated. Rostow was succeeded by fellow CPD stalwart Kenneth Adelman, a foreign policy hawk whose nomination was fiercely opposed by Democrats. Nitze, the great survivor, remained in place.[48]

Shultz felt that the hardliners were curbing Reagan's inclination to approach the Soviets. He aligned himself with the moderates—Baker, Bush, and Deaver—who also viewed Clark and Weinberger as a hindrance. Aware of Deaver's close relationship with Reagan and the First Lady, Shultz built a rapport with the deputy chief of staff. By early 1983, Shultz had obtained personal access to Reagan, a luxury that was not granted to Haig.[49] Although the rivalries continued, it marked the start of a shift in the power struggle, one away from the hard-shell conservatives and toward the pragmatists—a category that would increasingly feature the president.

Shultz believed that it was time to engage with Moscow. Domestically, the administration had suffered heavy criticism and a string of political defeats. Reagan's military buildup was a potential casualty. Internationally, the passing of Brezhnev offered at least the possibility of a change in the Soviet approach. Shultz knew that the existing U.S. policies were unproductive and untenable. "I wanted to develop a strategy for a new start with the Soviet Union," he recalled. "I felt we had to try to turn the relationship around: away from confrontation and toward real problem solving."[50] Shultz was dissatisfied with NSDD-75. Two days after it was issued, he sent Reagan a memo titled: "U.S.–Soviet Relations in 1983." Its central thrust differed from the directive. Rather than reversing Soviet "expansionism" through military and economic pressure, Shultz proposed the start of "an intensified dialogue" with Moscow, based on realism and mutual interests. He outlined a detailed agenda which focused on four main areas: human rights, arms control, regional issues (e.g., the Middle East), and bilateral relations (e.g., trade and cultural exchanges).[51] In the weeks to follow, Shultz would develop these ideas in further papers to the president.[52]

By contrast, a memo from William Clark offered only broad brushstrokes on how to proceed. Yet he too felt that it was time to open a dialogue with the Soviets. Clark told Reagan: "On the whole I believe it would be worthwhile because it would make clear that you are not ideologically against solving problems with the Soviet Union; it would show that you are at least willing to try."[53] But Clark was lukewarm in his enthusiasm. By May he was telling Reagan of his "serious reservations" about Shultz's plan to engage with the Soviets.[54] There would be plenty of difficulties ahead. The U.S. ambassador in Moscow, Arthur Hartman, reported that Andropov's outlook had "departed in no way from the Brezhnev policy."[55] Rumors circulated about Andropov's ill-health. Though it remained a state secret in early 1983, the Soviet leader was undergoing treatment for kidney disease, and spent several hours a day connected to a dialysis machine. His disorder was linked to other ailments, including heart disease and diabetes, and did not bode well for hopes of a sustained dialogue.[56]

Reagan appeared open to the idea of doing something to repair bilateral relations. On February 12, Shultz persuaded him to meet privately with Dobrynin. Shultz suspected (correctly) that a personal encounter with a Soviet official would yield greater dividends than a policy round-table, in which Reagan was susceptible to hardline views.[57] The notion of a U.S. president speaking with a Soviet ambassador in Washington was hardly audacious. But given the non-activity of the past two years, Reagan's response was significant.

On February 15, Reagan and Dobrynin discussed the most pressing issues in U.S.–Soviet relations. Although Shultz was present, he rarely interjected. Reagan suggested opening a private channel of communication between Shultz and Dobrynin, so that views could be more easily exchanged. "Probably, people in the Soviet Union regard me as a crazy warmonger," Reagan said. "But I don't want a war between us, because I know it would bring countless disasters. We should make a fresh start." As proof of the Soviet readiness to engage, he requested that seven Pentecostal Christians (who had taken refuge at the U.S. embassy in Moscow in 1978) be allowed to emigrate. He said that American perceptions of the Soviets would change if the families were allowed to leave. As for Soviet views of the Reagan administration, Dobrynin explained: "We regard the huge rearmament program in the United States now under way, amidst political tension between the two countries, as a real threat to our nation's security." He scolded Reagan for speaking of Soviet ambitions for a "communist-controlled world." "We are not proclaiming a world crusade against capitalism," Dobrynin remarked.[58]

This was Reagan's first meeting with a Soviet official, which lent a certain piquancy to the occasion. While no major breakthrough was achieved, it offered the possibility of a platform for bilateral talks, away from the cut and thrust of the Geneva sessions. Reagan's show of initiative had at last provided Shultz with a diplomatic opening. "The president was personally engaged," he noted. "I felt this could be a turning point with the Soviets." Dobrynin relayed the exchanges to Andropov, and recommended that the "special subject" (i.e., the Pentecostals) be addressed. The Pentecostal families were soon granted permission to leave the USSR.[59]

EVIL EMPIRE

Further bilateral progress did not follow. Soviet doubts over Reagan were restored within weeks of the Dobrynin meeting. During a speech in Orlando on March 8 (to the National Association of Evangelicals), the president referred to the Soviet Union as "an evil empire" and "the focus of evil in the modern world." The words rank among Reagan's most famous, attracting media attention at home and abroad.

Less well remembered is the domestic context which gave rise to the rhetoric. The evangelicals were one of Reagan's most important political constituencies, and the NAE was the largest umbrella group for conservative Protestants. Though purportedly designed to address religious issues, the aim of his speech was to sway public opinion against the nuclear freeze. Reagan needed the help of Christian right leaders. Democratic success in the midterm elections had ensured the passage of a freeze resolution in the House, and the campaign enjoyed the support of many American churches. In 1982, the National Conference of Catholic Bishops began releasing drafts of a pastoral letter on war and peace which condemned nuclear weapons. (The final letter was published in May 1983.) The Episcopal House of Bishops and the United Methodist Council of Bishops had both issued similar pastoral letters supporting a nuclear freeze and excoriating the arms race. And the Synagogue Council of America (representing six leading groups of Conservative, Reform, and Orthodox organizations) released a statement declaring that the United States was "morally bound" to reduce the danger of nuclear war. Moreover, Billy Graham had recently made a series of evangelistic trips to the USSR and Eastern Europe, where he publicly denounced the arms race. Fearing that others might follow his lead, the administration decided to take action.[60] White House aides said that Reagan's speech was intended as "a rebuttal to recent criticism of administration policy by church officials, notably the Roman Catholic hierarchy."[61]

Reagan urged evangelical ministers to support his approach. His utterances of the Soviets as "evil" were part of the same passage in which he appealed for a rejection of the freeze: "So, in your discussions of the nuclear freeze proposals, I urge you to beware the temptation of pride—the temptation of blithely declaring yourselves above it all and label both sides equally at fault, to ignore the facts of history and the aggressive impulses of an evil empire, to simply call the arms race a giant misunderstanding and thereby remove yourself from the struggle between right and wrong and good and evil."[62] Reagan called the nuclear freeze "a very dangerous fraud," and warned against "simple-minded appeasement." "A freeze would reward the Soviet Union for its enormous and unparalleled military buildup," he declared. The speech was written by Anthony Dolan, a young Pulitzer Prize-winning journalist who authored Reagan's address in London the previous year. The White House pragmatists who read the speech draft were unsettled. David Gergen, the director of communications, recalled some "outrageous statements." One official drew a giant X across the Soviet piece in a bid to remove it from the draft, and returned it to Dolan. When this was sent to Reagan, he restored the hardline version and according to Dolan, actually "toughened" the section on the Soviet Union.[63] None of which pleased the Soviet leadership. Dobrynin, noting the Kremlin's proclivity for engaging in propaganda, felt that Reagan was giving them "a dose of their own medicine."[64]

STAR WARS

The "evil empire" speech was not the only Cold War issue bound up in domestic politics in early 1983. On March 23, Reagan unveiled a proposal for a Strategic Defense Initiative (SDI) in a nationally televised address. The first half of his speech sought to justify the defense budget. Reagan talked up the threat posed by the Soviet Union and Fidel Castro, the bête noire of U.S. presidents. In the second half, he announced plans for a program to counter the "awesome Soviet missile threat" using defensive measures. Reagan asked: "What if free people could live secure in the knowledge that their security did not rest upon the threat of instant U.S. retaliation to deter a Soviet attack, that we could intercept and destroy strategic ballistic missiles before they reached our own soil or that of our allies?" He called on the American scientific community "to turn their great talents now to the cause of mankind and world peace, to give us the means of rendering these nuclear weapons impotent and obsolete." Reagan would direct "a comprehensive effort" to form a research and development program to achieve the goal of eliminating the threat posed by strategic nuclear missiles. It held the promise of "changing the course of human history."[65]

The idea of deploying a missile defense system was nothing new. The onset of the military space race in 1957 (the year of Sputnik) would spawn years of ballistic missile defense (BMD) research. Over the next two decades, the United States spent an average of $1.3 billion per year on various missile defense programs. Policymakers and scientists (such as Edward Teller, father of the Hydrogen bomb) researched the possibility of building a defense against nuclear attack via missiles and radar and computer systems. Reagan's "astrodome" plan, projected to cost hundreds of billions of dollars, would attempt to destroy inbound missiles via lasers, particle beams, and other energy weapons, which would be deployed in space.[66] It aimed to achieve his longtime goal: to eliminate the threat of Mutual Assured Destruction (MAD) by rendering nuclear weapons obsolete.

Reactions at home and abroad were unfavorable. Opponents of the idea (political, military, and scientific) argued that the construction of an impenetrable shield against incoming missiles was impossible. The *New York Times* dismissed the proposal as "a pipe dream, a projection of fantasy in policy."[67] The press labeled it "Star Wars," an allusion to the George Lucas film.[68] (When the label stuck, the administration christened it the "Strategic Defense Initiative.") Democrats derided Reagan's speech.

"The only thing the President did not tell us last night was that the Evil Empire was about to launch the Death Star against the United States," said Rep. Tom Downey (D-New York). His House colleague Ed Markey (D-Massachusetts) was even more withering: "The forces of evil are the Soviets. They are Darth Vader. We are Luke Skywalker and the force of good. We are now listening to the original E.T.—Edward Teller."[69] The veteran diplomat George Ball offered a more sober view, calling it "one of the most irresponsible acts by any head of state in modern times."[70]

Allied reactions were not much kinder. SDI was met with anger and criticism. The reasons were manifold. Firstly, the announcement had been made unilaterally, with no prior consultation with European leaders. Secondly, it presented a direct challenge to the ABM Treaty, highly valued by NATO partners who deemed it the most important arms control agreement to date. Thirdly, it raised fears that European security would be decoupled from that of the United States. Finally, it appeared to symbolize American isolationism: a move away from East–West arms control talks toward a new, unilateral pursuit of military and techno- logical supremacy.[71] British Prime Minister Margaret Thatcher (a former research chemist) was a notable critic. She did not share Reagan's vision of a world free of nuclear weapons, calling it "an unobtainable dream." Moreover, Thatcher believed in the deterrent value of MAD, regarding it as central to Britain's national security.[72]

THE ORIGINS OF SDI

The origins of SDI tend to be explained with rhetorical ease, often ascribed to Reagan's idealism. Reagan had long been uncomfortable with the concept of MAD, which invited nuclear bluffing ("brinkmanship"). He expressed hope for a world free of nuclear weapons.[73] As Raymond Garthoff notes, the idea of "unleashing technological genius to provide a total defense" appealed to Reagan's nostalgic desire for an impenetrable, self-reliant America.[74] But if the aims of SDI reflected idealism, its imme- diate origins stemmed from political concerns. The announcement was sudden and unexpected. In his speech, Reagan told the nation that his proposal was made "after careful consultation with my advisers."[75] In fact, almost the entire government was omitted from proceedings. Not a single NSC meeting had been held in advance. High-ranking officials at State, the CIA, and the Pentagon were informed just prior to the address.[76] Why, more than two years into Reagan's term, was SDI so hastily unveiled?

According to Martin Anderson (Reagan's friend and campaign adviser), the SDI idea was born during a visit to the NORAD base in July 1979. Reagan was shocked to find that there was no defense against a Soviet missile strike. Amid talk of U.S. "vulnerability," candidate Reagan vented frustration at the lack of defense against nuclear weapons.[77] In February 1980, his military adviser Daniel Graham proposed an alternative to the MAD doctrine: the creation of a defense system in space.[78] Reagan's political aides "liked the substance of the idea," wrote Anderson, but decided the timing was not right, since it risked attack from Democrats in an election year.[79] But Graham was undeterred. After Reagan won office, he pushed his strategic defense idea to friends in government, including Allen, Haig, and the Army chief of staff, General Edward Meyer. None were enthused, but Graham found a more sympathetic ear in Karl Bendesten, a businessman, CPD member, and former Army colonel. A panel of consultants (including Edward Teller) was formed to study the possibility of a space-based missile defense system.[80]

Bendesten had friends in high places. They included high-profile Reagan supporters such as Joseph Coors (the brewery owner) and Jaquelin Hume, a grocery magnate and colleague of Meese. To oversee their project, Graham and Bendesten established a group called High Frontier, which operated under the umbrella of the Heritage Foundation, a conservative think tank with close ties to the administration. By mid-1981, High Frontier had won the backing of some top Reagan aides: Allen, Anderson, Meese, and George Keyworth, the president's scientific adviser. On January 8, 1982, the panel was given a twenty-minute meeting with Reagan at the White House, where Bendesten made his case for a space-based BMD program. But Bendesten and his panel were to be disappointed. Reagan listened but made no commitments, merely remarking that he would consult with his advisers. In a meeting chaired by Meese three days later, Keyworth and James Nance (assistant national security adviser) expressed their misgivings about the idea. Reagan sent a polite letter to Bendesten and nothing followed.[81] The matter would remain dormant in the White House for a year. In his memoirs, Anderson effortlessly glosses over the time lapse. But the SDI idea languished. As Weinberger recalled: "We did little until 1983, contenting ourselves with some minor research designed to try to improve the effectiveness of the 1970s-vintage ground-based Sprint and Spartan defensive missile systems. However, the effort was very minor [...] Not until early 1983 did we begin serious work to initiate a program for deploying a defensive system that could protect [...] from the horrors of Soviet nuclear missiles."[82]

What changed the dynamics was not events overseas but at home, where a grim set of circumstances faced Reagan in early 1983. The breakthrough of the nuclear freeze movement, waning support for his defense programs, the rejection of the MX proposals, heavy congressional defeats, a flagging economy, and record low approval ratings—all had converged in the New Year. It is well to remember that this was the political context in which the SDI proposal emerged. It was kept secret from the likely skeptics, with only a handful of Reagan's advisers privy to developments.

As noted in Chapter 5, the first six months of 1982 had seen the freeze campaign achieve national prominence. Its evolution from a grassroots crusade to a coast-to-coast political movement caught the administration by surprise. So did the speed with which congressional Democrats seized on the issue. The demonstrations in Central Park on June 12 were a vivid illustration of the growing opposition to Reagan's military buildup. On June 16, Edward Teller appeared on William F. Buckley's *Firing Line*, a long-running public affairs TV show. Teller pushed his case for the greater role of science and technology in aiding U.S. defense. His goal was to develop a secret weapon which could neutralize an incoming nuclear attack. Teller said that his research was stymied by a lack of funds and government interest, and criticized supporters of a nuclear freeze—remarks topped with a sprinkling of references to Neville Chamberlain, Hitler, and Soviet strength. "Scientists outside the few who work for Defense are not sufficiently interested. This is the demoralization," Teller complained. "We are not making progress fast enough, even though we have indications that the Soviets are ahead of us. They will know how to defend themselves; we won't. And if the nuclear freeze movement succeeds, we will be fools; the Soviets won't." Teller concluded: "If there should be such a [nuclear] war, the Soviets would probably be able to kill more than 50 percent of the American people. We would be able to kill five percent of the Soviets."[83]

Reagan learned of Teller's remarks and expressed concern. Within weeks, his counsellor Edwin Meese attended an address at the Hoover Institute, in which Teller spoke of his plan for new defensive weapons.[84] After the New York protests, Teller informed Keyworth (his former pupil) of his "deep concern about the implications of the nuclear freeze movement and the administration's ability to proceed with restoration of an adequate defense."[85] With Keyworth's encouragement, Teller wrote to Reagan on July 23, 1982. He explained that "an important new class of defensive weapons" was on the horizon. Scientists were developing the means for converting the energy of small hydrogen bombs into "unprecedented forms," which could then be directed against enemy targets. The advantage of these defensive weapons was that it would be enemy warheads, rockets, and satellites which would be destroyed, rather than human lives. Teller warned Reagan of the "extraordinary potential" of Soviet technology, which he suggested was "a few years ahead" of the United States. He appealed for a mandate to "vigorously explore and exploit" the opportunities, to bring an end to the reliance on MAD. There were political benefits at stake. "Commencing this effort may constitute a uniquely effective reply to those advocating the dangerous inferiority implied by a nuclear freeze," he told Reagan.[86] Six days later, Keyworth wrote to Clark, recommending that Teller be given a personal meeting with the president. Reagan's response was positive. "We should take this seriously and have a real look," he told Clark. "Remember, our country once turned down the submarine."[87]

But little emerged from the exchanges. Almost three months passed before Teller visited the White House, where he briefed Reagan on his latest idea: a nuclear-driven, X-ray laser defensive weapon.[88] Their conversation did not go well. The other attendees—Keyworth, Clark, and Meese—cut the meeting short after Teller appealed for increased funds for his Livermore Laboratory. "There were lots of interruptions," Teller recalled. "I don't think I had a chance to put a good case before Reagan."[89] Nothing followed, perhaps because so few of Reagan's advisers believed in the plan. Among the skeptics was Weinberger, who bluntly told Graham: "We are unwilling to commit this nation to a course which calls for growing into a capability that does not currently exist."[90] Richard DeLauer, the Pentagon's research director, warned that Teller's study "grossly underestimated" the time and money required, and felt that such a system would still be vulnerable to attack. Scientists also doubted its feasibility. Michael May, associate director at Livermore, deemed it "quite unlikely" that a laser space station could survive an attack by near-undetectable ASATs. Military analysts were equally dubious. Harold Brown, defense secretary under Carter (and a former Livermore director), said that a space-based laser system for missile defense would "not be feasible before the next century, if ever, and would cost on the order of $100 billion."[91]

The administration instead focused its efforts on countering the freeze campaign and securing funding for the MX. The former failed in the November midterm elections; the latter in December, when Congress rejected the "Dense Pack" basing mode. The defeats led to a series of events which would culminate in SDI. By then, Reagan held a record low approval rating for an elected postwar president in his second year. The economic recession was the major factor, but foreign and defense policies were also important. A Lou Harris poll in January revealed that two-thirds of Americans believed Reagan was doing an unsatisfactory job in arms control. Fifty-seven percent worried that the United States might become embroiled in a nuclear war.[92] "Politically, diplomatically, and militarily, Reagan needed a bold stroke to escape his stalemate and put life back into his foreign policy," noted author Hedrick Smith.[93]

One of the chief initiators of SDI was Bud McFarlane, who felt that "the politics of deploying ICBMs was becoming too difficult." After the MX defeat, McFarlane told Reagan that he was working on a concept to "outflank the freeze movement," while improving the U.S. position in strategic arms talks. Reagan encouraged him to find a solution and report back in January.[94] Instead of concentrating on offensive weapons, which had met with such domestic opposition, McFarlane concluded that the administration should seek to develop a *defensive*, antimissile system. He would later ascribe the initiative to a number of factors: "the East–West political dynamic, congressional politics, trends in domestic thinking, and arms control strategy."[95] Jack Matlock (soon to become NSC adviser on Soviet affairs) said that McFarlane viewed SDI as "a scam," but pushed it because of the congressional obstruction of the MX. "McFarlane's highest priority was to obtain a 50 percent cut in Soviet heavy ICBMs," Matlock explained. "Since we couldn't get a basing mode approved for the MX, we did not have a heavy ICBM to trade. Therefore, we would tell the Soviets that we would build a defense that would make their ICBMs unusable."[96]

Clark and his military assistant, John Poindexter, liked the strategic defense idea, having become gloomy about the prospects for passing the MX through Congress. "I became concerned that we simply were not going to be able to gain the public or congressional support," Poindexter recalled. "We just could not overcome the public apathy and fear of [. . .] basing nuclear weapons on U.S. soil."[97] Aware that a strategic defense proposal needed an advocate on the Joint Chiefs of Staff (JCS), they called on Admiral James Watkins, chief of naval operations. Watkins had led a JCS review on the MX, and grew exasperated by the political road-blocks. He was also a devout Catholic, and noted the efforts of Catholic Bishops to develop a pastoral letter on war and peace. As Watkins saw it, a defensive system could provide the perfect solution: avoiding the domestic political obstacles and offsetting the Soviet advantage in land-based ICBMs.[98]

With Watkins on board, Clark organized a meeting between Reagan and the Joint Chiefs for February 11. Ahead of the meeting, Watkins lunched with Teller, who told him of his "Excalibur" idea, which promised to destroy incoming missiles via nuclear-driven X-ray lasers. Watkins knew that Teller's plan of deploying nuclear devices in space was a political nonstarter. But he felt that strategic defense offered a way out of the MX stalemate and would be more amenable to the public. Watkins thus incorporated some of Teller's points into a "white paper," which was passed to the other Joint Chiefs: Army General John Vessey and Air Force General Charles Gabriel. To his surprise, Vessey and Gabriel, exhausted and dispirited about the MX, unanimously adopted the paper for the Reagan meeting.[99]

On February 11, the Joint Chiefs, Weinberger, and McFarlane briefed the president. Vessey outlined Watkins's proposal for missile defense (SDI), calling it "a middle ground between the dangerous extremes of (a) threatening a preemptive strike; or (b) passively absorbing a Soviet first strike." Defense was "more moral and therefore more palatable to the American people." Disingenuously, McFarlane interjected: "Wait a minute. Are you saying that you think it's possible that we might be able to develop an effective defense against ballistic missiles?" Watkins replied, "Yes, that's exactly what I'm saying." McFarlane turned to Reagan and said: "I believe that Jim is suggesting that new technologies may offer the possibility of enabling us to deal with a Soviet missile attack by defensive means." "I understand," Reagan replied. "That's what I've been hoping for." The meeting ended with the president telling his advisers to "go back and look at this and get ready to push it hard."[100]

Henceforth, the prime mover was Reagan. He was genuinely taken with the strategic defense idea as an alternative to MAD. Yet he was also enduring the most difficult phase of his presidency to date. SDI was an example of how Reagan's idealism and pragmatism could coexist. Reagan placed his faith in the ingenuity of American science, hoping to bring an end to the reliance on MAD and nuclear weapons. But he also saw the practical need for swift action to counter growing discontent with his foreign policy. For Reagan, SDI could both lessen the nuclear threat and offset his domestic opposition—shoring up the administration's left and right flanks simultaneously. As author Strobe Talbott noted: "To those conservatives who worried primarily about the Soviet threat, the president could present the program as a way of disarming the communist enemy. To liberals, he could offer not just a new, more humane basis for deterrence but a way of eliminating the danger of nuclear war."[101] Reagan displayed his anxiety at an NSC meeting in late February, when he vented anger at public perceptions, and the "ridiculous and harmful" criticism of his policies. He was upset by accusations that the administration was "saber-rattling" and lacked a strategic plan. Reagan singled out "the latest propaganda threat," a film produced by Helen Caldicott, associate of his daughter Patti. "This is the type of criticism to which U.S. security planning is continually subjected to," Reagan bemoaned. He called for a public affairs campaign to show the asymmetrical trend in defense procurement vis-à-vis the Soviets, and put the "anti-defense lobby on the defensive."[102]

By March 1983, Reagan could not announce SDI soon enough. "Reagan's view of the political payoff was sufficient rationale as far as he was concerned," McFarlane recalled. "By that I mean, providing the American people with an appealing answer to their fears—the intrinsic value of being able to tell Americans: 'For the first time in the nuclear age, I'm doing something to save your lives. I'm telling you that we can get rid of nuclear weapons' [...] He was less worried about details such as changing strategic doctrine or how it would affect the Allies."[103] McFarlane claimed that the ploy of using SDI as a bargaining chip with the Soviets was *his* idea and had not even occurred to Reagan, who was concerned about providing a shield against nuclear attack.[104] He was taken aback by the speed with which Reagan called for an announcement. It had been assumed that SDI would not be unveiled until the Scowcroft Commission completed its work on the MX in April. But Reagan pressed ahead. He was due to deliver a speech on the defense budget on March 23, and told McFarlane that he wanted to give a broader address in which he could "break something new" to the public—providing them with something reassuring and halting the momentum of the freeze movement.[105] "Reagan wanted it out as soon as possible," recalled McFarlane. "He was so swept away by his ability to stand up and announce a program that would defend Americans that he couldn't wait."[106]

Reagan ditched the draft speech prepared by the Defense Department. Instead, McFarlane wrote the portion of the new address in which Reagan outlined his vision for strategic defense. He consulted with Keyworth, who was "dumbfounded" when told that the president would make an announcement so soon.[107] The Joint Chiefs were stunned and embarrassed. They had assumed that the meeting on February 11 would prompt "a re-examination of allocation of resources to put more emphasis on defense," but no more. "The speech caught us all by surprise," Vessey recalled. "It was clear that more study had to be done."[108] But Vessey's

efforts to postpone the address were resisted. To avoid any delays, Clark
ensured that Weinberger (who had made his opposition known) and
Shultz (a likely skeptic) were not told of proceedings until shortly before
the speech. Even Teller was kept in the dark. "Edward, you're going to like
it," was all Reagan told him.[109] When informed on March 21, an alarmed
Weinberger asked for a delay so that European allies could be prepared.
His request, pursued by Perle, succeeded in delaying the speech for just
24 hours.[110]

Shultz also learned of the speech on March 21, and was livid. He
had sent Reagan two papers earlier that month, which outlined the
new four-part agenda to improve U.S.–Soviet relations.[111] Arriving on
the heels of the "evil empire" remarks, the unveiling of SDI threatened
to derail the bilateral dialogue no sooner than it had begun. At worst, it
could encourage hardliners in Moscow to push the case for a first strike
before the defensive shield was built. "You guys are leading the
President out on a limb and people will saw it off," Shultz told Clark
and McFarlane. "The Chiefs should have their necks wrung."[112] He
called Keyworth a "lunatic" for encouraging Reagan's utopian
vision.[113] Shultz also feared that a sudden shift to a defensive doctrine
(without any consultation with the Europeans) would rupture the
Atlantic alliance. But these considerations barely figured in the decision-
making process. For SDI was as much a response to a political crisis as
a strategic one.

SOVIET REACTIONS

From the Soviet viewpoint, the "evil empire" remarks and SDI reflected
a continuing hardline U.S. policy, with the military buildup at its core.
While Soviet commentators reacted with fury to the "evil" vilification, it
was Reagan's new defense program which most alarmed the Kremlin.[114]
Andropov was already facing the arrival of the "Euromissiles" later in
the year. The administration's public talk of "winning" a nuclear war, and
now the SDI proposal, had upped the military ante still further. Soviet
leaders grappled with the question: Was the United States ready to abandon the concept of Mutual Assured Destruction? On March 26,
Andropov accused Reagan of telling "a deliberate lie" about Soviet military strength. In an interview with *Pravda*, he claimed that SDI would
"open the floodgates of a runway for all types of strategic arms, both
offensive and defensive [...] Engaging in this is not just irresponsible, it is
insane." Andropov said that Reagan's plan was to achieve the means of

destroying the Soviet strategic system, "to deny it the capability to mount a retaliatory strike."[115]

Leading Soviet scientists such as Evgeny Velikhov argued that SDI was unrealistic and could be nullified with countermeasures. But the Politburo "could not ignore" the realities of power politics, noted Andrei Aleksandrov-Agentov, foreign policy adviser to Andropov. "Whether it was a practical idea or not, they had to account for reality—the real factor in the policy of the United States. That's why this Star Wars declaration was a contribution to the substantial worsening of our relations."[116] Dobrynin claimed that despite the scientific skepticism, Soviet leaders were convinced of the "great technical potential" of America, and treated SDI as a genuine threat. But the ambassador saw domestic political motives when Deaver spoke with him about SDI on March 26. "[Deaver] saw it as a campaign issue," Dobrynin recalled, "because it held out hope to American voters that the nuclear threat would be neutralized, blunting Democratic attacks on Reagan as a warmonger."[117]

Nonetheless, SDI was viewed by the Kremlin as the latest in a string of provocative American moves, one more dangerous and uncertain. The possible militarization of space and departure from traditional nuclear deterrence worried the Soviet leadership. Defense Minister Dmitry Ustinov quickly commissioned a study of the SDI proposal and Soviet countermeasures. In May, the Politburo agreed to intensify propaganda at home and abroad, to counter the "anti-Soviet fabrications" of the United States. A "peace offensive" aimed to win support in the West and fracture the Atlantic alliance.[118] The Soviets met the perceived threat by pledging more military spending. Andropov promised to match the Americans "development for development" in new weapons.[119] This did nothing to help the stagnant Soviet economy. For the past decade, energy exports accounted for 80 percent of the USSR's hard currency earnings, a boom resulting from the global oil shocks. Much of it was spent on a vast military buildup and the war in Afghanistan. But the "petrodollars" dried up. Chronic energy shortages in the early 1980s were compounded by the decline in Siberian oil output and in world oil prices. Despite Andropov's attempts at limited reform, the Soviet economy and living standards continued to slump. Soviet infrastructure was crumbling and the labor force grew dispirited.[120]

The Soviet overreaction to SDI would play into the hands of the Reagan administration, lending the plan a degree of credibility that it did not possess at home or in Western Europe.[121] The consequences were serious.

It provoked consternation among European allies, who feared that Moscow could take aggressive action in response, before SDI was in place. In the arms control talks, SDI would pose a major obstacle to Soviet negotiators, who refused to make reductions in offensive nuclear forces so long as the United States sought to build its defensive "shield."[122]

7

The Most Dangerous Year

Nineteen eighty-three marked fifty years of diplomatic relations between the United States and the Soviet Union. But the anniversary could hardly have been less fitting. The world's two nuclear powers remained locked in a struggle for supremacy, in which efforts to expand their stockpiles still outpaced those of negotiation. Mounting U.S.–Soviet tensions would raise public fears of nuclear war. The year saw President Reagan denounce the USSR as an "evil empire," and up the military ante by unveiling a proposal for a Strategic Defense Initiative. The Soviet destruction of a Korean airliner on September 1 would cost the lives of all 269 passengers (sixty-two of them American). Soon after, Reagan ordered the invasion of Grenada and the overthrow of its pro-Marxist government. A conjuncture of events in November saw bilateral relations reach their nadir. *Able Archer*, a NATO military exercise spanning Western Europe, was misinterpreted by Soviet leaders, who placed their forces on the nuclear alert. Two weeks later, the arrival of U.S. missiles in Western Europe led the Soviet Union to storm out of INF talks and withdraw from START negotiations. The mutual hostility and risk of miscalculation led Robert Gates (deputy director for intelligence) to describe 1983 as "the most dangerous year" of the second half of the Cold War.[1]

There is much evidence to support Gates's view. Yet it tends to obscure a development quite as significant: Reagan's growing awareness of the political context (at home and abroad), and signs of a readiness to depart from the hardliners' positions. With Shultz's prompting, the president sought to initiate a dialogue with Moscow and became more receptive to the idea of modifying the U.S. approach to arms control. He opted for a restrained reaction to the KAL disaster, and as the year progressed,

displayed a newfound aversion to publicly attacking the Soviets. Even
before the November crisis there had been a discernible change in
Reagan's attitude. It reflected his own moderate views, a desire to improve
relations, and an increased sense of his domestic imperatives. Idealistic
though it was, SDI had emerged largely from concerns that the administration was losing the public relations battle to the nuclear freeze movement. Congressional pressures, public criticism, and Reagan's willingness
to listen to the moderates (including his wife, Nancy) were gradually
brought to bear. His appointment of Jack Matlock as chief adviser on
Soviet affairs—to replace the hawkish Richard Pipes—signaled a different
outlook. So too did his selection of Bud McFarlane (and not Jeane
Kirkpatrick) to succeed William Clark as national security adviser. The
evolution was subtle. A new approach would not be developed or publicly
articulated until 1984. But as his election campaign began, Reagan the
pragmatist was emerging.

HARDLINERS VERSUS PRAGMATISTS: CENTRAL AMERICA

U.S. policy toward Central America remained a hotly contested issue. As
noted, the Democratic-led Boland Amendment (December 1982) aimed to
thwart Reagan's attempt to fund the Contras for the purpose of
overthrowing the leftist government in Nicaragua (the Sandinistas).
While hawks such as Henry Jackson supported Reagan's effort, most
Democrats were strongly opposed to military action. There was also
a split within the administration. Hardliners sought to maintain pressure
against the Sandinista regime by finding ways to work around the Boland
Amendment. They tied the fight against communism in the region to the
battle for supremacy with the Soviets. The moderates worried about an
escalating U.S. presence in the region (especially the domestic political
ramifications) and downplayed the notion of linkage.

The debate was renewed in early 1983, when intelligence sources
reported that the Sandinistas were being aided by 2,000 Cuban military
advisers. Soviet military supplies to Cuba had risen sharply due to
the increased U.S. involvement in the region.[2] Clark and Kirkpatrick
now demanded that more military aid be sent to the Contras and the
Salvadoran army. CIA Director William Casey (another hardliner) suggested that a fully funded Contra force could overthrow the Sandinistas by
the end of the year. Morton Blackwell produced a political action plan,
"Winning in Central America," which argued for the escalation of military assistance to the Contras. "The key to winning in Central America is

to win in Congress," wrote Blackwell. "If the people of Central America believe the President cannot get the Congress to support their resistance to communist aggression, it will be a matter of weeks before U.S. helicopters will be evacuating U.S. personnel from our embassy roof in San Salvador."[3] The hawks urged Reagan to apply pressure on Congress, and persuaded him to remove Tom Enders, the assistant secretary of state for Inter-American affairs.[4] Clark took control of Central American policy over the summer. He convinced Reagan to launch Operation *Big Pine II*, a large-scale training maneuver in Honduras involving 12,000 U.S. troops.[5]

All of which displeased the pragmatists. Baker and Deaver grew concerned by the increased military involvement, which they believed could cost Reagan reelection. At the start of Reagan's term, Baker told Deaver: "Those guys in the National Security Council want to get us into a war in Central America. We'll be out of here so fast it'll make your head spin if we get involved in a war down there [. . .] We'll keep him out of a war, and he'll be a two-term President."[6] Reagan's policies were ideologically driven, rooted in his anti-communism and his willingness to use American power to enforce change. But while he believed in arming the Contras, Reagan remained averse to the idea of direct military intervention. When a reporter asked about the conditions under which he might consider sending U.S. troops, Reagan quipped: "Well, maybe if they dropped a bomb on the White House, I might get mad."[7] Deaver, who knew Reagan better than most, recalled: "I thought of him as a moderate man in almost everything. His rhetoric was sometimes more strident than his actions, but I knew him as a moderate guy with moderate views, with common sense on national defense."[8]

Partisan disputes waged throughout 1983. Reagan linked the U.S. fight against communism in Central America to the Cold War struggle with the Soviet Union. "If we cannot defend ourselves there, we cannot expect to prevail elsewhere," he told Congress. "Our credibility would collapse, our alliances would crumble, and the safety of our homeland would be put in jeopardy."[9] But Reagan's efforts were unsuccessful. On May 3, the Democratic-led House Intelligence Committee voted to cut off all U.S. assistance to the Contras. Reagan lamented the "very dangerous precedent [. . .] taking away the ability of the executive branch to carry out its constitutional responsibilities."[10] In the Senate, however, liberals did not command a majority. Some $24 million in Contra aid was approved for 1983–84. Yet there was a caveat: legislators prohibited the administration from using any funds for the purpose of overthrowing the

Nicaraguan government. House Speaker Tip O'Neill and Senate Minority Leader Robert Byrd wrote to Reagan, conveying their unease.[11] Democrats were alarmed by the launch of *Big Pine II* and the formation of military bases in Honduras. These measures reflected the administration's apparent lack of interest in following the intent (if not the letter) of the Boland Amendment. "Reagan thinks he's John Wayne," O'Neill complained. "He thinks he can go down there and clean the place out."[12]

The administration appointed a bipartisan commission, chaired by Henry Kissinger, to rally support for its position. Yet by late 1983, opinion polls showed wide public disapproval of Reagan's policies toward Central America.[13] Shultz was sent to Capitol Hill on a damage limitation exercise. Acknowledging the failure to consult with Congress ahead of *Big Pine II*, Shultz pledged that if the Hondurans or Nicaraguans initiated an attack, U.S. forces would withdraw immediately. But Democratic pressure told in October 1984, when a second Boland Amendment was enacted. Congress voted to end funding for the purpose of supporting—directly or indirectly—military operations in Nicaragua by any nation, group, or organization. Reagan called the legislative restrictions "irresponsible."[14]

INF

By March 1983, European criticism of U.S. policy had prompted demands for a negotiated solution on INF. Some 572 Pershing and Cruise missiles were due to be deployed in Western Europe (beginning with West Germany in November), a decision which met with public opposition across the Atlantic. West German Chancellor Helmut Kohl (under pressure from the SPD ahead of local elections) called on Reagan to adopt a more measured position, by making the first step toward an interim INF agreement. So too did British Prime Minister Margaret Thatcher, whose support had "softened" over the winter.[15] Thatcher wrote to Reagan on February 18, suggesting that a "major new initiative" should be tabled after the West German elections in early March.[16] Like Kohl, Thatcher had domestic political concerns. A Gallup poll published in the *Daily Telegraph* (a conservative broadsheet) on February 10 found that a majority of Britons were opposed to the deployment of cruise missiles, and Thatcher was contemplating an early general election.[17]

George Bush's visit to Europe in early February revealed allied expectations for a fresh U.S. plan on INF. Dennis Blair, deputy director at the NSC's European Affairs Directorate, recommended that a new proposal be unveiled by late March.[18] The arguments were summed up by the U.S. ambassador in Brussels, Charles Price, who warned Clark: "If we lose European support, we will have neither deployments nor an arms control agreement. The Soviets will have won a great victory, the Alliance will be fragmented, and the credibility of American leadership eroded." European allies wanted to keep the elimination of U.S. and Soviet missiles as the overriding objective. But they did not want to impose a requirement that Moscow accept reductions to zero as a precondition for any interim agreement setting equal levels above zero. Price added: "The European view is obviously moving toward the perception that our zero-zero position is inflexible and the Soviets [position] more flexible."[19]

The European calls for a compromise were backed by most Democrats and many Republicans. "There is no point in letting the Soviets score a propaganda coup by being the first to move away from their current position," declared Charles Percy (R-Illinois), chairman of the Senate Foreign Relations Committee.[20] On March 30, Reagan relented on the "zero-zero" option. He offered instead an interim agreement, permitting the deployment of equal numbers of U.S. and Soviet INF warheads "on a global basis" at the "lowest possible levels." But Soviet officials spurned the proposal, citing familiar objections. They insisted that British and French forces had be included in the limitations, and rejected the notion of global ceilings because of its implications for Soviet missiles deployed in Asia.[21]

HARDLINERS VERSUS PRAGMATISTS: THE SOVIET UNION

The struggle between the hardliners and pragmatists also intensified over the Soviet Union. It would culminate in a summer showdown between Shultz and Clark. Reagan's willingness to back Shultz over his longtime friend marked a shift in the bureaucratic struggle for authority. It also reflected the president's wish to move toward a less confrontational stance with Moscow. Clark's position was undermined, and before long Reagan would seek a new national security adviser.

In mid-March, Richard Wirthlin reported of a sharp erosion in public confidence in Reagan's management of foreign affairs. A Harris poll, conducted after the SDI speech, found that 60 percent of Americans disapproved of his handling of foreign policy. By a 64–29 percent margin, Reagan received a negative rating on his efforts to manage the nuclear arms talks. His SDI proposal had failed to galvanize domestic support—striking a responsive chord only with a conservative minority in Congress, which had always backed military spending. Administration officials acknowledged that the arms buildup and anti-Soviet rhetoric was prompting fears that Reagan was a "warmonger," willing to risk confrontation.[22] Diplomat and historian George Kennan called the administration's attitude toward the USSR "inexcusably childish, unworthy of people charged with the responsibility for conducting the affairs of a great power in an endangered world." The two nations, he warned, were on "a march toward war."[23]

Shultz was worried about the effects of the SDI announcement. On March 25, he held a private meeting with Reagan to reinforce the arguments of his earlier memo, titled "Next Steps in U.S.–Soviet Relations." Over the next two months Shultz continued to push for a dialogue with Moscow, to explore possibilities on human rights, arms control, trade, and regional issues. The hardliners disapproved of Shultz's ideas and resented his growing influence on policy. In a handwritten note to Reagan, Clark warned: "Mr. President, if our plans for the Soviets (or any other issue in my area of responsibility) are not coordinated with Cap [Weinberger], Bill [Casey], and Jeane [Kirkpatrick], we will fail."[24]

On April 6, Reagan met with his top advisers to discuss "long-term and immediate short-term" relations with the Soviet Union. The president said he was prepared for a "step-by-step effort toward a more constructive relationship." The plan was to "proceed in a manner consistent with a summit in early 1984." Working back from that time frame, it was necessary to have "a number of matters well in train" so that the summit could have substance. A visit by Shultz to Moscow in July for a meeting with Gromyko might prompt a reciprocal visit from Gromyko to Washington in September, after the UN General Assembly. If successful, these exchanges could pave the way for an election year summit between Reagan and Andropov. It was thus agreed that Shultz would meet Dobrynin and propose new talks in line with his four-part agenda.[25]

Shultz sent Reagan a further memo on May 21. To improve relations with the Soviets, he recommended the pursuit of a new cultural agreement and the opening of a consulate in Kiev.[26] The hardliners objected. Four days later, Clark told Reagan that he had "serious reservations" about initiating talks with Moscow on new agreements. Given the Soviet intransigence on arms control and human rights, he claimed that Shultz's approach would "manifest the administration's engagement in a creeping return to détente."[27] But Reagan now leaned toward Shultz's views. After the meeting on April 6, he wrote in his diary: "Some of the NSC staff are too hardline and don't think any approach should be made to the Soviets. I think I'm hardline and will never appease, but I do want to try and let them see there is a better world if they'll show by deed they want to get along with the free world."[28]

Publicly, the administration tried to maintain the stance of "no business as usual without significant concrete changes in Soviet behavior." But as the INF position was being modified, rumors spread about a broader policy shift. Leaks to newspapers became so commonplace that Richard Darman began calling for the use of polygraphs, "to help test the veracity of various key players." Reagan groused about having it "up to my keister" with revelations of internal debates.[29] Comments made by Brent Scowcroft, chairman of the Presidential Commission on Strategic Forces, were published in the *Washington Post*. "My perception is that U.S.–Soviet relations are really very bad," Scowcroft told the press after a meeting with Reagan on May 23. But he added that Reagan was "sincerely interested in making progress on arms control" and was now "prepared to make a deal."[30]

The administration moved to quell the speculation. On June 15, Shultz testified to the Senate Foreign Relations Committee about the position on U.S.–Soviet relations. He parried criticism of Reagan's record by arguing that the existing tensions were the result of Soviet practices: a large military buildup, the failure to abide by the Helsinki Accords, "spoiling" activities in the Third World, and violations of existing arms agreements. But Shultz confirmed that the administration would now embark on a new course. He outlined the four-part agenda privately discussed with Reagan: human rights, arms control, bilateral relations (e.g., trade, cultural exchanges), and regional issues such as the Middle East. The latter was brought into focus by the bombing of the American embassy in Beirut on April 18, which killed sixty-three people. With civil war raging, Reagan had sent 1,200 U.S. Marines to Lebanon in 1982 as part of the Multinational Force. Israeli–Syrian fighting in Lebanon raised the prospect of a new U.S.–Soviet conflict, since Moscow had been supplying arms to Damascus. For numerous reasons, therefore, Shultz was ready to approach the Soviets. "Having begun to rebuild our strength, we now seek to engage the Soviet leaders in a constructive dialogue through which we hope to find political solutions to outstanding issues," he told Congress. "We do not want to, and need not, accept as inevitable the prospect of endless, dangerous confrontation with the Soviet Union. We can—and must—do better."[31] Shultz met with Dobrynin three days later, conveying Reagan's willingness to engage in serious talks.[32]

Shultz's testimony was perhaps the most lucid explanation of the administration's foreign policy to date. While demanding that the Soviet Union modify its behavior, at home and abroad, it also declared an interest in dialogue and negotiation. Since the text was cleared with Reagan beforehand, Shultz's vision marked a triumph for the pragmatists over the hardliners.[33] It was not to the liking of William Clark, who expressed his thoughts to Reagan in a handwritten message on July 9. Clark argued that the NSC, rather than State, should take charge of bilateral talks. "It was clear that the Russians have never taken any subordinate level seriously," wrote Clark, describing Shultz as "a solid economist." The national security adviser suggested that he (not Shultz) should visit Moscow for a high-level meeting. Shultz was already angry at how Clark was steering Central American policy. After learning of Clark's maneuvering for control over Soviet policy, he vented his fury to Reagan and threatened to resign: "Either you want a secretary of state who is an errand boy—and if that's what you want, it's not me—or you want somebody that you can have confidence in." Shultz gave Reagan a list of potential successors. "Bill Clark seems to want the job, because he is trying to run everything. There's also Jeane Kirkpatrick. Or Henry Kissinger." Reagan responded by reassuring Shultz, promising him greater authority and regular meetings at the Oval Office. Shultz found a useful ally in Nancy Reagan, who "didn't think Clark was qualified for the job," and spoke of her displeasure about his influence on Reagan. Clark's authority was irreparably damaged.[34]

The appointment of Jack Matlock as NSC adviser on Soviet affairs reflected the change in outlook. Few understood the Soviet Union better. Matlock, who arrived in June, had earlier served as deputy chief of mission at the U.S. embassy in Moscow, and as the ambassador in Prague.[35] He offered a far more practical take on U.S.–Soviet relations than his predecessor, Richard Pipes, whose hawkish views helped inform Reagan's thinking in 1981–82. "When I started my job at the NSC, I found that Pipes and his successor had consistently advised against any serious negotiation, and particularly against seeking a summit meeting," Matlock recalled. "Yet one of the first meetings I had with Reagan was a secret one, during which he told us that he wanted to meet the Soviet leader 'to prove that I am not the sort of person to eat his grandchildren.' I was told when asked to take the job that Reagan had decided that it was time to negotiate with the Soviet Union."[36] Matlock broadly agreed with Shultz's views. The new approach would be based on "realism, strength, and dialogue."[37]

REAGAN REACHES OUT

In early July, the focus moved to the pros and cons of a possible summit. By the mid-point of Reagan's third year, contact with the Soviet leader remained minimal. Donald Fortier (NSC director of politico-military affairs) argued that a successful meeting would serve diplomatic and domestic purposes "by showing the President's willingness to engage in dialogue with the Soviet leadership for peace."[38] Reagan's political strategists agreed. "The concern mentioned most often on the Hill is our lack of commitment to serious arms control negotiations," reported Kenneth Duberstein (congressional liaison), citing "growing evidence of slippage [in support] among moderate Democrats" for the MX.[39] Wirthlin was still warning of the slide in public support for Reagan's handling of foreign affairs. By August, Walter Mondale (the likely Democratic candidate) had moved to within two percentage points of Reagan in the polls.[40]

Clark was leery of the summit idea. He told Reagan that he saw only "limited gains" from a meeting with Andropov, and little prospect of a breakthrough. "Our confrontation with the Soviet Union is and will continue to be a protracted one," he wrote. To relieve the domestic pressures, Clark suggested approaching members of Congress privately, to persuade them to avoid pressing publicly for a summit.[41] But Reagan was now open to the summit idea. He decided to reach out to Andropov. In a handwritten letter on July 11, Reagan wrote: "We both share an enormous responsibility for the preservation of stability in the world. I believe we can fulfil that mandate, but in order to do so, it will require a more active level of exchange than we have heretofore been able to establish [...] Historically our predecessors have made better progress when they communicated privately and candidly. If you wish to engage in such communication you will find me ready." It emerged that Reagan's draft letter had proposed talks directed toward eventually eliminating *all* nuclear weapons. Clark, shocked by the language, deleted the passage and redrafted Reagan's letter in formulaic style.[42]

Reagan's letter received a mixed reaction. To the Kremlin, it reflected a consistent paradox. On the one hand, the president was embarking on a massive new military program. On the other hand, he was proposing significant cuts in nuclear arms. Moscow viewed it as part of a "one-sided" U.S. objective, which targeted an overhaul of the Soviet military arsenal. "In Soviet eyes, arms control was a means of regulating military competition and codifying parity, a process combining continuity with quiet diplomacy," Dobrynin recalled. "We therefore believed Reagan was not serious about arms control, and many in the West and even in the United States shared that impression."[43] Andropov replied to Reagan on August 4. He explained that an agreement was possible "so long as the United States has not begun deploying its missiles in Europe."[44] Shortly thereafter, modest steps were taken to try to improve relations. U.S. and Soviet negotiators finalized a new long-term grain agreement—a deal which Moscow knew had more to do with ongoing pressure from the American farm belt. "The farmers were pushing for it," Shultz admitted. "So it wasn't a big concession. And the Soviets knew that very well."[45] On Shultz's recommendation, Reagan made a gesture of goodwill by ending the U.S. embargo on the sale of equipment to Moscow for construction of the Soviet gas pipeline. Again the impact was minimal, since the pipeline was already virtually complete.[46]

Reagan wrote to Andropov on August 22. He questioned the Soviet concern about the British and French nuclear arsenals, which were "not in the same category" as the land-based SS-20s. "How could you possibly consider them a threat, given the tremendous nuclear arsenal which you possess," Reagan asked.[47] On August 27, Andropov made a formal offer. In the "European part" of the USSR, all medium-range missiles to be reduced under the Soviet proposal would be destroyed. These included the Soviet SS-20s, which would be limited to the level of the British and French missiles. Andropov described it as "a serious step" toward an agreement, and called on the United States to make a reciprocal move.[48] Shultz was skeptical. "The basic problems in the Soviet position remain," he told Reagan. Among them were the inclusion of British and French forces, a ban on U.S. INF deployments, and no new limits on the Soviet SS-20s in the Far East. "The Soviet aim is primarily directed toward public opinion," Shultz concluded. "Both here and in Europe, it will likely generate additional pressures."[49] But before Reagan could reply, U.S.–Soviet relations were plunged into crisis.

THE KAL DISASTER

On August 31, Korean Air Lines flight 007 left Anchorage to make its way toward Seoul. The planned route was a familiar one: the R-20 airway across the Pacific Ocean (which veered close to Soviet airspace), over Japan, before descending into the South Korean capital. But after five hours in the air, the plane strayed 300 miles off course—eventually drifting into Soviet airspace over the Kamchatka Peninsula. Soviet air defense forces mistakenly believed the civilian aircraft to be a U.S. reconnaissance plane, RC-135, which was built on a similar Boeing 747 airframe. Three Soviet SU-15 fighters and one MiG-23 were soon airborne to confront the intruder. As the plane neared Sakhalin, Major Gennady Osipovich (aboard an SU-15) issued a "friend or foe" signal. But since the aircraft could not read the frequency, no response was forthcoming. Rather than contacting the plane on the international distress frequency, Osipovich was ordered to fire warning shots. Yet none were visible to the marooned airliner. Soviet ground controllers, convinced that the plane was trying to escape, ordered Osipovich to destroy the target. At 3.25 am on September 1, KAL 007 was shot down over the Sea of Japan. All 269 passengers and crew were killed. Among the victims were sixty-two Americans, including Rep. Larry McDonald (D-Georgia).[50]

The event sparked condemnation at home and abroad.[51] Margaret Thatcher, Reagan's closest international partner, felt that it "vividly illustrated the true nature of the Soviet regime."[52] Although outraged, members of Congress were divided over how to respond. Some called for strong countermeasures. "The president should demand the immediate closing of the Russian embassy and recall of the Russian ambassador," argued Rep. Bill Patman (D-Texas). Rep. Newt Gingrich (R-Georgia) called the Soviets "barbarians" and said the incident was "deliberate murder." Senate Minority Leader Robert Byrd (D-West Virginia) demanded the cancellation of a new $10 billion grain sale agreement just signed with Moscow. Henry Jackson also called for swift action, but died of a heart attack soon after holding a press conference, in which he denounced the Soviets for the shootdown. Others appealed for a more measured outlook. Rep. Bill Frenzel (R-Minnesota) wrote to Reagan, arguing that unilateral embargoes would hurt Americans the most, and that nuclear arms talks were too important to be compromised.[53] Despite the "reprehensible" incident, Senate Majority Leader Howard Baker reminded Reagan that he had "an obligation to continue the dialogue with the Soviet Union in the quest for peace."[54]

The administration was also divided over how to proceed. Shultz rejected several draft speeches which he found "dangerously overdrawn, couched in an ominous tone that might suggest some form of U.S. military retaliation." He sought to avoid confrontational rhetoric, and decided to proceed with a scheduled meeting with Gromyko in Madrid on September 8. "We were not going to pull out of INF and START talks," Shultz recalled. "This was not going to be easy to manage. The knee-jerk reaction of Cap and other hardliners was to stop all contacts."[55] Weinberger argued that all meetings with the Soviets should be canceled, citing the need for "a very high penalty."[56] John Lenczowski, the NSC director of European and Soviet affairs, criticized Shultz for "eluding the question" of motivation, and suggested that "U.S. policy encouraged the Soviets to commit the crime." He told Clark: "The Soviets are under no illusion as to what U.S. policy is achieving: it serves to legitimize the criminal Soviet regime, and it serves to demonstrate American political, moral (and military) weakness to the world [...] They have seen that around the President are advisers who have urged him to tone down his rhetoric." Lenczowski called for a withdrawal from arms talks and for "drastically reduced" diplomatic relations. Clark approved the memo and sent it to Reagan.[57]

Reagan was awakened in the middle of the night at his California ranch by a phone call from Clark. Although horrified by the news, the president sounded a cautious note. "Let's pray that it's not true," he said. "But if this has occurred, we must guard against overreaction in our response."[58] Reagan consulted with Shultz, Matlock, and Gergen to prepare his statement. He used only small parts of a hardline draft text provided by his speechwriter, Anthony Dolan.[59] In a televised address to the nation on September 5, Reagan condemned the Soviet attack as "a massacre," and "an act of barbarism, born of a society which wantonly disregards individual rights and the value of human life, and seeks constantly to expand and dominate other nations."[60]

Despite the tough rhetoric, Reagan agreed with Shultz that U.S. sanctions should be minimized. The incident would not be used as a pretext for ending a dialogue on arms control. Countermeasures were modest: the cancellation of a U.S.–Soviet transportation agreement, and a request for an international investigation. As author Don Oberdorfer noted, it was the perfect strategy for Reagan, who "performed best when declaiming powerful words and sweeping verities but was uncomfortable with ordering drastic action."[61] It also made political sense. The Soviet action had already provoked outrage across America; seizing on it would only escalate tensions and invite further questions about Reagan's willingness to steer a more peaceful path. "We shouldn't overplay it," advised Howard Baker. "The KAL incident will become, on its own momentum, our best support for the administration's hard line."[62] Behind the scenes, Nancy Reagan was an important moderate voice, nudging her husband to "tone down" the rhetoric and engage with Soviet leaders. "With the world so dangerous, I felt it was ridiculous for these two heavily armed superpowers to be sitting there and not talking to each other," she later wrote.[63] Deaver recalled her persistently asking, "What are we doing about the Soviet thing?"[64] He ensured that the First Lady received daily updates on the media coverage of Reagan's handling of the KAL crisis.[65]

The downing of the KAL was not a "terrorist act," as Reagan had claimed. But it was a blunder of the first magnitude from the Soviet military, who believed that the plane was engaged in a reconnaissance mission. Moscow compounded the error by shamefully attempting to deflect responsibility. Far from issuing an apology, the Soviet response was to deny and cover up. The Politburo was opposed to any admission of wrongdoing, and persuaded Andropov against making any verbal concession.[66] What followed was days of denials and counteraccusations in Soviet official statements and press commentaries.[67] On September 6, TASS acknowledged that the civilian airliner was mistakenly shot down by a Soviet fighter jet. But it persisted with the allegation that the intruder was on a spy mission organized by the U.S. government.[68] Anti-Soviet sentiment was galvanized on both sides of the Atlantic.

Reagan was praised by the media for his stewardship of the crisis. The *New York Times* applauded his "tough but restrained" reaction. Tom Wicker commended Reagan for resisting the political pressures of his conservative base ("the great temptation") by refusing to break off talks with Moscow.[69] The *Los Angeles Times* cited "statesmanship" and "forceful restraint," while the *Chicago Tribune* commented on the political benefits for Reagan: "It is clear that there are likely to be short-term effects both on the relationship between President Reagan and Congress on defense spending, and on the campaign for the presidency in 1984 [...] If the President is successful in achieving a balance [in foreign policy], his position as a candidate will be strengthened enormously."[70] Rep. Les Aspin (D-Wisconsin) admitted that support for Reagan's positions on defense and arms control would be strengthened. But he claimed that the president still had everything to prove in his dealings with the Soviets. "It'll buy him some time," Aspin said. "But it doesn't get him off the hook. He's still got to come up with an arms control proposal that moderate people on both sides say is a serious thing."[71]

WORSENING RELATIONS

The prospects for progress on arms control remained bleak. The Soviet leadership seized on the forceful U.S. rhetoric after the KAL shootdown, which led to a new wave of anti-American sentiment. Many attributed it to Reagan's "crusade" to gain political support for his military programs. The Kremlin's adviser on American affairs, Georgy Arbatov, dismissed the notion of a U.S. push for a thaw in relations. "The administration has nothing in mind except a number of ruses that it needs in view of the upcoming election in 1984," he complained on Soviet television. Despite the limited American countermeasures, the mutual suspicion and hostility increased. Charges and counter-charges became a daily occurrence. Political elites in Washington and Moscow blamed one another for the worsening relations.[72]

The tension was apparent at the Shultz–Gromyko meeting in Madrid on September 8. In an angry exchange, Gromyko refused to discuss either the KAL incident or the plight of Soviet dissident Anatoly Shcharansky, which were raised by Shultz early on. Dialogue descended into monologue, with both men intent on sticking to their respective agendas. "The world situation is now slipping toward a very dangerous precipice," Gromyko warned. "In our opinion, the U.S. should re-evaluate its policies, and the president and his administration should look at international affairs in a new way." After two fruitless hours, the meeting ended. A furious Shultz described the Soviet explanation for the downing of the airliner as "preposterous." He declared: "Gromyko's response to me today was even more unsatisfactory than the response he gave me in public yesterday. I find it totally unacceptable." For his part, Gromyko judged it "the sharpest exchange" of the fourteen meetings he had held with a U.S. secretary of state.[73]

Bilateral relations worsened as the month progressed. On September 17, Gromyko canceled his annual visit to the UN General Assembly, after the governors of New York and New Jersey refused to allow his jet to land at Kennedy or Newark Airport. Most of the Soviet delegation did travel—using alternative routes such as a U.S. military airbase or via Mexico City.[74] On the same day, in a radio address to the nation, Reagan deplored the Soviet "crime and cover up" on the KAL shootdown. "We may not be able to change the Soviets' ways, but we can change our attitude toward them," he declared. "We can stop pretending they share the same dreams and aspirations we do. We can start preparing ourselves for what John F. Kennedy called a 'long twilight struggle'."[75]

Four days later, George Bush attacked the USSR during a speech in Vienna. His address coincided with the first-ever visit to the United States of a Hungarian foreign minister (Péter Várkonyi). Bush denied that the Yalta Conference of 1945 had divided the continent into spheres of influence. Instead he blamed the split on Soviet behavior. "We recognize no lawful division of Europe. Soviet violation of these [Yalta] obligations is the prime root of East–West tensions today [...] The United States will engage in closer political, economic, and cultural relations with those countries such as Hungary and Romania, which assert greater openness or independence." After referring to the "brutal murder" of the 269 KAL casualties, Bush questioned whether the Russians were really European, having not experienced any of "the three great events in European history"—the Renaissance, the Reformation, and the Enlightenment.[76]

Bush's speech was criticized by the Kremlin, the Western European press, and (privately) by allied diplomats, who presumed it to be an official U.S. policy statement. Yet that was not the intention. The original text, drafted by the State Department, did not contain a single mention of the Soviet Union. But despite the efforts of Richard Burt and other State officials, Bush (a moderate) asked his speechwriter to prepare a new address that would "reinforce a tough image" to impress hardline Republicans. Aides of Várkonyi (who met with Shultz) told the *Washington Post* that Bush's speech was "aimed at American domestic politics."[77] TASS accused the vice president of having abused and insulted the people of Eastern Europe.[78] Andropov charged Reagan with using the KAL incident to press his case for a new arms buildup. The president, he said, was "on a militarist course that represents a serious threat to peace [...] If anyone had any illusion about the evolution for the better in the policy of the administration, recent events had dispelled them completely."[79] According to Dobrynin, Soviet leaders had reached the conclusion that any agreement with Reagan was impossible.[80]

Further signs of Soviet agitation emerged in October. Matlock met with Sergei Vishnevsky, a *Pravda* columnist with links to the CPSU and KGB. Vishnevsky's view was that U.S.–Soviet relations had "deteriorated to a dangerous point." Many Soviet people were asking if war was imminent. The USSR was led by an ageing triumvirate—Andropov, Ustinov, and Gromyko—all of whom were "rigid" on policy issues. "President Reagan is mentally and physically ten years younger than his age," Vishnevsky said. "Our leaders are ten years older [...] The leadership is convinced that the Reagan administration is out to bring their system down and will give no quarter; therefore they have no choice but to hunker down and fight back."[81] After a meeting between Hartman and Gromyko on October 19, Matlock warned: "The major thrust of Gromyko's comment was that Soviet leaders are convinced that the Reagan administration does not accept their legitimacy, and that it is not prepared to negotiate seriously with the USSR, but is actually dedicated to bringing down the system."[82]

GRENADA

On October 23, a terrorist attack in Beirut killed 241 U.S. military personnel, stationed in Lebanon as part of the Multinational Force. The public reaction was somewhat offset by the U.S. invasion of Grenada two days later. A militant Marxist group had seized control of the tiny Caribbean island on October 12, and within days had killed Prime Minister Maurice Bishop. After the Beirut bombing, the State Department feared for the 600 American students enrolled in a private medical college in the capital, St. George's. Reagan promptly ordered an invasion. "He was very unequivocal," McFarlane recalled. "He couldn't wait."[83] So much so that Margaret Thatcher was not informed until after U.S. forces had already been dispatched. Since Grenada was a member of the British Commonwealth, the action angered and embarrassed the prime minister.[84] "The Americans are worse than the Soviets," she told the Irish prime minister, Garret Fitzgerald. "That man! After all I've done for him, he didn't even consult me."[85]

Nineteen hundred U.S. Marines (followed later by 4,000 troops) quickly achieved the goal of liberating what Reagan declared a "Soviet-Cuban colony."[86] U.S. troops withdrew in December after the installation of a Democratic government. The low-risk mission would be the only time that Reagan authorized a conventional military operation. Following so soon after the Beirut bombing, the American public were generally supportive. Despite criticism from liberals, Reagan savored the first U.S. military victory since the Vietnam War. "I probably never felt better during my presidency than I did that day," he recalled, likening the action in Grenada to the liberation of France and Italy from Nazism in the Second World War.[87]

NUCLEAR FEARS: THE SOVIET UNION AND WESTERN EUROPE

Late 1983 was dominated by nuclear tensions and the mutual distrust between Washington and Moscow. The United States now possessed more than ten thousand strategic nuclear weapons capable of hitting the Soviet Union via long-range missiles or bombers. The Soviets had almost eight thousand strategic weapons which could strike America. Together, the nuclear arsenals of both nations accounted for 97 percent of all nuclear weapons, the equivalent of more than 1 million "Hiroshimas."[88] The chief root of Soviet concern was the impending arrival of INF missiles in Europe. Official statements and press releases emphasized the danger of nuclear war. This was partly for public consumption, within the USSR and in Western Europe, where a large antinuclear movement gathered pace. But it also reflected genuine worries about U.S. intentions. Reagan was, after all, the most avowedly anti-communist president in American history, overseeing the largest peacetime military buildup. Together with the launch of SDI, it had fostered a climate of suspicion and resentment among Soviet leaders.[89] After the U.S. invasion of Grenada, Vice President Vasili Kuznetsov accused Washington of "nurturing delirious plans for world domination," and "pursuing a policy with no brakes [...] pushing mankind to the brink of catastrophe." The Soviet press compared Reagan to Hitler.[90] By late summer, signs indicating the location of air raid shelters were ubiquitous. Kremlin-approved broadcasts on the radio and television suggested the possibility of a nuclear attack. A U.S. intelligence review stated that the Soviet leadership "appeared to be bracing the population for the worst."[91] Editors of journals were inundated with letters from concerned Soviet citizens. For their part, political elites in Washington tended to dismiss the Soviets' expressed fears about a nuclear conflict as mere "propaganda." It all exacerbated the mutual misunderstandings.[92]

The potential for miscalculation was illustrated on the night of September 26, when Soviet early-warning systems detected an incoming U.S. missile strike. The duty officer, Lt. Col. Stanislav Petrov, was finishing his supper when a siren suddenly began to boom; a louder noise unlike the sound usually heard in exercises. The klaxon howled as huge red letters flashed on the screen, announcing in Russian: "Launch ... Launch ... Launch." Computer read-outs indicated that several intercontinental ballistic missiles had been launched from somewhere in the United States. The protocol for the Soviet military would have been a retaliatory nuclear strike, under the authorization of senior leaders. Petrov was terrified. "It's 1983 and our relations with the United States are very tense," he thought. But Petrov sensed that the algorithm in his early-warning system had wrongly detected the missiles. ICBMs were typically visible to Soviet reconnaissance satellites for about three minutes after a launch. There had been no such signs. Optical images from the satellite did not denote any fires or flares from a rocket. Suspecting that it was a false alarm, Petrov communicated with the Soviet military command center. As he was on the phone, the klaxon reappeared on the screen, denoting a second missile launch. This time the message read: "Missile Attack ... Missile Attack ... Missile Attack." Petrov followed his instincts and reported a false alarm. A third, fourth, and fifth launch would be picked up by the satellite. Petrov held firm in his belief that the system was failing. Eventually the klaxon stopped, and a missile event no longer registered. Petrov proved to be correct: the Soviet early-warning system had mistaken the sun's reflections on high altitude clouds (passing over an Air Force base in Wyoming) for a U.S. missile launch. The incident would remain classified for fifteen years. Petrov received belated recognition in 2013, when he was awarded the Dresden Peace Prize. The following year a movie titled *The Man Who Saved the World* premiered, documenting Petrov's role in averting nuclear catastrophe.[93]

Concerns over nuclear war were not confined to Moscow. On October 22–23, some two million Europeans protested against the INF deployment.[94] London was brought to a standstill, where more than a quarter of a million people (including Labour Party leader Neil Kinnock) participated in three marches which converged on Hyde Park. It marked the largest antinuclear demonstrations in British history.[95] Antony Acland, head of the diplomatic service, told the ambassador in Washington, Oliver Wright, about "worrying shortcomings" in U.S. foreign policy and the administration's "serious failure to project its aims." The Foreign Office warned Margaret Thatcher of growing anti-American sentiment among the British public.[96] Despite the fallout over Grenada, the prime minister backed the arrival of U.S. cruise missiles in Britain. Following the antinuclear protests, Thatcher scheduled a hearing in parliament to firm up support for the deployment.[97] By contrast, the French pacifist movement was low-key—owing to the government's exclusive control of foreign affairs. President François Mitterrand called the East–West crisis the "most serious" since the Cuban Missile Crisis of 1962. Despite supporting the INF deployment, Mitterrand criticized Reagan's actions over Grenada, which he felt were badly explained and "added to the perverse impression that the U.S. is the troublemaker in the world."[98]

The biggest crowds were in West Germany, where over 600,000 people took to the streets in protest. Egon Bahr (disarmament "expert" in the opposition SPD) urged allied leaders to reach a settlement by endorsing Andropov's offer of matching the Soviet missiles with the combined French and British forces. "In the entire postwar period we have lived with the threat from the Soviet Union," Bahr wrote. "What is now new is the concern that peace could be threatened by our principal ally—the United States." Détente had been placed "on the index of banned words" in Washington. The SPD ignored a plea from former chancellor and party leader, Helmut Schmidt, whose support for the INF deployment contributed to the collapse of his government. It marked the end of a foreign policy consensus between the Social Democrats and the

governing Christian Democrats, led by Chancellor Helmut Kohl. Schmidt
praised America for having rebuilt democracy in West Germany after the
Second World War, and urged his party to steer the Reagan administration away from a "missionary ideological course." Despite SPD opposition, Kohl's center-right coalition held a majority in favor of the INF
deployment. In mid-November, the West German parliament voted to
approve the "Euromissiles."[99]

NUCLEAR FEARS AND DOMESTIC POLITICS

But nuclear fears also gripped America. As the real 1984 loomed, parallels
were drawn with George Orwell's fictional world: a militarized culture,
propaganda, and the specter of war.[100] Scarcely a week passed without
journalists or political commentators speculating on his gloomy presenti-
ment. Bomb shelter sales were on the rise. FEMA designed elaborate
evacuation plans to help save communities from potential radiation
sickness.[101] Doomsday scenarios were portrayed in print and film, illustrating the likely effects of nuclear catastrophe. On November 20, ABC
screened *The Day After*—a graphic two-hour drama depicting the consequences of a nuclear war on a small town in Kansas. The central theme
was despair. Crops no longer grew; the farmland was awash with con-
taminated ash; infants were born deformed; and for radiation sickness
there was no cure.

The movie was viewed by more than 100 million people, and coincided with the deployment of INF missiles in Europe. It thus attracted
national attention, deepening the political wedge between proponents
and opponents of a nuclear freeze. "ABC is doing a $7 million adver-
tising job for our issue," said Janet Michaud, director of the Campaign
Against Nuclear War, a Washington-based disarmament group. "We
couldn't begin to reach as many people as they reach if we pooled all
our resources." Actors Paul Newman and Meryl Streep starred in TV
adverts advocating a nuclear freeze, specially produced to coincide
with the movie. Rep. Ed Markey (D-Massachusetts), who sponsored
the freeze resolution, called it "the most powerful television program
in history." "People will be irrevocably changed in terms of their
attitude about nuclear war," Markey declared. "Anyone who advocates limited survivable nuclear war is not going to be happy with this
movie."[102]

Many Republicans considered *The Day After* to be politically motivated. On ABC's *Viewpoint*, William F. Buckley suggested that the purpose

of the movie was "to launch an enterprise that seeks to debilitate the United States." (Scientist Carl Sagan countered that a real nuclear war would be much worse than was depicted.)[103] As a former actor, Reagan was aware of the potency of images in the public mind. He was downbeat after watching an advance copy of the movie. "It has Lawrence, Kansas, wiped out in a nuclear war with Russia," Reagan wrote in his diary. "It is powerfully done [...] very effective and left me greatly depressed."[104] Reagan's advisers agreed on a low-key approach, conscious of the administration's vulnerability on defense issues. "We should not attack the network for showing the film, nor should we attack the film itself," noted James Baker after holding a meeting. "We agree with the premise that nuclear war is horrible; the key question is how we should prevent it."[105]

David Gergen contacted William Greener, director of communications for the Republican National Committee. A letter was dispatched to all party chairmen, defending the administration's position.[106] Shultz gave an interview to ABC's *Viewpoint* as part of the public relations battle against supporters of an "immediate freeze." Bush, Weinberger, and Adelman wrote op-ed pieces in major newspapers. Daniel Graham's High Frontier group organized commercial spots, and sent a short documentary to forty television stations affiliated with ABC. Meanwhile, the American Security Council wrote to ABC requesting an advisory before the screening of the movie. The aim was to inform viewers that the network did not take a position in the debate between advocates of a nuclear freeze, and those who favored a "strengthened defense."[107]

The public interest generated by *The Day After* was consolation for the nuclear freeze campaign, whose legislative progress had ground to a halt—despite the passage of a resolution in the House in May 1983. On October 31, Ted Kennedy's version of the freeze resolution was rejected by the Senate by a vote of fifty-eight to forty. Kennedy lamented that while arms control negotiators dallied, "their governments have developed and deployed new missiles with more warheads, greater accuracy, and shorter warning time." He again teamed up with Sen. Mark Hatfield (R-Oregon), staging a forum in Washington on December 8 alongside American and Soviet scientists. They warned the public that nuclear war would lead to a climactic disaster, known as "nuclear winter." Large explosions would produce great volumes of dust and smoke particles, effectively blocking out the sun. "A nuclear war of any scope would mean either the disappearance of mankind, or its degradation to a level below the prehistoric one," declared Vladimir Aleksandrov, of the Soviet Academy of

Sciences.[108] The "nuclear winter" argument spread after Carl Sagan published an article in *Parade* magazine, warning of the potentially deadly climactic changes.[109]

For Democrats, Republicans, and freeze activists, concerns over a nuclear war became a key campaign issue. Freeze activists unveiled their strategy in December at a national conference in St. Louis. Their aim was to elect a pro-freeze Congress—and a president who supported the cause. An independent Political Action Committee, Freeze Voter '84, was launched. "We're Not Just Going to Change the Politicians' Minds; We're Going to Change the Politicians," read their slogan. The freeze movement now boasted 1,000 local groups across the nation, while 38 state campaigns formed their own Freeze Voter PACs. They included the Council for a Liveable World, PeacePAC, SANE, and Women's Action for Nuclear Disarmament. Together, these antinuclear PACs would raise more than $6 million from individual donors and direct mail. Three antinuclear organizations based in Boston formed a lobbying group, the Professionals Coalition for Nuclear Arms Control. While officially bipartisan, the freeze campaign's hopes rested on the influence it could muster within the Democratic Party.[110] The election of 1984 was "the final big test for the freeze movement," according to its founder Randall Forsberg.[111]

Democratic presidential hopefuls fought to present themselves as the candidate of disarmament. Though all but one supported a nuclear freeze, each candidate defined it differently. There were also ranging views on the adequacy of the American nuclear arsenal. Sen. John Glenn (Ohio), for example, supported a freeze on the testing, production, and deployment of nuclear weapons. But his idea of a freeze allowed for force modernization (e.g., the Midgetman and B-1 bomber), which diverged from that of grassroots activists. Other candidates defined a nuclear freeze as one that barred the modernization of nuclear forces. They included former South Dakota senator George McGovern, and Sen. Alan Cranston (California), who made arms control the core issue of his campaign. Rev. Jesse Jackson declared that he would "fight for a bilateral, verifiable arms freeze," while Reubin Askew (ex-governor of Florida) was alone in opposing the freeze idea. "I respect the freeze movement," said Askew. "Without it, President Reagan would not have moved. But we're going to have to be able to do some modernizing as we attempt to negotiate."[112]

The views of Walter Mondale, favorite for the party nomination, were less clear. In 1983, he argued in favor of a host of programs, such as the

Midgetman, cruise missiles, the Trident submarine, and stealth bombers (although he opposed the MX). But he also declared that these weapons should be "subject to arms control, including a mutual verifiable freeze." The former vice president struggled to reconcile his support for these two positions.[113] Mondale hailed from the liberal wing of the party and his foreign policy credentials were not strong. He therefore courted the Coalition for a Democratic Majority—the neoconservative group which had long criticized Carter's pursuit of arms control with the Soviets. In a speech to the CDM, laden with references to Scoop Jackson, Mondale declared: "The Soviet leaders are cynical and dangerous. They repress their people. In Afghanistan, they murder. In Syria, they arm terrorists. From Angola to Central America, their proxies exploit instability."[114]

The Democratic Party were more divided over other foreign issues. Tip O'Neill, for example, had angered liberals by initially supporting Reagan's actions in Lebanon. But he alienated the conservative faction by leading the charge against U.S. policy toward Central America.[115] Pollster Vut Fingerhut suggested to O'Neill and Byrd that foreign policy should not be pushed as a major campaign theme.[116] But most party insiders held the view that it represented Reagan's prime weakness. After all, a steady economic recovery in 1983 had bolstered the president's prospects, nullifying an alternative line of attack. Further emphasis would thus be placed on undermining Reagan's credibility on foreign affairs. O'Neill did his bit in a *New York Times* interview: "Reagan has caused us continuous harm. He's got a million people in Europe marching against our policies. He has no knowledge of things that are happening out there [...] He only works three hours a day. He doesn't read his briefing papers. It's sinful that this man is the President."[117]

"CHARTING A MIDDLE COURSE"

The Reagan administration anticipated the Democratic charges. Stabilizing U.S.–Soviet relations, and easing public fears of a nuclear war, ranked among its top priorities for 1984. The administration's record here was unimpressive. Bilateral relations were now worse than in 1980. The INF negotiations were collapsing. Antinuclear protests had mushroomed on either side of the Atlantic. And with the arrival of U.S. missiles in Europe, the prospect of a Soviet withdrawal from arms talks loomed large.

The prospects for START, which had resumed on June 8, were also gloomy. In April, following pressure from the freeze movement, the

Scowcroft Commission recommended a more flexible approach known as "build-down." It was designed to show the administration's commitment to arms control, and formed part of a "quid pro quo" for Democratic support for Reagan's defense program. But no progress had been achieved in the Geneva talks. In September, Democrats renewed their calls for modifications to the U.S. position, and threatened to withdraw their support for defense programs (such as the MX) in the upcoming appropriations cycle. Key moderate Democrats such as Sen. Al Gore (Tennessee) warned Duberstein that the MX coalition would "rupture quickly" unless Reagan displayed "good faith" on arms control.[118]

NSC and State officials began devising formulas to offset domestic criticism and make the U.S. position more amenable to the Soviets. "It is apparent that there is not a good understanding of our current negotiating position, either on the Hill or with the public," warned an NSC memo. "Some believe that pressures on the Hill to adopt 'build-down' and to change our START position are deeply held, and transcend the current international political circumstances [...] Pressures may be such that we will now need to take the steps which could precipitate the conditions for achieving progress in START in the coming months."[119] On September 27, the START Interagency Group recommended modifications to the U.S. position, "to demonstrate its reasonableness" on strategic arms. They included greater limits on SLCMs (sea-launched cruise missiles), the elimination of the proposed 2,500 sub-limit on ICBM warheads, and further limits on the size of ALCM forces (air-launched cruise missiles). "Charting such a middle course can blunt criticism," the Interagency Group argued. "Modifications to the U.S. position would demonstrate to domestic critics that everything is on the table and help to engage the Soviets more seriously in the negotiations. The reason for taking a more forthcoming approach now is to lessen our vulnerability to Soviet and domestic criticism that our START position is not comprehensive [...] Until we do so, we are vulnerable to charges that the administration is taking a rigid, unrealistic approach."[120] Clark suggested pursuing a Vladivostok-type agreement on the way to a full START treaty, along with new build-down provisions. "Its acknowledgment costs us nothing and would help us on the Hill," he told Reagan.[121]

On September 29, Reagan held a meeting to provide START negotiator Ed Rowny with some flexibility. He had already proposed a mutual annual 5 percent reduction in the number of ballistic missile warheads, down to the 5,000 level. Reagan now felt the need to "go a bit further," by showing "a willingness to seek additional build-down rules designed to encourage movement." Among his directives were reductions tied to modernization, such as a two-for-one build-down for new MIRVed ICBM warheads, and a three-for-two build-down for new warheads on SLBMs. Reagan was intent on moving toward a more moderate position: "I recognize that some in the Administration have differing views on just how flexible we should be at this time. However, I believe the approach I have outlined is necessary and appropriate; and I want it clearly understood that I expect my decisions to be supported by everyone. I don't want the press playing up differences or floating 'sour grapes' stories."[122]

*

Reagan's decision to replace William Clark with Robert McFarlane was a further sign of his readiness to inject some adaptability into U.S. policy. Clark, whose authority had diminished, resigned as national security adviser in mid-October. A vigorous debate ensued over who would succeed him. Shultz and Deaver hoped that the president would select James Baker, his chief of staff. They shared Baker's view that a positive change in U.S.–Soviet relations was the top priority for 1984. Although Reagan approved of the idea, it was opposed by Casey and Weinberger, who preferred the hardline Jeane Kirkpatrick. As a result, Reagan decided that Baker (who was directing the election campaign) should remain in place. But he did not opt for ideological continuity by naming Kirkpatrick as Clark's successor. Reagan instead chose Clark's deputy, "Bud" McFarlane, who had served under Kissinger in the Nixon administration, and under Brent Scowcroft, Ford's national security adviser. Despite McFarlane's military background, he held more moderate views on foreign affairs.[123]

Reagan's chief advisers—Shultz, Baker, Matlock, and McFarlane—encouraged a more pragmatic approach. The president was told that he could not rely on the "anti-Carter" vote as in 1980. Coalition-building was needed to expand Reagan's base of support from the right toward centrist voters, who were less than satisfied with his handling of arms control.[124] McFarlane informed Reagan that there was little appetite for another large military buildup, owing to the vast sums already spent on rearmament.[125] The administration had failed to achieve any major agreements with the Soviets, and foreign policy themes were being couched in banal generalities, such as "deterrence and peace."[126] In a memo to Reagan's political troika, Wirthlin warned: "The President's handling of foreign policy and the fear of a possible unwanted war underlie apprehension toward his reelection." By a distance, opposition to the arms race was

the issue with "the most cutting political edge." "Over half of the negative
responses focused on foreign policy," Wirthlin explained. "The highest
mention is war and defense policies, specifically the fear of the United
States getting involved in a war, poor foreign policy, an increase in the
arms race, and an increase in defense spending."[127] Stuart Spencer,
Reagan's campaign strategist, shared Wirthlin's views. When Nancy
Reagan asked Spencer if her husband could win a second term, his upbeat
response was tempered by warnings about Reagan's vulnerability on his
dealings with the Soviets. The First Lady had high regard for Spencer's
judgment, which reinforced her own instincts. As author Lou Cannon
recalled, "improving U.S.–Soviet relations became Nancy Reagan's special cause."[128]

In October, Baker and Wirthlin finalized the election campaign plan.
The thrust of the foreign policy approach was that words had to be
accompanied by actions. "We must strongly position the President on
the 'peace' side of the peace through strength formula," they argued. "The
most powerful and unpredictable shocks to the administration are likely
to be generated in foreign affairs. We recently saw the political chessboard
rearranged overnight when the Soviets shot down the Korean airliner. We
should continue to neutralize nuclear freeze advocates by emphasizing
that our goal is to do more than simply freeze the production and deployment of nuclear arms; it is to reduce them. We need to launch some foreign
policy initiatives that dramatically symbolize 'peace'." Reagan was told
that in the last six presidential elections, the subjects of war and peace
were of more concern to the public than "bread and butter" issues.
The campaign plan concluded: "A year from now the claim that the
Reagan administration has maintained peace would be fortified if we
could show some progress in negotiating an arms settlement."[129] As
1984 approached, the president was eager to "get relations with
Moscow on a constructive track."[130] Before long, in official statements,
interviews, and a televised speech, Reagan's tone would shift significantly.

ABLE ARCHER 83

If Reagan needed any further incentive to rethink his foreign policy,
it arrived in November. A NATO military exercise spanning Western
Europe was misinterpreted by Moscow as a possible prelude to a
U.S. nuclear strike. Early in the month, the United States and its NATO
allies launched *Able Archer 83*, which was designed to test the procedures
for the simulated release of nuclear weapons in a conflict with the Soviets

in Europe. It was one of several exercises under the umbrella of *Autumn Forge*, and was carried out at the height of U.S.–Soviet tensions (November 7–11), when the leadership in Moscow had reached a state of agitation over the INF missiles. The original plan was to involve Reagan and Bush in the direction of the exercise. But when McFarlane was made aware of the Soviet unease, he dropped the idea. Instead, on November 18, Weinberger and Vessey briefed Reagan on the updated Single Integrated Operational Plan (SIOP), which outlined the U.S. procedures to fight a nuclear war.

Reagan was first briefed on the SIOP in the spring of 1982. Options for a retaliatory attack to a Soviet nuclear strike (it was assumed that Moscow would fire first) involved the launch of hundreds of ICBMs and scores of bombers. One idea was to target Soviet economic and industrial centers, which would destroy many cities and inflict a huge number of casualties. A further option was to target the Soviet political leadership and their command and control centers ("nuclear decapitation"), limiting the chance of a Soviet response while reducing the amount of civilian deaths. The SIOP called for U.S. nuclear missiles to be directed at nearly 50,000 Soviet targets: 25,000 military targets, 15,000 economic-industrial targets, and some 5,000 focused on the Soviet leadership.[131] It was, Reagan recalled, "a most sobering experience." His views were at odds with those of the hardliners, who claimed that Soviet fears of nuclear war were no more than propaganda. Reagan wrote in his diary: "I feel the Soviets are so defense minded, so paranoid about being attacked that, without being in any way soft on them, we ought to tell them no one here has any intention of doing anything like that."[132]

While *Able Archer* was underway, reports of Soviet anxiety emerged from KGB defector Oleg Gordievsky. Although serving as the deputy KGB chief in London, Gordievsky doubled up as a spy for Britain's MI6. On November 8–9, he reported to Westminster and Washington on the state of panic in the Kremlin. Moscow's KGB center had sent flash telegrams to its stations in Western Europe, requesting information about U.S. plans for a nuclear attack on the Soviet Union.[133] The telegram warned of a "very short" seven- to ten-day window between a U.S. decision to launch an attack and the delivery of a nuclear strike. Agents were given a checklist of indicators that a countdown to a nuclear attack was in motion.[134] "The Gordievsky briefs were quite shocking," McFarlane recalled. "There was widespread fear, anxiety, and alarm on the Soviet side about the United States' intentions of possibly launching a first strike."[135] CIA Director William Casey reported on a GRU (Soviet

military intelligence) directive to all posts to obtain information about
U.S. military preparations. Casey warned Reagan that the KGB and GRU
information reflected "a Soviet perception of an increased threat of war,
and a realization of the necessity to keep intelligence information flowing
to Moscow during wartime, or after a rupture in diplomatic relations."[136]

The risk of miscalculation was growing. Only six weeks earlier, the
Soviet early-warning system had malfunctioned by interpreting the
sun's reflections on high altitude clouds for a U.S. missile launch.
With Andropov now seriously ill, high-ranking Soviet officials publicly
expressed concern. On November 19, Defense Minister Dmitry Ustinov
warned: "The dangerous character of military exercises conducted
in recent years by the U.S. and NATO draws attention. They are
characterized by vast scope, and it becomes more and more difficult
to distinguish them from the real deployment of armed forces for
aggression."[137] Soon after *Able Archer* had ended, the Soviet commander of the Warsaw Pact forces, Marshal Viktor Kulikov, criticized
the "irresponsible, extremely dangerous activity." "The U.S.-NATO
military and political leadership must realize that whatever means
they elaborate for unleashing an aggressive war and conducting combat
operations, the Soviet Union and its allies will be capable of a fitting
response."[138] Vladimir Kryuchkov, the deputy KGB chairman, recalled
"a really tense moment," though it did not push the Soviets to the
brink. "It was a matter of what conclusions were to be made. One
couldn't exclude the possibility of a war with the use of nuclear
weapons."[139]

At the time, U.S. intelligence downplayed the Soviet alarm. On
December 30, Casey rowed back on his earlier comments to Reagan.
He claimed that Moscow was "playing up the war danger" for propaganda purposes, in a bid to increase resistance to the INF deployment
and "deepen cleavages within the Atlantic alliance."[140] In May 1984,
a report was led by fellow hawk Fritz Ermarth, who had just become
the national intelligence officer on the Soviet Union. Of the crisis in
late 1983, Ermarth concluded: "We believe strongly that Soviet actions
are not inspired by, and Soviet leaders do not perceive, a genuine danger
of imminent conflict or confrontation with the United States." The
Soviets were "just rattling their pots and pans."[141]

But Ermarth's view was debunked in 2015, when "The Soviet
War Scare Report" was declassified. The report was produced by the
President's Foreign Intelligence Advisory Board (PFIAB) in 1990.
Although many details remain redacted, the PFIAB stated that Warsaw

Pact military reactions to *Able Archer* were "unprecedented" and "unparalleled in scale." The Soviet Union had conducted at least thirty-six intelligence flights over the Norwegian, North, Baltic, and Barents Seas to detect the presence of U.S. naval forces in support of *Able Archer*. Soviet nuclear fighter bombers were placed on standby at airfields in East Germany and Poland. The USSR suspended all flight operations from November 4 to 10 (except intelligence collections), in order to have as many aircraft available as possible for a potential conflict. Military personnel began transporting nuclear weapons from storage sites to delivery units by helicopter. On November 5, Politburo member Grigory Romanov declared: "The international situation is at present white hot, thoroughly white hot. Perhaps never before in the postwar decades has the atmosphere in the world been as tense as it is now."[142]

The PFIAB was scathing in its criticism of Ermarth's report, deeming it "over-confident, particularly in the judgments pertaining to Soviet leadership intentions—since little intelligence, human or technical, existed to support them." Ermarth's interpretations "were defended by explaining away facts inconsistent with them." The PFIAB cited a memo from Casey to Reagan in June 1984—a month after Ermarth's report—which offered a different view of events. Casey had by then revised his opinion. He pointed to "a stunning array of indicators" of "increasing aggressiveness in Soviet policy and activities." The abnormal military behavior added "a dimension of genuineness to the Soviet expressions of concern that is often not reflected in intelligence issuances." When told, Reagan described the events as "really scary."[143]

The PFIAB was "deeply disturbed" by the American handling of the crisis. It concluded:

We believe the Soviets perceived that the correlation of forces had turned against the USSR, that the U.S. was seeking military superiority, and that the chances of the U.S. launching a nuclear first strike—perhaps under cover of a routine training exercise—were growing. We also believe that the U.S. intelligence community did not at the time, and for several years afterwards, attach sufficient weight to the possibility that the war scare was real. As a result, the President was given assessments of Soviet attitudes and actions that understated the risks to the United States [...] In 1983 we may have inadvertently placed our relationship with the Soviet Union on a hair trigger.[144]

Reagan's chief adviser on Soviet affairs was worried. On December 12, Matlock wrote to Oliver North (NSC deputy director for political-military affairs), after reading a briefing of the next exercise, *Night Train 84* (scheduled for April).[145] "We are concerned with the political implications of this exercise," he warned. "The scenario itself—if it should leak—will be used by critics of the administration both here and elsewhere in the world as evidence that we are planning for a nuclear war. This could seriously undercut the President's image as a peacemaker." Matlock was so concerned about the political optics that he suggested altering the exercise, to produce "a scenario which culminates not in a nuclear exchange, but in a peaceful solution."[146] (*Night Train* would proceed as originally planned.) The next day, Matlock briefed McFarlane on a report from an unnamed American academic in Moscow, who had spent the past ten days with Soviet officials. "Fear of war seems to affect the elite as well as the man on the street," the academic wrote. "Paranoia seems rampant among high officials, and the danger of irrational elements in Soviet decision-making seems higher." The U.S. presidential election had become "the central determining factor in Soviet foreign policy."[147]

Against this unflattering backdrop, it is not surprising that few senior figures have been willing to broach *Able Archer* in their memoirs. Indeed, as these events occurred "on their watch," most avoid it entirely. But not Ronald Reagan. "Simply put, it was a scenario for a sequence of events that could lead to the end of civilization as we knew it," he recalled. "In several ways, the sequence of events described in the briefings paralleled those in the ABC movie [*The Day After*]. Yet there were still some people at the Pentagon who claimed a nuclear war was 'winnable'. I thought they were crazy."[148] Robert Gates, the deputy director for intelligence, wrote: "The hottest year of the last half of the Cold War—the period when the risk of miscalculation, of each side misreading the other, and the level of tension were at their highest—was 1983 [...] After going through the postmortems and the documents, I don't think the Soviets were crying wolf. They may not have believed a NATO attack was imminent in November, but they did seem to believe that the situation was very dangerous. And U.S. intelligence had failed to grasp the true extent of their anxiety."[149]

*

November 1983 marked the fiftieth anniversary of U.S.–Soviet diplomatic relations. But there was little to celebrate. On November 23 the first set of Pershing II missiles arrived in West Germany. That same day, Soviet diplomats walked out of the INF talks in Geneva. On December 8, citing a change in the strategic situation, the Soviet delegation left the START negotiations without setting any date for their resumption. For the first time since 1968, there were no strategic arms control talks in motion.

U.S.–Soviet relations had plunged to a new low. The front cover of *Time Magazine* pictured Reagan and Andropov stood with their backs turned to each other, the "Men of the Year" stern-faced and solemn.[150]

Notwithstanding the tension, U.S. foreign policy in 1983 had entered a transitional phase. It was the year in which Reagan gradually broke ranks with the hardliners, aligning himself with the moderate, pragmatic wing. Pipes and Clark were replaced by Matlock and McFarlane. Shultz, who devised a four-point plan to improve bilateral relations, was elevated to the top of the policymaking process. The president wrote to Andropov and opted for a measured response to the KAL disaster. But Reagan's evolving views had yet to translate into any major policy shifts. On the contrary, the launch of SDI and deployment of INF missiles were viewed by Moscow as the latest in a litany of provocative American moves. Indeed, the most notable changes (modifications rather than genuinely new proposals) were those either imposed on the administration by domestic forces, or under duress from Western Europe. The Scowcroft Commission, and its call for a more moderate approach to START, was the culmination of pressure from Democrats and the nuclear freeze campaign. Compliance with the "build-down" policy was a quid pro quo for congressional support for the funding of Reagan's strategic defense program. These were factors in Reagan's decision to adopt a more "flexible" START position in late September. The adoption of an interim INF proposal (which proved to be fruitless) emerged only after sustained pressure from key European allies such as West German Chancellor Helmut Kohl.

As the events mounted (public attacks, SDI, the KAL shootdown, INF deployments), Washington and Moscow began to misread each other's intentions. The *Able Archer* "war scare" suggested that bilateral relations were, at the very least, in a state of serious disrepair. The INF talks were in crisis. START was not living up to its acronym. The president had not held a single meeting with a Soviet leader or foreign minister during his first three years in office. This was hardly statesmanship. While taking the plaudits for an economic recovery, Reagan's struggle for credibility on foreign affairs continued. "The policies, quite simply, had not succeeded in their own avowed terms," noted Strobe Talbott. "In 1980 Ronald Reagan had promised that as president he would promptly and purposefully begin negotiations leading to arms reductions. His proposals emerged anything but promptly, and their nature contributed both to a breakdown in negotiations and to a buildup in rearmaments, Soviet as well as American [. . .] The Reagan policies had, by the end of 1983, touched off a backlash against the administration both at home and abroad."[151] But changes were imminent. With U.S.–Soviet relations at their nadir, the president would shift gear in 1984. Reagan, as with Carter, would follow the logic of the intermestic in his election year.

8

To the Center

Reagan's third year had seen a gradual tempering of the confrontational approach. Amid public concern over nuclear war, *Able Archer* had further focused his mind. "I was even more anxious to get a top Soviet leader in a room alone and try to convince him we had no designs on the Soviet Union and Russians had nothing to fear from us," Reagan recalled.[1] In 1984, U.S. foreign policy would move to the center with far greater urgency, as the need to avert a major crisis combined with domestic imperatives. The pragmatists grasped the symbiosis. If his ambition of reducing nuclear arms was to be realized, Reagan would need to win a second term. His immediate political interests would be served by forging a more flexible, constructive approach with Moscow. Reagan would now emphasize the peaceful side of "peace through strength"—a candidate who could be peacemaker and statesman.[2]

The Cold War paradigm was inverted. In 1980, Reagan and Carter had sought to project military strength.[3] Four years on, with public dismay about the direction of nuclear arms talks (and new defense programs in place), diplomacy and peace became the central themes. "1984 was not so much about formulating policy to win the Cold War but, instead, devising a political campaign to win Reagan the Electoral College," argues author Paul Kengor.[4] But the shift did not stem solely from political maneuvering. Reagan was genuinely worried by the state of U.S.–Soviet relations. He was appalled by the military plans drawn up by the Pentagon, which toyed with the notion of "winning" a nuclear war.[5] Election year would see the president embark on a course corrective, which would complement his foreign and domestic aims. As historian Julian Zelizer notes, "politics and strategy were moving along the same lines."[6]

The fourteen-month period from January 1984 to March 1985 marked some important developments. A major televised address in the New Year saw Reagan's public tone shift dramatically—a contrast from the fiery rhetoric of much of his first three years. Within weeks, Andropov was replaced by Konstantin Chernenko, the latest in a line of infirm Soviet leaders. Following a policy review, Reagan decided to adopt a more flexible approach in negotiations with Moscow. Despite a Soviet boycott of the Olympic Games in Los Angeles, talks on a wide range of bilateral issues were in place by midsummer. Many of the sanctions imposed by Carter in 1980 were gradually reversed. Reagan invited Foreign Minister Andrei Gromyko to the White House in September—his first-ever meeting with a top-ranking Soviet official. A landslide reelection victory was achieved six weeks later. By early 1985, the arms control talks had resumed.

These events did not yield a major agreement or diplomatic break-through. But 1984 did witness a thaw in U.S.–Soviet relations, in which the sense of fear, paranoia, and distrust were eased. Orwellian scenarios did not come to pass. The Reagan "turn" was not triggered by a bilateral quid pro quo. Nor was it in keeping with the concept of "reciprocity." On the contrary, the change in approach followed a long period of Soviet intransigence: the attack on the Korean airliner, walkouts from the INF and START talks, public condemnations of American actions, and viola-tions of existing arms agreements. Reagan's outlook in 1984 was a conscious departure from NSDD-75, which placed the onus on the Soviets to initiate a change in course, and warned against "yielding to pressures to take the first step."[7] What occurred in his fourth year was the logical acceleration of a more politically expedient course; one that began in 1983 but which had still to be defined and implemented. The Second Cold War was not quite over. But by the time of Gorbachev's arrival, Reagan's initiative had helped to defuse the East–West crisis.

DEFICITS AND DEFENSE BUDGET REFORM

Nineteen eighty-four brought Reagan two key domestic challenges: a major fight for reelection, and a tough battle on Capitol Hill for approval of his defense budget. The president held the aces. A Gallup poll in December gave Reagan an approval rating of 53 percent—a 17-point rise since the beginning of the year. The turnaround stemmed from the economic recovery in 1983, which created a "feelgood factor" that was depicted in campaign commercials. For the past two years, pollster Richard Wirthlin had posed a key question: "Are you better off than you were in 1980?" Republicans juxtaposed "Morning in America" with the sense of "malaise" under Carter (e.g., inflation, unemployment, the hostage crisis). Reagan faced none of the intraparty fissures which plagued his predecessor. Commanding solid support among Republicans, he would run virtually unopposed as the party nominee. But despite the economic revival, Reagan had failed to fulfill his promises of balancing the budget and reducing the deficit, which reached $208 billion in the fiscal year 1983.[8] The outcome derived chiefly from high military spending combined with a commitment to low taxes. "Stockman, Darman, and Baker all realized that the budget numbers didn't add up and that the second term was going to be terrible," recalled Ed Rollins, Reagan's national campaign director. But the president did not. As biographer Lou Cannon notes, "Reagan had never computed the costs of the progress he was peddling."[9]

Advisers warned that the defense budget clash gave Democrats "an easy club with which to politically bludgeon the President."[10] On December 21, sixteen House Democrats wrote to Reagan, threatening to vote against legislation to increase the government's borrowing authority unless he participated in "good faith" efforts to curtail spending.[11] The trimming of the Pentagon budget and raising of taxes were their prime goals.[12] The former had become an attractive target. Widespread perceptions of Reagan's indiscriminate spending, combined with deficit records, discredited the rhetoric that "every dollar is necessary" when it came to defense. On top of this, Weinberger was requesting a $48 billion increase in budget authority ($13 billion after inflation), claiming that it would take another decade to "level out" defense spending with the Soviets after "a decade of neglect."[13] It compelled many members of Congress (even those allied with the Pentagon) to argue for a halt in defense spending. "More and more members of Congress were finding excess to be trimmed from the defense budget regardless of what the Soviets were up to," noted author Daniel Wirls.[14] The result was that key programs such as the MX missile remained in limbo. "I think the MX will be slowed down in the Senate, and the House may very well defeat it," remarked Sen. Sam Nunn (D-Georgia), a "boll weevil" Democrat who had supported rearmament. "People back home care about the economy and deficits and rising interest rates, and they feel defense should play a role in getting those deficits under control."[15] On April 12, the House Armed Services Committee voted to reduce the weapons budget for FY 1985 by almost $9 billion.[16] The Reagan administration was also thwarted in its call for the production of at least thirty MX missiles in 1984. Democrats argued that its value as a "bargaining chip" was diminished by the fact the Soviets had withdrawn from arms control talks.[17] The fate of the MX would remain unresolved in election year.

A NEW TONE

International challenges were more considerable. Three years of rearmament, sanctions, and tough rhetoric had failed to induce any positive change in Soviet policy. Bilateral relations were in disarray. For the first time in fifteen years strategic arms talks were off the agenda, increasing public unease about a nuclear war. Soviet leaders felt "humiliated" by the KAL incident, and blamed Reagan for "personally orchestrating" the international reaction. The INF deployment and *Able Archer* had given the Kremlin even less reason to pursue avenues that might aid his campaign. So much so that the KGB mounted a covert operation designed to prevent Reagan's reelection.[18] Donald Fortier, the NSC director of politico-military affairs, foresaw no departures in Soviet policy. While Soviet leaders saw themselves "under attack" internationally, their internal position—for all the USSR's economic problems—remained extremely secure. Efforts to "hurt the president politically" would intensify, as would attempts to disrupt INF deployments in Europe.[19] "The odds are very much against a summit or major progress in arms reductions for the next 6 to 9 months," warned McFarlane in November. "For negotiations to be possible in 1984, two conditions must be met: the Soviets must be convinced that the President is very likely to be reelected; and they must be convinced that there is a realistic chance to reach some agreements that they could accept."[20]

The moderate wing now pushed for greater flexibility, without undermining the substance of the U.S. position. By late 1983, the attitudes of Reagan's top foreign policy advisers bore no resemblance to those who were in place at the start.[21] They urged Reagan to give assurances (in public and private) about his willingness to improve relations with Moscow. The president embraced this task on either side of the New Year. He did so despite learning of an "increasingly disturbing pattern" of Soviet noncompliance on a host of commitments.[22] Soviet violations extended to arms control provisions of the Helsinki accords, chemical and biological weapons conventions, the SS-25 and SS-16 missiles, and nuclear testing (the Threshold Test Ban Treaty). All were the subject of NSC meetings, reflecting the "very serious, very sobering realities about

Soviet activities and intentions."[23] Pressure to scrutinize Soviet noncompliance had mounted since the KAL incident, mainly from advocates of
a more hawkish foreign policy. In December, right-wing senators Jesse
Helms (R-North Carolina) and James McClure (R-Idaho)—both chasing
reelection in 1984—succeeded in amending the ACDA authorization act.
Their intervention required Reagan to submit a report to Congress on the
Soviet record of (non)compliance on existing arms agreements.[24]

But the pragmatists were undeterred. Matlock chaired the first in
a series of Saturday breakfast meetings at the State Department, based
on the four-part framework devised by Shultz. They concluded that
Reagan needed to publicize his desire for better relations with the
Soviets.[25] "I developed the structure of the policy during Shultz's secret
Saturday morning meetings," Matlock recalled. "That was not only
where we would put our emphasis—cooperation to achieve common
goals—but also what we would not do. Specifically, we were not to
question the legitimacy of the Soviet system, we were not to seek military
superiority, and we were not to try to change Soviet governance [...] The
substance of our proposals did not change, but we maintained flexibility
and we presented them as cooperative efforts to solve common
problems."[26] Where earlier reviews had been carried out in a ponderous
manner, there was now a sense of urgency and direction. In one of a string
of memos to the president, McFarlane wrote: "We must stress in public
your call for dialogue and your desire to reduce tensions and solve problems. Tangible progress and a summit that produced positive results could
be helpful if the Soviets decide to bite the bullet and adjust their policies
sufficiently. But if they continue to resist negotiation, you must be in
a position by late summer to make it clear that this was their fault, not
yours."[27]

The first step was a choreographed interview with *Time Magazine*,
devoted to foreign policy, in which Reagan struck a rueful tone. When
asked about the wisdom of his "evil empire" remarks, the president
explained: "I thought at the time that they [Soviet leaders] really had to
know and understand how we felt [...] No, I would not say things like that
again. Even after some of the things that have been done recently."[28]
Measures were taken behind the scenes. The State Department and NSC
engaged with American citizens who had contacts in the Kremlin. One
intermediary was Suzanne Massie, author of a cultural history of Russia,
who would tell Soviet officials of the administration's desire to restart
talks.[29] The "breakfast group" also recommended that Reagan deliver
a major public speech on U.S.–Soviet relations.[30] The central aim, Shultz

explained, was to demonstrate that the administration was ready to talk, "even if the Soviets are not." He told Reagan that the speech "should stress our determination to pursue a dialogue and to achieve positive results." Provocative rhetoric had to be avoided.[31] McFarlane wrote to Reagan again on December 18. "Virtually all pundits and many travellers to the Soviet Union are writing alarmist columns about 'escalating tensions' and the risk of war," he warned. "It is useful to reassure the Americans and to give them an understanding that you enter 1984 committed to trying to solve problems. It would also be very well received in Europe. Finally, it could have an impact on Soviet thinking."[32]

Reagan was receptive. He was ready to move beyond words and take action to improve relations—if the Soviets were also willing to compromise. He followed up on Shultz's suggestion by writing to Andropov before Christmas, proposing ways to open a dialogue.[33] Reagan's letter was quite unlike his previous messages, which cited Soviet misbehavior such as noncompliance, human rights abuses, or Third World intervention. On this occasion all were absent. On Matlock's advice he even omitted a reference to the KAL attack, which had been included in a draft version. Reagan expressed hope for a Shultz–Gromyko meeting in January, which could establish "a pattern of regular high-level exchanges and confidential exchanges." To prepare the groundwork, he suggested sending a "personal emissary" to Moscow to discuss issues such as arms reductions.[34]

Andropov, however, was now gravely ill. The Soviet leader had disappeared from public view, and was reportedly on dialysis for advanced kidney disease. "His long-term medical prognosis isn't very good," remarked a U.S. government source.[35] One of Andropov's last visitors was Mikhail Gorbachev, a high-ranking Politburo member who was in charge of economic reform. "When I entered his room he was sitting in an armchair and made a weak attempt to smile," Gorbachev recalled. "The change since my last meeting with him was striking. He was puffy-faced and haggard; his skin was sallow. His eyes were dim, he barely looked up, and sitting was obviously difficult. I exerted every effort to glance away, to somehow disguise my shock."[36] With no response forthcoming, Reagan focused his attention on the public speech on U.S.–Soviet relations.

*

Walter Mondale, Reagan's likely domestic opponent, was also talking foreign policy. Addressing the National Press Club on January 3, he launched a scathing attack on the administration. In a speech titled

"A Safer World," Mondale pointed out that Reagan was the first president since Herbert Hoover not to meet with his Soviet counterpart. The absence of communication "increased the risk of nuclear war." Mondale declared that he would hold annual summits with Soviet leaders if elected president. He proposed a mutual, verifiable freeze on the deployment of nuclear weapons, the resubmission of the SALT II agreement for Senate approval, and backed Nitze's "Walk in the Woods" proposal on INF.[37] Mondale cast himself as the candidate who could deliver peace. But greater emphasis was placed on denouncing Reagan's record. "Do we live in a safer world than we did three years ago?" he asked, paraphrasing a Reagan line from 1980. "Are we further from nuclear war? After a thousand days of Mr. Reagan, is the world anywhere less tense, anywhere closer to peace?" Mondale answered his own questions: "The Middle East and Central America are at war. A wave of terrorism is breaking around the world. U.S.–Soviet relations are in crisis. Arms control talks with Moscow have collapsed [...] Three years into his term, there hasn't been one single advance made toward meaningful arms control. Instead, we have an extremely dangerous and escalating arms race. Nowhere else is Mr. Reagan's record more appalling."[38]

But on January 16, Reagan struck a tone of moderation. His internationally televised speech ("Address to the Nation and Other Countries on U.S.–Soviet Relations") signaled a turning point in the U.S. attitude toward Moscow. To preempt accusations of domestic politicking it was delivered in the late morning—thereby reaching peak audiences in Europe and the USSR. Unlike previous addresses it was drafted by policy experts—principally Jack Matlock—rather than conservative speechwriters such as Anthony Dolan. The watchword was "peace" (it was mentioned twenty-five times) and the president called for "constructive cooperation" between the two nations. Twice in the same passage he referred to the goal of compromise. "Soviet leaders know it makes sense to compromise only if they can get something in return," Reagan announced. "Well, America can now offer something in return [...] Our negotiators are ready to return to the negotiating table to work toward agreements in INF, START, and MBFR. We will negotiate in good faith. Whenever the Soviet Union is ready to do likewise, we'll meet them halfway."

Reagan's speech contained no mention of an "evil empire." Instead, he declared that 1984 was "a year of opportunities for peace." He outlined the principles which would guide the American approach—realism, strength, and dialogue; themes stressed by Shultz and Matlock over recent months. While acknowledging the different philosophies of the two nations, Reagan spoke of the "imperative" need to begin a dialogue. On Matlock's advice, he invoked an excerpt from John F. Kennedy's speech at American University in 1963. (Reagan frequently quoted JFK, a habit which annoyed Ted Kennedy.[39]) In drawing an analogy between 1984 and the improved climate after the Cuban Missile Crisis, Reagan was, noted a senior official, "expressing what ought to be possible in U.S.–Soviet relations."[40]

Then came the peroration, written by Reagan himself:

Just suppose with me for a moment that an Ivan and an Anya could find themselves, oh, say, in a waiting room, or sharing a shelter from the rain or a storm with a Jim and Sally, and there was no language barrier to keep them from getting acquainted. Would they then debate the differences between their respective governments? Or would they find themselves comparing notes about their children and what each other did for a living? Before they parted company, they would probably have touched on ambitions and hobbies and what they wanted for their children and problems of making ends meet. And as they went their separate ways, maybe Anya would be saying to Ivan, 'Wasn't she nice? She also teaches music'. Or Jim would be telling Sally what Ivan did or didn't like about his boss. They might even have decided they were all going to get together for dinner some evening soon. Above all, they would have proven that people don't make wars. People want to raise their children in a world without fear and without war [...] If the Soviet Government wants peace, then there will be peace. Together we can strengthen peace, reduce the level of arms, and know in doing so that we have helped fulfill the hopes and dreams of those we represent and, indeed, of people everywhere. Let us begin now.[41]

Folksy and saccharine, it was quintessential Reagan. But some insiders were baffled. "Who wrote this shit?" exclaimed a White House staffer after reading the parable.[42] Had Reagan chosen to deliver this sort of speech in January of 1981, 1982, or even 1983, it could have provided the impetus for the development of a more positive U.S.–Soviet relationship. That it arrived in the heat of election season made the Soviet leadership extremely skeptical.[43] "At any other time, such a speech by an American president would have been a tangible step toward improving relations with the Soviet Union," recalled Dobrynin. "But with all the other negative factors, to say nothing of the imminent presidential election, it was hard to believe in Reagan's sincerity."[44]

Publicly, U.S. officials cited the "changed" military balance as the rationale for the policy turn: only now, after a period of rearmament, was the administration able to begin substantive talks. With American missiles stationed in Europe and strategic defense plans ahead, Reagan could claim to be in a position of strength to negotiate peace—his stated goal at the outset. But the argument was specious. In reality, the United States was not nearly as weak as Reagan and others had claimed upon taking office. It was more or less as powerful in 1981 as it was at the start of 1984.[45] At no point was the nation in danger of losing its hegemony. The Soviet Union was in prolonged economic and social decline, and trailed far behind America in advanced military technologies, despite the claims peddled by alarmists.[46] Dobrynin noted that, in retrospect, the speech *did* mark an "evolution" in Reagan's views on relations with the Soviets. Yet the context in which it emerged prompted scorn from Moscow, and from Reagan's domestic opponents.[47]

TASS charged Reagan with using "peaceful rhetoric to cover a militaristic policy" and "indulging in election-year propaganda." "The speech does not contain any new ideas or constructive proposals," the Soviet press agency stated.[48] Noting the reaction in Moscow, Suzanne Massie told McFarlane: "They simply do not understand our President and do not trust him. They are deeply suspicious of his motives and all of his initiatives, however reasonable. Given the state of communication between our two countries, this will not be an easy perception to dispel."[49] Western reactions were very favorable, with the British and West German governments, among others, hailing the change in tone. Foreign ministers Geoffrey Howe and Hans-Dietrich Genscher welcomed the speech as a message of goodwill to the Soviets. In September 1983, Margaret Thatcher had reminded Reagan that "we all have to live on the same planet." "We needed to ask ourselves how we could influence Soviet thinking," she said. "It was clear that we could not do so unless we had a reasonable relationship."[50] The broad European view was that Reagan had finally struck a balance between firmness and negotiability.[51]

Domestic reactions broke largely along party lines. Republicans praised Reagan for offering Moscow "an olive branch." Democratic presidential hopefuls accused him of lurching from confrontation to peace for campaign purposes. "You can't bop them with one hand, and at the same time hold out the other to shake hands," remarked Sen. John Glenn (Ohio). Sen. Gary Hart (Colorado) queried Reagan's claim that his policies had made the world safer "because all the evidence points to just the opposite." Mondale treated the speech as an election year move. "Once again, President Reagan is trying to deal with the politics of a problem instead of the problem itself," he declared.[52]

While moderate conservatives welcomed the speech, the hardline ideologues were less keen on what they perceived to be the "new"

Reagan. The Committee on the Present Danger grew anxious after learning of his planned address. In a letter to Reagan on January 11, Charls
Walker (the executive committee chairman) warned of the "increasing
pressures" during election year—including calls for the administration to
moderate its negotiating stance and demonstrate seriousness about arms
control. "There will be pressure on us to negotiate with ourselves while
the Soviets look on in silent approval, offering nothing and collecting
whatever concessions they can," Walker wrote. "We would be foolish
to relinquish unilaterally at the negotiating table what had been dearly
won in the larger arena." Reagan's reply was vague and polite.[53] But if the
president's approach with Moscow was evolving, the man himself was
not. Reagan was an optimist who, Shultz recalled, "appealed to people's
best hopes, not their fears, to their confidence rather than their doubts."[54]
Although Reagan had accepted membership of the CPD, he was never an
active participant. His outlook diverged from the neoconservatives,
whose worldview "assumed a stable, malevolent Soviet Union that was
immune from drastic change." Indeed, they would continually dismiss the
reforms undertaken by Gorbachev in Reagan's second term.[55] By then,
with the administration following a moderate course, many hawks were
disenchanted with the direction of U.S. foreign policy.[56]

But that was later. In 1984 Reagan had to manage the politics of the
Cold War. The administration deemed it wise to balance the speech with
at least a gesture to the hardliners. It thus expedited its report to Congress
on Soviet noncompliance—which was issued within days of Reagan's
"Ivan and Anya" address. On January 23, the president's message to
Congress was made public, along with a fact sheet alleging Soviet violations of six arms control agreements. Reagan pledged that the United
States would work toward "better treaty drafting" in future negotiations,
and more workable verification provisions. He said it was "fundamentally
important that the Soviets take a constructive attitude toward
compliance."[57] The juxtaposition of the "soft" speech and "hard" noncompliance report was no coincidence. After learning of Reagan's impending speech in early January, hardline senators (e.g., Helms, McClure) had
pressured the White House for a prompt release of the report. By complying
with this request directly after the speech, the administration aimed to
mollify those opposed to Reagan's new emphasis on better relations with
the Soviets.[58] But the report would prove the exception to the rule. In 1984
the accent was on diplomacy. Some administration officials had even
sought to delay making the noncompliance claims public, on the grounds
that it would hamper attempts to resume talks with Moscow.[59]

SHULTZ MEETS GROMYKO

A sign of the new push for progress in U.S.–Soviet relations emerged on January 13. An NSC meeting was held to discuss the stalemated Mutual and Balanced Force Reduction talks, which were due to resume in March. (The Soviet "walkout" from START and INF did not extend to MBFR, which focused on conventional arms and had been underway since 1973.) The background was unpromising. McFarlane explained Moscow's "unresponsiveness" to a U.S. proposal in the summer and the "general Soviet recalcitrance" following the KAL attack. Reagan had made minor modifications to his INF and START positions in 1983. Shultz and McFarlane now wanted more flexibility on MBFR. "Movement now makes sense, and will help to stem Congressional pressures for troop reductions—which are a constant concern to us," Shultz told Reagan. A more moderate approach would also enjoy the "strong support" of allies, helping to generate greater Western unity. Weinberger argued against making a move, citing the Soviet walkout from the Geneva talks. But Reagan sided with his secretary of state. He called for "something concrete in hand that demonstrates responsiveness and flexibility," directing officials to prepare a new proposal for the MBFR talks.[60]

Minimal progress was made in Stockholm, where Shultz and Gromyko met on January 18 at the Conference on Disarmament in Europe (CDE). Beforehand, the Soviet foreign minister publicly criticized Reagan's speech. "What is needed is deeds and not verbal acrobatics," Gromyko declared. "They are clearly a sign of short-term considerations." He called for a change in U.S. policy from "militarism and aggression" to "peace and cooperation."[61] Shultz fended off the criticism. In response to a press question—also linking Reagan's speech to election-year politics—he said that the president "didn't need the Russian embrace to be reelected."[62] The two foreign ministers held a five-hour talk—their first meeting since the tempestuous affair in Madrid. A range of issues were traversed, including human rights. Shultz raised concern about rising anti-Semitism, noting that large numbers of Soviet Jews were still being denied the right to emigrate. Gromyko would not brook interference in Soviet "internal affairs," though he was willing to engage on other issues, such as the possible reopening of consulates and broader cultural relations. Arms control was broached tentatively. The Soviets were not prepared to resume talks on START or INF, but were open to receiving new proposals. In the meantime, Shultz and Gromyko agreed to restart MBFR negotiations on March 16.[63]

On January 30, Dobrynin handed Shultz a message from Andropov, in response to Reagan's letter the previous month. Andropov accepted the need for dialogue but repeated previous criticisms, including "the militarization of outer space" (i.e., SDI). He said that the "extremely unfavorable" state of relations was the result of U.S. policies, and called for "practical deeds" to match the readiness for talks.[64] Democrats were also skeptical. Dobrynin was visited by Jimmy Carter, who described the peace rhetoric as "a pure campaign maneuver." Carter was "utterly convinced" there would be no arms control agreement while Reagan remained in power. So was Tip O'Neill, who told Dobrynin that no effort should be spared to prevent "that demagogue Reagan" from being reelected. "Reagan will give vent to his primitive instincts and give us a lot of trouble, probably put us on the verge of a major armed conflict," O'Neill remarked. "He's a dangerous man." In a more measured assessment, George Kennan told Dobrynin that Reagan had become a "peace candidate" largely because of the antinuclear campaign and the public reaction to *The Day After*. Kennan advised Dobrynin to take the president at his word, place him on the defensive, and publicly demonstrate the Soviet readiness to reach agreements.[65]

WITHDRAWAL FROM LEBANON

Policy shifts took place elsewhere in early 1984, forming part of the new emphasis on "peace initiatives." The continued U.S. military action in Lebanon was viewed as a serious political liability for Reagan. On October 23, 1983, a suicide bomber had killed 241 U.S. military personnel in their barracks in Beirut. In December, the administration's report to Congress was accompanied by a presidential letter, which stressed the value of continued participation in the Multinational Force. An NSC memo argued that a premature withdrawal would "damage seriously the credibility of the United States and its partners."[66] But the strategic arguments were overtaken by the groundswell of public opinion against military involvement. Public and congressional debate increased after the leaking of the (highly critical) Long Commission report on the Beirut bombings, together with the JCS proposals on U.S. redeployment.[67] Reagan fumed: "I have to say I am pretty mad about the way we are reduced to considering redeployment of our forces in Lebanon in response to a public debate stimulated by leaks from within our government."[68]

House Speaker Tip O'Neill announced that he was reconsidering his support for the eighteen-month limit for the Marine deployment.

Moderate Democrats who had earlier backed Reagan's position, such as Rep. Les Aspin (D-Wisconsin), warned that their commitment was not open-ended. They accused Reagan of overstating the American stake in Lebanon, and of not pushing hard enough to secure a diplomatic solution to the crisis.[69] "We find our domestic support unraveling and the social fabric in Lebanon is in turmoil," McFarlane told Reagan on January 3. There was now "a growing crescendo of criticism from liberals and conservatives [...] Virtually all of the serious press has turned against us—some because they seek a quick withdrawal; others because they argue we are not pressing Syria hard enough."[70]

O'Neill confronted Reagan at a meeting on January 25, in full view of Republicans and Democrats. "Every time I talk to you, you say things are going well," O'Neill said. "Yet there's nothing but deterioration over there." The Speaker blamed Reagan for the plight of the U.S. Marines. "You either underestimated it, or you failed to follow through." Days later, House Democrats agreed on a resolution calling for the "prompt and orderly withdrawal" of the Marines from Beirut. Republicans joined in the criticism. Senate Majority Leader Howard Baker (R-Tennessee) told Shultz that Reagan had to reconsider his Lebanon policy by the end of January— or else face congressional efforts to impose a change. Senate Foreign Relations Committee chairman Charles Percy (R-Illinois)—who was fighting for reelection—threatened to table a resolution calling for "an accelerated process of withdrawal for all forces in Lebanon."[71] James Baker, Reagan's campaign director, appealed for a prompt U.S. withdrawal. "The support for the Marine presence has not just eroded, it has vanished. We need movement," he wrote. "The worst thing in the world would be to have to act *following* congressional approval. It would be a terrible indictment of our inability to conduct foreign policy. We must *lead*, not follow. We have 4 weeks or so!"[72] Reagan duly cut his losses. On February 7, he ordered the Marines to begin withdrawing, much to the anger of neoconservatives. His decision undercut the credibility of the U.S. invasion of Grenada, which Reagan had linked to the situation in Lebanon.[73]

CHERNENKO FOR ANDROPOV

On February 9, Yuri Andropov died aged 69. The elderly trio of Gromyko, Ustinov, and Tikhonov endorsed the 72-year-old Siberian Konstantin Chernenko, who became the new Soviet general secretary. The preservation of the conservative old guard meant frustration for Mikhail Gorbachev, who was mooted for the leadership by reform-minded apparatchiks.

Chernenko's election was both understandable and baffling. He was the senior secretary in terms of length of service in the Politburo, and chaired the meetings during Andropov's many absences. He was efficient and dutiful. Conservatives in the central committee deemed Chernenko a safe bet, someone less likely to wring changes in the power structure than the more vigorous, imaginative Gorbachev. "Kostya [Chernenko] is an easier person to deal with than Misha [Gorbachev]," Nikolai Tikhonov (prime minister) explained to Ustinov.[74] Yet they backed Chernenko fully aware that he was an ill man. Chernenko suffered from severe emphysema and, like Brezhnev, was pumped with painkillers. He struggled to read the eulogy at Andropov's funeral (his first public address), gasping for breath in mid-sentence. Foreign leaders in attendance—which did not include Reagan—saw a figure even frailer than Andropov, who had kept his illness discreet. Chernenko, it was clear, would be a short-term Soviet leader.[75]

Chernenko's failing health meant that Gromkyo retained control over Soviet foreign policy. When Bush met with Chernenko after the funeral, the foreign minister had dominated the discussion.[76] Still, the vice president was upbeat. "Chernenko is no pushover," Bush told Reagan. "But he does seem open and treated us graciously. He gave the impression that there is somebody at home in the Kremlin with whom we can do business."[77] Sen. Howard Baker, also part of the delegation in Moscow, suggested that Chernenko entered office "without the burden of deeply seated personal animosity against the United States."[78] Yet Chernenko's letter to Reagan on February 23 was hardly encouraging. The principles governing the Soviet approach would remain: "peaceful coexistence" between the socialist and capitalist states, and the protection of Soviet security interests. Chernenko stressed the importance of "exercising restraint" to avoid aggravating the "dangerous situation." He called for "a dialogue aimed at finding concrete and mutually acceptable solutions in those areas where it proves realistically possible."[79]

POLICY REVIEW

The arrival of a new Soviet leader prompted a U.S. policy review, in line with the tone set by Reagan in January. It took place amid a report from Wirthlin, who warned that despite the buoyant economy, "worries over foreign policy generally have never run so broad and deep." The president, he wrote on February 16, was "less strong today politically than he was a month ago." Reporting to Reagan's campaign directors, Wirthlin explained that despite holding "a good margin of support over Mondale

[...] there remains lingering concern about the likelihood of his starting an unnecessary war and his ability to balance the federal budget." While a Gallup poll in early February placed Reagan's approval rating at 52 percent, foreign affairs was still "the major political liability." A Harris poll produced similar findings. Reagan received a 59–36 percent negative rating on his handling of nuclear arms talks, and a 58–37 negative score for his management of relations with the Soviets. By 59–38 percent, the majority of Americans disapproved of Reagan's handling of foreign policy.[80]

The "breakfast group"—led by Shultz, McFarlane, and Matlock—identified opportunities for progress with the Soviets in 1984. They felt that the Soviets had likely recognized the need for their own policy readjustments, and that Chernenko's arrival could advance this process. But the Kremlin still harbored "a deep and fundamental hostility" to the administration, and was reluctant to do anything which might facilitate Reagan's reelection. The three advisers recommended pursuing a range of issues with the Soviets: from key matters such as arms control to more "peripheral" areas such as human rights, cultural exchanges, and regional affairs. The tabling of new ideas on a START framework, they explained, could hasten the return of a genuine dialogue by the summer. Demonstrating a willingness to negotiate seriously would maximize the chances for agreements in 1984, and provide a basis for progress in 1985. The "breakfast group" told Reagan: "We should move rapidly to put more content into the dialogue and to search for more efficient modalities. We should stick to the broad agenda set forth in your January speech, but we need to concentrate particular attention on issues where the Soviets can find a direct interest in responding."[81]

There was now an urgency, flexibility, and level of detail that had been conspicuously absent in the administration for the past three years. A checklist of twenty-nine U.S.–Soviet issues was compiled across four broad areas, with analysis of the immediate prospects for each.[82] McFarlane sent Reagan a "Plan of Action for 1984" (written by Matlock), which contained a suggested timetable of events from early March up to September, with monthly proposals, trade-offs, and ideas for bilateral meetings. Reagan was told that he faced a fundamental choice: (1) to engage with low expectations and focus simply on the peripheral issues or (2) to attempt to achieve some major breakthroughs. The first option (the "modest scenario") would require new steps in bilateral areas where a solution would favor long-term U.S. interests (e.g., consulates, cultural exchanges). The "ambitious scenario" would, in addition, require some movement by the administration on its arms control positions. Reagan's advisers endorsed the ambitious course, "leaning forward to make clear our commitment to solving problems." They recommended an attempt to get START and INF "off dead-center" by proposing a new START framework and showing a readiness to accept a modified "Walk in the Woods" solution to INF—including the removal of some planned Pershing II deployments. Progress would provide the basis for a summit between Reagan and Chernenko (or Gromyko), which could lead to renewed talks. If the Soviets balked, the initiatives could be made public in advance of the election to prove Moscow's intransigence.[83]

Reagan welcomed the memos. At a foreign policy meeting on March 2, he expressed interest in holding a summit with Chernenko "as rapidly as possible."[84] One idea Reagan had in mind was to invite the Soviet leader to be his special guest at the opening of the Olympic Games in Los Angeles in July.[85] But there were mixed signals emerging from Moscow. Speeches by Gromyko and Chernenko in late February lurched from harsh condemnations of U.S. policy to expressions of interest in reducing tensions.[86] Jack Matlock (who was proving to be a far more constructive adviser than Richard Pipes) spoke with two Soviet officials, who made it clear that the post-Andropov leadership *was* interested in negotiation. "Now is a good time to make a fresh start," he was told by Vadim Zagladin, of the CPSU Central Committee.[87] Matlock was primed by Lawrence Horowitz, an aide to Ted Kennedy who had recently met with Zagladin in Moscow.[88] Kennedy was so worried by the deterioration of relations that he considered these matters "above politics." At a time when most Democrats were denouncing Reagan's handling of foreign affairs, Horowitz continued to keep Matlock informed of his contact with Soviet officials.[89] Senators Joe Biden (D-Delaware) and William Cohen (R-Maine), who visited Moscow after Andropov's funeral, said that the Soviets were "profoundly suspicious" of Reagan's motives. They urged the administration to make a "significant gesture" by following through on the tone set out in Reagan's January address. To be effective, U.S. initiatives should proceed through confidential backchannels, thus avoiding accusations of domestic politicking.[90]

Reagan and his advisers supported a private approach. They arranged for General Brent Scowcroft to visit Moscow on March 8, as a member of the Dartmouth Group of foreign policy experts. Matlock requested that Scowcroft be received at a high level—if possible with Chernenko himself. As such, Scowcroft would carry a letter from Reagan addressed to the Soviet leader. Reagan's letter was conciliatory, with none of the ideological baggage that had marked many of his earlier messages. The United States, he wrote, had no desire to threaten the security of the Soviet Union and its allies. Reagan was now prepared to discuss "trade-offs" to "bridge the proposals of both sides." If the Soviets had new ideas on how to proceed with START and INF talks, he was "ready to give them serious consideration." He told Chernenko that the administration had new ideas in other areas (MBFR, chemical weapons, and CDE) to "move the process ahead." Reagan was willing to discuss the Soviet concerns over SDI—but only after the arms control talks in Geneva had resumed. He called for the "intensification" of a dialogue on regional issues (such as the Iran–Iraq conflict), for the establishment of consulates in Kiev and New York, and for a new bilateral exchanges agreement. Reagan told Chernenko that he was touched by the gesture to release the Pentecostal families in 1983. Similar humanitarian gestures in 1984 would do much for U.S. opinion of the Soviet Union. He hoped for "a turn toward steady and good relations."[91]

On March 7, Shultz handed Reagan's letter to Dobrynin, explaining the U.S. willingness to discuss trade-offs, including START and INF. Dobrynin called it "a good effort [...] the most detailed discussion in three or four years." He promised to report back, but warned Shultz about the Soviet leadership situation. Chernenko was struggling to adapt to his new responsibilities. And while Gorbachev was showing promise, Gromyko remained a central part of the power structure. "It would be a mistake to try and avoid Gromyko, since this might turn him into a wrecker," Dobrynin warned.[92] By the time Scowcroft arrived in Moscow, it was clear that the Soviet foreign minister was an obstacle to progress. Shultz had asked Gromyko to arrange a meeting between Chernenko and Scowcroft (Reagan's personal emissary). Affronted at being bypassed, Gromyko rejected the request. He offered only a meeting with his deputy, Georgy Korniyenko, which Scowcroft spurned.[93] "The Scowcroft mission was seen as a U.S. trick," Dobrynin explained. "Gromyko viewed it as an effort to go around him."[94]

Chernenko replied to Reagan on March 19. The Soviet leader saw no change in the U.S. position on the INF missiles deployed in Europe. "This step has become the main obstacle on the path of negotiations," Chernenko wrote. "It has undermined the general process of limiting and reducing nuclear arms." There were other grievances, notably Reagan's SDI plans. Chernenko called for "a resolute and unequivocal renunciation of the very idea." He proposed talks aimed at reaching an agreement to "prevent the militarization of outer space."[95] Hopes for a summit meeting appeared to have been dashed. "[Chernenko] was cut from the same cloth as Brezhnev and Andropov—a tough old-line communist," Reagan recalled.[96]

<h2 style="text-align:center">"WE WILL BUILD A RECORD"</h2>

Despite receiving the "cold shoulder," Reagan was not discouraged. Gone were the days of confrontation. "I think this calls for a very well thought out reply and not just a routine acknowledgment that leaves the status quo as is," he wrote.[97] The views of Shultz, McFarlane, and Matlock were well known to the president. McFarlane now directed members of the SACPG (Senior Arms Control Policy Group) to present their thoughts on how to proceed with START and INF. Reagan had formed the SACPG in mid-1983 in a vain effort to ease the bureaucratic feuding over national security.[98] The verdicts of his defense secretary and arms control team (which were addressed to Reagan) arrived on March 23. All were mired in domestic political considerations.

START negotiator Ed Rowny argued that while a full-fledged U.S.–Soviet deal prior to the election was "clearly unrealistic," an agreement on the guidelines for talks could be achieved. What he envisaged was an accord similar to the aide memoire agreed at Vladivostok in 1974. There were "major political benefits" at stake. "Resumption of the negotiations would, by itself, provide a certain amount of positive political fallout," Rowny explained. "Such an agreement would demonstrate concretely that the President's policies [. . .] offer the best prospect for reaching agreement with the Soviets. It would solidify support in Congress and among the public for the Administration's defense and arms control positions." An agreement would also win the approval of European allies, reinforcing solidarity on the INF deployments, while keeping the antinuclear movement on the defensive. Rowny listed potential trade-offs and called for the process to be expedited. "In view of the relatively short time remaining, we need to begin discussions with the Soviets on this matter soon," he advised. "The President should, in a factual but measured way, explain the virtues of the START proposal and his personal commitment to arms control—not wait until the Democratic candidate puts him on the defensive."[99] Rowny's arguments were backed by Kenneth Adelman, the ACDA director. Adelman told Reagan that domestic opponents were portraying the administration as the only one since the Second World War without a significant arms control achievement. It was a record that was damaging the pursuit of strategic programs such as the MX. "We can and should make moves that will demonstrate our interest in arms control, without prejudicing our substantive positions and without asking the Soviets to 'eat crow'."[100]

Opposing these views were INF negotiator Paul Nitze and Defense Secretary Caspar Weinberger. Nitze warned of a negative domestic reaction if the administration was seen to be rewarding the Soviets for having broken off talks. The Kremlin would view any concessions as a sign of American weakness. Since the "Euromissiles" were the immediate concern of the Soviets and Europeans, Nitze suggested that any new initiative should focus on INF. Such a move, he wrote, would help Reagan's allies in Congress, who were under pressure to demonstrate movement on arms control to their constituents. Nitze felt that it was "risky" to conduct serious talks with the Soviets in an election year. Any new proposal should be cosmetic, he argued, "formulated in such a way that it could be advanced unilaterally and not require actual negotiation."[101]

However, the greatest resistance emerged from the Pentagon. In a six-page memo, Weinberger warned Reagan that he had more to lose by shifting gear. "As we approach the national conventions there is a risk that we shall lose the initiative—that a vigorous explanation of our policies mounted in the aftermath of the Democratic attack on them will sound defensive and unpersuasive." He pointed to 1980, when Jimmy Carter had "abruptly changed" his policies toward the Soviet Union—withdrawing the SALT II Treaty from Senate consideration, instituting sanctions, and proposing a five percent growth in defense spending. The change had come "too late" to regain the confidence of American voters. "Carter's shift seemed to vindicate the criticism that led up to it," Weinberger argued. "By abandoning his established policies and appearing to embrace new and contradictory ones, Carter himself seemed to acknowledge that he had been weak in the face of Soviet strength."[102] Weinberger drew a parallel with Reagan's own election-year turn. He questioned the new "policy of restraint," which "deliberately played down the Soviet walkout from Geneva and its record on compliance." The results of the strategy unveiled in January, he claimed, had been "disappointing." "We must not drift toward November in the hope that a late breakthrough will obviate the need for a reassertion of this administration's record and philosophy," Weinberger told Reagan. He cited a report by CIA Director William Casey, which was pessimistic about Moscow's willingness to engage in talks.[103] The defense secretary instead appealed for a vigorous counterattack. The Democratic National Committee was running television slots portraying Reagan as the first president since John F. Kennedy who was not presiding over a nuclear arms negotiation. Weinberger bemoaned that the administration was "inaudible" in its self-defense.[104]

Reagan read the memoranda and summoned an NSC meeting on March 27. Weinberger recited his argument that the Soviets would not negotiate in 1984. "Chernenko is not only not responding, he wouldn't even receive the letter that Scowcroft carried," he told the president. Rowny argued that the Soviets might return to the table "when they see that there really is something in it for them. If we show a little ankle, maybe a little thigh, then you get movement." Shultz urged Reagan to continue setting "positive messages" on his readiness to deal—including on START and INF. He rebuked Weinberger for his negativity. "We should be prepared to take parts of the Soviet position and shouldn't be against everything in SALT. The secretary of defense uses the word 'framework' as if it's a swear word."

But the most significant input was from Reagan, who said that the new course, based on flexibility, would be pursued. He knew that Soviet leaders were doing their best to make him look "non-cooperative," yet added: "We can't go on negotiating with ourselves. We can't be supplicants crawling. We can't look like failures. I do not intend to make unilateral concessions to get them back to the table, but I believe we must have a full, credible agenda on arms control. Maybe we could build a record." Reagan accepted that it was unlikely the Soviets would strike a deal on START or INF before the election. The administration therefore needed to achieve progress on "lesser things": MBFR, chemical weapons, confidence building, ballistic missile testing, agreement not to encrypt, CDE, and a range of nonmilitary issues. On the key matters of START and INF, Reagan called for "solid, flexible positions." He designated Shultz as "public spokesman on arms control," and said that the "good aspects" of SALT II should not be ignored. "We need a position which takes part of their [Soviet] approach and melds it with ours, so that they have a fig leaf for coming off their position," Reagan explained. He told Nitze and Rowny to begin private talks with Moscow, and to table the chemical weapons treaty as soon as possible. He directed the SACPG to "accelerate their work," and present new options on START and INF within a few weeks. "I think we should work in private channels," Reagan said. "But we will not crawl. We will build a record."[105]

THE MONDALE CAMPAIGN

Reagan's move to the center posed a question for his political opponents: should they embrace or disparage his "year of peace" plans? In general,

Democrats chose the latter course, focusing on the broad effect of Reagan's first three years. "Relations with the Soviet Union are the worst they have been since the end of World War II," Tip O'Neill declared. "I've never felt so badly about anything as I feel right now with regard to the Cold War."[106] Walter Mondale, favorite for the party nomination, queried the diplomatic pivot ahead of the Iowa caucus. "Mr Reagan has started talking about talking to the Soviets. But at three minutes to midnight, it's past time to talk about talking—it's time to *start* talking."[107] The theme of Mondale's January address, "A Safer World," became the core of his stump speech.[108] Reagan's Strategic Defense Initiative was a focal point of criticism. "The clock is ticking," Mondale warned ahead of the Ohio primary. "In less than 200 days, if Reagan is elected, the arms race on earth will be extended to the skies." The former vice president offered a plan "to stop the heavens from being militarized." He targeted a ban on anti-satellite weapons, and called for a reaffirmation of the U.S. commitment to the ABM Treaty. Mondale proposed a temporary moratorium on the testing and deployment of all weapons in space, which he hoped could lead to a verifiable agreement with Moscow.[109]

There were other avenues of attack. While U.S. forces had withdrawn from Lebanon, military involvement in Central America remained a highly charged issue. Mondale accused Reagan of pursuing "misguided" and "blundering" policies that were leading the nation into war. He called for the withdrawal of all U.S. combat forces and invoked the Vietnam analogy. Reagan's policies were "widening, militarizing, and Americanizing the conflict." After revelations that Nicaraguan harbors had been secretly mined by CIA-sponsored commandos, Mondale warned: "If this pattern of irresponsibility and deception continues, I predict America could be involved in a full-scale war in Central America."[110]

But Democrats were wary of being labeled too dovish on national security. Of all the candidates, only civil rights activist Jesse Jackson favored actual reductions in defense spending. The Mondale team believed that even the suspicion of wavering on the defense budget "would play into Republican hands." The party platform document on foreign policy was carefully worded. It stressed the need for arms control and a dialogue with Moscow, while ensuring that the nominee could not be accused of "naivety" about the Soviet Union. To bridge the internal divisions over arms control, the platform pledged the party to the same approach: the proposal of a "quick freeze" with the Soviets on selected weapons systems in order to get comprehensive freeze negotiations started. In straddling these political considerations, the document was deliberately vague.[111]

Mondale fended off Sen. Gary Hart (Colorado) and Jackson to win the party nomination. At O'Neill's prompting, Rep. Geraldine Ferraro (New York) became his running mate, the first woman to be nominated for national office by a major party. Mondale also had the support of the nuclear freeze movement. Helen Caldicott pronounced the Mondale–Reagan race as "the most important vote of the nuclear age." Peace groups, which raised about $6 million for the 1984 elections, began pouring in activists to work for the campaign (in some states the freeze staff outnumbered Mondale's).[112] Yet there were other issues on which to run. Inequality had risen during Reagan's term, with average income among the poorest one-fifth of families having declined by eight percent. By 1984, some thirteen million children lived below the poverty line— more than when Lyndon Johnson launched the "war on poverty" in 1964.[113] At his acceptance speech in July, Mondale berated Reagan's "unfair" economic policies and the budget deficit: "Let's tell the truth. Mr. Reagan will raise taxes and so will I. He won't tell you. I just did."[114] Along with tax increases, Mondale promised to reduce defense spending to $30 billion, the savings of which could be diverted into social programs, education, and the environment.[115]

But his campaign was struggling. The Democratic coalition which had fractured during the 1970s remained deeply divided. Working-class and middle-class Americans who previously voted Democrat had switched their loyalty to the GOP under Reagan and had not returned.[116] Mondale talked of taxes and deficits but failed to couch his message in a positive, optimistic tone (Jeane Kirkpatrick labeled him "bad news Fritz"). In contrast, Reagan could pursue a feel-good campaign, revolving around an economic recovery, low inflation, falling unemployment, and catchy patriotic slogans: the Olympian motto "Go for the Gold," and his campaign ad "It's Morning Again in America."[117] Mondale recalled: "By the spring of 1984 the economy had recovered from the 1980–82 recession, and Reagan's polls, which had dipped into the thirties for a time, were recovering nicely. It was Morning in America and he was pretending that we didn't exist." By June, as the Democratic Convention beckoned, Mondale had secured the delegates to become the party candidate. But he was now twenty-five points behind Reagan in the polls.[118]

FROM HAWK TO OWL

Despite holding the whip hand, Reagan's campaign team urged caution. Mondale's triumph in Pennsylvania during April, coupled with a lack of progress in foreign affairs, gave rise to reports about a narrowing race. "Peace through strength was the appeal Reagan sought to make in foreign policy," wrote the *Washington Post*'s Joseph Kraft. "But the peace dividend supposed to come with strength has not followed. The Russians have given the wet mitten to Washington's appeals in the arms control field. Dispatches from Moscow belie the administration's hope that the Soviets will come round soon."[119] As Reagan's chief of staff and campaign director, James Baker was by far the most important among the "troika" of political advisers. He had persuaded the president to withdraw U.S. forces from Lebanon (against the advice of Shultz), and continued to sound warnings about the foreign policy record.[120] The "hyping" of events in Central America by Democrats called for a "tricky balancing act." "We have to defend our policy, credibly suggest the threat to America ('on our own continent, with a 300-mile open border'), without going so far as to raise the specter of Vietnam," Baker advised. On issues such as East–West relations there was little sense of achievement, prompting awkward questions. "What have we really accomplished? Is the world really safer? My opinion remains that we must put extremely high priority on finding a way to show positive accomplishment."[121]

For ideas McFarlane reached out to Richard Nixon, whose election-year exploits in 1972 had yielded arms control agreements and a Moscow summit. Nixon suggested that Reagan actively support Senate approval of the Threshold Test Ban Treaty, and express his willingness to have a Comprehensive Test Ban. ("Why not?" Reagan wrote.) Given the Soviet concerns over SDI, Nixon recommended that Reagan offer to share whatever technology the United States developed in the field. He likened the idea to Eisenhower's "Open Skies" proposal in 1955. "They would probably turn it down," Nixon added. But the offer itself would "completely demolish" the Soviet argument that the concept was based around offensive missiles.[122]

SDI was emerging as a major obstacle to progress. Dobrynin told Shultz that the issue could become "the most dangerously destabilizing factor" in the relationship. The Soviets wanted to begin talks to avoid "the militarization of outer space," and proposed a moratorium on anti-satellite tests. The Reagan administration was willing to discuss the matter privately—but not in public—until the START and INF negotiations had resumed. U.S. policymakers stressed the relationship between offensive and defensive missiles.[123] Reagan was not (yet) ready to take up the suggestion of sharing technology on ballistic missile defense research. He skimmed over the subject in a letter to Chernenko on

April 16, claiming that the Soviets had been engaged in similar research efforts for years. Instead, Reagan pointed to the "considerable flexibility" the United States was displaying elsewhere. He expressed disappointment that the Soviets had not shown the same degree of compromise, or taken up the offer of private talks on arms control. But the thrust of his message was again positive. "We are prepared to consider any equitable outcome [...] and to halt, reverse, or eliminate entirely our deployments of Pershing and cruise missiles in the context of an agreement between the two sides." In his postscript, Reagan tried the human touch, reflecting on "the tragedy and scale of Soviet losses in warfare through the ages."[124]

Chernenko did not respond for nearly two months. The delay was no surprise. The Soviets were biding their time as they monitored U.S. political developments. From the Kremlin's viewpoint there was no urgency to expedite talks. But it did arrive at another decision during April: to withdraw the USSR from the 1984 Olympic Games in Los Angeles. Soviet leaders had long recognized that top-level international sport was tied to the intricacies of diplomacy. The World Cup and Olympics played such a role in Soviet foreign relations. In 1973, the Soviet soccer team was drawn to play Chile (then led by the socialist government of Salvador Allende) in a qualification decider for the 1974 World Cup finals. The Soviets won the first leg in Moscow. But by the time of the second leg in Santiago, the Allende government had been overthrown in a military coup d'état. The Chilean national stadium was used as a giant prison: socialists, communists, and other resisters were executed on the field. After FIFA refused Moscow's request to move the game to a neutral venue, the Soviets withdrew their participation.[125]

The decision to boycott the Los Angeles Olympics was linked to retribution (for the U.S. boycott of the 1980 Moscow Olympics) and to underscore the poor state of bilateral relations ahead of the election. In late April, the Soviet media and sports officials alleged that the U.S. had "violated" the Olympic charter and was seeking to make political capital out of the games. The State Department refuted the charges, instructing American embassies in Eastern Europe to emphasize that athletes from all nations were welcome.[126] Reagan wrote to Chernenko on May 3. He explained that he had assured IOC President Juan Antonio Samaranch that all Soviet athletes would be welcomed and that the Olympic charter would be upheld.[127] But his efforts were for nought. The USSR officially announced its withdrawal five days later, claiming that the Reagan administration "does not intend to ensure the security of Soviet athletes."

Fourteen Soviet allies followed suit. A statement by the Soviet Olympic Committee accused the administration of being in "direct connivance" with extremist groups seeking to create "unbearable conditions" for Soviet participants. It claimed that anti-Soviet propaganda and threats against athletes were part of the U.S. plan to use the Olympics for "political gain." Officials further alleged that right-wing groups in Los Angeles were attempting to help Soviet athletes to defect.[128]

Reagan took it in his stride. On a European tour soon after, he told the Duke of Edinburgh: "Communist morality supports whatever enhances Communism. Therefore, whatever enables Soviet and East European athletes to win, including drug-taking, is good." Over lunch, British Ambassador Oliver Wright suggested to Reagan that the Soviet withdrawal would "backfire" and aid his election bid. "You can say that again!" Reagan replied with a large laugh. But the president switched tone. He talked about the Soviet fear of invasion, their experiences in the Second World War, and his efforts to engage Chernenko. Reporting to London, Wright observed: "While he has not changed suddenly from a hawk to a dove, it is also very clear that he realizes we have to live with the Russians on the same planet and is searching in his mind for ways of doing business with them. Maybe he has become an owl."[129]

DIPLOMATIC OFFENSIVE

While progress on START and INF was being stymied, the administration worked on building a record of agreements elsewhere, as per Reagan's directive. A series of bilateral accords were pursued through diplomatic backchannels. The aim was to restore U.S.–Soviet contact levels to those which existed prior to the invasion of Afghanistan. New proposals were expedited in other areas of arms control. A draft chemical weapons treaty was tabled at the Committee on Disarmament in Geneva on April 18. A modified MBFR proposal was presented to the Soviets in Vienna. And on CDE issues, James Goodby (head of the U.S. delegation) traveled to Moscow to listen to Soviet ideas. There was also a hive of diplomatic activity on nonmilitary issues. They ranged from new agreements on cultural exchanges and reopening consulates in Kiev and New York, to cooperative agreements on agriculture, the environment, fishing, health, and housing. Factsheets on the record of U.S. attempts to engage the Soviets since January 1984 were circulated internally for use as talking points.[130] In total, the administration proposed joint activities in sixteen areas with the Soviet Union—something that Reagan was not shy about expressing on the campaign trail.[131]

Reagan approved these initiatives despite the worsening human rights situation in the USSR. The most prominent dissident, Andrei Sakharov (a nuclear physicist), was planning a hunger strike in a bid to force Soviet authorities to allow his wife, Yelena Bonner, to leave the country to receive medical treatment. Bonner, who suffered from a heart condition, was a founding member of the Moscow Helsinki Watch Group. When Sakharov was exiled to the closed city of Gorky in 1980, she became an outspoken critic of the Soviet human rights record. In April 1984, Bonner sent letters to the U.S. embassy in Moscow, explaining Sakharov's protest and appealing for temporary refuge. But housing Bonner during the hunger strike would pose political problems. Shultz told Reagan: "It would be very difficult for the Soviets to give her exit permission while she was staying in our embassy. The major diplomatic confrontation that would ensue would very likely bring the rest of our dialogue to a standstill." The Sakharov case reflected the plight of Soviet Jewry (and human rights activists generally), and Reagan received letters from special interest groups on their behalf. He was not insensitive. Reagan had raised the human rights issue in a letter to Chernenko two days before learning of the Sakharov–Bonner case. A further draft letter to Chernenko was prepared for Reagan's consideration—specifically appealing for the Soviets to grant Bonner an exit permission—but there is no record of it being sent.[132]

Human rights in the USSR would not begin to improve until 1985, with the arrival of a new Soviet leader. (Bonner was duly allowed to travel to America.) In the meantime, Reagan sanctioned increased U.S.–Soviet contacts, as his administration pursued a string of bilateral agreements. The initiatives prompted some opposition from within government agencies. A leading critic was John Lenczowski, the hardline NSC director of Soviet and European Affairs, who noted the departure from NSDD-75. "How can we conduct business-as-usual with the USSR when it has been behaving so abominably," he complained.[133] "Taken together, these [initiatives] add up to a relationship of wholesale cooperation with the Soviets which amounts to a revival of the détente relationship established by President Nixon." Lenczowski pointed to the Soviet war in Afghanistan, the KAL shootdown, human rights abuses, and noncompliance with arms treaties. He questioned why the administration was now ditching the policy of sanctions it had pursued over the past three years. "Perhaps the strategy underlying this has appeared in secret documents which I have not seen," Lenczowski wrote. "What I have been able to see is a rather under-articulated policy of 'intensified dialogue'."[134]

Matlock rejected the argument. There was, he acknowledged, a political need to counter anti-Reagan propaganda. But Matlock believed the initiatives would also yield long-term benefits. The expansion of contacts with Soviet citizens was part of a strategy which aimed to apply pressure on the Kremlin over the coming years. "Cutting the Soviet Union off from contact with us is simply not in our long-term interest," Matlock argued. He saw little point in continuing sanctions which were undermining U.S. attempts to deal with the Soviets.[135] On February 18, Matlock and McFarlane drew Reagan's attention to an article by James Billington, director of the Wilson Center and an expert on Russian history. Billington called on the administration to think strategically, and reach out to the Soviet public by expanding bilateral exchanges. New agreements would help expose the younger generation to American life, and might over time lead to "more realistic and less rigid Soviet policies." Billington's arguments chimed with Shultz's four-part framework. The bilateral initiatives could serve as the basis for a more fruitful relationship—once the long-anticipated generational shift took place in Moscow. Chernenko's illness was no secret, and the younger, reform-minded Gorbachev was the favorite to succeed him.[136] To highlight the new efforts to promote contacts, Reagan delivered a speech to a specially organized "American Conference on U.S.–Soviet Exchanges" at the White House on June 27. Although most were renewals of earlier (pre-1980) agreements, he listed the "sensible and comprehensive proposals to improve the U.S.–Soviet dialogue and our working relationship."[137]

Since January, the Soviets had done everything possible to avoid contributing to Reagan's effort to persuade the public that relations with Moscow were improving. But by June the Kremlin had grudgingly concluded that Mondale's campaign was doomed; a Gallup Poll in late May gave Reagan a handsome lead over his Democratic opponents.[138] Moreover, a new American anti-satellite weapons (ASAT) system was about to enter its early testing stage. Thus, in addition to discussing bilateral projects, Soviet leaders grew receptive to the idea of reopening arms talks and a possible high-level meeting. The Soviet logic was that it was better to deal with Reagan in flexible campaign mode, rather than after the election when U.S. views might stiffen. Moscow showed increased interest in anti-satellite and antimissile space weaponry, and proposed a moratorium agreement on testing.[139] "It was important that we reckoned on Reagan as the likely winner," recalled Dobrynin. "It was simply bad politics to be too brutal to someone we would probably have to deal with for another four years. The Politburo came to the same conclusion."[140] On July 5, a Soviet embassy official in Belgrade told the State Department that "last month" Moscow had decided to "unfreeze" relations with the United States before the election.[141]

Chernenko's reply to Reagan's letter (April 16) finally arrived on June 6. It was likely drafted by Gromyko and the tone was defensive. Chernenko criticized the U.S. response to Soviet proposals to avoid "the militarization of outer space." He complained that the USSR was "encircled by a chain of American military bases" and by the INF missiles "on our doorstep."[142] But Chernenko promised to send delegations to negotiate on chemical weapons in Geneva and on MBFR in Vienna. On June 29, Dobrynin proposed that the two sides hold a conference in September to deal with SDI. Reagan called it "an excellent idea."[143] But the plans broke down for familiar reasons. The administration argued that SDI could not be discussed independently of START and INF; negotiations on defensive and offensive missiles were interrelated. Nitze claimed that this "linkage" tactic was the best way of pressuring the Soviets ("the demandeurs") to make concessions on the issues of interest to America—the reduction of strategic and intermediate-range nuclear forces.[144] Additionally, the United States resisted Soviet demands for a moratorium on testing space weapons, offering only to try to agree on "limitations."[145] Soviet officials declared that bilateral relations were "hostage to the extreme right-wing" of the Republican Party. Hardliners such as Perle and Weinberger were blamed for blocking attempts at a serious dialogue.[146] The Department of Defense, which was originally appalled by SDI, had by now transformed its views. Weinberger called it "an inspired vision."[147]

*

While these diplomatic volleys were not yet yielding concrete results, the broad effect was important. The two sides were engaging publicly and more intensively about arms talks than at any stage since at least mid-1983.[148] Moreover, a string of nonmilitary, bilateral agreements were due to be renewed. A thaw in U.S.–Soviet relations had gradually developed over the first seven months of 1984. The improved atmosphere was reflected by a new push for a summit ahead of the election—at home and abroad. Western leaders called on Reagan to meet with the Soviets. In early March, Helmut Kohl encouraged Reagan to "probe" for a summit with Chernenko, believing the Soviets would respond positively.[149] At the Economic Summit in London in June (where a crowd of 50,000 protested against the INF missiles), Canadian Prime Minister Pierre Trudeau told the president to be "more forthcoming" with Moscow. Irritated, Reagan removed his glasses and snapped: "Damn it Pierre, I've said everything! What the hell more can I do to get those guys back to the table? You're telling me we haven't done it?"[150]

Domestic pressure for a top-level meeting was also growing. Reagan's personal popularity was not translating to the Republican Party. Under-pressure politicians, up for reelection, urged the president to hold a summit with Chernenko in line with the broad wishes of the public.[151] Among the most vocal were Senate Majority Leader Howard Baker (R-Tennessee) and Charles Percy (R-Illinois), chairman of the Senate Foreign Relations Committee. Percy was trailing Democratic rival Paul Simon in his fight for political survival. On June 13, he and Baker launched a public appeal for Reagan to meet with the Soviet leader, regardless of the state of arms talks. After holding court with Reagan, the senators took their case to the press from the White House driveway. "Let's just get together and talk about the world situation, because we've got to figure out some way not to blow each other up," declared Baker (who was retiring his seat). "When you have changed circumstances, you ought to change your strategy." He said it was "anachronistic" for Reagan to insist on the promise of results as his price for a summit. Percy denied that political motives were behind his appeal. "It's been five years since we met with our chief adversaries," he argued. "We ought not to wait any longer. This is the time to make that initiative."[152]

Reagan was moved to defend himself that evening at a press conference, where he stated his readiness for a summit.[153] But behind the scenes the administration was sending out feelers to Moscow. With his reputation as a budding reformer, Mikhail Gorbachev had been targeted as an interlocu-tor. Bush sought to arrange a meeting with him in Geneva. (The administra-tion kept this quiet, fearing accusations of "political posturing.")[154] In a private conversation, Bush told Viktor Israelyan (Soviet ambassador to the Committee on Disarmament) that he would welcome a meeting with "your next leader, Gorbachev." But Israelyan worried that the Soviet foreign ministry would view a Bush–Gorbachev meeting as an American ruse, and decided not to relay the message to Moscow.[155]

Reagan was warned about appearing too eager for a meeting. "We must carefully avoid any actions which lead the Soviets to believe that you need a summit for your reelection," wrote McFarlane and Matlock. "The political pressures on you are of course evident to them, but [...] if the Soviets conclude your motivation is largely political, they will either refuse to play or will ask an exorbitant price and be attracted to strategems to embarrass you."[156] It was not until August that an opening emerged. The administration received signals from Soviet diplomats that Gromyko (who was due to attend the UN General Assembly in New York) would welcome a meeting with Reagan. Gromyko had not been received at the White House since the invasion of Afghanistan. Shultz relayed the news to Reagan on August 13. "We would be reinstating something without a change in Afghanistan," he explained. "But if we could get something going that would be a little more constructive, that would be helpful. Perhaps you'd like to consider whether to invite Gromyko this fall." Reagan did not hesitate. "It's the right thing to do," he replied. "Try to work it out."[157]

Reagan's decision to invite Gromyko was made days after an embarrassing political gaffe. On August 11, Reagan veered off-script during his weekly radio address, delivered from his California ranch. While testing out the microphone he jokingly remarked: "My fellow Americans, I am pleased to tell you today that I've signed legislation that will outlaw Russia forever. We begin bombing in five minutes." The words were recorded by CBS and CNN, among others. The faux pas seemed to vindicate the strategists' insistence on a cautious, low-key campaign: the risks in "letting Reagan be Reagan" appeared to outweigh the advantages. As Lou Cannon recalled, Reagan's advisers "were convinced by mid-summer that he could not be defeated unless he did something to beat himself."[158] It was not the first such incident. During a radio voice check in October 1982, Reagan described the Polish military government as "a bunch of lousy no good bums"—words that were broadcast by ABC and NBC.[159] The Soviets called the latest remarks "unprecedentedly hostile to the USSR and dangerous to the cause of peace," citing "doctrines of protracted nuclear war." TASS charged Reagan with having "babbled out" real attitudes which he had been forced to recently keep quiet because of the election. In response, the State Department accused Moscow of "blowing the subject way out of proportion for propaganda exercises."[160] But behind the scenes, Republican strategists winced. "I don't think it's very funny," Mondale told the press. "What does Mr. Reagan really believe? What he says when he knows the camera's on, or when he thinks the microphone's off?"[161]

REAGAN MEETS GROMYKO

The microphone incident had died down by the time Andrei Gromyko arrived in New York. Soviet foreign minister since 1957, he was the Cold

War's great survivor. At 75, Gromyko had served under Stalin, Khrushchev, and Brezhnev, and was nine years older than the Soviet Union itself. His diplomatic career stretched back to 1939, when he came to America as a chargé d'affaires. George Shultz was then a freshman at Princeton and Ronald Reagan was starring in *Naughty but Nice*. The Byelorussian had met with every U.S. president dating back to Franklin Roosevelt, and fourteen secretaries of state. One of his former counterparts, Cyrus Vance, suggested that Gromyko gave the Soviets "the advantage of an institutional memory, a memory that helps protect you from pitfalls you've experienced in the past."[162] But by 1984, his longevity was more a problem than a virtue. Shultz viewed Gromyko as a symbol of communism's "tragic flaw." "He believed the Marxist dogma he preached," Shultz recalled. "To him, the laws, institutions, and values of the West were bourgeois deceptions [...] He was comfortable with the Cold War. His mind was lodged somewhere around 1948, but these were the 1980s."[163]

With Chernenko in failing health (his emphysema and heart arrhythmia had worsened), Gromyko was still leading Soviet foreign policy. He shook hands with Reagan at a UN reception on September 23. It was the president's first direct contact with a top-ranking Soviet official during nearly four years in office. Reagan told Gromyko that he wanted "a realistic, constructive, long-term relationship," but their brief talk was drowned out by the piano tune, *Take the A Train*.[164] The next three days saw Reagan deliver a conciliatory speech at the UN, while Gromyko met with Shultz and Mondale. The Democratic presidential nominee told the press that it was "pretty pathetic" that Reagan's first encounter with a Soviet leader would be with the foreign minister rather than the "top man" Chernenko.[165]

On September 28, Reagan met with Gromyko for two hours in the Oval Office. Despite the press coverage there were no expectations for a major breakthrough. And none would be achieved. The meeting was more symbolic than substantive. Reagan tried to convince the foreign minister of his dream for "a world without nuclear arms." He told Gromyko: "We can't accomplish anything talking about each other. We have to talk *to* each other." Gromyko called nuclear disarmament "the question of all questions," agreeing that the ultimate goal should be the elimination of all nuclear weapons. Their conversation did not drift into details, and both men were happy to focus instead on general principles.[166] While no new agreements were reached, the meeting had been amicable. Gromyko found Reagan to be "very courteous" and detected "no frostiness." Arthur Hartman, who spoke with Reagan after-ward, recalled the president's relief at having passed "the Gromyko test." Reagan joked that having debated the Soviet foreign minister, Mondale would not be a problem. After the meeting, the two men attended a pre-lunch reception, where they were greeted by Nancy Reagan. As the event drew to a close, Gromyko took the First Lady aside. "Does your husband believe in peace?" he asked quietly. "Yes of course," she replied. "Then whisper 'peace' in your husband's ear every night," Gromyko said. "Oh sure," replied the First Lady. "But I'll whisper it in your ear too." She leaned over with a smile and whispered, "Peace." Gromyko's face broke into a wide grin.[167]

REAGAN VERSUS MONDALE

Reagan took it easy on the campaign trail, as was his wont. Speeches and audiences were carefully prepackaged, and the president rarely expressed original thoughts. He took an eighteen-day vacation at Rancho del Cielo between late July and mid-August, and was well rested for the home straight. Perhaps too well rested. When the first televised debate began, the "great communicator" was out of practice. He fluffed lines, overused statistics, and failed to make coherent arguments. This was the downside of not "letting Reagan be Reagan." David Broder of the *Washington Post* likened Mondale's display in Louisville to that of Kennedy against Nixon in 1960. Mondale, he wrote, "managed to sound and look sharper than his older, better-known and more credentialed opponent." Reagan's strategists had a rethink, and brought in media guru Roger Ailes ("Dr. Feelgood") to help restore morale.

By the time of the second debate in Kansas City, Reagan had recovered his poise. In a more assured (but not vintage) performance, he placed Mondale on the defensive. Reagan acted upon Nixon's suggestion, stating his willingness to share SDI technology with the Soviet Union. He also added a touch of wit. The moderator, Henry Trewhitt, noted that Reagan (73) was the oldest president in U.S. history, and had been criticized for looking tired in the first debate. "I recall [...] that President Kennedy had to go for days on end with very little sleep during the Cuban Missile Crisis," Trewhitt said. "Is there any doubt in your mind that you would be able to function in such circumstances?" Reagan replied: "Not at all, Mr. Trewhitt. And I want you to know that I will not make age an issue of this campaign. I am not going to exploit, for political purposes, my opponent's youth and inexperience." The audience and Mondale broke into laughter.[168] Reagan was on course for reelection, and the one-liner had been the coup de grâce. On November 6, Reagan won 525 electoral votes (to Mondale's 13) and carried forty-nine states. He secured 58.8 percent of the popular vote, having won the support of large swathes of southern Democrats. The Republican Party was less successful. Democrats kept control of the House (although the GOP won sixteen seats), while Republicans retained their grip on the Senate despite losing two seats. Among the casualties was Charles Percy (R-Illinois), chairman of the Senate Foreign Relations Committee.[169]

THATCHER, GORBACHEV, AND THE RETURN TO ARMS TALKS

The landslide victory strengthened Reagan's negotiating hand at home and abroad. In late 1984 and early 1985, he launched a two-pronged offensive: pressing the Soviets to engage in serious arms talks, while lobbying Congress to fund new weapons systems (the MX and SDI) to aid U.S. diplomatic efforts.[170] Soon after the election, Washington and Moscow agreed to resume formal arms control talks in Geneva in January 1985. It scotched rumors that Reagan would reverse his policy of seeking accommodation with the Soviets now that he had won a second term. There were, however, changes in personnel. James Baker, a success as chief of staff, left the White House for the relative sanctuary of the Treasury. He swapped places with Treasury Secretary Don Regan, a combative figure whose spell as chief of staff would prove to be an unhappy experience. Edwin Meese also left the White House (to become Attorney General), while Jeane Kirkpatrick prepared to step down as ambassador to the UN, bequeathing her position to Vernon Walters.

But the election did nothing to resolve the long-running feud between Shultz and Weinberger. Reagan's decision to back Shultz's strategy— pursuing closer bilateral ties and agreeing to meet Gromyko—had angered the defense secretary and other hardliners (e.g., Casey, Kirkpatrick, Perle, Lenczowski), who felt that the United States should not be rewarding the Soviets until they changed their policies. Weinberger took his case to conservative allies, who duly told Reagan of their dissatisfaction with Shultz. The secretary of state, they claimed, had "gone soft with the Russians."[171] Reagan dismissed the idea of removing Shultz. But a series of leaks to the press from the Defense Department (intelligence information concerning the USSR) brought the issue to a head.[172] Shultz marched into the Oval Office to tell Reagan: "We have to have a unified posture, and you have to do something about it [...] It's a good time to go. I've been here

now a certain amount of time. I'll go and do something else." Reagan said
he would think about it but made it clear that he wanted Shultz to remain.
The president would never "lay it out" to Weinberger, to whom he was
personally close. But there was no doubt as to where Reagan placed his
trust. He told McFarlane: "If I were to fire George and put Cap over at
State, I would get bad policy. So I'm not going to do that. George is the man
I want there. But I'm not going to fire Cap. He's my friend." Looking to
McFarlane as an intermediary, Reagan asked him to "make it work."[173]

Reagan called several NSPG meetings ahead of the Geneva talks. As
with earlier rounds in 1984, Reagan's input was far greater than in the
previous three years, when he tended to play a peripheral role. All of the
usual suspects attended, including Paul Nitze, who became the president's
new "special adviser" on arms control. The 77-year-old had been a fixture
of the diplomatic establishment for four decades, serving as Truman's
director of policy planning in the State Department, and authoring NSC-
68, which became the blueprint for U.S. policy in the Cold War. The idea
for a new role came from Shultz, who held Nitze in high regard and
wanted to avoid further interagency squabbles. Decisions would now be
made through the Reagan–Shultz–Nitze axis. To outflank Weinberger,
Shultz installed Nitze in an office on the seventh floor of the State
Department, just around the corner from his own.[174] Nitze was not
universally popular. The hardliners considered him soft, citing his
"Walk in the Woods" gambit, while some moderates found him implacable. Richard Burt (assistant secretary of state for European affairs)
groaned to Shultz: "What's behind the Nitze thing? He's 77. He doesn't
take orders. He's too iconoclastic." Shultz waved away the complaints.[175]

The main topic of debate was how to broach SDI, a prime source of
Soviet concern. Moscow had agreed to return to negotiations on the
understanding that both nuclear and space arms would be on the agenda.
This condition dismayed the likes of Weinberger, who felt that SDI should
not be up for discussion. Reagan's views were straightforward: all nuclear
weapons should be eliminated, and strategic defense should serve as
deterrence. He said that SDI gave the U.S. "a great deal of leverage"
over the Soviets. "We have no objections to their having defenses, but
we have to look at defenses for ourselves," Reagan told officials. "They
are afraid of SDI. We must show them how defenses are not threatening
[...] make it clear that we are not seeking advantage, only defense."
Assuaging Soviet fears would be no easy task. The administration was
struggling to promote SDI domestically, with opposition from within
Congress and the media. "The Russians may bet that the United States

cannot sell its SDI program at home," McFarlane argued. "We need to get support for strategic defense." Reagan joked: "We can start by canceling our subscriptions to the *Washington Post*." While the president was willing to show flexibility elsewhere, he remained attached to SDI. He said it should not be used as "the price for [arms] reductions," likening the situation to "a duel between two gunfighters." "Our policy of MAD could get us both killed," Reagan warned. "It's just too dangerous."[176]

Reagan's views on SDI were not shared by Margaret Thatcher, who invited Mikhail Gorbachev to Britain in December. Gorbachev was effectively in charge at the Politburo, with Chernenko gravely ill.[177] He was the most prominent in a younger generation of political figures intent on reforming the Soviet system. Overlooked for the top job in February, Gorbachev arrived at Chequers (Thatcher's country retreat) knowing that he was next in line to succeed Chernenko. Here was an early chance to weaken Gromkyo's grip on foreign policy. By going to England, "we'll gradually erode the monopoly," Gorbachev told his adviser, Anatoly Chernyaev.[178] An intense discussion went even better than British diplomats could have expected. Thatcher and Gorbachev disagreed on plenty— trading blows over ideology, economics, and human rights. But the prime minister came away impressed. She found Gorbachev "attractive and charming." Gorbachev's humor, energy, and readiness to discuss all manner of things was a contrast from the usual staid approach of Soviet apparatchiks. Thatcher also enjoyed the intellectual tête-à-tête—something she never experienced in her meetings with Reagan. "I like Mr. Gorbachev. We can do business together," Thatcher told the press afterward.

Arms control and strategic defense were hotly debated at Chequers. Thatcher told Gorbachev that Reagan's "dream" of ridding the world of nuclear weapons was "not viable." The pursuit of a ballistic missile defense would "lead to a fresh twist in the arms race spiral." Gorbachev noted the gap between Reagan and Thatcher's views on SDI, and played to her sense of independence. He quoted Lord Palmerston's famous dictum: "Nations have no permanent friends or allies; they only have permanent interests." "Tell your friend Reagan not to go ahead with space weapons," Gorbachev said to Thatcher. Otherwise, "the Russians would either develop their own, or more probably, develop new offensive systems superior to SDI." Gorbachev cited the influence of Perle and Weinberger, complaining that in four years of Reagan "not a single step forward has been taken in U.S.–Soviet relations."[179]

On December 22, Thatcher traveled to Camp David to brief Reagan on the Gorbachev meeting. "I certainly found him a man one could do business with. I actually rather liked him," she explained. But Thatcher added: "I got the impression that in some ways he was using me as a stalking horse for you [...] he was on the look-out for possible divergences of view between us." Thatcher said that she had warned Gorbachev against trying to drive a wedge between the allies. She believed the Soviets were "genuinely fearful" about the costs of the technological advances of the arms race, and were "prepared to negotiate seriously on nuclear weapons if they believe that you are politically committed to reductions." Thatcher did not repeat what she had uttered to Gorbachev about Reagan's "dream" of a nuclear-free world. But she did tell Reagan of her "real worries about SDI's impact on deterrence." Indeed, Thatcher doubted that the system was feasible: "In the past, scientific genius had always developed a counter system. Even if an SDI system proved 95 percent successful [...] over 60 million people would still die from those weapons that got through." An awkward silence followed. "Reagan was taken aback," McFarlane recalled. "He had heard it through us, but it was palpable across the table from the prime minister." Reagan listened but was not for turning on SDI. He agreed to a four-point press statement (hoping to quell reports of disagreements), and duly set off for his New Year's holiday in Palm Springs.[180]

Shultz broadened the U.S. delegation for the Geneva meeting on January 7, 1985. In a bid to improve teamwork, all of the key players were invited. They included "dissenters" such as Perle and Adelman, and moderates such as Burt and McFarlane. The prospect of archrivals traveling together attracted media attention. The plane carrying the U.S. team was dubbed "the ship of feuds," a tribute to the battle of the "two Richards" (Burt and Perle).[181] But the figures who mattered most in Switzerland were Shultz and Gromkyo. In a six-hour session they discussed three broad arms subjects: strategic weapons (START), the intermediate-range missiles in Europe (INF), and the newer area of space weaponry (SDI). The latter was the main source of disagreement. Following Reagan's lead, Shultz tried to convince Gromkyo that strategic defense systems "could contribute to the goal of eventually eliminating all nuclear weapons." Gromyko would have none of it. "The U.S. calls this a defensive concept, but the Soviet Union does not share this view. We see it as part of a general offensive plan [...] Isn't it simpler to eliminate nuclear weapons themselves? Why should our two countries spend their material and intellectual resources developing such a system?" Gromyko knew that the Soviets trailed America in economic power and advanced military technologies. He told Shultz: "The U.S. wants to gain advantage over the Soviet Union, and the defensive system if developed would be used to bring pressure on us. Let us not mince words: the system would be used to blackmail the USSR."[182]

There was a further dispute about whether the three areas (START, INF, and SDI) were interrelated. Gromyko accepted that there was a natural connection between offensive and defensive weaponry. But he insisted on a double linkage of the areas. There could be no agreement on INF, he said, without a deal on START. And there could be no agreement on either of those weapons systems without an accord on "space weapons." Shultz rejected the demands, stressing that progress in one area should not prevent movement in others. Sensing that talks were going nowhere, the two sides agreed to a joint communique, so vague and abstract that nobody could quite fathom what it meant. The text merely outlined the parameters for talks, with the tough debates postponed for the next round. But the outcome satisfied both delegations, allowing them to announce an agreement to restart negotiations. After the lows of 1983, that itself was progress.[183]

*

Reagan's move to the center had proved a success. By early 1985, the United States and the Soviet Union had moved toward a less confrontational relationship. Reagan's shift—dispensing with bellicose rhetoric; indicating new flexibility on START and INF; pursuing a wide range of bilateral agreements; inviting Gromyko to the White House—had lowered tensions and brought the Soviets back to arms talks, without conceding ground on matters of substance. He made these decisions without any real movement from Moscow. As Matlock recalled, "there was no fundamental change in Soviet policy." Still, in Geneva the Soviets had accepted the "organic relationship" between offensive and defensive weapons. It marked a change from their previous insistence on treating SDI separately from START and INF. The Reagan administration could continue to use SDI as leverage in the quest to reduce Soviet offensive weapons.[184] A sign of the improving relations was the visit of a Soviet parliamentary group to America in early March. It was led by Vladimir Shcherbitsky, the Ukrainian Communist Party chief, who became the first Politburo member other than Gromyko to visit Washington since 1973. His tour included a meeting with Reagan on March 7, in which they discussed the wartime cooperation between their nations.[185] Three days later Chernenko died, aged 73. A new leader was installed and with it, a new era in Soviet politics began.

9

Conciliation

In the early hours of March 11, Reagan was awakened by a phone call from McFarlane. He was told that Chernenko had died, and Mikhail Gorbachev was the new "head man" in the Kremlin. The news came as no surprise. Chernenko had been seriously ill for months, with Gorbachev acting as the de facto number two. Reagan would contend with the fourth different Soviet leader since taking office. "How am I supposed to get anyplace with the Russians if they keep dying on me?" he asked his wife, Nancy.[1] For the past decade, Soviet leaders had been too infirm to fully carry out their duties. Andropov's modest set of reforms lost momentum after his death in early 1984, as the conservative old guard resisted calls for change. The Soviet leaders' physical frailties seemed to personify the nation's problems: a declining economy, a disastrous war in Afghanistan, opposition from within Eastern Europe, and a range of negative social trends (declining life expectancy for males, rising infant mortality rates, and rampant alcoholism).[2]

Unlike his predecessors, Gorbachev sought to implement genuine economic and political reform. The direction it would take owed much to the Soviet leader and the new generation that held power in Moscow. In the USSR, there was little overt pressure from "below" to institute major changes. Had one of the conservative, nationalist elites succeeded Chernenko (such as Grigory Romanov or Viktor Grishin), Soviet policies in the late 1980s—and the Cold War—would have looked very different. Such was the hyper-centralized nature of the Soviet system.[3] Gorbachev knew that his domestic goals could not be achieved without adjusting foreign policy, and reducing the military expenses which drained the Soviet budget. A sign of his intent was the appointment of the reform-minded Shevardnadze as foreign minister in place of the veteran Gromyko. Between 1985 and 1989, Gorbachev would emerge as the critical agent of change in the Soviet Union and in the Cold War struggle with the United States. As author James Wilson notes, "[Gorbachev] pressed forward not because of SDI but in spite of it."[4]

For the newly reelected president, Gorbachev's arrival was perfectly timed. Riding a wave of popularity and political strength, Reagan stood by the policy of engagement and moderation. He rejected the advice of hardliners who persisted in opposing realistic negotiation. Weinberger continued to view the Soviet Union as a permanent enemy "bent on world conquest."[5] Despite his early misgivings, Reagan soon realized that Gorbachev was a "somewhat different breed" of Soviet leader.[6] The Geneva summit of November 1985—the first meeting of a U.S. and Soviet leader in six and a half years—marked a milestone in the late Cold War. Although no agreement on arms control emerged (none was expected), the meeting set a new tone for U.S.–Soviet relations. It provided a base for trust between two men with different backgrounds and philosophies.[7] Reagan and Gorbachev viewed the summit as a personal breakthrough. There were many issues to resolve, and Gorbachev's policies would evolve gradually. But the events of 1985 did much to allay the tension and mutual suspicion between the two nations.

ENTER GORBACHEV

Mikhail Gorbachev was born to a peasant family in 1931 in the Stavropol region of the North Caucasus. The family had suffered hardships. One of his grandfathers was deported to Siberia for failing to meet the government's sowing quota; the other grandfather, a collective farm organizer, was imprisoned as "an enemy of the people" during the Stalinist purges of the late 1930s. Gorbachev was 10 years old when the Nazis invaded the Soviet Union. His father (also a farmer) was conscripted into the Red Army to fight the Wermacht, leaving the young Mikhail at home with his mother. The Gorbachev family endured the occupation of their village (Privolnoye) by German armies from mid-1942 to early 1943. Gorbachev's father was wounded in battle, but ultimately survived.

Rather than continuing the family occupation, the ambitious Gorbachev set his sights beyond provincial life. He received top grades at school and worked the fields during the summer, earning the Order of the Red Banner of Labor. The award helped Gorbachev win a place at Moscow State University in 1950, where he would study law and meet his future wife, a philosophy student named Raisa Titarenko. He took to politics, joining the Communist Party in 1952—a time when Soviet ideology was imbued with the spirit of the "Great Patriotic War." Gorbachev was "deeply moved" by Stalin's death only months later. But during the early Khrushchev years, he came to view Stalin in a different light, noting that his own family were victims of the terror unleashed in the 1930s. Soon after graduating, Gorbachev ditched his pursuit of a legal career to join the Communist Youth League (Komsomol). Over the next two decades he rose rapidly through the political ranks. In 1970, Gorbachev became party chief for the Stavropol province in southern Russia. The political ascendance allowed him to travel overseas to gain a firsthand view of "bourgeois" nations such as France and Italy. Although Gorbachev believed that public education and health services were organized "more fairly" in the USSR, he was struck by the gulf in wealth between his nation and those in the West. "Why," he wondered, "do we live worse than other developed countries?" Gorbachev had a more cosmopolitan air than his Soviet contemporaries. He devoured the foreign political literature made available to top Soviet officials. He drew upon books written by West European communists for his intellectual development, and articles by social democrats such as Willy Brandt and François Mitterrand.[8]

By the 1970s, Gorbachev had struck up a relationship with Yuri Andropov, the powerful KGB chief. In 1978, he was promoted to the Central Committee as secretary for agriculture, becoming (at 47) the youngest member of the Politburo. Gorbachev was keen to bring about reform. He met with economists, hoping to decentralize authority and provide farmers with more responsibility and independence. But with the Politburo in "total disarray," little could be achieved. Brezhnev was too ill to organize serious initiatives, and most of the elderly hardliners were not keen on instituting change. The early 1980s saw a power struggle emerge between the conservative old guard and the younger reformers who were eager to explore new ideas. When Andropov succeeded Brezhnev in late 1982, Gorbachev was placed in charge of implementing modest economic reform. But Andropov was also an ill man, and his protégé concluded that serious reform was not yet possible. "[Andropov] was too deeply entrenched in his own past experience," Gorbachev noted. "It held him firmly in his grasp."[9] The Chernenko interlude saw Soviet economic and social problems worsen. Gorbachev presided over Politburo meetings in the general secretary's many absences, and fended off attacks from the hardliners. However, others were more sympathetic. "Everything's rotten. It has to be changed," he was told by Eduard Shevardnadze, first secretary of the Communist Party in Georgia, who had known Gorbachev since their days in the Komsomol.[10]

With the death of Ustinov (in December 1984) and Chernenko, the old guard gave way to a new generation of leaders. "An understanding was growing that the country could no longer endure another man of Chernenko's intellectual and political weakness," recalled Georgy Arbatov. "The country was so tired of the grey anonymity of the leadership that the problem of a successor was on everyone's mind. By the time of Chernenko's death the prevailing opinion was that the only worthy candidate was Mikhail Gorbachev."[11] Aged 54, Gorbachev was two decades younger than Chernenko (and Reagan), and thirteen years younger than the average age of the ten voting members of the Politburo. Gorbachev was appointed general secretary at a late-night Politburo meeting on March 10. He arrived back at his dacha outside Moscow at 4.00 am, where wife Raisa was awaiting his return. "I came to Moscow hoping and believing that I would be able to do something, but so far I haven't accomplished much," he told her. "It's impossible to achieve anything substantial, the things the country is waiting for. It's like coming up against a wall. If I really want to change anything, I have to accept the position. We just can't go on living like this."[12]

REAGAN AND GORBACHEV: THE EARLY EXCHANGES

The CIA had viewed Gorbachev positively since his emergence as Andropov's protégé in 1983. Thatcher's endorsement in late 1984 (after meeting Gorbachev at Chequers) only strengthened their conviction. But old verities died hard. U.S. intelligence worried that they were overlooking something fundamental about Gorbachev. Any protégé of Andropov had to have a tough exterior. "I don't much care for the way we are writing about Gorbachev," Gates told Robert Blackwell (CIA expert on Soviet affairs) in February 1985. "We are losing the thread of what toughness and skill brought him to where he is. This is not some Gary Hart or Lee Iacocca. We have to give the policymakers a clearer view of the kind of person they may be facing."[13] The CIA's first comprehensive analysis of Gorbachev would not arrive until mid-June.[14]

Reagan had no intention of going to Moscow for Chernenko's funeral. Aware of Chernenko's poor health, he had decided weeks earlier that the "funeral delegation" would consist of Bush, Shultz, and Hartman.[15] Instead he wrote a letter to Gorbachev, which was delivered by Bush and

Shultz at the Great Kremlin Palace on March 13. "You can be assured of my personal commitment to work with you and the rest of the Soviet leadership in serious negotiations," Reagan wrote. "In that spirit, I would like to invite you to visit me in Washington at your earliest convenient opportunity."[16] In a lively meeting, Gorbachev told the U.S. delegation that the Soviet Union was not interested in confrontation. He challenged the administration to demonstrate seriousness in the arms talks. "Is the United States really interested in achieving results at the talks or does it need them to implement its rearmament programs?" he asked. Bush conveyed Reagan's readiness to work with Moscow and his invitation to Gorbachev to visit Washington. While Gorbachev made no commitments, his response was positive. With both leaders beginning new terms in office, it was "a unique moment." Gorbachev added: "I am ready to return U.S.–Soviet relations to a normal channel. It is necessary to know each other, to find time for meetings to discuss outstanding problems, and to seek ways to bring the two countries together."[17]

The new Soviet leader spoke with an intensity and vigor that impressed the U.S. delegation. "In Gorbachev we have an entirely different kind of leader in the Soviet Union than we have experienced before," Shultz told Bush. Gorbachev was "quicker, fresher, more engaging" than his predecessors. He was also confident in his abilities, exchanging jokes with Gromyko during the meeting. Bush found Gorbachev to be "a smooth performer," informal and at ease when exchanging views. After a period of reflection, Shultz told the press on March 15: "Gorbachev is totally different from any Soviet leader I've met. But the U.S.–Soviet relationship is not just about personalities."[18] Privately, Gorbachev was more skeptical. "The general impression that the American delegation left is, I tell you honestly, quite mediocre. This is not a very serious team," he informed the Conference of Secretaries of the Communist Party. "When I touched upon questions that were outside of the text Bush had, he got lost. The only issue the Americans kept pushing was that President Reagan wishes to meet with the Soviet leadership, wishes to conduct negotiations. However, the message from the U.S. President is quite amorphous and general."[19]

But Gorbachev's reply to Reagan on March 24 was upbeat. He welcomed the idea of a summit, although he deferred a decision on the time and venue. Gorbachev stressed the need for joint efforts at the top level, "to give a proper impetus to our relations." Both sides had to tone down the rhetoric and avoid "whipping up animosity." The development of a more "peaceful, calm" relationship, he wrote, would help generate an atmosphere of mutual trust. Shultz was again impressed. He noted the complete absence of polemics, which contrasted with the correspondence of Gorbachev's predecessors.[20]

*

Just as progress seemed possible, U.S.–Soviet relations hit a new snag. On March 24, an American liaison officer, Major Arthur Nicholson, was killed by a sentry while photographing Soviet military material through the window of a tank storage facility in the East German town of Ludwigslust. The young Soviet soldier had shot him in the stomach and refused to allow Nicholson's driver (whom he held at gunpoint) to administer first aid. By the time medics arrived, Nicholson had bled to death. Nicholson was a member of the U.S. military liaison mission, stationed in Potsdam since 1947 with a mandate to observe activities in what was once the Soviet zone of occupied Germany.[21] The 1947 agreement allowed freedom of travel in occupation zones of the other side, but forbade entry into "places of disposition of military units without escort or supervision." It was the first time in many years that a military liaison officer was killed, and Washington and Moscow pointed the finger of blame at each other.[22]

Soviet diplomat Vladimir Kulagin issued a statement claiming that Nicholson had entered a prohibited area and disregarded warnings to halt. After attempting to escape he was then shot. Outraged U.S. officials rejected the explanation. Burt called the shooting "totally unjustified," stating that Nicholson's death was tantamount to "murder."[23] Weinberger likened the incident to the KAL shootdown. He demanded that negotiations with the Soviets be terminated (the arms talks had only resumed on March 14[24]) and that compensation be paid to Nicholson's family.[25] Other hardliners followed suit. Lenczowski alerted McFarlane to a *Wall Street Journal* article—duly relayed to Reagan—which claimed that the order to kill Nicholson was issued by the Politburo.[26]

Reagan rejected the advice. He said that the commanders of both sides in Germany should meet, regardless of a Soviet apology or compensation, to avoid a repetition of the incident. The suggestion for a meeting came from Soviet officials and had the support of the State Department, NSC, and the Joint Chiefs of Staff. Weinberger refused to comply, calling it a "love and kisses" session with the murderers of a U.S. officer. He publicly expressed dismay at "opinion-leaders" for "measur[ing] the effect of Nicholson's murder on the atmosphere of East–West relations."[27] Reagan told Shultz that he was being "clobbered" by

Weinberger and the hardliners for wanting to meet with Gorbachev.[28] But rather than making him unwilling to have a summit, Reagan said the incident made him "more anxious to go to one."[29] Shultz was supportive. "We protested vigorously and immediately," he recalled. "But I would not let 'linkage' come into play; our movement toward a better overall U.S.–Soviet relationship would not be derailed."[30] On April 4, Reagan sent another letter to Gorbachev. The president reiterated his hope for a more constructive relationship between the two countries. "I believe that new opportunities are now opening up in U.S.–Soviet relations. We must take advantage of them," Reagan wrote. "There are such opportunities in every area of our relations, including humanitarian, regional, bilateral, and arms control issues." Reagan was "appalled" by the "senseless killing" of Nicholson, and suggested that the two sides take steps to prevent any reoccurrence.[31]

Reagan's letter would be delivered on April 10 by Tip O'Neill, who was visiting Moscow as head of a congressional delegation. In the meantime, Gorbachev gave his first public reaction to his correspondence with Reagan. The Soviet leader told *Pravda* that both sides had expressed a "positive attitude." "I am convinced that a serious impulse should be given to U.S.–Soviet relations at a high political level," Gorbachev explained. "Confrontation is not an inborn defect in our relations. It is, rather, an anomaly. There is no inevitability that it should remain." Gorbachev used the occasion to push two arms control initiatives. He announced a six-month moratorium on the deployment of Soviet intermediate-range missiles in Europe, which could be made permanent if the United States agreed to stop placing Pershing IIs and cruise missiles in Europe. The White House flatly rejected the idea. The Soviet deployment of SS-20s was already far advanced, while NATO was still in the early stages of its deployment. The Reagan administration claimed that the proposal was "nothing new," and would give the Soviets a 10–1 advantage in nuclear warheads in Europe. Soon after, Gorbachev proposed a moratorium on all nuclear testing. Washington also rejected this idea. The Soviets had just concluded a series of tests, while U.S. officials were leery of unverified moratoria, citing Khrushchev's violations of an agreement with John F. Kennedy. Matlock believed that an unverified U.S.–Soviet moratorium could pose a threat to the broader arms talks, and was more likely to fuel a climate of "mutual suspicion and recrimination."[32]

O'Neill led a bipartisan delegation in a four-hour meeting with Gorbachev on April 10. In advance, Reagan had asked O'Neill to vouch for his sincere desire for arms control talks. (O'Neill's words would carry credibility, having told Dobrynin the previous year that Reagan was "a demagogue" and "a dangerous man."[33]) The Speaker delivered the letter and conveyed Reagan's thoughts. Gorbachev was "unyielding" on substantive issues, though he pledged to conduct talks in a practical manner. His prime concern was SDI, characterizing it as part of an offensive U.S. strategy, and threatening to deploy more missiles if Reagan proceeded with the plan.[34] "As long as you consider Star Wars we will have to build our nuclear capacity to make sure we can break through," Gorbachev explained. This offensive capacity, he said, would cost the USSR "20 times less" than the West would spend on SDI.[35] O'Neill had printed the phonetic pronunciation "Gor-ba-chov" on the heading of his notes, and found the Soviet leader "articulate, energetic, and tough." When O'Neill raised subjects such as economic policy and human rights, Gorbachev said he would not brook intrusion into Soviet internal affairs. Although the U.S. delegation did not yet see changes in policy, the Soviets were willing to talk about a range of issues in detail. Gorbachev was "serious" about arms control and again plugged his moratorium proposal. In contrast, a meeting with Gromyko the previous day was less smooth. The delegation reported on a "virtuoso performance" from the foreign minister, who delivered a "wide-ranging broadside" against U.S. foreign policy.[36]

Bilateral exchanges intensified. Shultz agreed to meet Gromyko in Vienna in mid-May to give some impetus to the arms talks, which were struggling to yield progress. On April 30, Reagan wrote a further letter to Gorbachev, addressing some of the issues raised by O'Neill in Moscow. Reagan felt that the Soviet proposal for a moratorium on deploying intermediate-range missiles was "unhelpful," providing "no basis for serious negotiation." He tried to assuage Gorbachev's fears about SDI, framing it as a defensive plan to protect Americans and move the world a step closer to nuclear abolition. "How are we ever to achieve that noble aim if nations have no defense against the uncertainty that all nuclear weapons might not have been removed from world arsenals?" Reagan asked. "Life provides no guarantee against some future madman getting his hands on nuclear weapons." Reagan told Gorbachev that the scientific research would take years and that there was "no possibility of a sudden, secretive, destabilizing move by the United States."[37] He reminded Gorbachev about his offer of a personal meeting, adding that "major formal agreements" were not a necessary precursor. Privately, Reagan doubted that Gorbachev was going to be a "different" Soviet leader. After a meeting with Ambassador Hartman on April 19, he noted: "[Hartman] confirms what I believe: that Gorbachev will be as tough as any of their leaders. If he wasn't a confirmed ideologue he would never have been chosen by the Politburo."[38]

CONGRESS AND THE MX

Reagan's conciliatory tone was reaping domestic rewards. In March, the administration secured authorization for the controversial MX program (twenty-one MX missiles at a cost of $1.5 billion), which had met fierce resistance from Democrats. The White House viewed the program as essential, both to offset the improved accuracy of Soviet missiles and for leverage in the strategic arms talks. Tip O'Neill publicly expressed his opposition to the MX, calling it "a waste of money." He dismissed the claims about a "window of vulnerability." "It'll be like Sputnik," O'Neill argued. "As soon as we get it, the Russians will increase their military spending and see if they can get something better."[39] Democrats had stymied Reagan's efforts to secure MX funding in early 1984. But Reagan's victory in November, and his efforts to forge a more peaceful path, had changed the political dynamics. Reagan and Shultz wrote to O'Neill ahead of the congressional votes. Both argued that the MX (Reagan called it "the Peacekeeper") was critical to the success of U.S. efforts at the Geneva talks.[40] Reagan invited conservative Democrats to the White House for cocktail parties, pitching the MX and SDI as necessary precursors to arms reductions.[41] Weinberger told the House Armed Services Committee that the Soviets "will have won the negotiations before it starts" if funding for the MX was defeated.[42] Conversely, liberals such as Paul Warnke and Clark Clifford (along with Gerard Smith, the SALT I negotiator) criticized the administration for "playing the Geneva card." They argued that the MX was neither militarily justifiable nor a useful bargaining chip, citing the U.S. superiority in strategic forces.[43]

But with the freeze movement on the wane after Reagan's reelection, a growing number of Democrats were wavering. Rep. Les Aspin (D-Wisconsin), chairman of the House Armed Services Committee, warned: "If Democrats want to spend the rest of their careers writing op-ed pieces and giving lectures in universities, then we continue to stroke our anti-defense image [...] Voters are not attracted to national security naysayers."[44] Politically vulnerable Democrats forged a middle ground by trading their votes on the MX for something concrete for themselves or their districts. (O'Neill told Reagan that he would not vote for the MX but neither would he "make an issue of it."[45]) On March 19–20, the Senate voted to approve the MX by 55 to 45. The following week in the House, Aspin said that a rejection of the MX would mean "giving help to the Soviet Union"—a comment which drew jeers from liberals and a standing ovation from Republicans. Six Democrats relented in the final few days, giving the administration a 219–213 victory. "We've all become afraid of being called a wimp," remarked Rep. Pat Schroeder (D-Colorado), a liberal who opposed the MX.[46]

However, the saga did not end there. Moderate and conservative Democrats who voted for the MX (such as Sam Nunn) warned that they would curtail further production. Their verdict was that it represented a bargaining chip rather than a military asset. Political trade-offs ensued. In May, the White House reluctantly accepted a Senate proposal to allow the purchase of twelve new MX missiles in the next fiscal year (Reagan had sought forty-eight missiles), and limit the operational force to fifty of the ten warhead weapons (the administration wanted to deploy 100). In June, the House voted to bar the purchase of any additional MX missiles during 1986.[47] As author Hedrick Smith noted, "the trading game left both sides with half a loaf." The administration gained fifty MXs, while the moderates (who had secured "build-down" via the Scowcroft Commission) achieved some flexibility in Reagan's arms control positions.[48]

"WHAT ABOUT THE SUMMIT?"

The buildup to the Shultz–Gromyko meeting was dominated by the question of a summit. Reagan had invited Gorbachev to Washington in his first letter and expressed hope for a response in his most recent correspondence. Matlock complained that the administration was creating the impression that the president was "desperate" for a summit.[49] Shultz therefore told Dobrynin that Reagan's offer remained open, but that he had nothing more to add. The Soviets could tell the administration when they were ready to discuss the details.[50] On May 8, Dobrynin told Matlock that Gromyko would have a summit proposal ready for his meeting with Shultz. He said that Gorbachev hoped to meet Reagan before the end of the year.[51] Days later, Reagan told John Poindexter (deputy national security adviser): "I feel very strongly that we should do no more to indicate we are begging for a meeting. We've invited them to a meeting in the U.S. (It's our turn.) The ball is in their court."[52]

On May 14, Shultz arrived at the Soviet embassy in Vienna for his sixth (and last) encounter with Gromyko. Shultz did not raise the question of a summit, reasoning that his counterpart would only use it to extract some concession in return.[53] However, Gromyko was under instruction to discuss the matter.[54] The meeting followed a familiar pattern. Shultz raised a number of issues which were not to Gromyko's liking, such as the Nicholson murder and Soviet human rights. Gromyko responded by stating that the important issue was arms control. For more than two hours he addressed a list of issues, mostly related to the negotiations on nuclear and space weapons. As Gromyko spoke, Shultz compiled a stack of papers, one for each of the subjects raised. When Gromyko ended his monologue the stack was three inches high. At that point, Shultz delved into his papers, calmly addressing each of the points raised. A rebuttal from Gromyko followed. By the time they concluded, the meeting had lasted six hours—twice its allotted time. Neither had moved on their arms control positions, nor did they want to be the first to raise the matter of the summit.

When it was time to adjourn, Shultz gathered his papers and headed for the door. As he did so, a Soviet delegate tapped him on the shoulder, telling him that Gromyko wanted a "private word." Shultz walked to the corner of the room where Gromyko was standing. "Is there anything you want to talk about?" Gromyko whispered. "No, we've covered everything," Shultz said. "What about the summit?" Gromyko asked. "What about it?" Shultz replied. Gromyko wanted to discuss a time and place. He ruled out Washington as a potential venue, lest it appear that Gorbachev was "paying court" to Reagan. Gromyko suggested that the president visit Moscow in November. "No way," Shultz replied. "It's your turn to come to Washington." "Out of the question!" Gromyko countered. "It should be in Europe, in a third country." The meeting ended with Shultz telling Gromyko that he would relay the proposal of a neutral venue to Reagan. Their three-minute conversation provided more impetus for U.S.–Soviet relations than the six hours which preceded it.[55]

A summit in Geneva (November 19–20) was announced on July 3. Dobrynin told the *Washington Post*'s Don Oberdorfer that things had improved since the "worst days of 1983." U.S.–Soviet relations were now back to "business as usual," albeit "not very good business."[56] The improved atmosphere was reflected by the visit of Secretary of Commerce Malcolm Baldrige to Moscow in late May. The two days of talks with senior Soviet officials was the first such top-level trade encounter in seven years. While no new agreement emerged, both sides were content that progress had been made. Gorbachev told Baldrige that it was "high time to defrost the potential of Soviet–American cooperation and [...] to stop the arms race and the escalation of hostility."[57] Meanwhile, Matlock reported on "growing evidence of tension" between Gromyko and Gorbachev—mostly gleaned from Soviet academics and Eastern European officials. He speculated that Gorbachev could move against Gromyko, to loosen his control over Soviet foreign policy.[58]

SALT II: "INTERIM RESTRAINT"

A trickier issue for Reagan was the unratified SALT II Treaty, which was due to expire at the end of the year. Although never enforced, both nations had agreed to abide by the restrictions it placed on the number of strategic weapons. But a new U.S. nuclear missile submarine was due to be commissioned, which would put America over the number of launchers allowed under SALT II unless an older nuclear submarine was deactivated. The question, therefore, was whether the United States should continue to observe the numerical limits, a policy known as "interim restraint." Yet again the administration was divided. The pragmatic wing—Shultz, McFarlane, Matlock, and Nitze (who had moderated his views)—favored continuation. They felt that the political risks of not adhering to SALT II outweighed the military arguments. For one thing, there was no necessity for an older submarine once the new one was in service. A U.S. violation of the agreement would threaten relations with allies, undermining the belief that the administration was truly committed to ending the arms race. Advisers noted that Reagan was the first president in years not to have an arms control agreement on his record; abrogating one of the major accords still in existence would hardly serve his political interests (particularly the pursuit of defense programs). Matlock explained that the public would blame Washington for discarding the restraints, disrupting the alliance, and creating further pressure over SDI. Moreover, a refusal to stay within the SALT II limits would free the Soviets completely from the treaty, allowing Moscow to wage a new propaganda campaign.[59]

But the hardliners (Weinberger, Perle, Adelman, and Rowny) wanted to free the United States from the restrictions of SALT II. In April they reminded Reagan of his own evaluation of the treaty ("fatally flawed"), arguing that the Soviets had already violated a number of provisions. "I've never liked SALT and neither have you," Weinberger told the president. "Never liked it at all," Reagan acknowledged. Weinberger claimed to speak for the whole of the Pentagon, despite the fact that the Joint Chiefs of Staff supported "interim restraint." He accused the State Department of seeking to "reaffirm" the SALT treaties—a charge refuted by Nitze and Shultz.[60] On June 10, Reagan announced that the United States would continue to abide by the unratified treaty—decommissioning one of the older nuclear submarines. In a bid to appease the hawks, Reagan denounced the Soviet treaty violations, promising "appropriate and pro-portionate responses to Soviet noncompliance" (indicating that a future withdrawal was possible). European allies welcomed Reagan's announce-ment. But the domestic reaction was divided. Hardline conservatives such as Sen. Steve Symms (R-Idaho) called the decision "unilateral disarma-ment and appeasement."[61] Reagan's qualified support for adherence to SALT II drew a firm response from Gorbachev. The USSR, he said, would not recognize the right of the United States to depart from the SALT II provisions in response to "reports on imaginary Soviet violations."[62]

GROMYKO OUT, SHEVARDNADZE IN

Gorbachev's spell as general secretary began cautiously. In his acceptance speech at the Politburo he declared that there was "no need to change policy." The status quo was the "true, correct, and genuinely Leninist" course.[63] But the remarks belied Gorbachev's inner sense of urgency. He was anxious to wring changes to the Soviet system, even if the measures that were required were not yet clear to him. At the Party Plenum in April and during a televised trip to Leningrad in May, Gorbachev spoke of the need for *perestroika* (restructuring). In 1985, this applied only to modest changes in economic management. Gorbachev assembled a new team to initiate a policy agenda. Out went political rivals such as Nikolai Tikhonov (Soviet prime minister), Grigory Romanov (Leningrad party secretary), and Viktor Grishin (Moscow party secretary). In came a trio of allies—Nikolai Ryzhkov, Yegor Ligachev, and KGB Chairman Viktor Chebrikov—who were elevated to the Politburo to exert pressure on would-be opponents.

A program of "conservative modernization" in Gorbachev's first two years would not radically differ from the plans envisioned by Andropov. One goal was to double investment in heavy industry, with the Politburo aiming to increase production by 20 percent over fifteen years. Other objectives were to combat corruption and improve work discipline. In a break with recent tradition, Gorbachev publicly named and shamed ministers for laziness or poor management, and openly criticized some of his Politburo colleagues. Part of the effort to increase productivity involved a national anti-alcohol campaign, which extended to the upper echelons. Alcohol was no longer served at Politburo meetings, a policy which was not universally popular. (Gorbachev rejected a request from Gromyko to exempt diplomatic functions from the ban.) But all of these initiatives proved financially disastrous. Later reforms—the deviation from a centralized planned economy toward a semi-free market system—produced an "economic halfway house," leading to severe shortages in output.[64]

The measures taken by Gorbachev in his first 100 days were enough for the CIA to describe him as "the most aggressive and activist Soviet leader since Khrushchev [...] Gorbachev is gambling that an attack on corruption and inefficiency, not radical reform, will turn the domestic situation around." In foreign affairs, Gorbachev's early impact was "mostly stylistic." Gambits such as the INF moratorium were considered "stale leftovers" from his predecessors. Meanwhile, Soviet forces remained engaged in a hopeless war in Afghanistan. But the CIA noted that Gorbachev had softened the Soviet conditions for a summit with Reagan, sanctioned increased bilateral exchanges, and met with several U.S. delegations. Gorbachev also sought to shore up relations with Warsaw Pact allies, receiving each of the leaders in Moscow after Chernenko's funeral. He publicly stressed the need for bloc unity and closer economic integration, and the security pact was renewed for another twenty years. However, at a Warsaw Pact summit in April, Gorbachev told party leaders of his dissatisfaction with corruption and "economic laxity."[65]

For advice on foreign affairs Gorbachev did not turn to veterans such as Boris Ponomarev, head of the Central Committee's International Department. Instead, he consulted with specialists advocating reform, such as Georgy Arbatov (director of the Institute for American Studies) and Aleksandr Yakovlev, who led the Institute of World Economy and International Relations. Yakovlev, who became head of the Party Propaganda Department, had spent time at Columbia University in the late 1950s as part of an academic exchange agreement. He was the most prominent of the "party intellectuals" who were developing ideas for modernizing the Soviet Union. They quietly abhorred the class-struggle ideology which polarized the world into capitalist and communist camps. They rejected the "Brezhnev Doctrine" to justify military intervention in the Eastern bloc, and the decision to go to war in Afghanistan. Indeed, the reformers' personal views were closer to those of critics of the Soviet system (such as Andrei Sakharov) than to the old guard which held power before Gorbachev. But their ideas complemented—rather than animated—Gorbachev's convictions: he would be the driving force behind the "new thinking" in Soviet foreign policy.[66]

In May, Gorbachev chose Lev Zaikov (Leningrad party first secretary) to head a Politburo Arms Limitation Commission, which included leaders responsible for defense, foreign affairs, security, and intelligence.[67] With Sergei Sokolov having succeeded Ustinov as defense minister, speculation surrounded the future of Gromyko, the last of the old guard. There were signs that his twenty-eight-year spell as foreign minister would soon be at an end. Gorbachev had abolished various Politburo commissions headed by Gromyko. And though Gromyko had supported his election, it was clear that Gorbachev wanted to depart from the rigid "old-line thinking" which had long governed Soviet foreign policy. Gromyko was finally ousted on July 2, shortly after the Geneva summit had been agreed upon. "Gorbachev rid himself of a minister who was a burden to him, whom he disliked, and whose presence and authority stood in the way of new thinking in foreign policy," Dobrynin recalled. "When new developments and a rapid transformation of the world called for a new approach, [Gromyko] gradually became an obstacle to the Soviet diplomacy he had directed for so many years. He finally realized this in his heart of hearts and suffered for it."[68]

Gromyko did not openly object—perhaps expecting that his deputy, Georgy Korniyenko, would succeed him. But Gorbachev instead chose an outsider, 57-year-old Eduard Shevardnadze, first secretary of the Georgian Communist Party. The two men had known each other for nearly twenty-five years, having served as Komsomol leaders in nearby regions. Shevardnadze called Gorbachev's proposal "the greatest surprise of my life." He was a "non-Russian," he told Gorbachev, without any diplomatic experience or foreign languages. But the Soviet leader was unconcerned. "Yes, you're a Georgian," Gorbachev replied, "but you're also a Soviet man. No experience? Well, perhaps that's a good thing. Our foreign policy needs a fresh eye, courage, innovation."[69] One man unimpressed by Shevardnadze's credentials was Anatoly Dobrynin. "Our foreign policy is going down the drain," he told Shultz. "They've named an agricultural type."[70] Gorbachev dismissed the misgivings over Shevardnadze. "He'll live and learn," the general secretary reasoned.[71]

Shevardnadze's entire career had been spent in Georgia, where he served as minister of the interior, acquiring a reputation for fighting corruption. Soft-spoken and courteous, his personal style differed from that of Gromyko. "Like Gorbachev, he seems to have a flair for PR," Matlock reported. "He may be adept at projecting an attractive image to foreign audiences, in sharp contrast to the dour Gromyko [. . .] As foreign minister he owes his position entirely to Gorbachev, so we can assume he will work as a faithful executor of Gorbachev's wishes." Matlock called Shevardnadze's appointment "a brilliant tactical move which puts [Gorbachev] in direct charge of Soviet foreign policy."[72] Meanwhile, Gromyko (aged 76) settled for the quiet life, accepting the ceremonial post of Chairman of the Soviet Presidium.

Shultz's first meeting with Shevardnadze was in late July in Helsinki, where foreign ministers gathered to celebrate the tenth anniversary of the Final Act. Shevardnadze greeted Shultz with a disarming smile. "We chatted in a friendly, open manner," Shultz recalled. "He reciprocated in a natural, easy way. No reservations. No guarded wariness." Shevardnadze's smile disappeared when Shultz delivered a hard-hitting speech on Soviet human rights violations in Finlandia Hall. "Did you have to give such a speech?" Shevardnadze asked Shultz during a break in the session. The two foreign ministers addressed the usual range of topics (arms control, bilateral relations, regional affairs) without deviating from their respective positions. But when they spoke alone, Shultz returned to the human rights issue. He told Shevardnadze: "Until the Soviet Union adopts a different policy, no aspect of our dealings will be truly satisfactory, nor will your society be able to progress as it can and should." Instead of responding furiously (as Gromyko might have done), Shevardnadze asked with a smile: "When I come to the United States, should I talk about black unemployment?" Shultz replied, "Help yourself." While the substance of Soviet policy was unchanged, Shultz noted the absence of polemics—indicating a new style and, he hoped, a new vein of thought. As the two men negotiated, their wives toured Helsinki together. The atmosphere contrasted with the Gromyko meeting in Vienna only weeks earlier. Shevardnadze even tried to discard the stack of papers he had taken to the meeting, telling a member of his staff that he wanted to "wing it" with Shultz. Dobrynin persuaded him to stick to the script, but in future meetings Shevardnadze would adopt a more informal approach.[73]

Shultz's warning about human rights seemed to have made an impact on the new-look Politburo. Within weeks, a meeting was held to discuss the high-profile case of Yelena Bonner, wife of Andrei Sakharov, the dissident and nuclear physicist who remained exiled in Gorky. Sakharov had requested permission for Bonner to travel to America to receive medical treatment for a heart condition. Politburo members urged Gorbachev to reach an early decision. KGB Chairman Viktor Chebrikov noted that delaying a decision until close to the summit would be viewed as a concession to Washington and was hence "undesirable." Some of the hardliners dissented. "You can't expect any decency from Bonner," said Party Secretariat Mikhail Zimyanin. "She's a beast in a skirt, an imperialist plant." But most members were in favor of granting an exit permission. Shevardnadze, Chebrikov, and Ryzhkov acknowledged the risks, but felt that releasing Bonner would be viewed favorably as a "humanitarian step." A stubborn refusal would only be detrimental to Soviet interests. Gorbachev agreed. Bonner could leave the USSR to receive medical treatment.[74] In late October, the Soviets announced their decision to allow Bonner to travel to Boston, where her mother, children, and grandchildren lived. By December 1986, Gorbachev had pardoned Bonner (once convicted of "anti-Soviet" activities) and released Sakharov from internal exile.[75]

REAGAN MEETS SHEVARDNADZE

While Shultz was in Finland, Reagan was recovering from a health scare. On July 13, he underwent surgery for colon cancer. Shortly thereafter skin cancer was discovered on his nose, for which he also received treatment. (Reagan would make a full recovery from both.) But in August, Reagan moved quickly to clear up comments made by McFarlane. In a rare speech, the national security adviser publicly blamed the Soviet system for the stalemate on arms control. McFarlane had veered from the policy agreed with Shultz and Matlock in late 1983, which sought to avoid questioning the legitimacy of the Soviet system.[76] "Without some changes in the Soviet approach to security issues, in fact in the thinking that underlies it, I fear that even incremental improvements in relations will be extremely hard to reach," declared McFarlane, who questioned the Soviet motives for their "brutal war" in Afghanistan.[77] The speech revived memories of Reagan's past rhetoric, and spurred press reports about a "hard-nosed" approach for the November summit.[78]

Reagan sought to repair the damage in an interview. "There's no question that the Soviet Union has made it plain that they are embarked on an expansionist program. They believe in the one-world communist state," Reagan said. "But at the same time, you have to wonder if this is not based on their fear and suspicion that the rest of us in the world mean them harm. Now, I think that we can present evidence to show that we have no such intention [...] We're the only two nations in the world that could bring about world peace, and I would think that that would be our task in history—to deal with that problem."[79] Reagan's balanced tone drew criticism from conservative commentators. George Will told ABC's David Brinkley: "Reagan really believes in a kind of open, American, genial, spirited, Western, liberal, democratic way that all the problems of the world result from misunderstandings [...] that the Cold War is this 68-year misunderstanding, that the clash between the United States and the Soviet Union is as much amenable to changes of personalities as is the tone of American politics. That's wrong." Brit Hume charged Reagan with "acknowledging a point that is advanced by liberals and apologists of the Soviet Union—that the Soviet behavior worldwide is the result not simply of its totalitarian, nasty ways, but its paranoia."[80]

But Reagan had not entirely dispensed with his earlier rhetoric. During 1985, he continued to invoke the notion of Soviet military superiority. The USSR, Reagan alleged, had "the greatest nuclear weapons arsenal in the world" and "the most sophisticated air defense system ever seen." The Soviets also boasted "the world's only missile defense system," and "the world's only operational killer satellite system."[81] At a press conference on September 17, Reagan told reporters: "In spite of some of the misinformation that has been spread around, the United States is still well behind the Soviet Union in literally every kind of offensive weapon, both conventional and in strategic weapons."[82] It is highly unlikely that Reagan actually believed these claims. But it served to "validate" his call for SDI and other defense programs, while offsetting some of the concerns raised by hardliners, who sensed that he was overly keen to reach a deal with Moscow. By hyping Soviet military power, Reagan was also hoping that Gorbachev might soften his negotiating position ahead of the summit. However, Reagan restated that he would not curtail SDI in exchange for Soviet reductions in offensive missiles.

Gorbachev also engaged in public diplomacy. Whereas past Soviet leaders were extremely cautious about dealing with the foreign media, Gorbachev spoke at length with Western journalists. "The situation in the world today is highly complex, very tense. I would even go so far as to say it is explosive," he told *Time Magazine* on August 28. SDI remained a chief concern. "The development of science and technology has reached a level where the broad-scale introduction of new achievements, particularly in the military field, can lead to an entirely new phase in the arms race," Gorbachev said. "If the present U.S. position on space weapons is its last word, the Geneva negotiations will lose all sense."[83]

*

The forerunner to the Geneva summit was a meeting between Reagan and Shevardnadze in Washington in late September. In advance, House Minority Leader Bob Michel (R-Illinois) sent the president a copy of Forrest Pogue's biography of George Marshall. Reagan quoted passages from the book at an NSC meeting, referring to the Second World War and the "Soviet historical fear of invasions and suspicions of foreigners." He agreed with Shultz that the biggest problem facing the Soviets was the poor state of their economy. The question was how far Gorbachev was prepared to go because of this. "We *want* peace. They *need* peace," Reagan commented.[84]

The Reagan–Shevardnadze meeting on September 27 was amicable. Reagan expressed his dismay at how America was being portrayed in the Soviet press. He wanted Moscow to get a "true picture" of who he was and what he stood for. (Reagan would soon give an interview to the Soviet government newspaper *Izvestiya* to clarify his position.) Shevardnadze handed Reagan a letter from Gorbachev, which outlined a new arms control proposal: a 50 percent reduction in offensive strategic weapons to a level of 6,000 warheads, accompanied by an agreement not to develop, test, or deploy "space-strike weapons." The proposal was unacceptable to the Reagan administration, since it required a complete ban on "space attack weapons" (i.e., SDI). Discussion of other matters (human rights, bilateral ties, regional conflicts) broke no new ground. But Reagan and Shevardnadze warmed to one another. Over lunch in the state dining room, Reagan pointed to the portrait of Abraham Lincoln, and the two men discussed the American and Russian civil wars. Reagan began telling jokes about communists, which drew laughter from the foreign minister.[85] (Shevardnadze found Reagan's sense of humor an especially endearing quality.[86]) The meeting ended with Shultz accepting an invitation to visit Moscow in early November for presummit talks. In the meantime, a new controversy arose over the ABM Treaty.

REINTERPRETING THE ABM TREATY

In the fall of 1985, a political tussle developed in Washington over how to interpret the 1972 Anti-Ballistic Missile Treaty. The question had significance for the future of SDI and the arms control negotiations with Moscow. The ABM issue surfaced in July during a Senate confirmation hearing for Donald Hicks, a defense contractor who was appointed as undersecretary of defense for research and development. At the hearing, Sen. Carl Levin (D-Michigan) raised concerns that the SDI program would violate the legal restrictions of the ABM Treaty. He cited the provision (article V, paragraph 1) of the treaty, which stated: "Each Party undertakes not to develop, test or deploy ABM systems or components which are sea-based, air-based, space-based or mobile land-based." If SDI was to progress, the administration would either have to withdraw from the treaty (risking international uproar) or find a way to circumvent the restrictions on a space-based system.[87]

Richard Perle (chair of the Interagency Committee on SDI) hired a young Pentagon attorney, Philip Kunsberg, to analyze the relationship between the ABM Treaty and strategic defense. Kunsberg had no arms control experience, having made his name as a district attorney in New York prosecuting drug dealers and pornographers. But he quickly opined that the treaty gave more leeway to SDI than the administration had earlier told Congress. Kunsberg argued that the Soviets had never accepted restrictions on space-based ABM systems if they employed "future technologies" (such as laser beams or energy-directed weapons). He claimed that the testing, development, and deployment of SDI were consistent with the treaty. Kunsberg's conclusion was heavily disputed by career government attorneys at the Defense Department and at the ACDA.[88] But the State Department's legal adviser, Abraham Sofaer, agreed that the language of the ABM Treaty was ambiguous, and did not reference specific future technologies. He told Shultz: "The President is not limited with regard to research, development, or testing of SDI." Sofaer's conclusion was music to the ears of the Perle–Weinberger wing, who argued for a much looser interpretation of the ABM Treaty than those commonly accepted. Perle championed a "broad" interpretation of the treaty, allowing the United States to not only conduct research but to develop and test prototypes of a space-based defense system. He invoked the Soviet radar at Krasnoyarsk, constructed during the Brezhnev era in violation of a corollary provision of the 1972 treaty, which remained an obstacle at the arms talks. "Why should we be bound if the other side clearly is not?" Perle asked.[89]

On October 4, the SACPG met to debate the ABM issue. Among those present was Paul Nitze, a veteran of the U.S. team that had negotiated the ABM Treaty and supported the "restrictive" interpretation. But after talking with Sofaer, Nitze shifted his position (not for the first time in his career) and agreed that a "broad interpretation" was justified. McFarlane also voiced support for the reinterpretation, believing it would "lay down a marker with the Soviets" and could be used as a bargaining chip.[90] Shultz raised no objections and accepted Sofaer's judgment. However, he was furious two days later when McFarlane told NBC's *Meet the Press* of the new "broad interpretation" that had been privately agreed upon. McFarlane's disclosure—made without authorization—provoked an angry response from Shultz. "You didn't get elected to anything," he told McFarlane. "When it comes to matters of this kind, that's for the President to decide, not for you or me or anybody else." "The Russians," Nitze added, "will use McFarlane's statement to show we are playing ducks and drakes with the treaty."[91]

On October 8, the White House confirmed that McFarlane's statement was administration policy. It was denounced by Democrats, European allies, and the Soviet Union. Helmut Kohl and Margaret Thatcher wrote to Reagan to express their disapproval. Rep. Dante Fascell (D-Florida), chairman of the House Foreign Affairs Committee, said that the new interpretation was "incredible" and spelled "serious and far-reaching consequences." Sen. Sam Nunn (D-Georgia), a past supporter of Reagan's arms buildup, called the decision a "complete and total misrepresentation" of the historical record. He warned of a congressional backlash against funding for SDI. (Congress would later vote to deny funds for any tests which exceeded the "restrictive interpretation" of the ABM Treaty.)[92]

The moderates in the administration were taken aback by the level of criticism. Shultz therefore requested authorization from Reagan to make a statement. He would explain that while the new interpretation was "justified legally," the United States would pursue the SDI program in accordance with the original "restrictive interpretation" of the ABM Treaty. Reagan agreed, aware that it would infuriate the hardliners. On October 14, Shultz clarified the U.S. position in a speech to the North Atlantic Assembly in San Francisco. Reagan wrote to Gorbachev, explaining that the strategic defense program would "remain in full accord with the ABM Treaty." (He also agreed with the idea of reducing strategic nuclear weapons by 50 percent.)[93] But it failed to assuage Soviet doubts. The Soviets' chief arms control negotiator, Viktor Karpov, accused Washington of creating a "Catch-22" situation by denying the original meaning of the treaty.[94]

The hawks bridled at Reagan's decision to follow the spirit of the "restrictive" interpretation. "Once again, we have succumbed to the appeasement policies of our so-called allies," decried Sen. Jesse Helms (R-North Carolina), who accused U.S. officials of "sneaking around and neutralizing" the building of a strategic defense.[95] Weinberger wrote an article in the *Christian Science Monitor*, warning Reagan not to compromise over SDI and to avoid committing himself to the ABM Treaty restrictions. "Thirteen members of the Politburo virtually exercise absolute control over the millions of our fellowmen," wrote Weinberger, who suggested Americans were "naïve" and "deluded" about the Soviet threat to freedom.[96]

SOVIET UNION 101

In preparation for the summit, Shultz and McFarlane met with Gorbachev in Moscow on November 5. By now, both sides had agreed to restore most of the contacts and joint projects which existed prior to the Soviet invasion of Afghanistan. But arms control remained a more difficult hurdle. In a feisty exchange, Gorbachev bemoaned the military-industrial complex which dictated American policy. He accused the United States of trying to use SDI to attain military supremacy over the Soviet Union, citing the reinterpretation of the ABM Treaty. "I'm amazed that you would base your judgment on the advice of a lawyer who had previously only experience prosecuting drug and pornography cases," Gorbachev remarked. Shultz explained that Reagan had ordered SDI activity to remain within the bounds of the 1972 treaty. He invoked the Soviet radar at Krasnoyarsk. "Look, we'll figure out for ourselves what our policy is on defense," Shultz said. "In fact, yours is the same. All you have to do is watch your programs. We don't see anything wrong with defending ourselves." Gorbachev rejected the argument. "We know what is going on," he replied. "You think you're ahead of us in technology and you can use these things to gain superiority over the Soviet Union [...] If you want superiority through your SDI, we will not help you. We'll let you bankrupt yourselves." Shultz sensed Gorbachev's commitment to communism as an ideology. But he was not discouraged by the combative approach. Shultz assumed that the Soviet leader would adopt a more measured style with Reagan. Gorbachev wanted to achieve something of substance in Geneva. He called for "a major political impetus to get a drastic improvement in our relations."[97]

Back in Washington, Reagan was learning his lines. From July to November the president read a series of papers compiled by Matlock ("Soviet Union 101"), which gave him new insights into the nation and its people. "I'm getting damn sick of cramming like a school kid," Reagan noted in his diary. "Sometimes they tell me more than I need to know."[98] But the crash course improved his command of Soviet history and culture. In a paper on Russian psychology, Matlock explained: "Yes, they lie and cheat. And they can stonewall a negotiation when it seems in their interest to strike a deal. They have a sense of pride and 'face' that makes the proverbial oriental variety pale in comparison." These traits often served a political purpose. Yet, Matlock continued: "In private with people he trusts, the Russian can be candid to a fault—groveling in his nation's inadequacies—and so scrupulously honest that it can be irritating, as when he makes a big deal over having forgotten to return a borrowed pencil."[99] Reagan read about the problems afflicting Soviet society, the instruments of political control, Gorbachev's domestic agenda, the USSR's international position, and the Soviet view of the United States.[100] He was told of the Soviet aims in Geneva: "Gorbachev's central objective is likely to be to promote the kind of positive atmosphere necessary for increased trade with the U.S. and our allies." While the Soviet leader would explore Reagan's views on bilateral relations and arms control, he was not expecting "major substantive breakthroughs."[101]

Reagan received advice from all quarters. Shultz described his experience with Gorbachev in Moscow and outlined the U.S. policy positions.[102] Robert Gates (deputy director for intelligence) briefed Reagan about strategy and geopolitics, and showed him a CIA-produced film on Gorbachev. According to Gates, Reagan was "alert but not very interested." He was more intrigued by a briefing from Kay Oliver, who described the Soviet Union in human terms, explaining everyday life and the hardships endured by the people.[103] Reagan also received counsel from familiar sources. Suzanne Massie continued to serve as an informal adviser (meeting Reagan at the Oval Office in September), while Richard Nixon told him not to back Gorbachev into a corner. "You have to leave them maneuvering room," Nixon explained to Reagan. "They have to save face back home."[104] Further afield, Margaret Thatcher forwarded a paper from Oleg Gordievsky, the Soviet KGB defector. He argued that the main Soviet concern over SDI was not that they considered it a physical threat. Rather, Soviet leaders felt that it would force them to accelerate their own program in a way they could ill afford if they were to tackle their economic problems. (Gordievsky's view was broadly shared by Matlock and McFarlane.)[105] The Heritage Foundation took a different approach. In a specially prepared briefing book, think-tankers advised Reagan against signing "proclamations of good intentions lacking enforcement mechanisms." They argued that Stalin had played upon the guilt of Western allies for the Red Army losses in the Second World War, which led to the installation of a communist government in Poland. "Do not succumb to Soviet manipulation by guilt," Reagan was warned.[106]

By the time he boarded the plane for Switzerland, Reagan had mastered his brief. The president dictated his thoughts about Gorbachev and the summit. "I believe Gorbachev is a highly intelligent leader totally dedicated to traditional Soviet goals," Reagan said. "He will be a formidable negotiator and will try to make Soviet foreign and military policy more effective." Reagan felt that Gorbachev wanted to "reduce the burden of defense spending," and anticipated more resistance over SDI because "he doesn't want to face the cost of competing with us." The president was also wary of the domestic perceptions of what would constitute a successful summit. "In the world of PR we are faced with two domestic elements," Reagan continued. "One argues that no agreement with the Soviets is worth the time, trouble, or paper it's written on, so we should dig in our heels and say 'nyet' to any concession. On the other side are those so hungry for an agreement that they would advise major concessions because a successful summit requires that. My own view is that any agreement must be in the long-term interest of the United States and our allies. We'll sign no other kind."[107]

Reagan flew to Geneva on November 16 to give himself time to overcome any travel fatigue. But he was soon reminded of the domestic naysayers. The *New York Times* and *Washington Post* published a letter from Weinberger to Reagan (dated November 13), urging him not to give Gorbachev a commitment that the United States would abide by the SALT II and ABM treaties.[108] Rumors spread that Weinberger had leaked the letter in protest at being omitted from the U.S. delegation, in addition to his desire to scupper the summit. McFarlane, off the record, told reporters that the leaker was indeed the defense secretary. He considered the letter "treasonous."[109] Shultz and Matlock were seething. Here was a public display of Weinberger's lack of confidence in Reagan's judgment. The Soviets were also furious. Gorbachev's adviser, Georgy Arbatov, called it "a direct attempt to torpedo the whole arms control process." (The feeling was shared by Reagan's chief advisers.)[110] Reagan was angry, but had grown used to Weinberger's public salvos. When an official raised the article with him, the president responded with a rhetorical shrug: "Doesn't everybody know what Cap thinks?"[111]

REAGAN AND GORBACHEV: THE GENEVA SUMMIT

November 19 was bitterly cold as Reagan (the nominal host) waited for Gorbachev at the Château Fleur d'Eau, a gray-stone villa overlooking Lake Geneva. As the media assembled near the driveway, a debate ensued among the U.S. delegation. Reagan was trying to decide whether to wear his overcoat when he stepped outside to greet the Soviet leader. His counsel was divided. The president looked out the window at the gray clouds, put on his overcoat, and promptly took it off again. Moments later Reagan strode outside to meet his counterpart. Gorbachev emerged from his car coated, scarved, and hatted. "Where is your coat?" asked Gorbachev, doffing his fedora. "It's inside," replied Reagan, motioning toward the château. As they shook hands, photographers captured the moment: a bald, slightly paunched Gorbachev, bundled against the cold; Reagan (at 74) standing upright and coatless, with thick hair brillantined in the 1940s fashion. The president, although twenty years older, looked more vigorous.[112]

Reagan directed Gorbachev to the sitting room for a private discussion—only their interpreters were present. It was supposed to last fifteen minutes, but the two leaders (good talkers and listeners) chatted for a full hour. Both agreed that arms control would be addressed at the larger sessions, so Reagan focused on making a personal connection. He spoke of the "similar" humble beginnings from which they emerged, and of the need for mutual trust. "Countries do not mistrust each other because of arms," Reagan said. "Rather, they build up their arms because of the mistrust between them." He explained that both nations could follow their own system of government, but with peaceful competition. Reagan said he understood the Soviet fear of war because of the enormous sacrifices made during the fight against Nazi Germany. "Americans hate war too," he added. Gorbachev emphasized the importance of their meeting. Six and a half years had passed since the last summit and "many problems had developed in U.S.–Soviet relations in that period." Gorbachev said he wanted more meetings at all levels—dialogue instead of talking through the press. "This is your idea, Mr. President: talk *to* each other, not *about* each other." He acknowledged "the fear of mutual destruction," but said that both sides could cooperate as they had done in the past, without changing their political systems, culture, or ideology.[113]

The plenary session was spent pinpointing the areas of mistrust. Gorbachev conceded that the USSR had its equivalent of the American military-industrial complex. "There are people linked to military affairs in both countries [...] people who earn their living from these matters," he said. Gorbachev's point was that such people should not be allowed to determine policy. He noted the economic upsurges in Japan and West Germany which followed a decline in military spending. "Soviet and American scholars have shown that one job in the military sector is three times as costly as in the civilian sector. More jobs can be created if the money is channeled into civilian areas." Gorbachev vented frustration at institutions such as the Heritage Foundation, which he claimed encouraged Reagan to use the arms race to ruin the Soviet economy. "This is a delusion," Gorbachev told the president. "The Soviet Union is an enormous country which will take care of its problems."

In response, Reagan defended the course of America's Cold War. The United States emerged from the Second World War as the only nation that had acquired a weapon of great destruction, the nuclear bomb, and had chosen not to use it. The U.S. had reduced its armed forces from 12 million to 1.5 million, Reagan said, and cut its navy by half. He told Gorbachev: "Eighteen times before this summit we had proposed meetings to discuss arms reduction and for twelve of those times the United States had nuclear superiority. The United States was willing to give it up. Most of these times we did not get cooperation from your predecessors." (Reagan's candor here about U.S. capabilities contrasted with his public claims of Soviet military supremacy.) The president mentioned other sources of mistrust, recalling that Soviet leaders had talked about a one-world communist state and "inspiring revolutions around the world." Reagan pointed to the example of Cuba, just ninety miles off American shores, before citing Afghanistan, Angola, Ethiopia, and Yemen.

Reagan dismissed Gorbachev's remarks about the U.S. military-industrial complex. "Our budget for humanitarian issues is greater than our total military budget," he argued. "Two-thirds of our military spending pays for manpower; only a small percentage is spent on equipment. The total military budget is a very small percentage of our GNP." But Reagan added: "Of course we would be better off without it [...] The United States has no economic interest in continuing a military buildup." Reagan said the Soviet arms buildup had given the American people reason to be fearful. "Maybe not fears of war, but that the Soviet Union could acquire such an imbalance of strength that it could deliver an ultimatum." He told Gorbachev that he was ready to address Soviet fears of the United States, if Moscow was willing to meet the concerns of Americans. "But more than words are needed," Reagan explained. "Only deeds can relieve mistrust."

Before breaking for lunch, Reagan raised the issue of strategic defense. Gorbachev had said that the United States was seeking a first-strike capability against the Soviet Union by building an antimissile shield which would destroy missiles before they hit the target. Reagan denied any such intent, insisting that SDI was a "defensive system." He suggested that the two sides cooperate on research: "The United States has a research program. The Soviet Union has the same kind of program [...] If one or both come up with such a system then they should sit down and make it available to everyone so no one would have fear of a nuclear strike. A mad man might come along with a nuclear weapon. If we could come up with a shield and share it, then nobody would worry about the mad man." Reagan made his pitch just before the interval, and promised Gorbachev the floor when the conversation resumed after lunch.[114]

After the early sparring the two leaders got down to business. Gorbachev charged the Reagan administration with overhyping Soviet power and its territorial ambitions. He made some encouraging noises over Afghanistan, though without drifting into detail. "We are ready to settle Afghanistan—get troops out, make a political settlement," Gorbachev said. "We have no plans for warm-water ports in the Gulf of Arabia." The Soviet leader then pivoted to SDI, taking issue with Reagan's public insistence on Soviet military superiority. "The United States has tripled the number of its nuclear weapons and has more nuclear weapons than the Soviet Union," he argued. "All institutes which study the problem, including the ISS [Institute for Strategic Studies] in London, conclude that there is strategic parity. Force structures are different, but they support different strategies." The Soviet Union wanted to maintain parity, Gorbachev said, but at a lower level. He called on Reagan to meet him halfway in a bid to reduce strategic weapons.

Gorbachev argued that SDI would lead to a new *offensive* arms race. "Space weapons will be harder to verify and will feed suspicions and mistrust. Scientists say that any shield can be pierced, so SDI cannot save us. So why create it? It only makes sense if it is to defend against a retaliatory strike. What would the West think if the Soviet Union was developing these weapons? You would react with horror." Gorbachev cited remarks by Weinberger, who had said that the West could not allow the Soviets to be the first to develop missile defense. "We cannot accept the rationale which says it is good if you do it and bad if we do it." Gorbachev saw that Reagan was "attached" to SDI, but warned him of the Soviet position. "If the U.S. embarks on SDI, the following will happen: (1) no reduction of offensive weapons; and (2) the Soviet Union will respond. This response will not be a mirror image of your program but a simpler, more effective system." Gorbachev knew precisely what he wanted to say about SDI and did not mince words. Hands gesturing and face reddened, this was a lecture he had spent a long time preparing. "It could unleash an uncontrollable process," he told Reagan. "You haven't thought this through. It will be a waste of money and will cause more distrust and more weapons."

Reagan waited for his counterpart to conclude. He tried to address Gorbachev's claims about nuclear parity. Reagan said it was true that America once had nuclear superiority. But he argued: "Since SALT I was signed, the Soviet Union added 6,000 nuclear warheads. Since SALT II, 3,850 have been added. Meanwhile, the U.S. has removed 2,400 warheads from Europe, while the Soviet Union threatened Europe with its SS-20s." "SDI," he told Gorbachev, "will never be used by the U.S. to improve its offensive capability or to launch a first strike."[115] But then Reagan could not speak for future U.S. presidents.

The debate wound down with Reagan suggesting a brisk walk. Gorbachev agreed. "Maybe some fresh air will bring some fresh ideas," he said. The pair strode toward the pool house, where a large fire was crackling. (This was not spontaneous; a "fireside chat" had been planned weeks in advance by the White House.) The discussion on strategic defense resumed. Reagan drew a parallel between the gas masks worn during wartime and the insurance of a "shield" to protect nations from nuclear missiles. Gorbachev was unimpressed. "We've read over everything you've ever said with regard to SDI," he replied. "I think I can understand you at a human level." Gorbachev saw that SDI had captured Reagan's imagination. But he could not agree to the concept, citing scientific analysis—Soviet and American. After an hour of deadlock, the two men put on their overcoats and ambled back to the château. As they approached the parking lot, Reagan proposed an agreement to hold future summits. He invited Gorbachev to come to Washington. The Soviet leader accepted and quickly proposed a follow-up summit in Moscow—to which Reagan promptly agreed. The president relayed the news to his team, who "almost went through the ceiling" in surprise.[116]

*

Reagan and Gorbachev reengaged the next morning to debate regional issues and human rights. The president was scathing about the Soviet conduct in Afghanistan. He rejected weak efforts to explain away the Soviet presence, lamenting that the war had created three million refugees. But human rights was broached far more tentatively. Reagan said several times that he did not want to interfere in Soviet internal affairs. He presented Gorbachev with a list of Soviet citizens (mostly Jewish) who were being denied permission to leave the country. However, Reagan did not press the matter further. "Reagan was not being Reagan. He was being messenger," recalled Kenneth Adelman. "Richard Nixon had convinced him that the only way to help Soviet dissidents was through 'quiet diplomacy'. So he mouthed the briefing material." For his part, Gorbachev raised unemployment and gender discrimination in the United States. "The most basic human right is everyone's right to a job," he said. "So much time has passed since the American Revolution, and yet women still do not have the same rights as men."[117]

The final session centered on arms control. Reagan and Gorbachev broadly agreed on the idea of 50 percent cuts in offensive strategic arms. However, the Soviets were still demanding that proposals for limits on INF forces had to include the British and French missiles. But strategic defense was the prime obstacle. "I don't know what is at the bottom of the U.S. position on SDI," Gorbachev complained. Maybe it was fueled by the "illusion" that America was ahead in the technology and information systems. Or maybe, he said, it was fed by the notion that the United States could employ SDI to obtain military superiority over the USSR. Gorbachev told Reagan of a conversation that he had with a Soviet scientist, who explained that SDI would produce between $600 billion and $1 trillion in new expenditures for the U.S. military-industrial complex. "Maybe that's the reason," Gorbachev said. Reagan called the financial estimates a "fantasy," defending his plans for a "shield" against nuclear weapons. Gorbachev found the arguments "unconvincing." "They contain many emotional elements," he said, "part of one man's dream." The Soviet leader believed that Reagan wanted peace. But he felt that SDI would trigger an arms race in space. "Describing these weapons as a 'shield' is only packaging," Gorbachev remarked.[118]

With a breakthrough out of reach, the delegations worked on a joint statement. But that also proved difficult. The working groups had stalled, as Soviet negotiators quibbled over language and began reneging on earlier agreements. In conversation with Gorbachev, Shultz named Georgy Korniyenko, the deputy foreign minister, as the chief culprit. Gorbachev immediately turned to Korniyenko and said, "Do it the way we discussed." For Reagan, who observed the scene, this was evidence that Gorbachev was "a man who was sure of himself and his power." Korniyenko slunk away "hushed and subdued." Negotiators stayed up until 5.00 am to craft a compromise statement. It did not mention SDI, instead citing general aims and principles. Reagan and Gorbachev agreed to "accelerate" negotiations "to prevent an arms race in space and terminate it on earth, to limit and reduce nuclear arms and enhance strategic stability." Both sides declared their intention to improve bilateral relations, including the promotion of cultural and educational exchanges. For the first time, "in the spirit of cooperation," the Soviets accepted the principle of discussions with the United States on human rights.[119]

*

The personal chemistry between Reagan and Gorbachev was more important than the statement. Despite some sharp exchanges, the two men warmed to one another. "The stuff really hit the fan," Reagan reflected at the end of the first day. "He was really belligerent and damn it I stood firm." But the longer they spoke, the more Reagan saw what Thatcher had perceived a year earlier: Gorbachev *was* someone he could do business with. "You could almost get to like the guy," the president remarked to Don Regan, his chief of staff. "Gorbachev and I and the interpreters went into a small room and wound up telling stories."[120] Some of the stories concerned Reagan's acting career. At an earlier press conference, Arbatov was asked whether Gorbachev had seen any of Reagan's movies. "Probably not," Arbatov replied, since these were "B movies." Reagan resumed the debate with Gorbachev. "Tell Arbatov, your PR guy, that I was in a lot of old movies that were good!" Reagan said. He cited *King's Row* as one of his best performances. Gorbachev said he had seen it recently and "liked it very much." "What does it feel like to see yourself in an old movie?" Gorbachev asked. "It's like seeing a son you never had," Reagan quipped.[121]

Reagan noted the absence of reference to a one-world communist state or the Brezhnev Doctrine. "There was a warmth in his face and style," Reagan wrote. "As we flew home I felt good. Gorbachev was tough and convinced communism was superior to capitalism. But after almost five years I'd finally met a Soviet leader I could talk to." Over dinner, Reagan saw similarities between Gorbachev and Tip O'Neill, his great domestic adversary. "[Gorbachev] could tell jokes about himself and even about his country, and I grew to like him more," Reagan recalled.[122] Seated to the other side of Gorbachev at dinner was Don Regan. He was taken aback when the Soviet leader "half apologized" for his "outburst" over SDI earlier in the day. Gorbachev explained that it was meant to show the intensity of his feelings on the issue. As the two leaders signed the joint statement, Reagan said to Gorbachev: "Your hardliners and my hard-liners are going to swallow very hard seeing us up here shaking hands and smiling." "You're so right," Gorbachev replied. "They won't like it."[123]

Epilogue

On his return to Washington, Reagan addressed a cheering Congress. He was speaking to Americans and to the world. "I can't claim that we had a meeting of minds on such fundamentals as ideology or national purpose," the president said. "But we understand each other better and that's a key to peace [...] We have a long way to go, but we're heading in the right direction."[1] Reagan won plaudits from both sides of the political aisle and the American public. A CBS News poll showed that 83 percent of respondents approved of his summit performance (a measure, perhaps, of the low expectations for success in U.S.–Soviet relations). Fifty-seven percent agreed with a questionnaire statement that Gorbachev was "a new kind of Soviet leader."[2] Reagan jotted in his diary: "I haven't gotten such a reception since I was shot."[3]

The Soviet reaction to Geneva was more restrained. Describing the initial tête-à-tête, Gorbachev thought Reagan was "not simply a conservative, but a political dinosaur." Yet over the course of their meetings, Gorbachev gained a better impression of his counterpart. The "fireside chat," followed by an agreement to hold summits in Washington and Moscow, had marked a fresh start. "Something important happened to each of us on that day, in spite of everything," Gorbachev recalled. "I think there had been two factors at work—responsibility and intuition [...] the 'human factor' had come into action. We both sensed that we must maintain contact and try to avoid a break. Somewhere in the back of our minds a glimmer of hope emerged that we could still come to an agreement."[4] On the plane back to Moscow, Gorbachev said that Reagan had impressed him as a "complex and contradictory" person, sometimes speaking his mind (as on SDI), and at other times mouthing propaganda dogmas. He was "stubborn and conservative," Gorbachev added. But the Soviet leader found it possible to establish a relationship with Reagan, a man who was "not as hopeless as some believed."[5]

Some of Gorbachev's top advisers were less convinced by events in Geneva. "It seemed to me that everything looked like theater," recalled Yakovlev, "and that in this theater there was a professional actor."[6] Yakovlev had a point. But then most summits are about style rather than substance. Meetings which yield agreements are no guarantee of success. U.S.–Soviet relations were in disarray within months of the Vienna summit in 1979, when Carter and Brezhnev hugged, kissed, and signed the SALT II Treaty. As Hedrick Smith noted in the *New York Times*: "No summit stands on its own. Its impact and legacy are defined by what follows. Good atmospherics without substantive underpinnings can be temporary."[7] In that sense, Gorbachev's post-summit ambivalence in a speech to the CPSU Central Committee—replete with hardliners and skeptics—was less important.[8] What mattered were his subsequent dealings with Reagan.

The pair exchanged letters in December, keen to build on the foundations laid in Geneva. For Gorbachev, the most significant achievement was to have "overcome the serious psychological barrier which had for a long time hindered a dialogue worthy of the leaders of the USSR and the USA."[9] The pace of events quickened. In January 1986, Gorbachev publicly proposed phasing out nuclear weapons and ballistic missiles by the year 2000. With the strains on the Soviet economy growing, Gorbachev set about alleviating his military burdens. "Our main goal now is to prevent the arms race from entering a new stage," he told advisers. "If we don't do that, the danger to us will increase. If we don't back down on some specific, maybe even important issues, if we don't budge from the positions we've held for a long time, we will lose in the end. We will be drawn into an arms race that we cannot manage. We will lose, because right now we are at the end of our tether."[10]

Gorbachev's readiness to strike a deal was illustrated at a remarkable summit in Reykjavik in October 1986. To the surprise of the U.S. delegation, Gorbachev was not only willing to destroy all intermediate-range missiles in Europe; he would also agree to a 50 percent cut in Soviet and American strategic weapons—without including the British and French forces. Reagan sensed a chance for a major breakthrough. He responded by offering to eliminate offensive ballistic missiles within ten years, as long the United States could retain the right to deploy defense systems against remaining nuclear arms (e.g., cruise missiles and bombers). Gorbachev raised the bet, proposing that the two sides abolish *all* nuclear weaponry by 1996. Reagan and Shultz were on board. "Let's do it," remarked the secretary of state. But the Soviet leader demanded one concession: that the United States confine further work on SDI to the laboratories for the ten-year period, in line with the ABM Treaty. Reagan balked, echoing the arguments he had made in Geneva. He wanted "a kind of gas mask against nuclear missiles." SDI was essential for deterrence "against the danger of nuclear maniacs." "I've heard all about gas masks and maniacs," replied Gorbachev. "But it still does not convince me." Reagan offered to share the benefits of space defense technologies with the USSR. But having publicly committed to SDI, and with the United States in a commanding position—economically, militarily, and technologically—the president refused to relent. "I have promised the American people I will not give up SDI," Reagan explained. "You're asking me to give up SDI [...] I cannot give in." So ended what Shultz called "the highest-stakes poker game ever played."[11] Reagan and Gorbachev emerged from Höfði House with disappointment etched on their faces. "I still think we can find a deal," Reagan said to Gorbachev as they parted ways. "I don't think you want a deal," Gorbachev replied. "I don't know what more I could have done." "You could have said yes," Reagan remarked.[12]

Both men returned home with an acute sense of letdown. An agreement to eliminate nuclear weapons had slipped away. "Reykjavik was too bold for the world," Shultz recalled. "It jarred people to think about no nuclear weapons."[13] But the disappointment subsided. In retrospect, the summit contained more positives than negatives. The initiative was a measure of just how much U.S.–Soviet relations had improved. (In any case, the complexities of effecting nuclear abolition would have been nigh impossible for Moscow and Washington to overcome.)[14] Reagan was philosophical. "The significance of that meeting in Reykjavik is not that we didn't sign agreements in the end," he told U.S. officials. "The significance is that we got as close as we did."[15] Moreover, the summit reconfirmed that in Gorbachev, Reagan had found a Soviet leader willing to compromise and help create a more stable international order.

It was Gorbachev who would make the concessions as the focus moved to INF talks. "No matter how difficult it is to do business with the United States, we are doomed to it," he told the Politburo in February 1987.[16] Gorbachev defied the hardliners opposed to his reforms. He agreed to eliminate one hundred medium-range warheads situated in the Asiatic part of the Soviet Union. (These were deployed to balance the U.S. nuclear weapons based in Asia and the Pacific.) With the Soviets having dropped their objections over the British and French nuclear arsenals, the INF Treaty was weighted in America's favor.[17] It was signed in December 1987 at the third Reagan–Gorbachev summit in Washington. Reagan was careful not to gloat, aware of Gorbachev's internal opposition. For the first time, an entire class of U.S. and Soviet nuclear weapons was eliminated.

Further summits (largely symbolic) followed in 1988. Reagan traveled to Moscow, where he strolled through Red Square arm-in-arm with Gorbachev. The Soviet leader visited New York in December and was warmly received by the American public. In a speech to the UN, Gorbachev announced a unilateral reduction of 500,000 troops in the Red Army and the withdrawal of six armored divisions stationed in Central Europe—having earlier ordered the withdrawal of all Soviet troops from Afghanistan (a process completed in February 1989). By then, Gorbachev was already embarking on a program of major economic and political reform. *Glasnost* (openness and transparency) and *perestroika* (restructuring) would usher in an unprecedented level of Soviet political liberalization, including individual rights such as freedom of speech and the introduction of elections. While the new freedoms facilitated the development of a civil society, the shift toward a "semi-market" system would prove an economic disaster. From January to September 1991, Soviet GNP fell by 12 percent, with basic consumer goods in short supply.[18]

As the foregoing facts suggest, Gorbachev was the principal human agent of change in the Cold War endgame. The question of why he chose to depart from traditional Soviet policy has sparked different interpretations. For the "triumphalists," the Soviet leader was outmaneuvered by the Reagan administration, which followed a carefully conceived strategy aimed at dismantling the USSR. The U.S. military buildup, allied with Reagan's tough negotiating posture and the threat of SDI, pushed the Soviet economy to breaking point and brought Gorbachev to heel.[19] This argument suffers from a lack of evidence. As historian Melvyn Leffler explains, the inner-workings of the National Security Council do not reveal a grand design to either "win" the Cold War or bring an end to the Soviet Union. On the contrary, they point to Reagan's nuclear abolitionism, and the administration's continued struggle to agree on a negotiating strategy to achieve arms reductions.[20] Robert Gates, then deputy director of the CIA, recalled that nobody in the U.S. government in January 1989 was predicting the events which subsequently occurred in

Eastern Europe.[21] Most of Gorbachev's top political and scientific advisers doubted the feasibility of SDI, and rejected the notion that the Soviet reforms were driven by Reagan's "dream"—as have many Sovietologists.[22]

Yet SDI was an important part of Soviet thinking. Gorbachev's fixation over "Star Wars" at Geneva and Reykjavik was not for nothing. In the minds of Soviet reformers, SDI reemphasized—in startling terms—the vastly superior American capabilities: technological, military, and economic. As Fredrik Logevall and Campbell Craig note, Soviet leaders could not simply ignore the issue, even if SDI remained a distant prospect and might never fully work. Defense Minister Dmitry Yazov, for example, railed against the U.S. effort "to attain military superiority over the USSR" and "use SDI to exhaust it economically."[23] For Gorbachev, SDI was part of the increasingly grim picture with which the Soviet Union had to contend, and underscored the need for reform. It was, however, of secondary importance in explaining the end of the Cold War.[24]

More persuasive is the argument that the key changes effected from 1989 (e.g., the relaxing of Soviet control in the Eastern bloc, the holding of free elections, and the eradication of the Berlin Wall) were primarily the result of factors originating in the USSR and elsewhere in Eastern Europe. These were factors largely (but not entirely) independent of the policies pursued by U.S. administrations. They include Gorbachev's own evolving predilections (reinforced by the Chernobyl nuclear disaster in April 1986); Soviet high politics; long-term structural problems besetting the Soviet economy; the role of non-state actors (Soviet and American); and the courageous efforts of citizens and peace groups across Eastern Europe.[25]

There was nothing inevitable about the change in Soviet policy or the collapse of the USSR. Quite the reverse. Notwithstanding its economic problems, the Soviet Union could (with some minor reform) have continued into the twenty-first century without great difficulty. Had one of the conservative, nationalist elites succeeded Chernenko in 1985, it is unlikely that Soviet policy (domestic or foreign) would have undergone serious reform. As Gorbachev took power, the USSR possessed more or less the same set of resources as a decade earlier. The Soviet leadership remained extremely secure, with little pressure from below for radical change.[26] As historian Stephen Kotkin notes: "In the 1980s Soviet society was fully employed and the regime stable. The country had low foreign debt and an excellent credit rating. It suffered no serious civil disorders until it began to reform and even then retained the loyalty of its shrinking but still formidable Armed Forces, Ministry of Interior, and KGB."[27]

Historian Archie Brown points out that while the Soviet system would sooner or later have reached crisis point, the direction of the resulting change could have gone the opposite way of *perestroika*.[28]

None of which is to diminish the important role played by Reagan (and subsequently George H. W. Bush) in bringing the East–West conflict to a peaceful resolution. Brown writes that "any American president with an ounce of common sense should, with Gorbachev as a partner, have been able to preside over the end of the Cold War."[29] The argument, while valid, fails to do justice to Reagan's handling of U.S.–Soviet relations. Nor does it contextualize the domestic political climate. As documented here, a significant rethink began in 1983–84—before Gorbachev held power—when Reagan departed from the rigid views of hardliners, aligning himself with the pragmatic wing. The result was an easing of the immediate tensions and a thaw in U.S.–Soviet relations. It was an example of crisis management that is too often overlooked.

Reagan continued to pursue a moderate course with Moscow in his second term. Freed from the burden of further elections, and with a new Soviet leader with whom to "do business," the president chose cooperation over confrontation. He rejected the counsel of powerful voices in his administration, the Republican Party, and the media, who were discomfited by the idea of negotiation. Weinberger, Casey, Gates, Ermarth, Clark, Poindexter, Perle, Lenczowski—none shared Reagan's desire to engage with Gorbachev. Nixon and Kissinger penned gloomy articles, warning Reagan of the pitfalls of dealing with the reformers in Moscow. "Any Western leader who indulges in the Soviets' disingenuous fantasies of a nuclear-free world courts unimaginable perils," the duo wrote in William F. Buckley's *National Review* in May 1987. Gorbachev, they claimed, was a traditional Soviet leader, whose foreign policy "can be said to be subtler implementation of historic Soviet patterns." In *Newsweek*, Kissinger suggested that Gorbachev's domestic reforms "may provide additional resources for expansionism and ideological challenges."[30] Reagan was attacked by conservatives for his handling of the Daniloff affair in 1986, when he struck a deal for the release of a U.S. reporter under arrest in Moscow in exchange for the release of a Soviet physicist arrested by the FBI. "George Shultz is a complete sellout and Ronald Reagan is behaving like a damn fool," bemoaned Howard Philips, chairman of the Conservative Caucus.[31]

For years, neoconservatives had issued calls to "let Reagan be Reagan." Now that Reagan *was* being Reagan, they did not like what they saw.[32] In his *Washington Post* column in April 1987, Charles Krauthammer wrote:

"Democratic leaders have a way of turning foolish in the presence of great dictators. Why is Gorbachev so readily extenuated by the leaders of the leading democracy? Because there is nothing that Western publics hunger for more than a communist with a human face. So when the smile reveals iron teeth, it is best to pretend we do not see them [...] Mr. Gorbachev, your iron teeth are showing."[33] Some "moderate" voices joined in the criticism. In a *Newsweek* article that same month, George Will argued: "Reagan seems to accept the core of the catechism of the antinuclear left, the notion that the threat to peace is technological, not political—the notion that the threat is the existence of nuclear weapons, not the nature of the Soviet regime [...] The prudent person's answer to Gorbachev's question— 'What are you afraid of'—is 'You—and perhaps Ronald Reagan'."[34]

The most sustained attack came from Weinberger, who chuntered angrily about the U.S. approach even after leaving the Pentagon. *Glasnost, perestroika,* and the removal of the Berlin Wall were not enough to placate him. In 1990, with the Brezhnev Doctrine dead, free elections underway, and Soviet republics seceding, Weinberger wrote: "Some attributed the Soviets' caving in to the changes in their leadership. But I was never able to accept that belief. My feeling has always been that no general secretary of the Communist Party of the Soviet Union will be allowed to alter in any fundamental way the basically aggressive nature of Soviet behavior." Gorbachev's concessions, he added, "do not mean that the USSR has given up its long-term aggressive designs."[35] A year later the USSR was dissolved.

The politics of foreign policy did not therefore disappear with Gorbachev's arrival in 1985. Anti-communism remained a useful political tool for the 1988 elections. As Democrats seized on the Iran-Contra scandal, hardline conservatives campaigned vigorously against ratification of the INF Treaty. Right-wing groups compared Reagan to Neville Chamberlain. Howard Philips continued to attack U.S. policy, calling Reagan a "useful idiot" for Soviet propaganda. The ideologues would lose the argument on INF. East–West relations were improving and the American public viewed Gorbachev positively. The Soviet leader was named *Time Magazine* "Man of the Year" for 1987, and by the time of the Moscow summit in May 1988, a Harris poll showed that 72 percent of American respondents had "a favorable impression" of Gorbachev. (The figure rose to 83 percent after the summit.)[36] But the Republican presidential candidate, George Bush (a moderate), pursued a "balancing act of courting right and center" to strengthen his credentials. Advisers told the vice president that anti-communism was the best means of appealing to middle class voters without alienating hardline conservatives.[37] Bush chose Indiana senator Dan Quayle as his running mate, a man who opposed the INF Treaty and claimed that Gorbachev was "no different from past Soviet leaders." *Perestroika*, Quayle said, was "nothing more than refined Stalinism."[38] Bush championed Reagan's national security achievements while projecting a far more hawkish image than his Democratic opponents. In November 1988, he defeated the Democratic candidate, Massachusetts Governor Michael Dukakis.

Reagan would downplay his contribution to the end of the Cold War, saying modestly that he had been 'dropped into a grand historical moment.'[39] But his role was more important than that. Reagan was willing to engage with the Soviets when others were not. He listened to the right people (George Shultz, Jack Matlock) and rejected the advice of naysayers opposed to negotiation, who cast Gorbachev as duplicitous and overhyped the Soviet threat. He was empathetic to Soviet fears of American military power, and conscious of the internal pressure Gorbachev faced from his own hardliners. Aware that the United States held the aces, Reagan told his foreign policy team to reach an agreement that did not "make [Gorbachev] look like he gave up everything." The Soviet leader, he said, must not be embarrassed or forced "to eat crow." "Let there be no talk of winners and losers," Reagan added. The aim was to establish a process of negotiation, "to avoid war in settling our differences in the future."[40]

The Geneva summit marked the end of the Second Cold War. As events drew to a close, Reagan sat down on the couch next to Gorbachev. "Mr. General Secretary, this is the first summit for both of us," he said. "Those leaders before us [at U.S.–Soviet summits] did not do so well. To hell with the old way of doing things. We'll do it our way and get something done." Gorbachev smiled broadly after hearing the translation. "I agree," he replied. Both men were true to their word.[41]

*

"The two men could hardly have been more different," recalled David Gergen. "Carter was a quiet, studious man who didn't try to fill a room. Reagan was a large, barrel-chested man who walked like John Wayne. Carter was inward-looking; Reagan loved to be 'one of the fellas'; Carter was Scotch-Irish; Reagan was all Irish."[42] Their policy instincts differed too. Both arrived in office with contrasting views on détente, arms control, military spending, strategic defense, human rights, and Third World intervention. But Carter and Reagan were pragmatic, subordinating ideology and principles for politics when needed. Nowhere was this more evident than in their approach toward the Soviet Union. Both presidents moved—Carter becoming more hawkish, Reagan more open to negotiation—by the end of their first terms, pushed by international affairs yet simultaneously incentivized by potential domestic gains to be found within their transformation.

To be sure, domestic politics was not the sole determinant. Foreign policy decisions rarely have monocausal roots. Ideology and strategy were often part of the mix. Some policies were the result of mainly external concerns (e.g., Carter's pursuit of the Panama Canal treaties; Reagan's response to the Polish crisis). But all major initiatives, however strategic or ideological, soon became bound up in domestic politics. Carter and Reagan made decisions on international issues based on political considerations throughout their presidencies. Carter was forced to placate his anti-détente critics (including those in his own party, such as Henry Jackson) in his bid to achieve a ratifiable SALT II agreement. Reagan, under pressure from farm belt senators and interest groups, removed the most economically effective of Carter's 1980 sanctions against Moscow (the grain embargo) within three months of taking office. His proposal for a Strategic Defense Initiative was as much a response to a political crisis as a strategic one. Reagan unveiled SDI amid a nationwide nuclear freeze movement, sagging approval ratings, an economic recession, heavy defeats in the midterm elections, and waning support for his military buildup. Just as Carter was forced to harden his defense posture by approving new military programs in 1979, so Reagan had to moderate his arms control positions in 1983—endorsing the findings of the Scowcroft Commission.

The political pressure intensified as election season began. Both administrations showed an increased urgency to align foreign policy with the public mood. Both presidents embarked on course correctives—introducing a string of new initiatives in 1980 and 1984. Carter lurched toward the right, adopting one hardline measure after another following the Soviet invasion of Afghanistan. Many were at odds with the principles he had earlier espoused. Reagan moved decisively toward the center, instituting changes in tone and policy. He began reversing the sanctions imposed on the USSR in 1980, directed officials to pursue a range of bilateral agreements (diplomatic and military), and invited Gromyko to a meeting at the White House. The diplomatic offensive was pursued despite worsening Soviet behavior at home and abroad, and veered from the formal strategy statements (e.g., NSDD 32 and 75).[43] Hardliners such as Weinberger and Lenczowski protested.[44] Reagan waved them away. Instead, he placed his trust in Shultz and in his own moderate instincts, reflecting a desire to improve relations and reduce nuclear arms.

The Carter and Reagan turns were dramatic moments in the late Cold War. But they were not equal in measure. Carter's policies in 1980 marked a full-fledged reversal from those pursued in 1977. The Reagan reversal was more modest, with the president able to embark on his course corrective without conceding major ground in the strategic arms talks. The disparity lay partly in their contrasting political fortunes. An economic recovery during 1983 had boosted Reagan's overall public support—even as confidence in his handling of foreign affairs remained low. By 1984, the "Reagan recession" had given way to "Morning in America." Carter's experience had been just the opposite. An economic recession and mounting inflation in 1979 (resulting from a new energy crisis) led to growing impatience with his administration. Carter's public approval ratings slumped. The Iran hostage crisis placed him under further pressure and came to symbolize America's problems. In the days and weeks thereafter, Carter was implored by his advisers to "personally take action."[45]

*

Shortly after the turn of the century, Robert McMahon argued that U.S. foreign relations history should be a "Janus-faced" field, looking inward as well as outward.[46] After all, that is how policymakers approach their craft: analyzing the context at home and abroad; weighing up costs and benefits; grasping the symbiosis between politics and policy. An overreliance on diplomatic exchanges and official statements can mislead—giving the impression that the makers and shapers of foreign policy paid little attention to public opinion, the election calendar, or how their decisions could affect them politically.[47] Decision-makers have always been averse to commenting on such issues. What is stated publicly seldom reflects what is said "behind closed doors." Anthony Lake, Bill Clinton's national security adviser, likened the discussion of domestic politics in U.S. foreign policy to the discussion of sex by the Victorians: "Nobody talks about it but it's on everyone's mind."[48] Politics was on the mind of Brzezinski and McFarlane, strategists whose memos were punctuated with references to credibility, timing, public opinion, Congress, elections, and rival candidates.

In general, rational democratic leaders do not stray far from public opinion, which rejects sustained extremes in foreign policy. This is particularly the case with first-term presidents (such as Carter and Reagan), when domestic incentives—personal and political—are brought to bear. The American electorate may have leaned toward firmness and distrust of Moscow, but was uncomfortable with unbridled hostility and protracted saber-rattling. Although U.S. presidents erred on the side of alarmism throughout the Cold War, they understood that political structures imposed bounds on permissible hawkish behavior. With an election looming in 1984, Reagan saw the need to temper his approach.[49]

Looking inward also reminds us that the American government is not a unitary actor, unfettered by internal division. The Carter and Reagan administrations faced powerful resistance on Capitol Hill and from within their respective parties—from liberals, moderates, conservatives, and neoconservatives. The push and pull of domestic pressures shaped foreign policy in ways that were undesired or unforeseen, from arms control and strategic defense to Lebanon and Central America. In the current era of hyper-partisanship, it is well to remember that bargaining and compromise have long played an important role in determining America's external actions. Only by assessing the full landscape—international *and* domestic—can we truly understand how the key figures operated: what influenced their risk calculus; why they chose certain policies over others; or why they decided to change course at a given time. Only by examining events at home and abroad can historians weigh the relative significance of diverse factors on the policymaking process. The convergence of these international and domestic dimensions (the "intermestic") is too often missing from historical scholarship.

In recent decades the "outward" (international, transnational history) has remained predominant, to a degree that obscures the centrality of American power and the vagaries of its political system. The United States was by far the most dominant nation in the post-1945 world, possessing more power (military, political, economic, ideological, social, cultural, scientific, and technological) than any other state. The wielders of that power—the presidency, cabinet, and executive agencies—merit deep and sustained attention. So, too, do domestic processes and events, which have often had a decisive impact on the course of U.S. foreign affairs.[50] International and transnational perspectives are vital, illuminating the results of U.S. actions around the globe, whether harmful or benign. But they do not necessarily bring us closer to understanding how and why American foreign policy is formed. On the contrary, they may have the opposite effect. To neglect the role of domestic politics is to ignore the internal sources of America's external behavior, limiting our perception of how and why the U.S. acts internationally. It is to distort the context in which policy is made, by downplaying the forces and constraints—real and perceived—with which decision-makers have to contend: public opinion, election campaigns, personal ambition, ideologies, rival candidates, the media, interest groups, and Congress, the world's most powerful legislative body.[51]

Back in 1977, Bayless Manning recognized that many policy issues blurred the lines between domestic and foreign.[52] In the new era of globalization, that international–domestic nexus has become more pronounced, not less. Populist leaders seize on intermestic affairs for political gain, from immigration and terrorism to war and trade. The United States has not been immune. A study on the politics of foreign policy in the Donald Trump years would require multiple volumes. But the reality is that American foreign policy has always been inherently political—that with rare exception there is no such thing as apolitical foreign policy.

Archives

Ronald Reagan Presidential Library (Simi Valley, CA)
RRPL

Lee Atwater Files
Howard Baker Files
James Baker Files
Morton Blackwell Files
William Clark Files
Richard Darman Files
Michael Deaver Files
Paula Dobriansky Files
Elizabeth Dole Files
Kenneth Duberstein Files
Executive Secretariat National Security Planning Group Files
Donald Fortier Files
David Gergen Files
George Keyworth Files
John Lenczowski Files
Robert Linhard Files
Jack Matlock Files
Robert McFarlane Files
Michael McManus Files
Edwin Meese Files
NSC Executive Secretariat Chron Files
NSC Executive Secretariat Head of State Files
NSC Executive Secretariat Meeting Files

NSC Executive Secretariat System Files
M. B. Oglesby Files
John Poindexter Files
Presidential Handwriting Files
Donald Regan Files

Jimmy Carter Presidential Library (Atlanta, GA)
JCPL

Bob Beckel Files
Zbigniew Brzezinski Donated Material
Landon Butler Files
Jimmy Carter Plains Files
Carter Presidency Project
Hedley Donovan Files
Hamilton Jordan Files
Frank Moore Files
NSA Brzezinski Material
NSA Staff Material
Presidential Handwriting Files
Gerald Rafshoon Files
Vertical Files
White House Central Files

Princeton University Mudd Library (Princeton, NJ)
PUML

David Aaron Papers
James Baker Papers
Don Oberdorfer Papers

Library of Congress (Washington, DC)
LOC

Stuart Eizenstat Papers
Paul Nitze Papers
William Odom Papers
Donald Regan Papers
Caspar Weinberger Papers

Boston College Burns Library (Boston, MA)
BCBL

Tip O'Neill Papers

Minnesota Historical Society (St. Paul, MN)
MNHS

    Walter Mondale Papers

United Kingdom National Archives (Kew, London)
UKNA

    Foreign and Commonwealth Office Records
    Prime Minister's Office Records

Digital National Security Archive (George Washington University)
NSA

Wilson Center Digital Archive (Washington, DC)
WCDA

Hoover Institution Archives (Stanford University)
HIA

Parallel History Project on NATO and the Warsaw Pact (ETH Zurich)
PHP

Miller Center of Public Affairs (University of Virginia)
MCPA

American Presidency Project (University of California, Santa Barbara)
APP

Foreign Relations of the United States (Washington, DC)
FRUS

Notes

INTRODUCTION

1. "The Political Report of the Central Committee of the CPSU to the Party Congress," Moscow, February 25, 1986, in Mikhail Gorbachev, *Toward a Better World* (New York: Richardson & Steinman, 1987), pp. 158–59.
2. Jimmy Carter, *White House Diary* (New York: Picador, 2010), p. 356.
3. ABC News–Harris Survey, "Kennedy Continues to Hold Wide Lead Over Carter in Race for Democratic Nomination," September 20, 1979, Vol. 1, No. 116. See: https://theharrispoll.com/wp-content/uploads/2017/12/Harris-Interactive-Poll-Research-KENNEDY-CONTINUES-TO-HOLD-WIDE-LEAD-OVER-CARTER-IN-1979–09.pdf
4. Presidential Job Approval, Jimmy Carter: The Gallup Poll, APP. See: www.presidency.ucsb.edu/statistics/data/presidential-job-approval
5. Betty Glad, *An Outsider in the White House: Jimmy Carter, His Advisors, and the Making of American Foreign Policy* (Ithaca: Cornell University Press, 2009), p. 197.
6. Transcript of Jimmy Carter Presidential Speech at University of Notre Dame, May 22, 1977, MCPA. See: https://millercenter.org/the-presidency/presidential-speeches/may-22–1977-university-notre-dame-commencement
7. Transcript of Jimmy Carter's "Meet The Press" interview on NBC, January 20, 1980, APP. See: www.presidency.ucsb.edu/ws/?pid=33060 See also: Robert Hunter to Brzezinski, "Speech on Soviet/Persian Gulf/Southwest Asia," January 11, 1980, ZB Donated Material, Geographical File, USSR; Afghanistan Reaction, Box 18, JCPL.
8. William Burr, "Jimmy Carter's Controversial Nuclear Targeting Directive PD-59 Declassified," September 12, 2012. See: http://nsarchive.gwu.edu/nukevault/ebb390/
9. For analysis of the "war scare" see: "The Soviet 'War Scare'," Report by the President's Foreign Intelligence Advisory Board, February 15, 1990, NSA. See: https://nsarchive2.gwu.edu/nukevault/ebb533-The-Able-Archer-War-Scare-

Declassified-PFIAB-Report-Released/2012-0238-MR.pdf; Marc Ambinder, *The Brink: President Reagan and the Nuclear War Scare of 1983* (New York: Simon & Schuster, 2018); Taylor Downing, *1983: The World at the Brink* (London: Little, Brown, 2018); Nate Jones (ed.), *Able Archer 83: The Secret History of the NATO Exercise That Almost Triggered Nuclear War* (New York: New Press, 2016); Benjamin Fischer, *A Cold War Conundrum: The 1983 Soviet War Scare* (Langley, VA: CIA Center for the Study of Intelligence, 1997).

10. Ronald Reagan, *An American Life: The Autobiography* (New York: Simon and Schuster, 1990), pp. 585–86.

11. John Mintz, "Doomsday Planning: From Bomb Shelters to Evacuation Routes," *Washington Post*, November 20, 1983.

12. David Hoffman, "In 1983 'War Scare,' Soviet Leadership Feared Nuclear Surprise Attack by U.S.," *Washington Post*, October 24, 2015.

13. Transcript of President Reagan's Address to the Nation and Other Countries on United States–Soviet Relations, January 16, 1984. See: https://reaganli brary.archives.gov/archives/speeches/1984/11684a.htm

14. Transcript of President Reagan's Address to the 39th Session of the United Nations General Assembly in New York, September 24, 1984. See: www .reaganlibrary.gov/sites/default/files/archives/speeches/1984/92484a.htm See also: Frances Clines, "Reagan, Meeting Gromyko, Asks for Closer Ties," *New York Times*, September 24, 1984.

15. Romesh Ratnesar, "Reagan's Message," Time's Annual Journey: 1989, *Time Magazine*, June 18, 2009.

16. Historians who refer to a "Second Cold War" or a "New Cold War" include: David Painter, *The Cold War: An International History* (Abingdon: Routledge, 1999); Olav Njølstad (ed.), *The Last Decade of the Cold War: From Conflict Escalation to Conflict Transformation* (Abingdon: Routledge, 2004); H. W. Brands, *The Devil We Knew: Americans and the Cold War* (New York: Oxford University Press, 1993); Campbell Craig and Fredrik Logevall, *America's Cold War: The Politics of Insecurity* (Cambridge, MA: Belknap Press/Harvard, 2009); Walter LaFeber, *America, Russia, and the Cold War, 1945–2002* (New York: McGraw-Hill, 2002); Kristina Spohr and David Reynolds (eds.), *Transcending the Cold War: Summits, Statecraft, and the Dissolution of Bipolarity in Europe, 1970–1990* (Oxford: Oxford University Press, 2016); John W. Young, *America, Russia and the Cold War, 1941–1998* (2nd ed.) (Harlow: Longman, 1999); Fred Halliday, *The Making of the Second Cold War* (2nd ed.) (London: Verso, 1986).

17. Excellent studies include: Raymond Garthoff, *Détente and Confrontation: American-Soviet Relations from Nixon to Reagan* (Washington, DC: Brookings, 1994); Raymond Garthoff, *The Great Transition: American-Soviet Relations and the End of the Cold War* (Washington, DC: Brookings, 1994); James Graham Wilson, *The Triumph of Improvisation: Gorbachev's Adaptability, Reagan's Engagement, and the End of the Cold War* (Ithaca: Cornell University Press, 2014); Don Oberdorfer, *From The Cold War to a New Era: The United States and the Soviet Union, 1983–1991* (Baltimore: Johns Hopkins University Press, 1998); Robert Service, *The End of the Cold*

War, 1985–1991 (New York: Public Affairs, 2015); Odd Arne Westad, *The Global Cold War: Third World Interventions and the Making of Our Times* (Cambridge: Cambridge University Press, 2005); Melvyn Leffler, *For the Soul of Mankind: The United States, the Soviet Union, and the Cold War* (New York: Hill and Wang, 2007); Louis Sell, *From Washington to Moscow: U.S.-Soviet Relations and the Collapse of the USSR* (Durham: Duke University Press, 2016). For wide-ranging international examinations of the late Cold War, see: Melvyn Leffler and Odd Arne Westad (eds.), *The Cambridge History of the Cold War: Volume 3: Endings* (New York: Cambridge University Press, 2010).

18. For analysis of the Soviet collapse, see: Archie Brown, *Seven Years that Changed the World: Perestroika in Perspective* (Oxford: Oxford University Press, 2007); Stephen Kotkin, *Armageddon Averted: The Soviet Collapse, 1970–2000* (Oxford: Oxford University Press, 2008); Vladislav Zubok, *A Failed Empire: The Soviet Union in the Cold War from Stalin to Gorbachev* (Chapel Hill: University of North Carolina Press, 2007); William Wohlforth, *Cold War Endgame: Oral History, Analysis, Debates* (University Park: Pennsylvania State University Press, 2003).

19. One of the few scholars to take issue with this notion was Beth Fischer in *The Reagan Reversal*. To date, this is the only work specifically addressing the Reagan "turn," but was written prior to the declassification of archival material. Fischer argued that U.S. policy had shifted before Gorbachev had arrived in power; that the Reagan administration decided on a new course of its own volition. In Fischer's view, the course adopted in 1984 was in direct response to the crisis in U.S.–Soviet relations in late 1983. The *Able Archer* war scare suddenly led the president to confront his fears about nuclear war and revise his attitude toward the Kremlin. "In essence [...] Reagan learned while in office." See: Beth Fischer, *The Reagan Reversal: Foreign Policy and the End of the Cold War* (Columbia: University of Missouri Press, 1997), pp. 1–2 & p. 148. Two works have specifically addressed the Carter "turn." Brian Auten rejects the theory that domestic politics, or *innenpolitik*, influenced the decision to change the complexion of defense policy. It was instead, he contests, "the result of a prudent (albeit late) change in the assessment of the Soviet's military power, and of its power projection capabilities." See: Brian Auten, *Carter's Conversion: The Hardening of American Defense Policy* (Columbia: University of Missouri Press, 2009), pp. 2–3. Conversely, David Skidmore does place the emphasis on domestic forces. However, as with Fischer's study on Reagan, it was written at a time when virtually no primary source material was available for research. See: David Skidmore, *Reversing Course: Carter's Foreign Policy, Domestic Politics, and the Failure of Reform* (Nashville: Vanderbilt University Press, 1996).

20. I refer to the literal, not the abstract—most subfields of history are at least to some extent "political." For example, the study of decision-makers, policy-makers, Congress, party politics, elections, and how they pertain to foreign policy. For a thought-provoking discussion on the subject, see:

Fredrik Logevall and Kenneth Osgood, "Why Did We Stop Teaching Political History?" *New York Times*, August 29, 2016.

21. Hal Brands, "The Real Gap," *The American Interest*, Vol. XIII, No. 1, September/October 2017, pp. 44–54.

22. Excellent studies include: Matthew Evangelista, *Unarmed Forces: The Transnational Movement to End the Cold War* (Ithaca: Cornell University Press, 1999); Daniel Thomas, *The Helsinki Effect: International Norms, Human Rights, and the Demise of Communism* (Princeton: Princeton University Press, 2001); Sarah Snyder, *Human Rights Activism and the End of the Cold War: A Transnational History of the Human Rights Network* (New York: Cambridge University Press, 2011); Niall Ferguson, Charles Maier, Erez Manela, and Daniel Sargent (eds.), *The Shock of the Global: The 1970s in Perspective* (Cambridge, MA: Belknap Press/Harvard, 2010); Joe Renouard, *Human Rights in American Foreign Policy: From the 1960s to the Soviet Collapse* (Philadelphia: University of Pennsylvania Press, 2015); Daniel Sargent, *A Superpower Transformed: The Remaking of American Foreign Relations in the 1970s* (New York: Oxford University Press, 2015).

23. Campbell Craig and Fredrik Logevall, *America's Cold War: The Politics of Insecurity* (Cambridge, MA: Belknap Press/Harvard, 2009), pp. 4–12.

24. See, for example: Barbara Keys, *Reclaiming American Virtue: The Human Rights Revolution of the 1970s* (Cambridge, MA: Harvard University Press, 2014).

25. For a fine examination of the interplay between structure and strategy in the late Cold War, see: Hal Brands, *Making the Unipolar Moment: U.S. Foreign Policy and the Rise of the Post-Cold War Order* (Ithaca: Cornell University Press, 2016).

26. Kyle Longley, "An Obsession: The Central American Policy of the Reagan Administration," pp. 211–31, in Bradley Lynn Coleman and Kyle Longley (eds.), *Reagan and the World: Leadership and National Security, 1981–1989* (Lexington: University of Kentucky Press, 2017).

27. For comparative studies of foreign policy, domestic and international influences, and executive leadership, see: Ryan Beasley, Juliet Kaarbo, Jeffrey Lantis, and Michael Snarr (eds.), *Foreign Policy in Comparative Perspective: Domestic and International Influences on State Behaviour* (Washington, DC: CQ Press, 2002); Ludger Helms, *Presidents, Prime Ministers and Chancellors: Executive Leadership in Western Democracies* (Basingstoke: Palgrave Macmillan, 2005).

28. For a good overview see: Eugene Wittkopf and James McCormick (eds.), *The Domestic Sources of American Foreign Policy: Insights and Evidence* (fifth edition) (Lanham: Rowman & Littefield, 2008).

29. Thomas Risse-Kappen, "Public Opinion, Domestic Structure, and Foreign Policy in Liberal Democracies," *World Politics*, Vol. 43, No. 4 (July 1991), pp. 479–512.

30. For insight into the legislative-executive relationship and foreign policy, see: James Lindsay, *Congress and the Politics of U.S. Foreign Policy* (Baltimore: Johns Hopkins University Press, 1994).

31. Thomas Schwartz, "Henry ... Winning an Election is Terribly Important: Partisan Politics in the History of U.S. Foreign Relations," *Diplomatic History*, Vol. 33, No. 22 (April 2009), pp. 173–90.
32. The literature remains thin, but see: Campbell Craig and Fredrik Logevall, *America's Cold War: The Politics of Insecurity* (Cambridge, MA: Belknap Press/Harvard, 2009); Julian Zelizer, *Arsenal of Democracy: The Politics of National Security – From World War II to the War on Terrorism* (New York: Basic Books, 2010); Robert David Johnson, *Congress and the Cold War* (Cambridge: Cambridge University Press, 2006); Andrew Johns and Mitchell Lerner (eds.), *The Cold War at Home and Abroad: Domestic Politics and U.S. Foreign Policy since 1945* (Lexington: The University Press of Kentucky, 2018); Andrew Johns, *Vietnam's Second Front: Domestic Politics, the Republican Party, and the War* (Lexington: The University Press of Kentucky, 2010).
33. Miroslav Nincic, "U.S. Soviet Policy and the Electoral Connection," *World Politics*, Vol. 42, No. 3 (April 1990), pp. 370–96; "Kennedy Attacks Nixon," *New York Times*, August 25, 1960.
34. Robert Divine, *Foreign Policy and U.S. Presidential Elections: 1952–1960* (New York: New Viewpoints, 1974), p. 44.
35. Melvin Small, *Democracy & Diplomacy: The Impact of Domestic Politics in U.S. Foreign Policy, 1789–1994* (Baltimore: Johns Hopkins University Press, 1995), pp. 93–97; Fredrik Logevall, "Domestic Politics," pp. 151–67, in Frank Costigliola and Michael Hogan (eds.), *Explaining the History of American Foreign Relations* (third edition) (New York: Cambridge University Press, 2016).
36. On the escalation of U.S. military intervention, see: Fredrik Logevall, *Choosing War: The Lost Chance for Peace and the Escalation of War in Vietnam* (Berkeley: University of California Press, 1999). On the role of domestic politics, see: Johns, *Vietnam's Second Front*.
37. Michael Armacost, *Ballots, Bullets and Bargains: American Foreign Policy and Presidential Elections* (New York: Columbia University Press, 2015), pp. 74–79; H. R. Haldeman, *The Haldeman Diaries: Inside the Nixon White House* (New York: Putnam, 1994), p. 223.
38. Douglas Brinkley and Luke Nichter (eds.), *The Nixon Tapes, 1971–72* (New York: Houghton Mifflin Harcourt, 2014), p. 607; Ken Hughes, *Fatal Politics: The Nixon Tapes, the Vietnam War, and the Casualties of Reelection* (Charlottesville, VA: University of Virginia Press, 2015); See also: http://tapes.millercenter.virginia.edu/clips/1972_0803_vietnam/
39. Samuel Beer, "A New Nationalism," *The New Republic*, January 27, 1979.
40. For analysis of neoconservatism and foreign policy, see: John Ehrman, *The Rise of Neoconservatism: Intellectuals and Foreign Affairs, 1945–1994* (New Haven: Yale University Press, 1995); Stefan Halper and Jonathan Clarke, *America Alone: The Neo-conservatives and the Global Order* (Cambridge: Cambridge University Press, 2004). For more information on the Committee on the Present Danger, see: Charles Tyroler (ed.), *Alerting America: The Papers on the Committee on the Present Danger* (New York: Permagon

Brassey's, 1984); Jerry Sanders, *Peddlers of Crisis: The Committee on the Present Danger* (Boston: South End Press, 1983).

41. Norman Podhoretz, "Making the World Safe for Communism," *Commentary*, April 1976.

42. Bayless Manning, "The Congress, the Executive, and Intermestic Affairs," *Foreign Affairs*, Vol. 55, No. 2, January 1977.

43. Armacost, *Ballots, Bullets and Bargains*, pp. 80–87; p. 104.

44. McFarlane to Reagan, "U.S.–Soviet Relations: A Framework for the Future," February 24, 1984, The Jack Matlock Files, Series I: Chron File, January–March 1984, Box 3, RRPL.

45. In *Choosing War*, historian Fredrik Logevall argues that credibility should be considered in terms of a three-part conception: domestically, internationally, and personally.

46. Armacost, *Ballots, Bullets and Bargains*, p. 106.

47. Brzezinski to Carter, "Reflections on Soviet Intervention in Afghanistan," December 26, 1979, ZB Donated Material, Geographic File, Southwest Asia; Persian Gulf, Box 17, JCPL.

48. Brzezinski to Carter, NSC Weekly Report: "U.S.-Soviet Relations," February 29, 1980, ZB Donated Material, Subject File, Box 42, JCPL.

49. Garthoff, *Détente and Confrontation*, p. 801.

50. Armacost, *Ballots, Bullets and Bargains*, pp. 41–42.

51. Zbigniew Brzezinski, *Power and Principle: Memoirs of the National Security Adviser, 1977–1981* (New York: Farrar, Straus & Giroux, 1983), pp. 427–29.

52. Brzezinski to Carter, "Strategic Reaction to the Afghanistan Problem," January 3, 1980, ZB Donated Material, Geographic File, Southwest Asia; Persian Gulf, Box 17, JCPL; Brzezinski to Carter, NSC Weekly Report: "Afghanistan: A Symptom or an Aberration?" March 28, 1980, ZB Donated Material, Subject File, Box 42, JCPL. The latter memo, written three months after the Soviet invasion, invoked "Russia's traditional push to the south," and "Molotov's proposal to Hitler in 1940 that the Nazis recognize the Soviet claim to pre-eminence" in the region. See also: Brzezinski, *Power and Principle*, p. 427.

53. Brzezinski to Carter, NSC Weekly Report: "Alert: The Arc of Crisis," December 2, 1978, ZB Donated Material, Subject File, Box 42, JCPL.

54. See: Garthoff, *Détente and Confrontation*, pp. 1046–75.

55. Fredrik Logevall, "Domestic Politics," p. 160, in Costigliola & Hogan (eds.), *Explaining the History of American Foreign Relations*.

56. Bernard Weinraub, "Mondale Pledges Immediate Effort for Arms Freeze," *New York Times*, September 6, 1984.

57. Lou Cannon and Margot Hornblower, "Reagan Defense Push May Backfire: Warmonger Image Resurfaces," *Washington Post*, April 7, 1983.

58. Wirthlin to Baker, Deaver, and Meese, "1984 Presidential Vote," September 2, 1983, The Michael Deaver Files, Series VI; Political Material, Box 65, RRPL.

59. "Reagan Campaign Action Plan," October 27, 1983, pp. 29–30, Series 10F: Reagan–Bush (General Election 1984), Box 136, Folder 1, The James Baker Papers, PUML.

60. Minutes of NSC Meeting, "Nuclear Arms Control Discussions," March 27, 1984. NSC Executive Secretariat Meeting Files, NSC 104-114, Box 11, RRPL.

61. Ronald Reagan, *Public Papers of the Presidents of the United States, 1984*, "Conference on U.S.-Soviet Exchanges", June 27, 1984 (Washington, DC: GPO, 1986), pp. 716–18.

62. "Presidential Directive/NSC-59: Nuclear Weapons Employment Policy," July 25, 1980, Vertical Files, JCPL.

63. Reagan, *An American Life*, pp. 585–86.

64. Memorandum by Kenneth Adelman (ACDA director) to Reagan: "Arms Control Possibilities in 1984," March 23, 1984. NSC Executive Secretariat Meeting Files, NSC 104-114, Box 11, RRPL.

65. NSDD-75, "U.S. Relations with the USSR," January 17, 1983. See: www.reaganlibrary.gov/sites/default/files/archives/reference/scanned-nsdds/nsdd75.pdf

66. Sell, *From Washington to Moscow*, pp. 133–34.

1 THE DWINDLING OF DÉTENTE

1. Jeffrey Frank, "The Primary Experiment: Jimmy Who?" *The New Yorker*, May 1, 2015.

2. Burton Kaufman and Scott Kaufman, *The Presidency of James Earl Carter Jr.* (Lawrence: University Press of Kansas, 2006), pp. 10–11.

3. Kandy Stroud, *How Jimmy Won: The Victory Campaign from Plains to the White House* (New York: William Morrow, 1977), pp. 185–87.

4. Robert Schulzinger, *U.S. Diplomacy Since 1900* (New York: Oxford University Press, 2002), p. 315.

5. Armacost, *Ballots, Bullets, and Bargains*, pp. 124–25; Christopher Lydon, "Carter Outlining Foreign Policy Views, Urges Wider Discussion," *New York Times*, March 16, 1976; Zelizer, *Arsenal of Democracy*, pp. 265–72.

6. Keys, *Reclaiming American Virtue*, p. 236; Stewart Patrick and Shepard Forman (eds.), *Multilateralism and U.S. Foreign Policy: Ambivalent Engagement* (Boulder: Lynne Rienner, 2002), p. 366. The argument cited by Anderson was originally attributed to Stuart Eizenstat, Carter's domestic policy adviser.

7. See Douglas Brinkley, *The Unfinished Presidency: Jimmy Carter's Journey Beyond the White House* (New York: Penguin, 1998).

8. Christian Peterson, *Globalizing Human Rights: Private Citizens, the Soviet Union, and the West* (New York: Routledge, 2012), p. 25.

9. Keys, *Reclaiming American Virtue*, p. 234; William Schmidli, *The Fate of Freedom Elsewhere: Human Rights and U.S. Cold War Policy Towards Argentina* (Ithaca: Cornell University Press, 2013), p. 88.

10. Garthoff, *Détente and Confrontation*, pp. 550–51.

11. Elizabeth Drew, "Human Rights," *The New Yorker*, July 18, 1977.

12. Craig and Logevall, *America's Cold War*, pp. 260–61.

13. Jussi Hanhimäki, *The Rise and Fall of Détente: American Foreign Policy and the Transformation of the Cold War* (Washington, DC: Potomac Books, 2013), p. 48.

14. John Lewis Gaddis, *Strategies of Containment: A Critical Appraisal of American National Security Policy during the Cold War* (New York: Oxford University Press, 2005), pp. 308–09.

15. Henry Kissinger, *The White House Years* (Boston: Little, Brown, & Company, 1979), p. 202.

16. Zubok, *A Failed Empire*, p. 220.

17. Young, *America, Russia and the Cold War, 1941–1998*, p. 159. The limits were as follows: 1,054 ICMBs for the United States and 1,618 for the USSR; 656 SLBMs for the United States and 740 for the USSR; 455 strategic bombers for the United States and 140 for the USSR.

18. LaFeber, *America, Russia, and the Cold War, 1945–2002*, p. 283.

19. Craig and Logevall, *America's Cold War*, pp. 268–69.

20. Zubok, *A Failed Empire*, p. 225.

21. Dan Morgan, "Jackson Emerges as Leader of Foreign Policy Opposition," *Washington Post*, October 22, 1973.

22. Ehrman, *The Rise of Neoconservatism*, pp. 33–34; Zelizer, *Arsenal of Democracy*, p. 245; Halper and Clarke, *America Alone*, pp. 40–68.

23. Brands, *The Devil We Knew*, pp. 149–50; Zelizer, *Arsenal of Democracy*, pp. 247–48.

24. Anatoly Dobrynin, *In Confidence: Moscow's Ambassador to America's Six Cold War Presidents* (New York: Times Books, 1995), p. 334.

25. Gerald Ford, *A Time to Heal* (New York: Harper & Row, 1979), p. 139.

26. Jimmy Carter, *Keeping Faith: Memoirs of a President* (New York: Bantam, 1982), p. 52.

27. See Glad, *An Outsider in the White House*, pp. 26–27.

28. Carter, *Keeping Faith*, p. 52.

29. Richard Burt, "Zbig Makes It Big," *New York Times*, July 30, 1978.

30. Interviews with Brzezinski and administration officials (1982), Carter Presidency Project, Box 62, JCPL; Cyrus Vance, *Hard Choices: Critical Years in America's Foreign Policy* (New York: Simon and Schuster, 1983), pp. 36–37.

31. Brzezinski, *Power and Principle*, pp. 147–49.

32. Scott Kaufman, *Plans Unraveled: The Foreign Policy of the Carter Administration* (DeKalb: Northern Illinois University Press, 2008), p. 18.

33. Brzezinski, *Power and Principle*, p. 3.

34. Bernard Gwertzman, "Vance and Brzezinski: Feuding Chapter by Chapter," *New York Times*, May 26, 1983.

35. Paul Warnke, "Apes on a Treadmill," *Foreign Policy*, Spring 1975, p. 16.

36. Robert Strong, *Working in the World: Jimmy Carter and the Making of American Foreign Policy* (Baton Rouge: Louisiana State University Press, 2000), pp. 13–44.

37. Paul Nitze, "Assuring Strategic Stability in an Era of Détente," *Foreign Affairs*, Vol. 54, No. 2, January 1976.

38. Brzezinski, *Power and Principle*, p. 21.

39. Interview with Jimmy Carter, November 29, 1982, Carter Presidential Oral History Project, MCPA.

40. Interview with Hamilton Jordan, November 6, 1981, Carter Presidential Oral History Project, MCPA.

41. John Dumbrell, *The Carter Administration: A Re-Evaluation* (Manchester: Manchester University Press, 1995), p. 30.

42. Kotkin, *Armageddon Averted*, pp. 48–50; Zubok, *A Failed Empire*, pp. 241–42.

43. For insight into Gromyko, see: McFarlane to Reagan, "Andrei Gromyko: The Consumate Soviet Diplomat," September 14, 1984, The Jack Matlock Files, Series I: Chron File, September-December 1984, Box 6, RRPL; David Remnick, "Gromyko: The Man Behind the Mask," *Washington Post*, January 7, 1985; Brzezinski to Carter, NSC Weekly Report: "Analysis of Gromyko," September 9, 1977, ZB Donated Material, Subject File, Box 41, JCPL.

44. Thomas, *The Helsinki Effect*, pp. 160–79; Zubok, *A Failed Empire*, pp. 254–55.

45. Garthoff, *Détente and Confrontation*, p. 647; Dobrynin, *In Confidence*, pp. 379–80.

46. Georgi Arbatov, *The System: An Insider's Life in Soviet Politics* (New York: Times Books, 1992), pp. 204–06.

47. John Newhouse, *War and Peace in the Nuclear Age* (New York: Vintage, 1990), p. 307.

48. Brzezinski to Carter, NSC Weekly Report: "Soviet Leadership Changes," May 26, 1977, ZB Donated Material, Subject File, Box 41, JCPL.

49. U.S.–Soviet Conference Transcript, p. 172, The Carter–Brezhnev Project, Fort Lauderdale (FL), March 23–26, 1995, Vertical Files, Box 115, JCPL; Garthoff, *Détente and Confrontation*, pp. 648–49.

50. Strobe Talbott, *Endgame: The Inside Story of SALT II* (New York: Harper & Row, 1979), p. 39; Garthoff, *Détente and Confrontation*, p. 624.

51. Dobrynin, *In Confidence*, pp. 379; The Carter–Brezhnev Project, "SALT II and the Growth of Mistrust," St. Simon's Island (GA), May 7–9, 1994, Transcript of Conference, pp. 40–41, NSA.

52. Vance, *Hard Choices*, pp. 48–49.

53. Brzezinski, *Power and Principle*, p. 50.

54. Carter to Brezhnev, January 26, 1977, Plains File, Carter–Brezhnev Correspondence, Box 17, JCPL.

55. Talbott, *Endgame*, p. 42; Glad, *An Outsider in the White House*, p. 48; Garthoff, *Détente and Confrontation*, pp. 884–85; Memorandum: "Moscow Commentary Lauds Statement on Limiting Nuclear Arms," January 27, 1977, NSA Brzezinski Material, Subject File: SALT, Box 52, JCPL.

56. For the Carter–Dobrynin meeting, see: U.S.–Soviet Conference Transcript, p. 170, The Carter–Brezhnev Project, Fort Lauderdale (FL), March 23–26, 1995, Vertical Files, Box 115, JCPL; Dobrynin, *In Confidence*, pp. 384–86; Carter, *Keeping Faith*, p. 217.

57. Brzezinski to Carter, "Summary of Conclusions of SCC Meeting," February 3, 1977, Vertical Files, Box 116, F: USSR, JCPL.

58. Bernard Gwertzman, "Choice of Arms Aide is Facing Opposition," *New York Times*, February 3, 1977; Strobe Talbott, *Endgame*, p. 56.

59. Robert Kaufman, *Henry M. Jackson: A Life in Politics* (Seattle: University of Washington Press, 2000), p. 361.

60. Carter to Brezhnev, February 14, 1977; Brezhnev to Carter, February 25, 1977; Carter to Brezhnev, March 4, 1977, Plains File, Carter–Brezhnev Correspondence, Box 17, JCPL.

61. Jackson to Carter: "Memorandum for the President on SALT," February 15, 1977, NSA Brzezinski Material, Subject File: SALT, Box 52, JCPL.

62. Kaufman, *Henry M. Jackson*, p. 363.

63. Carter to Jackson, 17 Feb. 1977, NSA Brzezinski Material, Subject File: SALT, Box 52, JCPL.

64. Dan Caldwell, *The Dynamics of Domestic Politics and Arms Control: The SALT II Treaty Ratification Debate* (Columbia: University of South Carolina Press, 1991), p. 40.

65. Talbott, *Endgame*, p. 53.

66. Sanders, *Peddlers of Crisis*, pp. 209–10; Bernard Gwertzman, "Choice of Arms Aide is Facing Opposition," *New York Times*, February 3, 1977.

67. Minutes of SCC Meeting, February 25, 1977, Vertical Files, Box 116, F: USSR, JCPL.

68. Brzezinski to Carter, "SCC Meeting," March 11, 1977, ZB Donated Material, Box 26, Meetings: SCC 9, JCPL; Brzezinski to Carter, NSC Weekly Report: "SALT," March 11, 1977, ZB Donated Material, Subject File, Box 41, JCPL; Talbott, *Endgame*, p. 57.

69. Talbott, *Endgame*, pp. 57–59.

70. Carter to Mondale, Vance, Brown, Warnke, and Turner: "Presidential Directive/NSC 7: SALT Negotiations," March 23, 1977, Vertical Files, Presidential Directives, Box 100, JCPL; Talbott, *Endgame*, pp. 60–61.

71. For the Carter–Kissinger meeting, see: The Carter–Brezhnev Project, "SALT II and the Growth of Mistrust," p. 59, NSA; Carter, *White House Diary*, pp. 34–35; Talbott, *Endgame*, p. 65.

72. Vance, *Hard Choices*, pp. 52–53; Dobrynin, *In Confidence*, p. 392.

73. Andrew Preston, *Sword of the Spirit, Shield of Faith: Religion in American War and Diplomacy* (New York: Alfred A. Knopf, 2012), pp. 575–79.

74. Stuart Eizenstat, *President Carter: The White House Years* (New York: St. Martin's Press, 2018), pp. 585–86.

75. Jordan to Carter, Memorandum, December 3, 1977, The Hamilton Jordan Files, Human Rights Policy, Box 34, JCPL.

76. The Carter–Brezhnev Project, "SALT II and the Growth of Mistrust," pp. 33–34, NSA.

77. Gaddis, *Strategies of Containment*, p. 346.

78. Garthoff, *Détente and Confrontation*, p. 624.

79. Christopher Wren, "Sakharov Receives Carter Letter Affirming Commitment on Rights," *New York Times*, February 18, 1977.

80. Bernard Gwertzman, "Carter and Mondale See Bukovsky, a Soviet Dissident," *New York Times*, March 2, 1977.
81. The Carter–Brezhnev Project, "SALT II and the Growth of Mistrust," p. 45, NSA.
82. Brezhnev to Carter, February 25, 1977, Plains File, Carter–Brezhnev Correspondence, Box 17, JCPL.
83. Brzezinski to Carter, NSC Weekly Report: "U.S.–Soviet Relations: A Preliminary Assessment," February 26, 1977; Brzezinski to Carter, NSC Weekly Report: "Opinions: U.S.–Soviet Relations," February 19, 1977, ZB Donated Material, Subject File, Box 41, JCPL.
84. Glad, *An Outsider in the White House*, p. 75; Dobrynin, *In Confidence*, p. 388.
85. Toon to Vance, "Brezhnev's Trade Union Speech: U.S.–Soviet Relations," March 21, 1977, NSA Brzezinski Material, Country File: USSR, Box 78, JCPL.
86. Dobrynin, *In Confidence*, p. 390; The Carter–Brezhnev Project, "SALT II and the Growth of Mistrust,' p. 57, NSA.
87. Vance, *Hard Choices*, p. 54; Dobrynin, *In Confidence*, p. 392; Bernard Gwertzman, "Vance and Brezhnev Open Moscow Talks," *New York Times*, March 29, 1977.
88. Andrei Gromyko, *Memoirs* (New York: Doubleday, 1989), p. 288.
89. Talbott, *Endgame*, p. 72.
90. The Carter–Brezhnev Project, "SALT II and the Growth of Mistrust," pp. 43–44, NSA.
91. Murrey Marder and Peter Osnos, "Vance and Soviets are Far Apart on Arms, Rights," *Washington Post*, March 29, 1977; "Excerpts from Secretary Vance's Press Conference on Arms Talks in Moscow," *New York Times*, March 31, 1977.
92. Garthoff, *Détente and Confrontation*, pp. 892–93. See also: Carter, *Keeping Faith*, p. 219.
93. David Shipler, "Gromyko Charges U.S. Seeks Own Gain in Arms Proposals," *New York Times*, April 1, 1977; David Willis, "Why Détente is Freezing Over this Summer," *Christian Science Monitor*, April 1, 1977.
94. Elizabeth Drew, *The New Yorker*, April 4, 1977, p. 112.
95. Vance, *Hard Choices*, p. 51.
96. Sanders, *Peddlers of Crisis*, pp. 191–203.
97. Craig and Logevall, *America's Cold War*, pp. 286–87; Zelizer, *Arsenal of Democracy*, pp. 273–74.
98. Paul Nitze, *From Hiroshima to Glasnost: At the Center of Decision – A Memoir* (New York: Grove Weidenfeld, 1989), p. 353.
99. "Common Sense and the Common Danger: Policy Statement of the Committee on the Present Danger," November 11, 1976, Tyroler (ed.), *Alerting America*, pp. 3–5.
100. Nicholas Thompson, *The Hawk and the Dove: Paul Nitze, George Kennan, and the History of the Cold War* (New York: Henry Holt, 2009), pp. 250–54.
101. Strong, *Working in the World*, pp. 23–24.

102. Strobe Talbott, *The Master of the Game: Paul Nitze and the Nuclear Peace* (New York: Alfred A. Knopf, 1988), pp. 152–53.
103. Tyroler (ed.), *Alerting America*, pp. 5–9.
104. Nitze, *From Hiroshima to Glasnost*, p. 354.
105. Caldwell, *The Dynamics of Domestic Politics and Arms Control*, pp. 102–03.
106. Sanders, *Peddlers of Crisis*, pp. 235–70; Ehrman, *The Rise of Neoconservatism*, pp. 97–136; Halper and Clarke, *America Alone*, pp. 40–68.
107. Caldwell, *The Dynamics of Domestic Politics and Arms Control*, pp. 102–03.
108. "What is the Soviet Union Up To?" April 4, 1977, Tyroler (ed.), *Alerting America*, pp. 10–15.
109. Talbott, *Endgame*, p. 82.
110. Dobrynin, *In Confidence*, pp. 394–95.
111. Carter later admitted that he should have "approached it differently, in a slower fashion." See: Interview with Jimmy Carter, November 29, 1982, Carter Presidential Oral History Project, MCPA.
112. Butler to Jordan, "SALT Politics," May 11, 1977, The Frank Moore Files, Senate Memoranda: SALT, Box 47, JCPL.
113. Minutes of SCC Meeting, "SALT," April 7, 1977, ZB Donated Material, Subject File, SCC Meetings, Box 26, JCPL; Memorandum by Brzezinski, "SALT," April 23, 1977, Vertical Files, Box 116, JCPL; Talbott, *Endgame*, p. 83.
114. Brzezinski to Carter, June 7, 1977, Vertical Files, Box 116, JCPL; Kaufman, *Plans Unraveled*, p. 42.
115. Vance, *Hard Choices*, p. 56.
116. Garthoff, *Détente and Confrontation*, pp. 894–95.
117. Coalition for a Democratic Majority, Open Letter to President Carter, May 14, 1977. Cited in: Sanders, *Peddlers of Crisis*, pp. 243–44.
118. Kaufman, *Plans Unraveled*, pp. 43–44.
119. Caldwell, *The Dynamics of Domestic Politics and Arms Control*, p. 104.
120. "Where We Stand on SALT," July 6, 1977, Tyroler (ed.), *Alerting America*, pp. 16–21.
121. Brzezinski, *Power and Principle*, p. 167; Butler to Jordan, "SALT Politics," May 11, 1977, The Frank Moore Files, Senate Memoranda: SALT, Box 47, JCPL.
122. Brzezinski to Carter, NSC Weekly Report: "U.S.–Soviet Relations," June 24, 1977, ZB Donated Material, Subject File, Box 41, JCPL; Brzezinski to Carter, NSC Weekly Report: "NSC Roundtable on the Future of the Soviet Economy," October 7, 1977, ZB Donated Material, Subject File, Box 41, JCPL.
123. Carter to Brezhnev, June 9, 1977; Brezhnev to Carter, June 30, 1977, Plains File, Carter–Brezhnev Correspondence, Box 17, JCPL.
124. The Carter–Brezhnev Project, "SALT II and the Growth of Mistrust," pp. 180–81, NSA; Brzezinski, *Power and Principle*, pp. 175–76.

125. Caldwell, *The Dynamics of Domestic Politics and Arms Control*, p. 104; Kaufman, *Henry M. Jackson*, pp. 364–65.

126. Rowland Evans and Robert Novak, "A Touchy Carter: Shades of Former Presidents?" *Washington Post*, August 13, 1977; Sanders, *Peddlers of Crisis*, p. 248.

127. Kaufman, *Henry M. Jackson*, p. 365.

128. Talbott, *Endgame*, pp. 123–24.

129. Record of Conversation between Gromyko and Carter, September 23, 1977, Archive of Foreign Policy, Russian Federation (AVP RF), Moscow, WCDA. See: https://digitalarchive.wilsoncenter.org/document/111256; Dobrynin, *In Confidence*, pp. 399–400; Carter, *Keeping Faith*, p. 220.

130. Record of Conversation between Gromyko and Carter, September 23, 1977, WCDA.

131. Gromyko, *Memoirs*, p. 289.

132. Carter, *Keeping Faith*, pp. 220–22.

133. Talbott, *Endgame*, pp. 131–32; Carter, *Keeping Faith*, p. 222; Gromyko, *Memoirs*, pp. 289–90; Dobrynin, *In Confidence*, p. 400.

134. Kaufman, *Plans Unraveled*, pp. 43–44.

135. Kaufman, *Henry M. Jackson*, pp. 365–66.

136. Letter by Carter to Jackson, October 20, 1977, Jimmy Carter Plains File, President's Personal Foreign Affairs File, USSR (SALT), 2-12/77, Box 5, JCPL.

137. Kaufman, *Henry M. Jackson*, p. 369; Dobrynin, *In Confidence*, pp. 400–01.

138. Carter, *Keeping Faith*, pp. 80–83.

139. Brzezinski and Moore to Carter, January 23, 1979, White House Central File, FO 6-1, JCPL.

140. Vance, *Hard Choices*, pp. 57–58.

141. Johnson, *Congress and the Cold War*, pp. 233–34.

142. Newhouse, *War and Peace in the Nuclear Age*, pp. 318–23.

143. Skidmore, *Reversing Course*, p. 46.

144. Newhouse, *War and Peace in the Nuclear Age*, pp. 309–10; Carter, *Keeping Faith*, p. 225.

145. Walter Pincus, "Neutron Killer Warhead Buried in ERDA Budget," *Washington Post*, June 6, 1977.

146. Brzezinski, *Power and Principle*, p. 303.

147. Strong, *Working in the World*, pp. 129–32.

148. NSC Memorandum to Brzezinski and Aaron, "SCC Meeting: Enhanced Radiation Weapon (ERW) and MBFR," November 14, 1977, ZB Donated Material, Subject File, SCC Meetings, Box 27, JCPL.

149. Brzezinski, *Power and Principle*, p. 302; Letter by Carter to Schmidt, September 19, 1977, Jimmy Carter Plains File, President's Personal Foreign Affairs, Box 1, Federal Republic of Germany, 9/77-11/80, JCPL.

150. Joe Renouard and Nathan Vigil, "The Quest for Leadership in a Time of Peace: Jimmy Carter and Western Europe, 1977–1981," pp. 314–15, in Matthias Schulz and Thomas Schwartz (eds.), *The Strained Alliance: U.S.-European Relations from Nixon to Carter* (New York: Cambridge University Press, 2010); Strong, *Working in the World*, pp. 135–38.

151. Eizenstat, *President Carter*, p. 619; Brzezinski, *Power and Principle*, p. 303; Richard Burt, "Neutron Bomb Controversy Strained Alliance and Caused Splits in the Administration," *New York Times*, April 9, 1978.

152. Memcon between Carter, Vance, Brzezinski, and Genscher, April 4, 1978, Jimmy Carter Plains File, President's Personal Foreign Affairs, Box 1, Federal Republic of Germany, 9/77-11/80, JCPL.

153. Helmut Schmidt, *Men and Powers: A Political Retrospective* (London: Jonathan Cape, 1990), pp. 63–64 and pp. 181–87; Kaufman, *Plans Unraveled*, p. 51.

154. Richard Burt, "President Decides to Defer Production of Neutron Weapons," *New York Times*, April 8, 1978; Strong, *Working in the World*, pp. 142–43; Kaufman and Kaufman, *The Presidency of James Earl Carter Jr.*, p. 115.

155. Transcript of Jimmy Carter Presidential Speech at University of Notre Dame, May 22, 1977, MCPA. See: https://millercenter.org/the-presidency/presidential-speeches/may-22-1977-university-notre-dame-commencement

156. The Carter–Brezhnev Project, "SALT II and the Growth of Mistrust," pp. 147–48, NSA.

157. Brzezinski to Carter, June 7, 1977, Vertical Files, Box 116, F: USSR, JCPL; "Summary of Conclusions at SCC Meeting," July 7, 1977, Vertical Files, Box 116, F: USSR, JCPL. See also: Garthoff, *Détente and Confrontation*, pp. 868–69; Glad, *An Outsider in the White House*, p. 57.

158. Presidential Directive/NSC-18: "U.S. National Strategy," August 24, 1977, Vertical Files, Presidential Directives, Box 100, JCPL. See also: Charles Mohr, "Carter Orders Steps to Increase Ability to Meet War Threats," *New York Times*, August 26, 1977.

159. Nancy Mitchell, "The Cold War and Jimmy Carter," in Leffler and Westad (eds.), *The Cambridge History of the Cold War: Volume III*, pp. 77–78. For an excellent study of Carter's policies toward Africa, see: Nancy Mitchell, *Jimmy Carter in Africa: Race and the Cold War* (Redwood City: Stanford University Press, 2016).

160. Brzezinski, *Power and Principle*, pp. 182–83; Memorandum of Conversation, SCC Meeting, February 14, 1978, Vertical Files, Box 117, JCPL.

161. Jimmy Carter, "The President's News Conference," March 2, 1978, *Public Papers of the Presidents*, pp. 440–42.

162. Brzezinski to Carter, "U.S.–Soviet Relations," April 7, 1978, ZB Donated Material, Subject File, Weekly Reports to the President, Box 41, JCPL. See also: Brzezinski to Carter, NSC Weekly Report: "The Psychology of Presidential Power," February 24, 1978, ZB Donated Material, Subject File, Box 41, JCPL.

163. Brzezinski to Carter, "SALT Uncertainties," April 14, 1978, ZB Donated Material, Subject File, Weekly Reports to the President, Box 41, JCPL.

164. Transcript of Carter's Address at Wake University in Winston-Sale, North Carolina, March 17, 1978, APP. See: www.presidency.ucsb.edu/documents/address-wake-forest-university-winston-salem-north-carolina; Transcript of Carter's Address at the U.S. Naval Academy, Annapolis, June 7, 1978,

APP. See: www.presidency.ucsb.edu/documents/address-the-commencement-exercises-the-united-states-naval-academy

165. Vance, *Hard Choices*, p. 88.
166. Garthoff, *Détente and Confrontation*, pp. 227–78; Craig and Logevall, *America's Cold War*, pp. 263–68.
167. Memcon between Jimmy Carter and Huang Zhen, February 8, 1977, Vertical Files, Box 40, JCPL.
168. Carter, *Keeping Faith*, p. 192.
169. Brzezinski to Carter, NSC Weekly Report: "Strategic Deterioration," February 9, 1978, ZB Donated Material, Subject File, Box 41, JCPL.
170. Carter to Mondale and Vance, March 16, 1978, Vertical Files, Box 116, JCPL; Carter, *Keeping Faith*, p. 194.
171. Brzezinski to Carter, NSC Weekly Report: "Human Rights in China," December 9, 1977, ZB Donated Material, Subject File, Box 41, JCPL.
172. U.S.–Soviet Conference Transcript, p. 128, The Carter–Brezhnev Project, Fort Lauderdale (FL), March 23–26, 1995, Vertical Files, Box 115, JCPL.
173. Memorandum of Conversation between Brzezinski and Deng Xiaoping, May 21, 1978, China, Vertical Files, JCPL; Kaufman, *Plans Unraveled*, p. 135; Leffler, *For the Soul of Mankind*, pp. 290–91; Glad, *An Outsider in the White House*, pp. 126–27.
174. Michael Schaller, *The United States and China in the Twentieth Century*, 2nd ed. (New York: Oxford University Press, 1990), pp. 207–08; Kaufman, *Plans Unraveled*, pp. 139–40.
175. Carter to Brezhnev, December 14, 1978, Plains File, Carter–Brezhnev Correspondence, Box 17, JCPL.
176. Garthoff, *Détente and Confrontation*, p. 782.
177. U.S.-Soviet Conference Transcript, pp. 131–33, The Carter–Brezhnev Project, Fort Lauderdale (FL), March 23–26, 1995, Vertical Files, Box 115, JCPL.
178. Dumbrell, *The Carter Administration*, p. 39.
179. Interview with Hamilton Jordan, November 6, 1981, Carter Presidential Oral History Project, MCPA.
180. Julian Zelizer, *Jimmy Carter* (New York: Times Books, 2010), p. 57.
181. Interview with Jimmy Carter, November 29, 1982, Carter Presidential Oral History Project, MCPA.
182. David Corbin, *The Last Great Senator: Robert C. Byrd's Encounters with Eleven U.S. Presidents* (Washington, DC: Potomac Books, 2012), pp. 170–73.
183. John Farrell, *Tip O'Neill and the Democratic Century* (Boston: Little, Brown, and Company, 2001), p. 452.
184. Dumbrell, *The Carter Administration*, p. 40.
185. Zelizer, *Jimmy Carter*, p. 58.
186. Jordan to Carter, "W.H. Staff Coordination Memo," January 1978, The Hamilton Jordan Files, Box 37, JCPL.
187. Moore to Rafshoon, October 12, 1978, Staff Offices, The Gerald Rafshoon Files, "Memoranda," Box 28, JCPL.

188. Harvey Summ and Tom Kelly (eds.), *The Good Neighbours: America, Panama, and the 1977 Canal Treaties* (Athens, OH: Ohio University Center for International Studies, 1988), p.60.
189. Kaufman, *Plans Unraveled*, p. 73.
190. Brzezinski to Carter, NSC Weekly Report: "Panama Canal Ratification Strategy: Or, the Taming of Byrd and Goldwater," August 26, 1977, ZB Donated Material, Subject File, Box 41, JCPL.
191. Butler to Jordan, "Foreign Policy Work Plans," June 25, 1977, The Hamilton Jordan Files, Box 34A, JCPL.
192. Johnson, *Congress and the Cold War*, p. 236.
193. Aragon to Jordan, "Status Report: Panama Canal Treaties Ratification Effort," November 30, 1977, The Hamilton Jordan Files, Box 36, JCPL.
194. Michael Hogan, *The Panama Canal in American Politics: Domestic Advocacy and the Evolution of Policy* (Carbondale: Southern Illinois University Press, 1986), p. 120; Skidmore, *Reversing Course*, pp. 113–14.
195. Craig and Logevall, *America's Cold War*, p. 295.
196. Adam Clymer, *Drawing the Line at the Big Ditch: The Panama Canal Treaties and the Rise of the Right* (Lawrence: University Press of Kansas, 2008), p. 56.
197. Mondale to Jordan, "Consultations with Senators on Foreign Policy Issues," August 2, 1977, The Hamilton Jordan Files, Box 36, JCPL; Jordan to Carter, "Status Report on the Panama Canal Treaty," August 1977, The Hamilton Jordan Files, Box 36, JCPL; Skidmore, *Reversing Course*, p. 117.
198. Aragon to Jordan, "Status Report: Panama Canal Treaties Ratification Effort," November 30, 1977, The Hamilton Jordan Files, Box 36, JCPL.
199. Jordan to Carter, "Meeting for Key People and Institutional Leaders," August 30, 1977; Jordan to Carter: "Update on Panama Canal/Revised Work Plan," October 1977, The Hamilton Jordan Files, Box 36, JCPL.
200. Carter, *Keeping Faith*, pp. 163–64.
201. Thomson to Jordan, "Presidential Telephone Calls to Senators," February 7, 1978, The Hamilton Jordan Files, Box 36, JCPL.
202. Johnson, *Congress and the Cold War*, p. 237.
203. Interview with Jimmy Carter, November 29, 1982, Carter Presidential Oral History Project, MCPA.
204. Moe to Mondale, Jordan, and Brzezinski, "SALT," April 10, 1978, The Hamilton Jordan Files, Box 37, JCPL.
205. Interview with Jimmy Carter, November 29, 1982, Carter Presidential Oral History Project, MCPA.
206. Interview with Hamilton Jordan, November 6, 1981, Carter Presidential Oral History Project, MCPA.
207. Transcript of Carter's Address at the U.S. Naval Academy, Annapolis, June 7, 1978, APP. See: www.presidency.ucsb.edu/documents/address-the-commencement-exercises-the-united-states-naval-academy
208. The Carter–Brezhnev Project, "SALT II and the Growth of Mistrust," p. 133, NSA.
209. Kaufman and Kaufman, *The Presidency of James Earl Carter Jr.*, pp. 121–22; Kaufman, *Henry M. Jackson*, pp. 355–56.

2 "IT'S ALL POLITICAL NOW"

1. Jordan to Carter, "SALT II Ratification Work Plan," January 30, 1979, The Hamilton Jordan Files, Box 53, JCPL.
2. Presidential Job Approval, Jimmy Carter: The Gallup Poll, APP. See: www.pr esidency.ucsb.edu/data/popularity.php?pres=39&sort=time&direct= DESC&Submit=DISPLAY;
3. Richard Neustadt, *Presidential Power and the Modern Presidents: The Politics of Leadership from Roosevelt to Reagan* (New York: Free Press, 1990), p. 240.
4. Adam Clymer, *Edward M. Kennedy: A Biography* (New York: Harper Perennial, 2009), pp. 268–69; Kaufman and Kaufman, *The Presidency of James Earl Carter Jr.*, pp. 166–67.
5. Carter, *White House Diary*, p. 283.
6. Kaufman and Kaufman, *The Presidency of James Earl Carter Jr.*, p. 167.
7. Brzezinski to Carter, NSC Weekly Report, "Midterm Assessment," January 26, 1979; Brzezinski to Carter, NSC Weekly Report: "Foreign Policy: Tone and Orchestration," February 24, 1979, ZB Donated Material, Subject File, Box 42, JCPL.
8. Brzezinski to Carter, NSC Weekly Report: "Alert: The Arc of Crisis," December 2, 1978, ZB Donated Material, Subject File, Box 42, JCPL.
9. Brzezinski to Carter, NSC Weekly Report: "Foreign Policy and Domestic Politics," April 12, 1979, ZB Donated Material, Subject File, Box 42, JCPL.
10. *Time Magazine*, January 1, 1979, pp. 12–41.
11. Glad, *An Outsider in the White House*, p. 130.
12. Kaufman, *Henry M. Jackson*, p. 380.
13. Carter, *Keeping Faith*, pp. 206–09.
14. Jimmy Carter, *Public Papers of the Presidents of the United States, 1979*, "The State of the Union: Annual Message to Congress," January 25, 1979 (Washington, DC: GPO, 1980), p. 158.
15. For the US planning see: Brzezinski to Vance, February 16, 1979, ZB Donated Material, Box 10, Sino-Vietnamese Conflict, JCPL; NSC Meeting, February 16, 1979, NSA Staff Material: Far East, Oksenberg File, Box 46, F: Meetings, 2/1–18/79, JCPL.
16. Carter to Brezhnev, February 17, 1979; Brezhnev to Carter, February 18, 1979, Plains File, Carter–Brezhnev Correspondence, Box 17, JCPL.
17. Craig Whitney, "Gromyko Says China Obstructs Improved U.S.-Soviet Relations," *New York Times*, February 27, 1979. See also: Glad, *An Outsider in the White House*, p. 133.
18. Dobrynin, *In Confidence*, pp. 418–19.
19. Nimetz to Moore, Beckel, and The White House, "Ratification Program for SALT II," October 6, 1978; Hodding Carter III to Nimetz, "Public Attitudes toward SALT: A Summary of the Poll Data," September 19, 1978, The Bob Beckel Files, Box 228, JCPL.
20. Moore and Beckel to SALT Working Group, "Congressional Planning and Outlook," October 12, 1978, The Hamilton Jordan Files, Box 54, JCPL.

21. Robert Byrd, *Child of the Appalachian Coalfields* (Morgantown: West Virginia University Press, 2005), pp. 396–97.
22. Jordan to Carter, "SALT II Ratification Work Plan," January 30, 1979, The Hamilton Jordan Files, Box 53, JCPL.
23. Brzezinski to Carter, NSC Weekly Report: "Foreign Policy and Domestic Politics," April 12, 1979, ZB Donated Material, Subject File, Box 42, JCPL.
24. Sanders, *Peddlers of Crisis*, p. 259; Tyroler (ed.), *Alerting America*, pp. 99–123.
25. Albright to Brzezinski, "Briefing for Roth Group Senators on SALT," March 21, 1979, ZB Donated Material, Subject File: SALT, Box 38, JCPL.
26. Newhouse, *War and Peace in the Nuclear Age*, pp. 318–23.
27. Brzezinski to Carter, NSC Weekly Report: "The U.S. Performance under your Leadership in the US–Soviet Rivalry," March 30, 1979; Brzezinski to Carter, NSC Weekly Report: "Foreign Policy and Domestic Politics," April 12, 1979, ZB Donated Material, Subject File, Box 42, JCPL; Brzezinski, *Power and Principle*, pp. 337–38.
28. Newhouse, *War and Peace in the Nuclear Age*, p. 304.
29. Johnson, *Congress and the Cold War*, p. 244.
30. Jack Matlock, *Reagan and Gorbachev: How the Cold War Ended* (New York: Random House, 2004), p. 11.
31. Newhouse, *War and Peace in the Nuclear Age*, p. 323.
32. Richard Burt, "Liberal Senators Say Arms Pact Would Not Curb Weapons Race," *New York Times*, March 5, 1979. See also: Caldwell, *The Domestic Dynamics of Arms Control*, p. 134.
33. Johnson, *Congress and the Cold War*, p. 244.
34. Cambridge Survey Research, "Results of miscellaneous questions on the February 1979 DNC survey," May 24, 1979; Cambridge Survey Research to the DNC, "The Political Situation and President Carter," May 25, 1979, The Hamilton Jordan Files, Box 33, Pat Caddell, JCPL.
35. Brzezinski, *Power and Principle*, p. 334.
36. Carter, *Keeping Faith*, p. 241.
37. Newhouse, *War and Peace in the Nuclear Age*, p. 323.
38. The Carter–Brezhnev Project, "SALT II and the Growth of Mistrust," p. 133, NSA.
39. Dobrynin, *In Confidence*, p. 420.
40. Vance to Carter, "Your Meetings with President Brezhnev in Vienna," June 8, 1979, The Carter–Brezhnev Project, "Global Competition and the Deterioration of US–Soviet Relations, 1977–1980," NSA.
41. Don Oberdorfer, "Two Great Powers, But Modest Aims," *Washington Post*, June 10, 1979.
42. Carter, *Keeping Faith*, pp. 241–42; Note by Brzezinski to Carter on Harriman memo, June 12, 1979, Jimmy Carter Plains File, Presidents Personal Foreign Affairs, Box 5, USSR, 9/77–12/80, JCPL.
43. Carter, *Keeping Faith*, p. 257.
44. Ibid., pp. 244–61; Dobrynin, *In Confidence*, p. 426.
45. For specific details of the treaty, see: Young, *America, Russia and the Cold War, 1941–1998* (2nd ed.), pp. 161–63; Dobrynin, *In Confidence*, p. 423.

For a record of the Vienna summit, see: "Memorandum of Conversation: Meeting between President Carter and President Brezhnev," June 16–18, 1979, Plenary sessions 1–5, The Carter–Brezhnev Project, "Global Competition and the Deterioration of U.S.–Soviet Relations, 1977–1980," NSA; "Memorandum of Conversation: Meeting between President Carter and President Brezhnev," June 16–18, 1979, Plenary sessions 1–5, Vertical Files, Box 116, F: USSR Rel. Docs, JCPL.

46. Carter, *Keeping Faith*, p. 261; Brzezinski, *Power and Principle*, pp. 343–44; Vance, *Hard Choices*, p. 139.
47. Dobrynin, *In Confidence*, p. 425.
48. Presidential Job Approval, Jimmy Carter: The Gallup Poll, APP. See: www.presidency.ucsb.edu/data/popularity.php?pres=39&sort=time&direct=DESC&Submit=DISPLAY; See also: Caldwell, *The Domestic Dynamics of Arms Control*, p. 91.
49. Don Oberdorfer, "Two Great Powers, But Modest Aims," *Washington Post*, June 10, 1979.
50. Kaufman, *Henry M. Jackson*, pp. 385–86; Dumbrell, *The Carter Presidency*, p. 185.
51. Jimmy Carter, *White House Diary*, p. 332.
52. Schulzinger, *U.S. Diplomacy Since 1900*, p. 327.
53. Kaufman and Kaufman, *The Presidency of James Earl Carter Jr.*, p. 177.
54. Text of President Carter's Address to the Nation on Energy and National Goals, July 15, 1979, APP. See: www.presidency.ucsb.edu/ws/?pid=32596
55. See for example: Edward Walsh, "Carter Finds Crisis of Confidence," *The Washington Post*, July 16, 1979.
56. Tip O'Neill, *Man of the House: The Life and Political Memoirs of Speaker Tip O'Neill* (New York: Random House, 1987), p. 318.
57. Dobrynin, *In Confidence*, p. 412.
58. Frank Church, "SALT II, Linkage, and National Security," *Arms Control Today*, The Arms Control Association, Vol. 8, No. 8, August/September 1978. The publication can be found in: The Bob Beckel Files, Box 220, JCPL. See also: LeRoy Ashby and Rod Gramer, *Fighting the Odds: The Life of Senator Frank Church* (Pullman: Washington State University Press, 1994), pp. 591–92.
59. Ashby and Gramer, *Fighting the Odds*, p. 593.
60. See: Jordan to Carter, "SALT II Ratification Work Plan," January 30, 1979, The Hamilton Jordan Files, Box 53, JCPL.
61. "A Safer U.S. With a SALT Treaty?" *U.S. News & World Report*, March 13, 1978.
62. Letter from Jackson, Nunn, and Tower to Carter, August 2, 1979, The Bob Beckel Files, Box 230, SALT II memo, JCPL.
63. Caldwell, *The Domestic Dynamics of Arms Control*, pp. 140–41.
64. "2,300-Man Soviet Unit Now in Cuba," *Washington Post*, August 31, 1979.
65. See also: Gloria Duffy, "Crisis Mangling and the Cuban Brigade," *International Security* (Summer 1983), Vol. 1, No. 1, pp. 67–87; David Newsom, *The Soviet Brigade in Cuba: A Study in Political Diplomacy*

(Bloomington: Indiana University Press, 1987); Strong, *Working in the World*, pp. 208–32.

66. Strong, *Working in the World*, p. 209.
67. Garthoff, *Détente and Confrontation*, p. 918.
68. Duffy, "Crisis Mangling and the Cuban Brigade," pp. 72–73.
69. David Binder, "Soviet Brigade: How the U.S. Traced It," *New York Times*, September 13, 1979.
70. Don Oberdorfer, "Cuban Crisis Mishandled, Insiders and Outsiders Agree," *Washington Post*, October 16, 1979.
71. Ibid.
72. David Binder, "Soviet Brigade: How the U.S. Traced It," *New York Times*, September 13, 1979.
73. Newsom, *The Soviet Brigade in Cuba*, p. 34.
74. Duffy, "Crisis Mangling and the Cuban Brigade," p. 78.
75. Ashby and Gramer, *Fighting the Odds*, pp. 590–92.
76. Vance, *Hard Choices*, p. 361.
77. Duffy, "Crisis Mangling and the Cuban Brigade," p. 79.
78. Newsom, *The Soviet Brigade in Cuba*, pp. 79–80. See Appendix D: "Text of Televised Remarks by President Carter," September 7, 1979.
79. Garthoff, *Détente and Confrontation*, p. 918.
80. David Binder, "Soviet Brigade: How the U.S. Traced It," *New York Times*, September 13, 1979.
81. Ibid., pp. 926–27.
82. Garthoff, *Détente and Confrontation*, p. 923; Dobrynin, *In Confidence*, p. 429.
83. U.S.–Soviet Conference Transcript, pp. 287–88, The Carter–Brezhnev Project, Fort Lauderdale (FL), March 23–26, 1995, Vertical Files, Box 115, JCPL. See also: Dobrynin, *In Confidence*, p. 429.
84. Robert Gates, *From the Shadows: The Ultimate Insider's Story of Five Presidents and How They Won the Cold War* (New York: Simon & Schuster, 1996), p. 159.
85. Carter to Brezhnev, September 25, 1979; Brezhnev to Carter, September 27, 1979. Plains File, Carter–Brezhnev Correspondence, Box 17, JCPL.
86. U.S.–Soviet Conference Transcript, p. 313, The Carter–Brezhnev Project, Fort Lauderdale (FL), March 23–26, 1995, Vertical Files, Box 115, JCPL.
87. Brzezinski to Carter, Memorandum, September 1979, ZB Donated Material, Geographic File, Box 10, Cuba 9/78-9/79, JCPL. See also: Brement to Brzezinski, "VBB: The Soviet Brigade in Cuba – Where do we go from here?" September 12, 1979, ZB Donated Material, Subject File, VBB meetings, Box 33, JCPL.
88. The "wise men" were as follows: George Ball, McGeorge Bundy, Clark Clifford, Roswell Gilpatrick, Averell Harriman, Nicholas Katzenbach, Henry Kissinger, Sol Linowitz, John McCloy, John McCone, David Packard, William Rodgers, Dean Rusk, James Schlesinger, Brent Scowcroft, and William Scranton. For Carter's handwritten notes on their meetings, see: Jimmy Carter, Plains File, Box 21, Cuba: Soviet Troops, September–October 1979, JCPL.

89. Hedley Donovan (Senior Adviser to the President) to Brzezinski and Cutler, September 27, 1979, NSA Brzezinski Material, Country File, Box 16, Cuba: Soviet Brigade (meetings), September 1979, JCPL.

90. McGeorge Bundy to Clark Clifford, September 26, 1979, The Landon Butler Files, Box 130, SALT Memoranda and Correspondence, JCPL.

91. Brzezinski, *Power and Principle*, p. 349.

92. Ibid., p. 349; Byrd, *Child of the Appalachian Coalfields*, p. 403.

93. Newsom, *The Soviet Brigade in Cuba*, pp. 81–86.

94. Robert Kaiser, "Senate Votes for Five Percent Defense Increase," *Washington Post*, September 19, 1979.

95. Brzezinski, *Power and Principle*, pp. 352–53. See also: Vance, *Hard Choices*, p. 364.

96. Gates, *From the Shadows*, p. 160.

97. Colman McCarthy, "Suddenly the President Began to Stagger. His Face Was Ashen," *Washington Post*, September 16, 1979.

98. Lake to Vance, "The Human Rights Policy: An Interim Assessment," January 16, 1978, White House Central Files, Box HU, Human Rights, JCPL.

99. Dumbrell, *The Carter Presidency*, p. 185; Cambridge Survey Research, "Results of Miscellaneous Questions on the DNC Survey," May 24, 1979, The Hamilton Jordan Files, Box 33, Pat Caddell, JCPL.

100. Caddell to Carter, Memorandum, September 25, 1979, Office of the Staff Secretary, President's Handwriting File, Box 149, JCPL. See also: Strong, *Working in the World*, pp. 221–22.

101. Alan Raymond to Beckel, Butler, and Rafshoon, "Memorandum: SALT II," August 20, 1979, The Landon Butler Files, Box 130, JCPL; Richard Sobel, *The Impact of Public Opinion on U.S. Foreign Policy Since Vietnam* (New York: Oxford University Press, 2001), p. 38.

102. Bill Smith to Beckel, "Some Thoughts on SALT Strategy and Tactics," August 2, 1979, The Bob Beckel Files, Box 230, SALT II memo, JCPL.

103. Butler to Jordan: "SALT II Work Plan for September," August 13, 1979, The Landon Butler Files, Box 130, JCPL.

104. Jordan and Moore to Carter, "SALT Outlook: Senate," August 1979, The Bob Beckel Files, Box 230, SALT II memos, 7/30/79-8/17/79, JCPL.

3 TO THE RIGHT

1. "Reagan Angered John Wayne," *New York Times*, March 16, 1987.

2. Carter, *White House Diary*, p. 318.

3. Garthoff, *Détente and Confrontation*, p. 1077.

4. Transcript of Jimmy Carter's "Meet The Press" interview on NBC, January 20, 1980, APP. See: www.presidency.ucsb.edu/ws/?pid=33060; See also: Robert Hunter to Brzezinski, "Speech on Soviet/Persian Gulf/Southwest Asia," January 11, 1980, ZB Donated Material, Geographical File, USSR; Afghanistan Reaction, Box 18, JCPL.

5. Clymer, *Edward M. Kennedy*, p. 276.

6. O'Neill, *Man of the House*, p. 326.
7. Edward M. Kennedy, *True Compass: A Memoir* (New York: Twelve, 2009), p. 367. An ABC–Harris Poll on September 20 showed the Massachusetts senator leading Carter by a 61–34 percent margin in the race for the Democratic nomination. ABC News–Harris Survey, "Kennedy Continues to Hold Wide Lead Over Carter in Race for Democratic Nomination," September 20, 1979, Vol. 1, No. 116. See: https://theharrispoll.com/wp-content/uploads/2017/12/Harris-Interactive-Poll-Research-KENNEDY-CONTINUES-TO-HOLD-WIDE-LEAD-OVER-CARTER-IN-1979-09.pdf
8. Carter, *White House Diary*, p. 356.
9. Farrell, *Tip O'Neill and the Democratic Century*, p. 532.
10. Paul Kengor, *The Crusader: Ronald Reagan and the Fall of Communism* (New York: Harper Perennial, 2006), p. 42.
11. Kiron Skinner, Annelise Anderson, and Martin Anderson (eds.), *Reagan, In His Own Hand* (New York: Touchstone, 2002), p. 15.
12. Ibid., pp. 84–85.
13. John Patrick Diggins, *Ronald Reagan: Fate, Freedom, and the Making of History* (New York: Norton, 2007), p. 158.
14. Caddell to Carter, "Recent Polls and Implications for Strategy," November 6, 1979, The Hamilton Jordan Files, Box 33, Pat Caddell, JCPL.
15. Leffler, *For the Soul of Mankind*, pp. 299–301.
16. Schulzinger, *U.S. Diplomacy Since 1900*, pp. 328–29.
17. Carter, *Keeping Faith*, p. 453.
18. Hamilton Jordan, *Crisis: The Last Year of the Carter Presidency* (New York: Putnam, 1982), p. 31.
19. Terence Smith, "Why Carter Admitted the Shah," *New York Times*, May 17, 1981.
20. Gaddis Smith, *Morality, Reason, and Power: American Diplomacy in the Carter Years* (New York: Hill and Wang, 1986), p. 198.
21. Carter, *Keeping Faith*, p. 459.
22. Eizenstat to Jordan, "Actions Toward Iran," November 9, 1979; McDonald to Jordan and Powell, "Food Exports to Iran," November 16, 1979; Jordan to Carter, Memorandum, November 1979 (n.d.), The Hamilton Jordan Files, Box 34, Iran, 11/79, JCPL.
23. Carter, *Keeping Faith*, pp. 459–60.
24. For SCC meetings discussing responses to the hostage crisis during November, see: ZB Donated Material, Subject File, SCC meetings, Box 30, JCPL.
25. Presidential Job Approval, Jimmy Carter: The Gallup Poll, APP. See: www.presidency.ucsb.edu/data/popularity.php?pres=39&sort=time&direct=DESC&Submit=DISPLAY
26. Carter, *White House Diary*, p. 377.
27. Clymer, *Edward M. Kennedy*, p. 277–79.
28. Carter, *White House Diary*, p. 367.
29. Jordan, *Crisis*, pp. 21–22.

30. David Farber, *Taken Hostage: The Iran Hostage Crisis and America's First Encounter with Radical Islam* (Princeton: Princeton University Press, 2004), pp. 163–64.
31. Ibid.
32. Chester Pach, "*Top Gun*, Toughness, and Terrorism: Some Reflections on the Elections of 1980 and 2004," *Diplomatic History*, Vol. 28 (September 2004), p. 553.
33. See Brzezinski's memo and Carter's handwritten response: Brzezinski to Carter, NSC Weekly Report: "Difficult Choices in Iran," December 21, 1979, ZB Donated Material, Subject File, Box 42, JCPL.
34. Jimmy Carter, *Public Papers of the Presidents of the United States, 1979* (Washington, DC: GPO, 1980), pp. 2239–40.
35. For a good analysis of Soviet–Afghan affairs in 1978–79, see: Garthoff, *Détente and Confrontation*, pp. 977–1046; Zubok, *A Failed Empire*, pp. 259–64.
36. Transcript of Brezhnev–Honecker summit in East Berlin (excerpt on Iran and Afghanistan), October 4, 1979, The Cold War International History Project (CWIHP), Bulletin 8–9 (Winter, 1996), pp. 156–57, WCDA.
37. Gromyko–Andropov–Ustinov–Ponomarev Report to CPSU CC, October 29, 1979, CWIHP, Bulletin 8–9 (Winter, 1996), pp. 157–58, WCDA.
38. Garthoff, *Détente and Confrontation*, p. 1036.
39. The Carter–Brezhnev Project, "The Intervention in Afghanistan and the Fall of Détente," Lysebu, September 17–20, 1995, Transcript of Conference, p. 73, NSA.
40. "Transcript of CPSU CC Politburo Discussions on Afghanistan," March 17, 1979, WCDA. See: http://digitalarchive.wilsoncenter.org/document/113260
41. "When and Why the Decision to Send Troops [to Afghanistan] Was Made" [from Georgy M. Kornienko, *The Cold War: Testimony of a Participant*, Moscow, Mezhdunarodnye Otnosheniya, 1994, pp. 193–95], NSA. See: https://nsarchive2.gwu.edu//dc.html?doc=5696259-Document-7-When-and-why-the-decision-to-send
42. "Summary of a meeting on Afghanistan," December 10, 1979, WCDA, A. A. Lyakhovskiy's "Plamya Afgana" ("Flame of the Afghanistan veteran," Iskon, Moscow, 1999); Translated for CWIHP by Gary Goldberg. https://digitalarchive.wilsoncenter.org/document/111780 ; Aleksandr Lyakhovsky, *The Tragedy and Valor of Afghan* (GPI Iskon, Moscow, 1995), pp. 109–12, "Soviet Decisions in December 1979," NSA. See: https://nsarchive2.gwu.edu//dc.html?doc=5696257-Document-5-Soviet-Decisions-in-December-1979; Garthoff, *Détente and Confrontation*, p. 1015.
43. The Carter–Brezhnev Project, "The Intervention in Afghanistan and the Fall of Détente," pp. 90–91, NSA.
44. Ibid., pp. 85–86.
45. Ibid., p. 95.
46. Vance, *Hard Choices*, p. 386.
47. The Carter–Brezhnev Project, "The Intervention in Afghanistan and the Fall of Détente," p. 38, NSA.

48. Ibid., p. 101.
49. Brzezinski to Carter, NSC Weekly Report: "Soviet Activities in Afghanistan," November 3, 1978; Brzezinski to Carter, NSC Weekly Report: "Alert: The Arc of Crisis," December 2, 1978, ZB Donated Material, Subject File, Box 42, JCPL.
50. Carter, *Keeping Faith*, p. 254.
51. See for example: Brown to Carter, "Memorandum: U.S. Military Presence in the Middle East/Persian Gulf," July 11, 1979; Sick to Brzezinski, "VBB: Middle East Force Presence," August 7, 1979; Harold Saunders to Vance, "U.S. Military Presence in the Indian Ocean/Middle East," August 1979, ZB Donated Material, Subject File, VBB meetings, Box 33, JCPL. See also: Ermarth and Sick to Brzezinski, "PRCs on Middle East/Persian Gulf," June 19, 1979, ZB Donated Material, Subject File, PRC meetings, Box 25, JCPL.
52. David Insberg, "The Rapid Deployment Force: The Few, the Futile, the Expendable," Cato Institute, Policy Analysis No. 44, November 8, 1984.
53. The Carter–Brezhnev Project, "The Intervention in Afghanistan and the Fall of Détente," p. 61, NSA.
54. Ibid., pp. 149–50.
55. Brzezinski to Carter, NSC Weekly Report: "Afghanistan: A Symptom or an Aberration?" March 28, 1980, ZB Donated Material, Subject File, Box 42, JCPL. For Brzezinski's recollections, see: Brzezinski, *Power and Principle*, p. 427.
56. Garthoff, *Détente and Confrontation*, p. 796.
57. Gates, *From the Shadows*. See pp. 131–32 & pp. 145–46.
58. The Carter–Brezhnev Project, "The Intervention in Afghanistan and the Fall of Détente," p. 103, NSA.
59. Garthoff, *Détente and Confrontation*, p. 1053.
60. The Carter–Brezhnev Project, "The Intervention in Afghanistan and the Fall of Détente," p. 119, NSA. As late as December 12, 1979, U.S. intelligence officials were skeptical about the likelihood of major military intervention in Afghanistan, despite the buildup of Soviet forces. See: CIA Intelligence Information Cable, "Appraisal of Situation in Afghanistan," 12 Dec. 1979, NSA Staff Material, North/South, Thornton, Country File, Box 91, Afghanistan: 5/78–12/79, JCPL.
61. Ibid., pp. 156–57.
62. Caldwell, *The Dynamics of Domestic Politics and Arms Control*, pp. 145–46.
63. Robert Kaiser, "Senate Committee Says SALT Not in America's Best Interest," *Washington Post*, December 21, 1979.
64. Sanders, *Peddlers of Crisis*, pp. 264–65.
65. Rosalynn Carter, *First Lady from Plains* (New York: Houghton Mifflin, 1984), p. 338.
66. Carter, *Keeping Faith*, p. 265.
67. Cutler and Donovan to Carter, "Iran: Memorandum to the President," December 18, 1979, The Hamilton Jordan Files, Box 34, Iran, 12/79-1/80, JCPL.
68. Ehrman, *The Rise of Neoconservatism*, p. 93.

69. Jeane Kirkpatrick, "Dictatorships and Double Standards," *Commentary*, November 1, 1979.
70. Ibid. For an excellent analysis of the article, see: Brands, *The Devil We Knew*, pp. 157–58.
71. For the Neoconservatives' dilemma, see: Peter Steinfels, *The Neoconservatives: The Origins of a Movement* (New York: Simon and Schuster, 2013); Ehrman, *The Rise of Neoconservatism*, pp. 131–36.
72. Adam Clymer, "GOP Presidential Aspirants Tour Nation to Denounce Carter's Foreign Policy," *New York Times*, February 20, 1979.
73. "Ronald Reagan's Announcement for Presidential Candidacy," November 13, 1979, Public Papers of Ronald Reagan, RRPL. See also: htt ps://reaganlibrary.archives.gov/archives/reference/11.13.79.html
74. Jordan, *Crisis*, pp. 365–66; Pach, "*Top Gun*, Toughness, and Terrorism," pp. 559–60.
75. The Carter–Brezhnev Project, "The Intervention in Afghanistan and the Fall of Détente," p. 141, NSA.
76. Brzezinski to Carter, "Reflections on Soviet Intervention in Afghanistan," December 26, 1979, ZB Donated Material, Geographic File, Southwest Asia; Persian Gulf, Box 17, JCPL.
77. Brzezinski to Carter, NSC Weekly Report: "Opinion," December 28, 1979, ZB Donated Material, Subject File, Box 42, JCPL.
78. Brzezinski to Carter, "Reflections on Soviet Intervention in Afghanistan," December 26, 1979, ZB Donated Material, Geographic File, Southwest Asia; Persian Gulf, Box 17, JCPL. An SCC Meeting on January 14, held without the participation of Vance, discussed the U.S. strategy toward Pakistan and the Persian Gulf region. See: SCC Meeting, "U.S. Strategy for South-West Asia and Persian Gulf," January 14, 1980, ZB Donated Material, Subject File, SCC Meetings, Box 31, JCPL.
79. Brzezinski, *Power and Principle*, p. 429.
80. Jordan, *Crisis*, p. 99.
81. Carter to Brezhnev, December 28, 1979; Brezhnev to Carter, December 29, 1979, ZB Donated Material, Geographic File, USSR, Afghanistan Reaction; Carter–Brezhnev Correspondence, Box 18, JCPL.
82. The Carter–Brezhnev Project, NSA, "The Intervention in Afghanistan and the Fall of Détente," p. 141.
83. Brzezinski, *Power and Principle*, p. 429.
84. Vance, *Hard Choices*, p. 388.
85. Brzezinski to Carter, "Reflections on Soviet Intervention in Afghanistan," December 26, 1979, ZB Donated Material, Geographic File, Southwest Asia; Persian Gulf, Box 17, JCPL.
86. Brzezinski, *Power and Principle*, p. 430.
87. Brzezinski to Carter, "Possible Steps in Reaction to Soviet Intervention in Afghanistan," January 2, 1980, ZB Donated Material, Geographic File, Southwest Asia; Persian Gulf, Box 17, JCPL.
88. Brzezinski to Mondale, Vance, Brown, Jones, and Turner: "Results of the NSC Meeting," January 2, 1980, ZB Donated Material, Geographic File, Southwest Asia; Persian Gulf, Box 17, JCPL.

89. "Text of the President's Address to the Nation," Office of the White House Press Secretary, January 4, 1980, ZB Donated Material, Geographic File, Southwest Asia; Persian Gulf, Box 17, JCPL.

90. Transcript of President's interview with Frank Reynolds on the Soviet reply, December 31, 1979, Volume I, Foundations of Foreign Policy, Document 133, FRUS, 1977–1980.

91. Donovan to Carter, January 2, 1980, The Hedley Donovan Files, Memos to the President, 8/21/79-8/14/80, Box 2, JCPL.

92. Sanders, *Peddlers of Crisis*, p. 283.

93. Transcript of Jimmy Carter's "Meet the Press" interview on NBC, January 20, 1980, APP. See: www.presidency.ucsb.edu/ws/?pid=33060

94. Transcript of President Carter's State of the Union Address, January 23, 1980, APP. See: www.presidency.ucsb.edu/ws/?pid=33079

95. Robert Hunter to Brzezinski, "Speech on Soviet/Persian Gulf/Southwest Asia," January 11, 1980, ZB Donated Material, Geographic File, USSR; Afghanistan Reaction, Box 18, JCPL.

96. Transcript of President Carter's State of the Union Address, January 23, 1980, APP. See: www.presidency.ucsb.edu/ws/?pid=33079

97. Ibid.

98. Brzezinski to Carter, "Strategic Reaction to the Afghanistan Problem," January 3, 1980, ZB Donated Material, Geographic File, Southwest Asia; Persian Gulf, Box 17, JCPL.

99. Peter Tarnoff to Brzezinski, "Memorandum for Dr. Brzezinski and the White House: U.S.-Soviet Relations and Afghanistan," December 31, 1979, ZB Donated Material, Geographic File, Southwest Asia; Persian Gulf, Box 17, JCPL.

100. Garthoff, *Détente and Confrontation*, p. 1040.

101. The Carter–Brezhnev Project, "The Intervention in Afghanistan and the Fall of Détente," p. 136 & p. 164, NSA.

102. Dobrynin, *In Confidence*, p. 446.

103. The Carter–Brezhnev Project, "The Intervention in Afghanistan and the Fall of Détente," p. 119, NSA.

104. Ibid., p. 138.

105. Ibid., p. 154.

106. Transcript of Meeting of the Politburo of the CPSU Central Committee, "Deterioration of Conditions in the Democratic Republic of Afghanistan and Possible Responses on Our Side," March 17, 1979, NSA. See: https://nsarchive2.gwu.edu/NSAEBB/NSAEBB57/r1.pdf

107. For details on the TNF deployment, see: Garthoff, *Détente and Confrontation*, pp. 935–74; Kaufman, *Plans Unraveled*, pp. 188–89.

108. Garthoff, *Détente and Confrontation*, pp. 1102–03.

109. Dobrynin, *In Confidence*, p. 446–47.

110. The Carter–Brezhnev Project, NSA, "The Intervention in Afghanistan and the Fall of Détente," p. 22.

111. David Mayers, *The Ambassadors and America's Soviet Policy* (New York: Oxford University Press, 1997), p. 236.

112. Brement to Brzezinski, "The Gromyko–Watson Exchange on Afghanistan,"
     February 6, 1980; Watson to Vance, "Meeting with Gromyko," January 30,
     1980, ZB Donated Material, Subject File, VBB Meetings, Box 34, JCPL. For
     Watson's recollections, see: Thomas Watson Jr., *Father, Son, & Co. My Life
     at IBM and Beyond* (New York: Bantam, 1990), pp. 424–36.
113. Vance to Gromyko, February 8, 1980, Plains File, Carter–Brezhnev
     Correspondence, Box 17, JCPL. See also: Vance, *Hard Choices*,
     pp. 394–95; Dobrynin, *In Confidence*, p. 449.
114. Gromyko to Vance, February 16, 1980, ZB Donated Material, Geographic
     File, Southwest Asia; Persian Gulf, Box 17, JCPL.
115. "Signals From Moscow," *The Christian Science Monitor*, February 29,
     1980. For the NSC view of Brezhnev's speech, see: Brement to Brzezinski
     and Aaron, "The Brezhnev Speech," February 27, 1980, ZB Donated
     Material, Geographic File, Southwest Asia; Persian Gulf, Box 17, JCPL.
116. Brzezinski, *Power and Principle*, pp. 435–36; Carter, *White House Diary*,
     p. 406. On the domestic political concerns, see also: Albright to Brzezinski,
     "SCC on SALT," February 27, 1980, NSA Staff Material, Press and
     Congressional Relations, Chronological File, Box 5, JCPL.
117. Carter, *White House Diary*, p. 406.
118. Brzezinski to Carter, NSC Weekly Report: "U.S.–Soviet Relations,"
     February 29, 1980, ZB Donated Material, Subject File, Box 42, JCPL.
119. Carter draft letter to Brezhnev, February 29, 1980, Plains File, Carter–
     Brezhnev Correspondence, Box 17, JCPL. Historian Betty Glad writes that
     this letter was sent by Carter to Brezhnev on March 1, 1980. See: Glad, *An
     Outsider in the White House*, pp. 202–03. I have found no evidence to
     support that claim. Further drafts of the letter were in fact produced over
     the following days. See, for example: Carter draft letter to Brezhnev,
     March 11, 1980, Plains File, Carter–Brezhnev Correspondence, Box 17,
     JCPL. Moreover, Vance's proposed messenger, Marshall Shulman, was
     never sent to Moscow. For Shulman's recollections of the aborted mission,
     see: U.S.–Soviet Conference Transcript, pp. 278–86, The Carter–Brezhnev
     Project, Fort Lauderdale (FL), March 23–26, 1995, Vertical Files, Box 115,
     JCPL.
120. Brzezinski, *Power and Principle*, p. 437.
121. Memcon between Brzezinski and Dobrynin, March 17, 1980, ZB Donated
     Material, Subject File, Alpha Channel (Miscellaneous) [1/80-3/80], Box 20,
     JCPL; Dobrynin, *In Confidence*, pp. 450–51; Glad, *An Outsider in the
     White House*, p. 203.
122. Brzezinski, *Power and Principle*, p. 437.
123. Nicholas Henderson (British Ambassador) to the FCO, "U.S. Presidential
     Campaign: Senator Edward Kennedy," January 29, 1980, PREM 19-1405,
     USA Internal Political Situation: The 1980 and 1984 Presidential
     Campaigns, UKNA.
124. Clymer, *Edward M. Kennedy*, pp. 291–92.
125. Henderson to FCO, "U.S. Presidential Campaign: Senator Edward
     Kennedy," January 29, 1980, PREM 19-1405, UKNA.

126. Albright to Brzezinski, "Meeting with Senator Moynihan," January 21, 1980, NSA Staff Material, Press & Congressional Relations, Chronological File, Box 5, JCPL. Moynihan's foreign policy statement on January 10 is attached with the note.

127. Ehrman, *The Rise of Neoconservatism*, pp. 134–36.

128. Paul Nitze, "Comments on the President's State of the Union Address," January 24, 1980, The Paul Nitze Papers, Box 20, LOC.

129. Laura Kalman, *Right Star Rising: A New Politics, 1974–1980* (New York: W. W. Norton, 2010), p. 345. See also: "Reagan Urges Senate to Reject Arms Pact, But His Tone is Softer," *New York Times*, September 16, 1979.

130. "Peace and Security in the 1980s," Address by Ronald Reagan to the Chicago Council on Foreign Relations, March 17, 1980.

131. Nicholas Sarantakes, *Dropping the Torch: Jimmy Carter, the Olympic Boycott, and the Cold War* (New York: Cambridge University Press, 2010), pp. 181–82.

132. Cited in: Small, *Democracy and Diplomacy*, p. 139.

133. Jordan, *Crisis*, p. 57.

134. Brzezinski to Carter, "Foreign Policy: Coherence and Sense of Direction," March 25, 1980, ZB Donated Material, Subject File, SCC Meetings, Box 32, JCPL.

135. "Presidential Directive/NSC-59: Nuclear Weapons Employment Policy," July 25, 1980, Vertical Files, JCPL.

136. *New York Times*, August 23, 1980. See also: Smith, *Morality, Reason, and Power*, p. 237.

137. Newhouse, *War and Peace in the Nuclear Age*, p. 286.

138. Glad, *An Outsider in the White House*, pp. 220–21.

139. Carter, *Keeping Faith*, pp. 251–52.

140. Newhouse, *War and Peace in the Nuclear Age*, pp. 286–89. See also: Richard Burt, "U.S. Stresses Limited Nuclear War in Sharp Shift on Military Strategy," *International Herald Tribune*, August 7, 1980; Michael Getler, "Carter Directive Modifies Strategy for a Nuclear War," *Washington Post*, August 6, 1980. For retrospective views from Brzezinski and Brown, see: Brzezinski, *Power and Principle*, pp. 454–59; Harold Brown, *Thinking About National Security: Defense and Foreign Policy in a Dangerous World* (Boulder: Westview Press, 1983), pp. 80–83.

141. Fred Kaplan, "Our Cold War Policy, Circa 1950," *New York Times*, May 18, 1980. For a good overview of NSC-68, see: Craig and Logevall, *America's Cold War*, pp. 108–14.

142. Cited in: Richard Burt, "Pentagon Chief Reassures Allies on War Strategy," *New York Times*, August 11, 1980; Paul Warnke, "The World According to Zbigniew Brzezinski," *Washington Monthly*, July/August 1986, p. 52.

143. Odom to Brzezinski, "Draft PD on Nuclear Targeting," March 22, 1980, ZB Donated Material, Subject File, Box 35, PD-59 [3/80-4/80], JCPL.

144. See for example: Odom and Welch to Brzezinski, "Draft PD on Nuclear Employment Policy," April 17, 1980, ZB Donated Material, Subject File, Box 35, PD-59 [3/80-4/80], JCPL.

145. Odom to Brzezinski, "Targeting PD Briefing for the President," July 24, 1980, ZB Donated Material, Subject File, Box 35, PD-59 [5/80-1/81], JCPL.

146. Brzezinski to Carter, NSC Weekly Report: "PD-59 Chronology," August 22, 1980, ZB Donated Material, Subject File, Box 42, JCPL.

147. Michael Getler, "Carter Directive Modifies Strategy for a Nuclear War," *Washington Post*, August 6, 1980.

148. Richard Burt, "The World: A New Order of Debate on Atomic War," *New York Times*, August 17, 1980; Richard Burt, "Pentagon Chief Reassures Allies on War Strategy," *New York Times*, August 11, 1980.

149. Brzezinski to Carter, "Flap with Muskie over PD-59," May 22, 1980, The William Odom Papers, Presidential Development: Defense Policy Development White House 1977–80, Box 36, LOC.

150. William Burr, "Jimmy Carter's Controversial Nuclear Targeting Directive PD-59 Declassified," NSA, September 12, 2012. See: http://nsarchive .gwu.edu/nukevault/ebb390/

151. Carter, *Keeping Faith*, p. 465.

152. Renouard and Vigil, "The Quest for Leadership in a Time of Peace: Jimmy Carter and Western Europe, 1977-1981," pp. 325–26, in Schulz and Schwartz (eds.), *The Strained Alliance*.

153. Carter, *Keeping Faith*, p. 466.

154. Ibid., pp. 486–87.

155. Kaufman and Kaufman, *The Presidency of James Earl Carter Jr.*, pp. 223–24.

156. Margaret Thatcher, *The Downing Street Years* (London: HarperCollins, 1993), p. 88. For Thatcher's general thoughts on Carter, see pp. 68–69.

157. Martin Berthoud (Head of FCO North American Department) to FCO, "U.S.–Soviet Relations," February 22, 1980, FCO 82-1025, Relations between the USA and the Soviet Union, UKNA.

158. Schmidt, *Men and Powers*, pp. 202–03.

159. Memcon between Vance and Schmidt on February 20 in Bonn (includes comments by Carter), February 25, 1980, ZB Donated Material, Geographic File, Southwest Asia; Persian Gulf, Box 17, JCPL.

160. Blackwill to Brzezinski and Aaron, "Schmidt and the Afghanistan Crisis," February 11, 1980, ZB Donated Material, Subject File, PRC Meetings, Box 25, JCPL.

161. Caddell to Les Francis (Deputy Chief of Staff), "Pre-Convention Polling," May 26, 1980, The Hamilton Jordan Files, Campaign Strategy; Pat Caddell Reports, Box 77, JCPL.

162. Eizenstat to Carter, "Proposed Grain Embargo," January 3, 1980, The Stuart Eizenstat Papers, Presidential Memoranda, Box 117, LOC; Jordan, *Crisis*, p. 100.

163. Brzezinski to Carter, NSC Weekly Report: "The Soviet Grain Embargo," June 27, 1980, ZB Donated Material, Subject File, Box 42, JCPL.

164. Brzezinski to Carter, NSC Weekly Report: "Foreign Policy and the Elections," August 7, 1980. ZB Donated Material, Subject File, Box 42, JCPL.

165. Transcript of Presidential Debate between Carter and Reagan in Cleveland, October 28, 1980, APP. See: www.presidency.ucsb.edu/documents/presiden tial-debate-cleveland
166. Dobrynin, *In Confidence*, p. 459.
167. The Carter–Brezhnev Project, NSA, "The Intervention in Afghanistan and the Fall of Détente," pp. 160–61. See also: Robert McFadden, "How Two Governors Reached Decision," *New York Times*, September 18, 1983.
168. Dobrynin, *In Confidence*, p. 460.
169. Zubok, *A Failed Empire*, pp. 266–67.
170. Gates, *From the Shadows*, p. 166. See also: "Summary of Conclusions of an Adhoc Meeting on Poland," December 3, 1980, Volume VI, Soviet Union. Document 311, FRUS, 1977–1980.
171. Carter to Brezhnev, December 3, 1980, Plains File, Carter–Brezhnev Correspondence, Box 17, JCPL.
172. Brzezinski, *Power and Principle*, pp. 466–67.
173. Zubok, *A Failed Empire*, p. 267.
174. Transcript of Jimmy Carter Presidential Speech at University of Notre Dame, May 22 1977, MCPA. See: https://millercenter.org/the-presidency/p residential-speeches/may-22-1977-university-notre-dame-commencement
175. Terence Smith, "The World has Changed and so has Jimmy Carter," *New York Times*, January 20, 1980.
176. Brzezinski to Carter, January 11, 1980, ZB Donated Material, Geographical File, Box 18, JCPL. See also: Transcript of Jimmy Carter's "Meet The Press" interview on NBC, January 20, 1980, APP. See: www.presidency.ucsb.edu /ws/?pid=33060
177. Smith, *Morality, Reason, and Power*, p. 242.
178. Pach, "*Top Gun*, Toughness, and Terrorism," p. 560.
179. Don Oberdorfer, "Vance Asks SALT Ratification to Avert Arms Race in 1980s," *Washington Post*, June 6, 1980.
180. The Carter–Brezhnev Project, "SALT II and the Growth of Mistrust," p. 116, NSA.
181. Interview by the author with Ambassador David Aaron, September 26, 2017.

4 CONFRONTATION

1. Edward Yager, *Ronald Reagan's Journey: Democrat to Republican* (New York: Rowman and Littlefield, 2006), pp. 12–13.
2. John Newhouse, *War and Peace in the Nuclear Age*, p. 334.
3. K. Skinner, A. Anderson, and M. Anderson (eds.), *Reagan, In His Own Hand*, p. 439.
4. Address by Ronald Reagan to the Veterans of Foreign Wars Convention, Chicago, August 18, 1980, APP. See: www.presidency.ucsb.edu/docu ments/address-the-veterans-foreign-wars-convention-chicago
5. Skinner et al, *Reagan, In His Own Hand*, pp. 10–12.

6. Donald Snow, *Thinking About National Security: Strategy, Policy, and Issues* (New York: Routledge, 2015), p. 28.

7. Stephen Knott and Jeffrey Chidester, *The Reagan Years* (New York: Facts On File, 2005), pp. 305–11. See: selected primary documents, "City Upon a Hill," Conservative Political Action Conference, January 25, 1974.

8. Address by Ronald Reagan to the Veterans of Foreign Wars Convention, Chicago, August 18, 1980, APP. See: www.presidency.ucsb.edu/documents/address-the-veterans-foreign-wars-convention-chicago

9. Schmidt, *Men and Powers*, p.247.

10. Lou Cannon, *President Reagan: The Role of a Lifetime* (New York: Simon and Schuster, 1991), pp. 285–86; Newhouse, *War and Peace in the Nuclear Age*, pp. 334–35.

11. Craig and Logevall, *America's Cold War*, p. 312.

12. Lou Cannon, "Ronald Reagan: The Pragmatist," *Los Angeles Times*, June 15, 2008.

13. Kalman, *Right Star Rising*, p. 345. See also: "Reagan Urges Senate to Reject Arms Pact, But His Tone is Softer," *New York Times*, September 16, 1979.

14. Sarantakes, *Dropping the Torch*, pp. 181–82.

15. Kyle Longley, "When Character Was King? Ronald Reagan and the Issues of Ethics and Morality," in Kyle Longley (et al), *Deconstructing Reagan: Conservative Mythology and America's Fortieth President* (New York: M.E. Sharpe, 2007), p. 91.

16. H. W. Brands, *Reagan: The Life* (New York: Doubleday, 2015), pp. 10–12. See also: Cannon, *President Reagan*, p. 212.

17. Reagan, *An American Life*, p. 21.

18. Ibid., p. 114.

19. Leffler, *For the Soul of Mankind*, pp. 344–45.

20. Reagan, *An American Life*, pp. 134–35.

21. Knott and Chidester, *The Reagan Years*, p. 217.

22. James Scott, *Deciding to Intervene: The Reagan Doctrine and American Foreign Policy* (Durham: Duke University Press, 1996), p. 17.

23. Robert Scheer, *With Enough Shovels: Reagan, Bush, and Nuclear War* (New York: Random House, 1982), p. 66.

24. Garthoff, *The Great Transition*, pp. 11–13.

25. For excellent studies on the broader subject, see: Sarah Snyder, *Human Rights Activism and the End of the Cold War: A Transnational History of the Helsinki Network* (New York: Cambridge University Press, 2011); Rosemary Foot, "The Cold War and Human Rights," in *The Cambridge History of the Cold War: Volume III*, pp. 445–65.

26. Tony Smith, *America's Mission: The United States and the Worldwide Struggle for Democracy* (Princeton: Princeton University Press, 2012), p. 286; Michael Schaller, "Reagan and the Cold War," in *Deconstructing Reagan*, p. 19.

27. Daniel Wirls, *Buildup: The Politics of Defense in the Reagan Era* (Ithaca: Cornell University Press, 1992), p. 32.

28. The Carter–Brezhnev Project, "SALT II and the Growth of Mistrust," p. 221, NSA; Wilson, *The Triumph of Improvisation*, p. 23.

29. Beal to Baker, Deaver, and Meese: "Strategic Planning Memorandum: President Reagan's 1982 Winter Campaign," December 10, 1981, The James Baker Papers, Series 6: Chief of Staff, Box 61, Folder 2, Office Files 1981, PUML.

30. John Dumbrell, *The Making of U.S. Foreign Policy* (Manchester: Manchester University Press, 1997), p. 74.

31. Wirls, *Buildup*, pp. 36–41; Leffler, *For the Soul of Mankind*, p. 346.

32. Johnson, *Congress and the Cold War*, pp. 252–60; *New York Times*, September 29, 1981.

33. Zelizer, *Arsenal of Democracy*, pp. 301–02.

34. Cannon, *President Reagan*, p. 116.

35. David Gergen, *Eyewitness to Power: The Essence of Leadership, Nixon to Clinton* (New York: Simon and Schuster, 2000), p. 153.

36. "Reagan Trying to be Sensitive to the Needs of Congress," *New York Times*, February 11, 1981.

37. Martin Anderson, *Revolution: The Reagan Legacy* (Stanford: Hoover Institution Press, 1990), pp. 289–90.

38. Richard Reeves, *President Reagan: The Triumph of Imagination* (New York: Simon and Schuster, 2005), pp. 13–15.

39. Cannon, *President Reagan*, pp. 145–47.

40. Garthoff, *The Great Transition*, p. 17.

41. Alexander Haig, *Caveat: Realism, Reagan, and Foreign Policy* (New York: Macmillan, 1984), pp. 26–27.

42. Ibid., p. 53.

43. Gerald Seib, "Reagan Pursues Old Ally Clark for a Post in State Department and May Stir Row," *Wall Street Journal*, January 12, 1981; Knott and Chidester, *The Reagan Years*, p. 139.

44. Caspar Weinberger, *Fighting for Peace: Seven Critical Years in the Pentagon* (New York: Warner, 1990), pp. 9–14.

45. George Wilson, "Weinberger, in His First Message, Says Mission is to Re-arm America," *Washington Post*, January 23, 1981.

46. Wirls, *Buildup*, p. 35.

47. Flora Lewis, "Foreign Affairs: Dispute and Drift," *New York Times*, February 21, 1982.

48. "Excerpts from Weinberger Statement on Military Budget Outlay," *New York Times*, March 5, 1981.

49. Scheer, *With Enough Shovels*, pp. 5–6; Weinberger, *Fighting for Peace*, pp. 34–35.

50. Sanders, *Peddlers of Crisis*, pp. 286–89.

51. Cannon, *President Reagan*, pp. 180–89; Lou Cannon and David Hoffman, "Reagan Tugged by Rival Strategists," *Washington Post*, April 17, 1983.

52. For more on the LSG see: The James Baker Papers, Series 6: Chief of Staff, Subseries 6D: Legislative Strategy Group 1981–84, PUML; The Richard Darman Files, Series I: Subject File, Box 3, RRPL.

53. Gergen, *Eyewitness to Power*, p. 182.

54. Walter Isaacson and Douglas Brew, "Calling Plays for the Gipper: Jim Baker's Strategy Group Nudges Policy Toward the Middle," *Time Magazine*, August 23, 1982.

55. Gergen, *Eyewitness to Power*, p. 182.
56. Robert Collins, *Transforming America: Politics and Culture During the Reagan Years* (New York: Columbia University Press, 2007), pp. 56–57.
57. Ann Reilly, "Reagan's Savvy Strategists," *Dun's Business Month*, March 1983.
58. Dick Kirschten, "Reagan's Legislative Strategy Team Keeps His Record of Victories Intact," *National Journal*, June 26, 1982.
59. Text of President Reagan's News Conference, January 29, 1981, APP. See: www.presidency.ucsb.edu/documents/the-presidents-news-conference-992
60. James Mann, *The Rebellion of Ronald Reagan: A History of the End of the Cold War* (New York: Viking, 2009), p. 28.
61. Dobrynin, *In Confidence*, p. 484.
62. Haig, *Caveat*, pp. 101–05.
63. Bernard Gwertzman, "Soviets Disclose Gromyko Letter Rebuking Haig," *New York Times*, February 12, 1981.
64. Dobrynin, *In Confidence*, p. 482.
65. Haig, *Caveat*, pp. 107–08; Dobrynin, *In Confidence*, pp. 486–87. See also: Allen to Reagan, Haig, Weinberger, Meese, and Baker, "Paper for NSC Meeting on February 11, 1981, and Minutes from NSC Meeting on February 6, 1981," February 10, 1981, NSC Executive Secretariat Meeting Files, Box 1, RRPL.
66. Garthoff, *The Great Transition*, p. 48.
67. Haig, *Caveat*, p. 105.
68. Robert Kaiser, "Kremlin's Expert on U.S. Can't Prolong Visit Here," *Washington Post*, April 2, 1981. For Arbatov's recollections, see: Arbatov, *The System*, p. 319. In his memoirs, Haig claimed that this decision was made "to protest the lack of American access to Soviet television." See: Haig, *Caveat*, pp. 109–10.
69. Dobrynin, *In Confidence*, p. 486.
70. Garthoff, *The Great Transition*, pp. 57–58.
71. Brezhnev to Reagan, March 6, 1981, NSC Executive Secretariat Head of State Files, Box 38: USSR, RRPL.
72. Reagan to Brezhnev, April 3, 1981; Brezhnev to Reagan, April 7, 1981, NSC Executive Secretariat Head of State Files, Box 38: USSR, RRPL.
73. Reagan, *An American Life*, pp. 269–70.
74. Reagan to Brezhnev, April 24, 1981, "Text of President Reagan's Handwritten Message to President Brezhnev," NSC Executive Secretariat Head of State Files, Box 38: USSR, RRPL.
75. Jack Matlock, *Reagan and Gorbachev: How the Cold War Ended* (New York: Random House, 2004), p. 21.
76. Reagan, *An American Life*, p. 271.
77. Reagan to Brezhnev, April 24, 1981 (Typed Letter); Brezhnev to Reagan, May 25, 1981, NSC Executive Secretariat Head of State Files, Box 38: USSR, RRPL.
78. Reagan, *An American Life*, p. 273.
79. Haig, *Caveat*, p. 160.

80. Brands, *Reagan*, p. 291. See also: Martin Schram and Michael Getler, "Haig's Actions Again Raise Concern Over his Conduct," *Washington Post*, April 1, 1981.

81. Lynn Rosellini, "Honey, I Forgot to Duck, Injured Reagan Tells Wife," *New York Times*, March 31, 1981; David Broder, "Reagan Wounded by Assailant's Bullet," *Washington Post*, March 31, 1981.

82. Peter Goldman, "America's Nightmare," *Newsweek*, April 13, 1981. See also: Collins, *Transforming America*, p. 71.

83. Farrell, *Tip O'Neill and the Democratic Century*, pp. 553–56.

84. Collins, *Transforming America*, p. 212.

85. Craig and Logevall, *America's Cold War*, pp. 317–18.

86. Minutes of NSC Meeting: "The Caribbean Basin," February 10, 1982, NSC Executive Secretariat Meeting Files, NSC 31–40, Box 4, RRPL.

87. John Coatsworth, "The Cold War in Central America, 1975–91," in *The Cambridge History of the Cold War: Volume III*, p. 211.

88. Cannon, *President Reagan*, pp. 358–65.

89. For an excellent study of the "Reagan Doctrine," see: Chester Pach, "The Reagan Doctrine: Principle, Pragmatism and Policy," *Presidential Studies Quarterly* (March 2006), Vol. 36, No. 1, pp. 75–88.

90. Brands, *Reagan*, p. 532.

91. Cannon, *President Reagan*, pp. 355–56.

92. Wirthlin to Baker, "A Political Action Plan: 1982," March 29, 1982, The Michael Deaver Files, Series 6, Political Material: Polling Information 1982, Richard Wirthlin, Box 65, RRPL.

93. Farrell, *Tip O'Neill and the Democratic Century,* pp. 611–14. See also: Zelizer, *Arsenal of Democracy*, pp. 312–13.

94. "A Secret War for Nicaragua," *Newsweek*, November 8, 1982; Farrell, *Tip O'Neill and the Democratic Century*, p. 614; Zelizer, *Arsenal of Democracy*, p. 315.

95. Friedersdorf to Baker, "Grain Embargo Meeting," February 21, 1981, The Kenneth Duberstein Files, Series 1, Box 1, RRPL.

96. Lee Lescaze, "Reagan to Lift Grain Embargo Today," *Washington Post*, April 24, 1981.

97. Friedersdorf to Baker and Meese, "Grain Embargo Meeting," February 18, 1981; Wright to Duberstein, "Farm Bill: Status in the House," April 2, 1981; Friedersdorf to Wright, "Grain Embargo," April 14, 1981, The Kenneth Duberstein Files, Series 1, Box 1, RRPL.

98. Haig, *Caveat*, pp. 110–11.

99. White House Staffing Memorandum: "U.S.-USSR Grain Agreement," July 13, 1982, The Kenneth Duberstein Files, Series 4, Box 27, RRPL.

100. White House Office of the Press Secretary, "Statement by the President: U.S.–USSR Grain Agreement," July 30, 1982, The Kenneth Duberstein Files, Series 4, Box 27, RRPL.

101. Garthoff, *The Great Transition*, p. 51.

102. Zubok, *A Failed Empire*, pp. 268–69.

103. Sell, *From Washington to Moscow*, pp. 109–10.

104. Douglas Brinkley (ed.), *The Reagan Diaries* (New York: HarperCollins, 2007), p. 30.
105. Seth Jones, *A Covert Action: Reagan, the CIA, and the Cold War Struggle in Poland* (New York: W.W. Norton, 2018), pp. 122–23.
106. Minutes of NSC Meeting: "Poland," December 21, 1981, NSC Executive Secretariat Meeting Files, Box 4, RRPL.
107. For background on the West Siberian gas pipeline agreement, see: "NSC Staff Summary: U.S. Position on the Siberian Pipeline," June 26, 1981, NSC Executive Secretariat Meeting Files, Box 2, RRPL. See also: Bruce Jentleson, *Pipeline Politics: Complex Political Economy of East-West Energy Trade* (Ithaca: Cornell University Press, 1986); Haig, *Caveat*, pp. 251–54; Tyler Esno, "Reagan's Economic War on the Soviet Union," *Diplomatic History*, Vol. 42 (April 2018), pp. 281–304. For a broader study of Western Europe and the late Cold War, see: John W. Young, "Western Europe and the End of the Cold War, 1979–89," in *The Cambridge History of the Cold War: Volume III*, pp. 289–310.
108. Weinberger to Reagan, "Oil and Gas Equipment and Technology for the USSR," September 8, 1981, NSC Executive Secretariat Meeting Files, Box 2, RRPL.
109. Haig, *Caveat*, p. 251.
110. Minutes of NSC Meeting: "East–West Trade Controls," July 9, 1981, NSC Executive Secretariat Meeting Files, Box 2, RRPL.
111. Minutes of NSC Meeting: "Poland," December 21 and 22, 1981, NSC Executive Secretariat Meeting Files, Box 4, RRPL.
112. White House Office of the Press Secretary, "Text of the Address by the President to the Nation," December 23, 1981, NSC Executive Secretariat Meeting Files, Box 4, RRPL; Brands, *Reagan*, p. 342.
113. Garthoff, *The Great Transition*, pp. 548–50; Pipes to Nance, "Measures to be Taken Against the Soviet Union," December 24, 1981, NSC Executive Secretariat Meeting Files, Box 4, RRPL; Steven Weisman, "Reagan Curtails Soviet Trade and Halts Technology Sales," *New York Times*, December 30, 1981.
114. Richard Aldous, *Reagan and Thatcher: The Difficult Relationship* (New York: W.W. Norton, 2012), pp. 62–63.
115. Text of a statement issued by the AFL-CIO, December 14, 1981. The Paula Dobriansky Files, Series I: Country Files, Poland: Memoranda (1981–83), RAC Box 3, RRPL.
116. Joseph Canzeri (Deputy Assistant to the President) to Deaver, "Satellite Program," January 19, 1982, The Paula Dobriansky Files, Series I: Country Files, Poland: Solidarity (01/19/1982-02/23/1982), RAC Box 4, RRPL.
117. NSC memorandum, "Strategy on Poland: Possible Next Steps Against the USSR," February 2, 1982, NSC Executive Secretariat Meeting Files, Box 4, RRPL.
118. Arch Puddington, *Lane Kirkland: Champion of American Labor* (Hoboken: Wiley, 2005), pp. 174–75.
119. Minutes of NSC Meeting: "Poland," December 21, 1981, NSC Executive Secretariat Meeting Files, Box 4, RRPL.

120. Puddington, *Lane Kirkland*, pp. 116–34; William Serrin, "Solidarity Day's Enigmatic Organizer," *New York Times*, September 19, 1981; Carl Bernstein, "The Holy Alliance: Ronald Reagan and John Paul II," *Time Magazine*, February 24, 1992.

121. NSC memorandum, "Strategy on Poland: Possible Next Steps Against the USSR," February 2, 1982, NSC Executive Secretariat Meeting Files, Box 4, RRPL.

122. Minutes of NSC Meeting: "Terms of Reference for High-Level USG Mission to Europe on Soviet Sanctions," February 26, 1982, NSC Executive Secretariat Meeting Files, Box 5, RRPL.

123. Clark to Reagan, "High Level Mission to Europe," March 1, 1982; "Report on Interagency Mission to Europe," March 13–20, 1982, NSC Executive Secretariat Meeting Files, Box 5, RRPL.

124. Minutes of NSC Meeting: "Debrief of Under-Secretary Buckley's Trip to Europe," March 25, 1982, NSC Executive Secretariat Meeting Files, Box 5, RRPL.

125. Halper and Clarke, *America Alone*, p. 165; Robert McMahon, *The Cold War* (New York: Oxford University Press, 2003), pp. 151–52.

126. Norman Podhoretz, "The Neoconservative Anguish over Reagan's Foreign Policy," *New York Times*, May 2, 1982.

127. "Executive Summary of the Conservative Political Conference: First Year Reagan Review," January 21, 1982, The Lee Atwater Files, Series I, Box 2, RRPL.

128. NSDD-54, "United States Policy Towards Eastern Europe," September 2, 1982. See: www.reaganlibrary.gov/sites/default/files/archives/reference/sca nned-nsdds/nsdd54.pdf

129. Jones, *A Covert Action*, pp. 136–39. See also: National Security Planning Group Meeting, "Poland; Latin America," November 4, 1982, Executive Secretariat National Security Planning Group Files, NSPG 0046, Box 93105, RRPL.

130. Gregory Domber, *Empowering Revolution: America, Poland, and the End of the Cold War* (Chapel Hill: University of North Carolina Press, 2014), pp. 109–10; Sell, *From Washington to Moscow*, pp. 112–13. See also: Gates, *From the Shadows*, pp. 237–39.

131. Bernstein, "The Holy Alliance," *Time Magazine*, February 24, 1992.

132. Christopher Andrew and Oleg Gordievsky, *KGB: The Inside Story* (New York: HarperCollins, 1990) p. 583.

133. For analysis of Operation RYAN, see: Taylor Downing, *1983: The World at the Brink* (London: Abacus, 2018), pp. 78–89.

134. Reagan to Brezhnev, September 22, 1981; Brezhnev to Reagan, October 15, 1981, NSC Executive Secretariat Head of State Files, Box 37: USSR, RRPL. See also: "Private Meeting between Secretary Haig and Minister Gromyko," New York, September 23, 1981, The William Clark Files, Box 3, RRPL.

135. For Schmidt's recollections, see: Schmidt, *Men and Powers*, pp. 277–79.

136. Strobe Talbott, *Deadly Gambits: The Reagan Administration and the Stalemate in Nuclear Arms Control* (New York: Alfred Knopf, 1984), pp. 56–57.

137. Minutes of NSC Meeting: "Theater Nuclear Forces," October 13, 1981, NSC Executive Secretariat Meeting Files, Box 3, RRPL. For Weinberger's reference to the Nobel Peace Prize, see the memoirs of Kenneth Adelman, who attended the meeting as a stand-in for the ambassador to the UN, Jeane Kirkpatrick: Kenneth Adelman, *The Great Universal Embrace: Arms Summitry – A Skeptic's Account* (New York: Simon and Schuster, 1989), p. 240. The reference is also mentioned in Strobe Talbott's earlier work. See: Talbott, *Deadly Gambits*, p. 71.

138. Newhouse, *War and Peace in the Nuclear Age*, p. 355.

139. Haig, *Caveat*, p. 229.

140. Minutes of NSC Meeting: "Theater Nuclear Forces," November 12, 1981, NSC Executive Secretariat Meeting Files, Box 3, RRPL. For an account of the meeting, see also: Talbott, *Deadly Gambits*, pp. 72–75.

141. Reagan, *An American Life*, p. 297.

142. Reagan to Brezhnev, November 17, 1981, NSC Executive Secretariat Head of State Files, Box 37: USSR, RRPL. See also: Remarks by Ronald Reagan to Members of the National Press Club on Arms Reduction and Nuclear Weapons, November 18, 1981, APP. See: www.presidency.ucsb.edu/docu ments/remarks-members-the-national-press-club-arms-reduction-and-nuclear- weapons

143. Talbott, *The Master of the Game*, pp. 170–72.

144. Brezhnev to Reagan, December 1, 1981, NSC Executive Secretariat Head of State Files, Box 37: USSR, RRPL.

145. Garthoff, *The Great Transition*, pp. 7–53; George Shultz, *Turmoil and Triumph: My Years as Secretary of State* (New York: Scribner's, 1993), p. 5; Interview by the author with Ambassador Jack Matlock, August 30, 2017.

5 THE NUCLEAR FREEZE MOVEMENT

1. Scheer, *With Enough Shovels*, p. 18.

2. John Kenneth Galbraith, "Ronald Reagan: The Nuclear Freeze's Best Friend," *Hartford Courant*, September 12, 1982.

3. Cannon, *President Reagan*, pp. 232–33. See also: Presidential Job Approval, Ronald Reagan: The Gallup Poll, APP. See: www.presidency.ucsb.edu/stat istics/data/presidential-job-approval

4. Adam Clymer, "Mondale Says Reagan's Policy Hurts NATO," *New York Times*, October 21, 1981; "Excerpts From Mondale Speech to Policy Group," *New York Times*, October 21, 1981.

5. Wirls, *Buildup*, pp. 56–57.

6. Angela Santese, "Ronald Reagan, the Nuclear Weapons Freeze Campaign and the Nuclear scare of the 1980s," *The International History Review*, Vol. 39, No. 3 (2017), pp. 496–520.

7. Lawrence Wittner, *Toward Nuclear Abolition: A History of the World Nuclear Disarmament Movement: 1971 to the Present* (Stanford: Stanford University Press, 2003), pp. 175–76.

8. Wirls, *Buildup*, pp. 72–73; David Meyer, *A Winter of Discontent: The Nuclear Freeze and American Politics* (New York: Praeger, 1990), p. 180.
9. Poll Results, NBC News Report, April 13, 1982, The Elizabeth Dole Files, Series 1, Box 40, National Citizens Participation Council: Nuclear Power, RRPL.
10. Wirls, *Buildup*, pp. 76–77.
11. Clymer, *Edward M. Kennedy*, pp. 320–21.
12. Meyer, *A Winter of Discontent*, p. 181.
13. Edward Kennedy, "Can a Freeze Halt the Arms Race? Yes: Only Such a Step Can Break the Impasse with the Soviet Union," *Los Angeles Times*, March 21, 1982.
14. Letter from Tip O'Neill to Harold Willens, August 11, 1982, The Tip O'Neill Papers, Series 2, Subseries A, Box 17, Subject Files: Nuclear Freeze, February–August 1982, BCBL.
15. Meyer, *A Winter of Discontent*, p. 101.
16. Wittner, *Toward Nuclear Abolition*, p. 176.
17. Colman McCarthy, "Heated Support for a Nuclear Freeze," *Washington Post*, March 21, 1982.
18. Douglas Waller, *Congress and the Nuclear Freeze: An Inside Look at the Politics of a Mass Movement* (Amherst: University of Massachusetts Press, 1987), pp. 129–35; Judith Miller, "Nuclear Freeze Stirring a Democratic Debate," *New York Times*, March 26, 1982.
19. William Knoblauch, *Nuclear Freeze in a Cold War: The Reagan Administration, Cultural Activism, and the End of the Arms Race* (Amherst, MA: University of Massachusetts Press, 2017), pp. 15–19.
20. Robert Kaiser, "Movement Against Nuclear Arms in Mushrooming," *Washington Post*, April 11, 1982; Meyer, *A Winter of Discontent*, p. 99; Peter McGrath, "The Nuclear Book Boom," *Newsweek*, April 12, 1982.
21. Collins, *Transforming America*, p. 198. See also: Paul Montgomery, "Throngs Fill Manhattan to Protest Nuclear Weapons," *New York Times*, June 13, 1982.
22. Wirls, *Buildup*, p. 77.
23. Judith Miller, "House Foreign Affairs Panel Seeks Nuclear Freeze," *New York Times*, June 24, 1982; Pat Towell, "House Panel Adopts Nuclear Freeze Measure," *Congressional Quarterly*, June 26, 1982.
24. Beal to Baker, Deaver, and Meese: "Strategic Planning Memorandum: President Reagan's 1982 Winter Campaign," December 10, 1981, The James Baker Papers, Series 6: Chief of Staff, Box 61, Folder 2, Office files 1981, PUML.
25. Wirthlin to Baker, "A Political Action Plan: 1982," March 29, 1982, The Michael Deaver Files, Series 6, Political Material: Polling Information 1982, Dick Wirthlin, Box 65, RRPL.
26. Hedrick Smith, "Subtle Shifts in Image for the President," *New York Times*, April 20, 1982.
27. Hedrick Smith, "The Nuclear Freeze," *New York Times*, April 1, 1982.
28. John Goshko, "Administration Opposes Nuclear Weapons Freeze," *Washington Post*, March 11, 1982.

29. Statement by Richard Burt, Director, Bureau of Politico-Military Affairs (State Department), March 10, 1982, The David Gergen Files, Box 7, RRPL.

30. Reagan, *An American Life*, pp. 552–53.

31. Wirls, *Buildup*, p. 104; Waller, *Congress and the Nuclear Freeze*, pp. 92–93.

32. Kraemer to Clark, "Possible Pro-Administration Nuclear Arms Control Resolution," March 19, 1982, The David Gergen Files, Box 7, RRPL.

33. Judith Miller, "58 Senators Back Alternative Plan on Nuclear Arms," *New York Times*, March 31, 1982.

34. Opening Statement on Nuclear Arms Reduction, March 30, 1982, The David Gergen Files, Box 7, RRPL.

35. Talbott, *Deadly Gambits*, p. 247.

36. Memo by START Interdepartmental Group to William Clark, April 10, 1982, NSC Executive Secretariat Meeting Files, Box 5, RRPL.

37. Haig to Reagan, "START: The Global Political Context," May 1, 1982, NSC Executive Secretariat Meeting Files, Box 6, RRPL.

38. Minutes of NSC Meeting: "Strategic Arms Reductions Talks (START)," April 21, 1982, NSC Executive Secretariat Meeting Files, Box 5, RRPL; Talbott, *Deadly Gambits*, pp. 248–51.

39. Talbott, *Deadly Gambits*, pp. 268–71.

40. Address by Ronald Reagan at Commencement Exercises at Eureka College in Illinois, May 9, 1982, APP. See: www.presidency.ucsb.edu/documents/address-commencement-exercises-eureka-college-illinois

41. Frances FitzGerald, *Way Out There In Blue: Reagan, Star Wars, and the End of the Cold War* (New York: Simon and Schuster, 2000), pp. 153–54; Sell, *From Washington to Moscow*, p. 154.

42. Leslie Gelb, "Washington: It's Time for Really Hard Bargaining," *New York Times*, June 13, 1982; Newhouse, *War and Peace in the Nuclear Age*, p. 346.

43. Brezhnev to Reagan, May 20, 1982, NSC Executive Secretariat Head of State Files, Box 38: USSR, RRPL.

44. Clark to Reagan, "Talking Points for Use at the April 16 NSC Meeting," April 15, 1982, NSC Executive Secretariat Meeting Files, Box 5, RRPL. See, for example: Robert Tucker, "The Middle East: Carterism without Carter?" *Commentary*, September 1981.

45. Norman Podhoretz, "The Neoconservative Anguish over Reagan's Foreign Policy," *New York Times*, May 2, 1982.

46. The Committee on the Present Danger, "Has America Become Number 2?" June 29, 1982. See: Tyroler (ed.), *Alerting America*, pp. 202–38.

47. See: Wilson, *The Triumph of Improvisation*, pp. 30–32; Talbott, *Deadly Gambits*, pp. 268–71.

48. Minutes of NSC Meeting, "NSDD 1–82," April 16, 1982, NSC Executive Secretariat Meeting files, Box 5, RRPL.

49. For the internal memos on NSDD-32, see: "U.S. National Security Strategy," (parts 1–3) NSC Executive Secretariat Meeting Files, Box 5, RRPL. See also: NSDD-32, "U.S. National Security Strategy," May 20, 1982. See: www.reaganlibrary.gov/sites/default/files/archives/reference/scanned-nsdds/nsdd32.pdf

50. Brinkley (ed.), *The Reagan Diaries*, p. 75.

51. Richard Halloran, "Pentagon Draws Up First Strategy for Fighting a Long Nuclear War," *New York Times*, May 30, 1982. For a good overview of the Defense Guidance, see: Garthoff, *The Great Transition*, pp. 36–39.

52. Richard Halloran, "Weinberger Confirms New Strategy on Atom War," *New York Times*, June 4, 1982.

53. FitzGerald, *Way Out There in Blue*, p. 187; Scheers, *With Enough Shovels*, p. 9.

54. Talbott, *Deadly Gambits*, p. 267.

55. Minutes of NSC Meeting, "NSDD 1-82," April 16, 1982, NSC Executive Secretariat Meeting Files, Box 5, RRPL.

56. Richard Pipes, *Vixi: Memoirs of a Non-Belonger* (New Haven: Yale University Press, 2003), pp. 166–67.

57. Craig and Logevall, *America's Cold War*, p. 314.

58. Clark to Reagan, "Memorandum to the President," April 22, 1982, The Robert McFarlane Files, RAC Box 1, Arms Control/Nuclear Freeze (1), RRPL.

59. Clark to Baker, Deaver, and Meese, "Policy Offensive on Arms Control and the Anti-nuclear Movement," April 22, 1982, The Robert McFarlane Files, RAC Box 1, Arms Control/Nuclear Freeze (1), RRPL.

60. Baker to Clark, "Nuclear Freeze and Related Arms Control and Defense Issues," April 28, 1982, The Robert McFarlane Files, RAC Box 1, Arms Control/Nuclear Freeze (1), RRPL.

61. Paul Bremer to Clark, "Public Affairs Strategy in Support of Administration's Nuclear Policy," May 5, 1982, The Robert McFarlane Files, RAC Box 1, Arms Control/Nuclear Freeze (2), RRPL.

62. Bistany to Gergen, "Anti-nuclear Movement," April 5, 1982, The David Gergen Files, Series 1: Gergen/Bistany Subject file, Box 1, RRPL.

63. The White House Office of the Press Secretary, "Radio Address by the President to the Nation," April 17, 1982, The Elizabeth Dole Files, Series 1, Subject file, Box 40, RRPL.

64. Address by Ronald Reagan to Members of the British Parliament, June 8, 1982, APP. See: www.presidency.ucsb.edu/documents/address-members-the-british-parliament

65. Raymond Walter Apple Jr., "President Urges Global Crusade for Democracy," *New York Times*, June 9, 1982.

66. Morton Blackwell to Jim Pinkerton, "1982 Elections," December 31, 1981, The Elizabeth Dole Files, Series 1, Subject file, Box 20, RRPL.

67. The White House Office of the Press Secretary, "Q and A with the President," December 10, 1982, The Elizabeth Dole files, Series 1, Subject file, Box 39, RRPL.

68. Memorandum of Conversation between Haig and Gromyko, "U.S.–Soviet Relations," June 18, 1982, The William Clark Files, Box 3, RRPL; Pipes to Clark, "Haig–Gromyko Meeting," July 23, 1982, The William Clark Files, Box 3, RRPL.

69. Reagan, *An American Life*, pp. 360–61.

70. Ibid., pp. 270–71. See also: Cannon, *President Reagan*, p. 204.

71. Knott and Chidester, *The Reagan Years*, pp. 227–28.

72. George Shultz, *Turmoil and Triumph: My Years as Secretary of State* (New York: Scribner's, 1993), p. 119.
73. Garthoff, *The Great Transition*, p. 50. See also: Matlock, *Reagan and Gorbachev*, p. 45.
74. Shultz, *Turmoil and Triumph*, pp. 122–23.
75. FitzGerald, *Way Out There in Blue*, pp. 270–71.
76. Talbott, *The Master of the Game*, p. 220.
77. Sell, *From Washington to Moscow*, p. 153; Newhouse, *War and Peace in the Nuclear Age*, pp. 355–56. For internal analysis of Nitze's INF proposal, see: Rostow to Reagan, "INF Package," July 30, 1982; Clark to Reagan, "INF Initiative," August 5, 1982, The William Clark Files, Box 3, RRPL.
78. Ibid.
79. Cannon, *President Reagan*, p. 204; Shultz, *Turmoil and Triumph*, p. 120; Weinberger, *Fighting for Peace*, p. 344.
80. Peter Pry, *War Scare: Russia and America on the Nuclear Brink* (Westport: Praeger, 1999), p. 4. For an alternative view of Andropov's time in Budapest, see: Raymond Walter Apple Jr., "Some Insights into Andropov Gleaned from Hungary Role," *New York Times*, December 28, 1982.
81. Zubok, *A Failed Empire*, p. 272.
82. John Burns, "The Emergence of Andropov," *New York Times*, February 27, 1983.
83. Matlock, *Reagan and Gorbachev*, p. 49.
84. Dobrynin, *In Confidence*, pp. 512–13.
85. Shultz, *Turmoil and Triumph*, p. 126.
86. Bernard Gwertzman, "Reagan Lifts Sanctions on Sales for Soviet Pipeline; Reports Accord With Allies," *New York Times*, November 14, 1982.
87. Haig, *Caveat*, p. 241.
88. John W. Sloan, "The Economic Costs of Reagan Mythology," in Kyle Longley (et al), *Deconstructing Reagan*, pp. 51–55; Zelizer, *Arsenal of Democracy*, p. 314.
89. Wirls, *Buildup*, pp. 103–05; Letter from Ed Rowny (START negotiator) to Rep. William Broomfield, August 2, 1982, The Robert McFarlane Files, RAC Box 1, Arms Control/Nuclear Freeze (4), RRPL.
90. Judith Miller, "House Supports Reagan on Arms, Adopting his Idea of Atom Freeze," *New York Times*, August 6, 1982.
91. Michael Hogan, *The Nuclear Freeze Campaign: Rhetoric and Foreign Policy in the Telepolitical Age* (East Lansing: Michigan State University Press, 1994), p. 192.
92. Wirls, *Buildup*, pp. 106–07.
93. McFarlane to Clark, "Public Affairs Strategy on the Nuclear Freeze," August 28, 1982, The Robert McFarlane Files, RAC Box 1, Arms Control/Nuclear Freeze (6), RRPL. In his memoirs, McFarlane gives a different take on the "success" of the anti-freeze campaign in 1982. See: Robert McFarlane, *Special Trust* (New York: Cadell & Davies, 1994), pp. 197–98.
94. Clark to Baker, "Nuclear Freeze," August 16, 1982, Box 7, The David Gergen Files, RRPL.

95. Matthew Wald, "Reagan Raises GOP Hackles," *New York Times*, August 8, 1982.
96. Wirls, *Buildup*, p. 105.
97. Remarks by Ronald Reagan in Columbus to Members of Ohio Veterans Organizations, October 4, 1982, APP. See: www.presidency.ucsb.edu/documents/remarks-columbus-members-ohio-veterans-organizations
98. Tom Wicker, "Enough is Enough," *New York Times*, October 8, 1982.
99. FitzGerald, *Way Out There in Blue*, p. 191.
100. Cannon, *President Reagan*, p. 233.
101. Matlock, *Reagan and Gorbachev*, p. 50.
102. Interview by the author with Ambassador Jack Matlock, August 30, 2017.
103. Garthoff, *The Great Transition*, pp. 54–84.
104. Thomas, *The Helsinki Effect*, pp. 211–12.
105. Shultz, *Turmoil and Triumph*, p. 5.

6 STAR WARS AND THE EVIL EMPIRE

1. Reeves, *President Reagan*, pp. 118–19.
2. *Gallup Reports* 208 (January 1983), p. 13. See also: Wirls, *Buildup*, pp. 147–48.
3. Richard Darman, *Who's in Control?: Polar Politics and the Sensible Center* (New York: Simon & Schuster, 1996), p. 113.
4. Ed Rollins to Meese, Baker, and Deaver, "Political Update," April 22, 1982, The Edwin Meese Files, Box 29, RRPL.
5. The David Broder Column, *Washington Post*, January 12, 1983.
6. Reeves, *President Reagan*, p. 132.
7. Brinkley (ed.), *The Reagan Diaries*, p. 117.
8. Joanne Omang, "Reagan Again Says Soviet Union Influences Anti-Nuclear Group," *Washington Post*, December 11, 1982.
9. Lou Cannon and David Hoffman, "Marshalling Support for Arms Buildup," *Washington Post*, February 14, 1983.
10. Joanne Omang, "Reagan Again Says Soviet Union Influences Anti-Nuclear Group," *Washington Post*, December 11, 1982.
11. Clymer, *Edward M. Kennedy*, p. 337.
12. Farrell, *Tip O'Neill and the Democratic Century*, pp. 598–99.
13. Lou Cannon and David Hoffman, "Marshalling Support for Arms Buildup," *Washington Post*, February 14, 1983.
14. Farrell, *Tip O'Neill and the Democratic Century*, pp. 598–99.
15. Garthoff, *The Great Transition*, p. 102.
16. Baker to Clark, "Co-ordination on Key Issues," January 12, 1983, The James Baker Papers, Series 6: Chief of Staff, Box 77, Folder 8, William Clark: General 1983, PUML. For Reagan's concern about the public perceptions of the defense budget, see: Minutes of NSC Meeting: "Discussion on Defense Program," January 28, 1983, NSC Executive Secretariat Meeting Files, Box 8, RRPL.

17. Darman to Baker, "Outreach Strategy Group," February 23, 1983, The James Baker Papers, Series 6: Chief of Staff, Box 60, Folder 4, Legislative Strategy 1983, PUML.

18. Spencer to Baker and Deaver, May 2, 1983. See attached memorandum, April 1983. The Michael Deaver Files, Series VI: Political Material; Election, Box 68, RRPL.

19. Wirls, *Buildup*, p. 113.

20. Brinkley (ed.), *The Reagan Diaries*, p. 113.

21. Richard Halloran, "Reagan Proposes 'Dense Pack' of 100 MX Missiles in Wyoming," *New York Times*, November 23, 1982.

22. The White House Office of the Press Secretary, "Statement by the President," November 22, 1982, The Elizabeth Dole Files, Series I, Subject File, Box 39, RRPL.

23. George Wilson, "Lobbying to Save MX Intensified: Panel Vote Today Spurs Pentagon, White House Blitz," *Washington Post*, December 2, 1982.

24. Dole to Baker, Deaver, Meese, and Clark, "MX Business Coalition," November 29, 1982, The Elizabeth Dole Files, Series I, Subject File, Box 39, RRPL.

25. David Hoffman, *The Dead Hand: Reagan, Gorbachev, and the Untold Story of the Cold War Arms Race* (New York: Doubleday, 2009), pp. 46–47.

26. McFarlane, *Special Trust*, p. 224.

27. Cannon, *President Reagan: The Role of a Lifetime*, p. 324.

28. Newhouse, *War and Peace in the Nuclear Age*, pp. 358–59.

29. The Scowcroft Commission was formally known as "The President's Commission on Strategic Forces." For the full report, see: Brent Scowcroft, *Report of the President's Commission on Strategic Forces*, April 6, 1983.

30. Lou Cannon, "Scowcroft Commission's Life is Extended for Two Years," *Washington Post*, June 4, 1983; Wirls, *Buildup*, p. 116.

31. AFL-CIO News Release, April 21, 1983, The Kenneth Duberstein Files, Series I, Box 8, RRPL.

32. Statement of Speaker Thomas P. O'Neill, 12 May 1983, The Tip O'Neill Papers, Series 6, Subseries D: Press Relations, Box 19, BCBL.

33. Meyer, *A Winter of Discontent*, p. 233.

34. David Maraniss, "House Passes Nuclear Freeze Resolution," *Washington Post*, May 5, 1983.

35. Wirls, *Buildup*, p. 117; Meyer, *A Winter of Discontent*, p. 234.

36. Clark to Reagan, "NSDD 11–82: Draft NSDD and Interagency Group Study," December 15, 1982, NSC Executive Secretariat Meeting Files, Box 7, RRPL. The memo contains a summary and draft of the directive (which became NSDD-75).

37. NSDD-75, "U.S. Relations with the USSR," January 17, 1983. See: www .reaganlibrary.gov/sites/default/files/archives/reference/scanned-nsdds/nsd d75.pdf

38. See for example: Norman Bailey, *The Strategic Plan That Won the Cold War* (McLean, VA: Potomac, 1998); Paul Kengor, *Crusader: Ronald Reagan and the Fall of Communism* (New York: HarperCollins, 2006); Richard Pipes, *Vixi: Memoirs of a Non-Belonger* (New Haven: Yale University Press,

2003); Peter Schweizer, *Reagan's War: The Epic Story of his Forty Year Struggle and Final Triumph Over Communism* (New York: Random House, 2002).

39. Wilson, *The Triumph of Imagination*, p. 198. See also: NSDD-32, "U.S. National Security Strategy," May 20, 1982. See: www.reaganlibrary.gov/si tes/default/files/archives/reference/scanned-nsdds/nsdd32.pdf

40. NSDD-75, "U.S. Relations with the USSR," January 17, 1983. See: www .reaganlibrary.gov/sites/default/files/archives/reference/scanned-nsdds/nsd d75.pdf

41. Garthoff, *The Great Transition*, p. 33.

42. Interview with Robert McFarlane, November 1, 1989, p. 3. The Don Oberdorfer Papers, Box 2, Folder 22, PUML.

43. NSDD-75, "U.S. Relations with the USSR," January 17, 1983. See: www .reaganlibrary.gov/sites/default/files/archives/reference/scanned-nsdds/nsd d75.pdf

44. Sell, *From Washington to Moscow*, pp. 133–34.

45. Shultz, *Turmoil and Triumph*, pp. 159, 166.

46. Philip Taubman, "The Shultz–Weinberger Feud," *New York Times*, April 14, 1985.

47. Cannon, *President Reagan*, p. 310. For Weinberger's admiration for Winston Churchill, see: Weinberger, *Fighting for Peace*, pp. 18–20.

48. Shultz, *Turmoil and Triumph*, p. 161.

49. Cannon, *President Reagan*, pp. 309–10.

50. Shultz, *Turmoil and Triumph*, p. 159.

51. Ibid., p. 162. See also: Wilson, *The Triumph of Imagination*, p. 69.

52. See for example: Shultz to Reagan, "U.S.-Soviet Relations: Where do we want to be and how do we get there?" March 3, 1983, The Robert McFarlane Files, Series I: Subject File, RAC Box 3, Soviet Union: Sensitive File, 1983 (02/15/1983–07/14/1983), RRPL; Shultz to Reagan, "Next Steps in U.S.-Soviet Relations," March 16, 1983, NSC Executive Secretariat System Files, No. 8307414, RRPL.

53. Clark to Reagan, "The Prospects for Progress in U.S.-Soviet Relations," February 4, 1983, The William Clark Files, U.S.–Soviet Relations, Working File Part 2, Box 8, RRPL.

54. Clark to Reagan, "U.S.-Soviet Relations: Next Steps," May 25, 1983, The William Clark Files, U.S.–Soviet Relations, Working File Part 7, Box 8, RRPL.

55. Hartman to Shultz, January 25, 1983, The William Clark Files, U.S.–Soviet Relations, Working File Part 2, Box 8, RRPL.

56. Victor Cohn, "Andropov Reported to be on Dialysis for Kidney Disease," *Washington Post*, December 28, 1983. See also: Oberdorfer, *From the Cold War to a New Era*, p. 20.

57. Cannon, *President Reagan*, p. 312.

58. For their recollections of the Reagan–Dobrynin meeting, see: Dobrynin, *In Confidence*, pp. 517–22; Reagan, *An American Life*, p. 558; Shultz, *Turmoil and Triumph*, p. 165.

59. Shultz, *Turmoil and Triumph*, p. 165.

60. Frances FitzGerald, *The Evangelicals: The Struggle to Shape America* (New York: Simon & Schuster, 2017), pp. 321–23; Hugh Gusterson, *Nuclear Rites: A Weapons Laboratory at the End of the Cold War* (Berkeley: University of California Press, 1996), pp. 60–61.

61. Francis Clines, "Reagan Denounces Ideology of Soviets as 'Focus of Evil'," *New York Times*, March 9, 1983.

62. Remarks by Ronald Reagan at the Annual Convention of the National Association of Evangelicals in Orlando, Florida, March 8, 1983, APP. See: www.presidency.ucsb.edu/documents/remarks-the-annual-convention-the-national-association-evangelicals-orlando-florida

63. Cannon, *President Reagan*, p. 317; Oberdorfer, *From the Cold War to a New Era*, pp. 23–24.

64. Dobrynin, *In Confidence*, p. 527.

65. Address by Ronald Reagan to the Nation on Defense and National Security, March 23, 1983, APP. See: www.presidency.ucsb.edu/documents/address-the-nation-defense-and-national-security

66. Craig and Logevall, *America's Cold War*, pp. 315–16; Newhouse, *War and Peace in the Nuclear Age*, p. 359.

67. Shultz, *Turmoil and Triumph*, p. 259.

68. "Star Wars: Will Space be the Next Battleground?" *Newsweek*, April 4, 1983.

69. Waller, *Congress and the Nuclear Freeze*, p. 191.

70. Collins, *Transforming America*, p. 202.

71. Garthoff, *The Great Transition*, p. 553.

72. Aldous, *Reagan and Thatcher*, p. 132; Thatcher, *The Downing Street Years*, pp. 463–73.

73. Brands, *Reagan*, pp. 416–17.

74. Garthoff, *The Great Transition*, p. 516.

75. Address by Ronald Reagan to the Nation on Defense and National Security, March 23, 1983, APP. See: www.presidency.ucsb.edu/documents/address-the-nation-defense-and-national-security

76. Hedrick Smith, *The Power Game: How Washington Works* (London: Collins, 1988), p. 603.

77. Martin Anderson, *Revolution* (New York: Harcourt Brace Jovanovich, 1988), pp. 80–99.

78. Daniel Graham, *To Provide for the Common Defense: The Case for Space Defense* (Louisville, KY: Frank Simon Company, 1986), p. 17.

79. Anderson, *Revolution*, pp. 86–87.

80. FitzGerald, *Way Out There in Blue*, p. 131.

81. Donald Baucom, *The Origins of SDI, 1944–1983* (Lawrence: University Press of Kansas, 1992), pp. 146–55; FitzGerald, *Way Out There in Blue*, p. 137.

82. Weinberger, *Fighting for Peace*, pp. 299–303.

83. Dorothy McCartney (research director) to Keyworth, July 7, 1982. Transcript of Edward Teller's interview with William F. Buckley on *The Firing Line*, which aired on PBS on June 16, 1982. The George Keyworth Files, RAC Box 16, RRPL.

84. Teller to Keyworth, July 23, 1982, The George Keyworth Files, RAC Box 16, RRPL.
85. Keyworth to Reagan, "Letter from Edward Teller," July 29, 1982, The George Keyworth Files, RAC Box 16, RRPL.
86. Teller to Reagan, July 23, 1982, The George Keyworth Files, RAC Box 16, RRPL.
87. Keyworth to Clark, "Request for Edward Teller to Meet with the President," July 13, 1982; Keyworth to Reagan, "Letter from Edward Teller," July 29, 1982. See handwritten note on letter by Ronald Reagan. The George Keyworth Files, RAC Box 16, RRPL.
88. Bruce Abell to Keyworth, "Fact Sheet on Involvement of Edward Teller with President's March 23 Speech on Strategic Defense," April 28, 1983, The George Keyworth Files, RAC Box 16, RRPL.
89. Paul Lettow, *Ronald Reagan and His Quest to Abolish Nuclear Weapons* (New York: Random House, 2005), p. 82.
90. Wirls, *Buildup*, p. 143.
91. Philip Boffey, "Pressures are Increasing for Arms Race in Space," *New York Times*, October 17, 1982.
92. FitzGerald, *Way Out There in Blue*, p. 191.
93. Smith, *The Power Game*, p. 605.
94. Baucom, *The Origins of SDI*, pp. 181–83; Talbott, *The Master of the Game*, pp. 200–08.
95. Talbott, *The Master of the Game*, p. 204.
96. Interview by the author with Ambassador Jack Matlock, August 30, 2017.
97. Cited in: Lettow, *Ronald Reagan and His Quest to Abolish Nuclear Weapons*, p. 91.
98. Baucom, *The Origins of SDI*, pp. 184–88.
99. Cannon, *President Reagan*, p. 328.
100. For accounts of Reagan's meeting with the Joint Chiefs on February 11, 1983, see: Frederick Hartmann, *Naval Renaissance: The U.S. Navy in the 1980s* (Annapolis: Naval Institute Press, 1990), pp. 254–56; Cannon, *President Reagan*, pp. 329–30; FitzGerald, *Way Out There in Blue*, p. 197; Baucom, *The Origins of SDI*, pp. 191–92; Smith, *The Power Game*, pp. 607–08; McFarlane, *Special Trust*, pp. 229–30; Weinberger, *Fighting for Peace*, p. 304.
101. Talbott, *The Master of the Game*, p. 194.
102. Minutes of NSC Meeting: "Briefing on Defense Guidance," February 25, 1983, NSC Executive Secretariat Meeting Files, No. 90221, RRPL.
103. Smith, *The Power Game*, p. 609.
104. FitzGerald, *Way Out There in Blue*, p. 198. In his memoirs, Reagan also dismissed the notion that he conceived of SDI as "a bargaining chip." See: Reagan, *An American Life*, pp. 547–48.
105. Baucom, *The Origins of SDI*, p. 193.
106. Cannon, *President Reagan*, pp. 330–31.
107. Baucom, *The Origins of SDI*, p. 194.
108. Cannon, *President Reagan*, p. 331; Smith, *The Power Game*, p. 613.
109. Talbott, *The Master of the Game*, p. 193.

110. Newhouse, *War and Peace in the Nuclear Age*, p. 361.
111. Shultz to Reagan, "U.S.-Soviet Relations: Where do we want to be and how do we get there?" March 3, 1983, The Robert McFarlane Files, Series I: Subject File, RAC Box 3, Soviet Union: Sensitive File, 1983 (February 15–July 14, 1983), RRPL; Shultz to Reagan, "Next Steps in U.S.-Soviet Relations," March 16, 1983, NSC Executive Secretariat System Files, No. 8307414, RRPL.
112. Shultz, *Turmoil and Triumph*, p. 254.
113. Smith, *The Power Game*, p. 614.
114. Garthoff, *The Great Transition*, pp. 111–12.
115. Dusko Doder, "Andropov Accuses Reagan of Lying About Soviet Arms," *Washington Post*, March 27, 1983.
116. Oberdorfer, *From the Cold War to a New Era*, p. 29–30.
117. Dobrynin, *In Confidence*, pp. 528–29.
118. Archie Brown, "The Gorbachev Revolution and the End of the Cold War," in *The Cambridge History of the Cold War: Volume III*, p. 252.
119. Newhouse, *War and Peace in the Nuclear Age*, p. 365.
120. On the Soviet economic problems, see: Kotkin, *Armageddon Averted*, pp. 15–30; Vladislav Zubok, "Soviet Foreign Policy from Détente to Gorbachev," in *The Cambridge History of the Cold War: Volume III*, pp. 89–111.
121. Newhouse, *War and Peace in the Nuclear Age*, p. 363
122. Matthew Evangelista, "Transnational Organizations and the Cold War," in *The Cambridge History of the Cold War: Volume III*, p. 419.

7 THE MOST DANGEROUS YEAR

1. Gates, *From the Shadows*, p. 258.
2. Drew Middleton, "Nicaragua Buildup: Regional Threat Seen," *New York Times*, March 9, 1983.
3. Morton Blackwell, "Winning in Central America," April 29, 1983, The Richard Darman Files, Series I, Subject File, Box 4, RRPL.
4. Christian Smith, *Resisting Reagan: The U.S. Central America Peace Movement* (Chicago: University of Chicago Press, 1996), pp. 30–31.
5. Raymond Bonner, "The Thousand Small Escalations of Our Latin War," *Washington Post*, September 16, 1984.
6. Interview with Michael Deaver, September 12, 2002, Reagan Presidential Oral History Project, MCPA.
7. Cannon, *President Reagan*, p. 361.
8. Interview with Michael Deaver, September 12, 2002, Reagan Presidential Oral History Project, MCPA.
9. William LeoGrande, *Our Own Backyard: The United States in Central America, 1977–1992* (Chapel Hill: University of North Carolina Press, 1998), pp. 213–14.
10. Lou Cannon, "Reagan Defends Nicaraguan Role," *Washington Post*, May 5, 1983.

11. Letter from Robert Byrd and Tip O'Neill to Reagan, July 28, 1983, The M.B. Oglesby Files, Box 8, RRPL.

12. Kyle Longley, "An Obsession: The Central American Policy of the Reagan Administration," pp. 218–21, in Coleman and Longley (eds.), *Reagan and the World*.

13. John Coatsworth, "The Cold War in Central America, 1975–1991," in *The Cambridge History of the Cold War: Volume III*, p. 212. See also: Johnson, *Congress and the Cold War*, pp. 276–77.

14. Longley, "An Obsession: The Central American Policy of the Reagan Administration," pp. 218–21.

15. John Vinocur, "In Europe, Bush Seeks to Keep Allies in Line," *New York Times*, February 6, 1983; R. W. Apple, Jr., "The Zero Option: Mrs Thatcher Softens Her Support," *New York Times*, January 20, 1983.

16. Letter by Thatcher to Reagan, February 18, 1983, WHORM: NSC Head of State File, Folder: Thatcher: Cables [2], Box 34, RRPL.

17. John Vinocur, "Bush, in London, Challenged by Nuclear Foe," *New York Times*, February 10, 1983.

18. Blair to Clark, "INF: Conclusions from the Vice President's Trip to Europe," February 10, 1983, The William Clark Files, Box 3, RRPL.

19. Memo from Ambassador Price to Clark (subsequently sent to Ronald Reagan), "Talking Points on INF," March 16, 1983, The William Clark Files, Box 3, RRPL.

20. Lou Cannon, "Administration Considers Proposal to Break Arms Negotiation Deadlock," *Washington Post*, March 15, 1983.

21. Ronald Powaski, *Return to Armageddon: The United States and the Nuclear Arms Race, 1981–1999* (New York: Oxford University Press, 2000), pp. 12–13.

22. Lou Cannon, "Warmonger Image Resurfaces: Reagan Defense Push May Backfire," *Washington Post*, April 7, 1983.

23. John Lewis Gaddis, *George F. Kennan: An American Life* (New York: Penguin, 2011), p. 660; Don Oberdorfer, "Envoy Extraordinaire," *Washington Post*, February 25, 1996.

24. Handwritten note by Clark to Reagan, March 26, 1983, The William Clark Files, U.S.–Soviet Relations, Working File Part 4, Box 8, RRPL.

25. "Meeting with the President," April 6, 1983, The William Clark Files, U.S.–Soviet Relations, Working File Part 5, Box 8, RRPL. The participants at the meeting were Reagan, Shultz, Clark, Baker, Meese, and Dam. See also: Oberdorfer, *From the Cold War to a New Era*, p. 35.

26. Shultz to Reagan, "Next Steps in U.S.-Soviet Relations," May 21, 1983, The William Clark Files, U.S.–Soviet Relations, Working File Part 7, Box 8, RRPL.

27. Clark to Reagan, "U.S.-Soviet Relations: Next Steps," May 25, 1983, The William Clark Files, U.S.–Soviet Relations, Working File Part 7, Box 8, RRPL.

28. Brinkley (ed.), *The Reagan Diaries*, p. 142.

29. Darman to Baker, "Protection of Classified Information," March 17, 1983, The Richard Darman Files, Series I: Subject File, Box 3, RRPL; Tom

Morganthau, Thomas DeFrank, and Eleanor Clift, "The Leaks at the White House," *Newsweek*, April 4, 1983.

30. Michael Getler, "Scowcroft Suggests Private U.S.-Soviet Talks," *Washington Post*, May 24, 1983.

31. "Excerpts from Shultz Statement on Soviets to Senate Committee," *New York Times*, June 16, 1983. See also: Shultz, *Turmoil and Triumph*, pp. 276–80.

32. Shultz to Reagan, "My Meeting with Dobrynin, 18 June," June 20, 1983, The William Clark Files, U.S.-Soviet Relations, Working File Part 14, Box 9, RRPL. See also: Leslie Gelb, "Expanding Contacts with Soviets: Shultz and Dobrynin Make a Start," *New York Times*, June 30, 1983.

33. Garthoff, *The Great Transition*, pp. 105–06.

34. Oberdorfer, *From the Cold War to a New Era*, pp. 40–42; Wilson, *The Triumph of Improvisation*, p. 75; Hoffman, *The Dead Hand*, p. 68. For Shultz's exchange with Reagan, see: Shultz, *Turmoil and Triumph*, pp. 311–14. For Nancy Reagan's views on Clark, see: Nancy Reagan, *My Turn: The Memoirs of Nancy Reagan* (New York: Random House, 1989), pp. 242–43.

35. Hedrick Smith, "Reagan Getting a Soviet Expert as New Adviser," *New York Times*, June 5, 1983.

36. Interview by the author with Ambassador Jack Matlock, August 30, 2017.

37. Matlock, *Reagan and Gorbachev*, pp. 61–62.

38. Memorandum by Donald Fortier, NSC Director of Politico-Military Affairs: "Goals and Objectives: The Soviet Union," July 6, 1983, The Donald Fortier Files, Soviet Project, RAC Box 14, RRPL.

39. Duberstein to McFarlane, "Upcoming MX Votes," July 18, 1983, The Kenneth Duberstein Files, Series I, Box 8, RRPL.

40. See for example: Wirthlin to Baker, Deaver, and Meese, "1984 Presidential Vote," September 2, 1983, The Michael Deaver Files, Series VI: Political Material: Polling Information, Dick Wirthlin, 1983–84, Box 65, RRPL; Wirthlin to Senator Paul Laxalt and Frank Fahrenkopf, "Presidential Performance," August 5, 1983, The Michael Deaver Files, Series VI: Political Material: Dick Wirthlin, 1983–84, Republican National Convention, Box 66, RRPL.

41. Clark to Reagan, "Summitry," June 1983, The William Clark Files, U.S.-Soviet Relations, Working File Part 15, Box 9, RRPL.

42. Reagan to Andropov, July 11, 1983, NSC Executive Secretariat Head of State Files, Box 38: USSR, RRPL; Reagan to Andropov, July 11, 1983, The Robert McFarlane Files, Series I: Subject File, RAC Box 3, Soviet Union: Sensitive File, 1983 (July 15–October 20, 1983), RRPL. See also: Martin Anderson and Annelise Anderson, *Reagan's Secret War: The Untold Story of His Fight to Save the World from Nuclear Disaster* (New York: Crown, 2009), pp. 137–38; Svetlana Savranskaya and Thomas Blanton, *The Last Superpower Summits: Gorbachev, Reagan, and Bush – Conversations that Ended the Cold War* (Budapest: Central European University Press, 2016), p. 5.

43. Dobrynin, *In Confidence*, pp. 531–33.

44. Andropov to Reagan, August 4, 1983, The Robert McFarlane Files, Series I: Subject File, RAC Box 3, Soviet Union: Sensitive File, 1983 (07/15/1983–10/20/1983), RRPL.

45. Interview with George Shultz, July 11, 1989, Segment I, p. 3, The Don Oberdorfer Papers, Box 3, Folder 2, PUML.

46. Marc Ambinder, *The Brink: President Reagan and the Nuclear War Scare of 1983* (New York: Simon and Schuster, 2018), p. 166.

47. Reagan to Andropov, August 22, 1983, The Robert McFarlane Files, Series I: Subject File, RAC Box 3, Soviet Union: Sensitive File, 1983 (July 15–October 20, 1983), RRPL. Note: the Reagan letter incorrectly states August 22, 1984, rather than 1983.

48. Andropov to Reagan, August 27, 1983, NSC Executive Secretariat Head of State Files, Box 38: USSR, RRPL.

49. Shultz to Reagan, "Andropov's Proposal to Destroy Missiles," August 29, 1983, NSC Executive Secretariat Head of State Files, Box 38: USSR, RRPL.

50. For excellent accounts of the KAL disaster, see: Sell, *From Washington to Moscow*, pp. 136–40; Hoffman, *The Dead Hand*, pp. 72–86.

51. For detailed foreign press reaction to the KAL incident, see: The Michael Deaver Files, Series IV: Subject File, The Korean Plane Incident, Box 45, RRPL.

52. Aldous, *Reagan and Thatcher*, p. 140.

53. Bill Patman to Reagan, September 1, 1983; Newt Gingrich to Reagan, September 1, 1983; Denny Smith to Reagan, September 2, 1983; Bill Frenzel to Reagan, September 2, 1983, The Michael Deaver Files, Series IV: Subject File, The Korean Plane Incident, Box 45, RRPL; David Shribman, "Senator Henry M. Jackson is Dead at 71," *New York Times*, September 3, 1983.

54. Michael Getler, "Reagan Demands an Explanation," *Washington Post*, September 2, 1983.

55. Shultz, *Turmoil and Triumph*, pp. 361–66.

56. Oberdorfer, *From the Cold War to a New Era*, p. 58.

57. Lenczowski to Clark, "The Korean Airliner, Soviet Motive, and U.S. Policy," September 3, 1983, The William Clark Files, KAL 007 Shootdown, Box 3, RRPL.

58. At the suggestion of Deaver, Clark wrote to Nancy Reagan informing her of the president's "measured" response to the KAL incident. See: Clark to Nancy Reagan, September 7, 1983, The William Clark Files, KAL 007 Shootdown, Box 3, RRPL. See also: Oberdorfer, *From the Cold War to a New Era*, p. 52.

59. Dolan to Clark, "Presidential Address: Downed Korean Airliner," September 4, 1983. For Matlock's suggested remarks, see: "Presidential Address, September 5, 1983: Matlock Suggestions," September 4, 1983, The Jack Matlock Files, Series I: Chron File, Box 1, RRPL.

60. "Transcript of President Reagan's Address on Downing of Korean Airliner," *New York Times*, September 6, 1983.

61. Oberdorfer, *From the Cold War to a New Era*, p. 59.

62. Shultz, *Turmoil and Triumph*, pp. 365–66.

63. Nancy Reagan, *My Turn*, pp. 63–64, 336–37.
64. Oberdorfer, *From the Cold War to a New Era*, p. 91.
65. Clark to Nancy Reagan, September 7, 1983, The William Clark Files, KAL 007 Shootdown, Box 3, RRPL. Copies of the U.S. media reports are attached.
66. Oberdorfer, *From the Cold War to a New Era*, pp. 56–57; Dobrynin, *In Confidence*, p. 537.
67. Garthoff, *The Great Transition*, p. 125.
68. Oberdorfer, *From the Cold War to a New Era*, pp. 59–60.
69. Tom Wicker, "Tough but Restrained," *New York Times*, September 9, 1983.
70. "Reagan: Forceful Restraint," *Los Angeles Times*, September 6, 1983; Jack Germond and Jules Witcover, "Soviet Trigger Finger and Peace," *Chicago Tribune*, September 7, 1983.
71. Helen Dewar and T. R. Reid, "Incident to Bolster the President's Hand, Congressmen Say," *Washington Post*, September 7, 1983.
72. Garthoff, *The Great Transition*, pp. 125–26.
73. For their respective views of the meeting, see: Shultz, *Turmoil and Triumph*, pp. 369–70; Gromyko, *Memoirs*, pp. 298–301. See also: Oberdorfer, *From the Cold War to a New Era*, pp. 60–61.
74. David Dunlap, "Diplomats Wary on Gromyko Move," *New York Times*, September 19, 1983.
75. Ronald Reagan, "Radio Address to the Nation on the Soviet Attack on a Korean Civilian Airliner," September 17, 1983, *Public Papers of the Presidents of the United States, 1983: Book 2* (Washington, DC: Office of the Federal Register, 1984), pp. 1295–96.
76. "Bush Promises Aid for East Bloc States with Independence," *New York Times*, September 22, 1983; Garthoff, *The Great Transition*, p. 128.
77. William Drozdiak, "Bush: U.S. Will Aid Maverick Soviet Bloc States," *Washington Post*, September 22, 1983; Garthoff, *The Great Transition*, p. 128.
78. UPI Archives, Moscow, September 22, 1983. See: www.upi.com/Archives/ 1983/09/22/Vice-President-George-Bush-abused-the-hospitality-of-the /8655433051200/
79. John Burns, "Andropov Attacks U.S. Missile Plan as Unacceptable," *New York Times*, September 29, 1983. See also: Hoffman, *The Dead Hand*, p. 87.
80. Dobrynin, *In Confidence*, p. 540.
81. Memorandum of Conversation between Jack Matlock and Sergei Vishnevsky, "U.S.-Soviet Relations," October 11, 1983, The Jack Matlock Files, Series I, Chron File: October 1983–December 1983, Box 2, RRPL.
82. Matlock to McFarlane, "Hartman-Gromyko Meeting," October 28, 1983. Attached is Hartman's report on the meeting with Gromyko on October 19. See: The Jack Matlock Files, Series I, Chron File: October 1983– December 1983, Box 2, RRPL.
83. Cited in: Cannon, *President Reagan*, p. 441.
84. See: Thatcher, *The Downing Street Years*, pp. 328–35; Geoffrey Howe, *Conflict of Loyalty* (London: Pan Books, 1995), pp. 325–37.

85. Aldous, *Reagan and Thatcher*, p. 156; John Campbell, *The Iron Lady: Margaret Thatcher: From Grocer's Daughter to Iron Lady* (London: Vintage, 2009), p. 270.

86. Hedrick Smith, "Reagan Says Cuba Aimed to Take Grenada," *New York Times*, October 28, 1983; Ronald Reagan, "Address to the Nation on Events in Lebanon and Grenada," October 27, 1983 See: www.reaganlibrary.gov/research/speeches/102783b

87. Reagan, *An American Life*, p. 457.

88. Oberdorfer, *From the Cold War to a New Era*, pp. 31–32.

89. Leffler, *For the Soul of Mankind*, pp. 357–58.

90. Garthoff, *The Great Transition*, p. 132.

91. David Hoffman, "In 1983 'War Scare', Soviet Leadership Feared Nuclear Surprise Attack by U.S.," *Washington Post*, October 24, 2015; "The Soviet War Scare," President's Foreign Intelligence Advisory Board, February 15, 1990, NSA. See: https://nsarchive2.gwu.edu/nukevault/ebb533-The-Able-Archer-War-Scare-Declassified-PFIAB-Report-Released/2012-0238-MR.pdf

92. Garthoff, *The Great Transition*, pp. 135, 174–75.

93. Taylor Downing, *1983: The World at the Brink* (London: Abacus, 2018), pp. 195–201; Ambinder, *The Brink*, pp. 178–84; Hoffman, *The Dead Hand*, pp. 6–11.

94. FitzGerald, *Way Out There in Blue*, p. 229. For analysis of U.S.–European relations during the Reagan years, see: Geir Lundestad, "The United States and Europe under Ronald Reagan," pp. 39–66, in David Kyvig (ed.), *Reagan and the World* (New York: Praeger, 1990).

95. R.W. Apple Jr., "Missile Protesters Jam Central London," *New York Times*, October 23, 1983.

96. Antony Acland to Oliver Wright, "Reagan and his Administration," May 24, 1983, FCO 82/1347, The Reagan Administration, UKNA.

97. Barnaby Feder, "Mrs Thatcher Plans Debate on Deployment of Missiles," *New York Times*, October 29, 1983.

98. Flora Lewis, "Foreign Affairs; Missiles and Pacifists," *New York Times*, November 18, 1983.

99. James Markham, "Vast Crowds Hold Rallies in Europe Against U.S. Arms," *New York Times*, October 23, 1983; James Markham, "Bonn Opposition Favors Soviet Missile Offer," *New York Times*, October 20, 1983; James Markham, "Schmidt's Party, in Revolt, Opposes Missiles," *New York Times*, November 20, 1983.

100. Edmond Van Den Bossche, "The Message for Today in Orwell's '1984'," *New York Times*, January 1, 1984.

101. John Mintz, "Doomsday Planning: From Bomb Shelters to Evacuation Routes," *Washington Post*, November 20, 1983.

102. Sally Bedell Smith, "ABC Film Depicting Consequences of Nuclear Attack Stirring Debate," *New York Times*, October 6, 1983.

103. Lisa Vox, *Existential Threats: American Apocalyptic Beliefs in the Technological Era* (Philadelphia: University of Pennsylvania Press, 2017), p. 119.

104. Brinkley (ed.), *The Reagan Diaries*, pp. 185–86.
105. Senior Staff Meeting Action Items: "The Day After," November 18, 1983, The James Baker Papers, Series 6: Chief of Staff, Box 73, Folder 1: Action Items 1983, PUML.
106. William Greener (RNC) to Gergen, "Upcoming Movie on ABC," November 17, 1983, The David Gergen Files, Series II, Subject File, Box 4, RRPL.
107. Gergen to Reagan, "Activities Relating to 'The Day After'," November 21, 1983, The James Baker Files, Series I: Memorandum File, Box 3: Communications, RRPL. See also: Sally Bedell Smith, "Film on a Nuclear War Already Causing Wide Fallout of Partisan Activity," *New York Times*, November 17, 1983.
108. Clymer, *Edward M. Kennedy*, p. 343.
109. Evangelista, *Unarmed Forces*, pp. 158–59. See also: Carl Sagan, "Nuclear War and Climatic Catastrophe: Some Policy Implications," *Foreign Affairs* (Winter 1983/84), pp. 258–92.
110. Meyer, *A Winter of Discontent*, pp. 241–44; Wirls, *Buildup*, pp. 118–21; Fox Butterfield, "Foes of Nuclear Arms Race Organize for '84 Campaign," *New York Times*, December 5, 1983.
111. Waller, *Congress and the Nuclear Freeze*, p. 294.
112. Robert Pear, "Democratic Candidates Disagree Over Adequacy of Nuclear Force," *New York Times*, November 6, 1983.
113. Ibid. See also: Mark Pellew to John Weston, "Democratic Views on Arms Control," October 14, 1983, FCO 82/1348, U.S. Presidential Election: 1984, UKNA.
114. "Remarks of Walter Mondale, Coalition for a Democratic Majority, Washington D.C.," November 15, 1983, FCO 82/1350, U.S. Internal Political Situation, UKNA.
115. T.R. Reid, "Democratic Sniping Troubles O'Neill," *Washington Post*, November 7, 1983.
116. Vut Fingerhut to Tip O'Neill and Robert Byrd, "Themes and Symbols for a Communications Strategy for Democratic Candidates in the Coming Year," November 15, 1983, The Tip O'Neill Papers, Series VI, Subseries D, Press Relations, Box 18, Democratic Response to State of the Union Address, December 1983–January 1984, BCBL.
117. James Reston, "The President is Going Down the Wrong Road: Q & A With the House Speaker," *New York Times*, November 1, 1983.
118. Memo by Duberstein to Baker, Meese, Deaver, and Clark: "Congressman Al Gore and Arms Control," September 20, 1983, The James Baker Files, Series I: Memorandum File, Subseries B, 1983–1983, Box 5, RRPL.
119. Memorandum by the NSC Senior Arms Control Policy Group, "NSC Meeting on Build-Down," September 8, 1983, NSC Executive Secretariat Meeting Files, Box 9, RRPL.
120. START Interagency Group Memorandum, "Potential Modifications to the U.S. START Position," September 27, 1983, Executive Secretariat National Security Planning Group Files, NSPG 0071 (START), Box 2, RRPL.

121. Clark to Reagan, "NSPG on START," September 29, 1983, Executive Secretariat National Security Planning Group Files, NSPG 0071 (START), Box 2, RRPL.
122. "President's Draft Talking Points," NSPG Meeting, September 29, 1983, Executive Secretariat National Security Planning Group Files, NSPG 0071 (START), Box 2, RRPL; Jason Saltoun-Ebin, *The Reagan Files: Inside the National Security Council* (Santa Barbara: Seabec, 2014), p. 258.
123. Cannon, *President Reagan*, pp. 429–35; Matlock, *Reagan and Gorbachev*, pp. 74–75.
124. Darman to State of the Union Group, "Five Thoughts and a Footnote," October 14, 1983, The Michael Deaver Files, Series IV: Subject File, State of the Union 1984, Box 58, RRPL.
125. Oberdorfer, *From the Cold War to a New Era*, p. 71.
126. Memo by Darman to Baker, Deaver, Duberstein, Gergen, McFarlane, and Meese: "Outline for State of the Union Address," December 8, 1983, The Edwin Meese Files, Box 27, RRPL; Memo: "Draft Outline of National Security Segment: State of the Union Address," November 2, 1983, The Michael Deaver Files, Series IV: Subject File, State of the Union 1984, Box 58, RRPL.
127. Wirthlin to Baker, Deaver, and Meese, "1984 Presidential Vote," September 2, 1983, The Michael Deaver Files, Series VI: Political Material: Polling Information, Dick Wirthlin, 1983–84, Box 65, RRPL.
128. Cannon, *President Reagan*, pp. 508–09.
129. "Reagan Campaign Action Plan," October 27, 1983, pp. 29–30, The James Baker Papers, Series 10F: Reagan-Bush (General Election 1984), Box 136, Folder 1, PUML.
130. Matlock, *Reagan and Gorbachev*, p. 75.
131. Oberdorfer, *From the Cold War to a New Era*, p. 65; Garrett Graff, *Raven Rock: The Story of the U.S. Government's Secret Plan to Save Itself—While the Rest of Us Die* (New York: Simon & Schuster, 2017), pp. 293–94; Downing, *1983: The World at the Brink*, pp. 60–64; Ambinder, *The Brink*, pp. 80–97.
132. Brinkley (ed.), *The Reagan Diaries*, p. 199.
133. Oberdorfer, *From the Cold War to a New Era*, p. 66; Garthoff, *The Great Transition*, p. 139. For Gordievsky's recollections, see: Andrew and Gordievsky, *KGB: The Inside Story*, pp. 583–600.
134. Andrew and Gordievsky, *KGB: The Inside Story*, pp. 502–03; Downing, *1983: The World at the Brink*, pp. 228–29.
135. Downing, *1983: The World at the Brink*, p. 260. British Foreign Secretary Geoffey Howe held a similar view of the Gordievsky briefs. See: Howe, *Conflict of Loyalty*, p. 350.
136. Gates, *From the Shadows*, pp. 271–72.
137. Garthoff, *The Great Transition*, p. 140.
138. Downing, *1983: The World at the Brink*, p. 248.
139. Ambinder, *The Brink*, p. 194.
140. Report by CIA Directorate of Intelligence: "Soviet Thinking on the Possibility of Armed Confrontation with the United States," December 30,

1983, The Jack Matlock Files, Series I: Chron Files, January 1984–March 1984, Box 3, RRPL.

141. Fritz Ermarth, "Observations on the 'War Scare' of 1983 from an Intelligence Perch," November 6, 1983. ETH Zurich Parallel History Project on NATO and the Warsaw Pact (PHP). See: www.php.isn.ethz.ch/lory1.ethz.ch/collec tions/colltopic320b.html?lng=en&id=17325&navinfo=15296

142. "The Soviet 'War Scare'," Report by the President's Foreign Intelligence Advisory Board, February 15, 1990, NSA. See: https://nsarchive2.gwu.edu/nukevault/ebb533-The-Able-Archer-War-Scare-Declassified-PFIAB-Report-Released/2012-0238-MR.pdf; See also: Downing, *1983: The World at the Brink*, p. 238.

143. "The Soviet 'War Scare'," Report by the President's Foreign Intelligence Advisory Board, February 15, 1990, NSA. See also: Downing, *1983: The World at the Brink*, pp. 222–56; Ambinder, *The Brink*, pp. 189–223.

144. Ibid. For further detailed information on *Able Archer*, see: Marc Ambinder, *The Brink: President Reagan and the Nuclear War Scare of 1983* (New York: Simon & Schuster, 2018); Taylor Downing, *1983: The World at the Brink* (London: Little, Brown, 2018); Nate Jones (ed.), *Able Archer 83: The Secret History of the NATO Exercise That Almost Triggered Nuclear War* (New York: New Press, 2016); Benjamin Fischer, *A Cold War Conundrum: The 1983 Soviet War Scare* (Langley, VA: CIA Center for the Study of Intelligence, 1997); For a skeptical take, see: Simon Miles, "The War Scare That Wasn't: Able Archer 83 and the Myths of the Second Cold War," *Journal of Cold War Studies*, Vol. 22, Issue 3 (Summer 2020), pp. 86–118.

145. Colin Powell (Military Assistant to the Secretary of Defense) to John Poindexter (Deputy National Security Adviser), "Significant Military Exercise: Night Train 84," December 8, 1983, The Jack Matlock Files, Series I: Chron File, October–December 1983, Box 2, RRPL.

146. Jack Matlock and Tyrus Cobb to Oliver North, "Exercise Night Train 84," December 12, 1983, The Jack Matlock Files, Series I: Chron File, October–December 1983, Box 2, RRPL.

147. Matlock to McFarlane, "American Academic on Soviet Policy," December 13, 1983. The full report is attached. The Jack Matlock Files, Series I: Chron File, October–December 1983, Box 2, RRPL.

148. Reagan, *An American Life*, pp. 585–86.

149. Gates, *From the Shadows*, pp. 258–73.

150. "Men of the Year: Ronald Reagan, Yuri Andropov," *Time Magazine*, January 2, 1984.

151. Talbott, *Deadly Gambits*, p. 343.

8 TO THE CENTER

1. Reagan, *An American Life*, p. 589.

2. David Ryan, "1984, Regional Crises, and Morning in America: The Predawn of the Reagan Era," p. 282, in Andrew Johnstone and

Andrew Priest (eds.), *U.S. Presidential Elections and Foreign Policy: Candidates, Campaigns, and Global Politics from FDR to Clinton* (Lexington: University Press of Kentucky, 2017).

3. See: Pach, "*Top Gun*, Toughness, and Terrorism," pp. 549–62.
4. Kengor, *The Crusader*, p. 200.
5. Reagan, *An American Life*, pp. 585–86.
6. Zelizer, *Arsenal of Democracy*, p. 327.
7. NSDD-75, "U.S. Relations with the USSR," January 17, 1983. See: www.reaganlibrary.gov/sites/default/files/archives/reference/scanned-nsdds/nsdd75.pdf
8. Chris Dolan, John Frendreis, and Raymond Tatalovich, *The Presidency and Economic Policy* (Lanham: Rowman and Littlefield, 2008), pp. 123–24.
9. Cannon, *President Reagan*, pp. 514–15.
10. John Carbaugh to McFarlane, "The Defense Budget Battle," December 12, 1983, The Robert McFarlane Files, Series II: Chronological Files, Chron (Official) December 1983, RAC Box 6, RRPL.
11. Letter to Reagan Signed by 16 House Democrats, December 21, 1983, The James Baker Papers, Series 6: Chief of Staff, Box 60, Folder 5, "Legislative Strategy 1984," PUML.
12. Steven Roberts, "16 House Democrats Warn Reagan of Action on Deficit," *New York Times*, December 21, 1983.
13. Mary McGrory, "At Least One Senator Realizes that Weinberger is Insatiable," *Washington Post*, February 2, 1984.
14. Wirls, *Buildup*, pp. 184–85.
15. Steven Roberts, "Experts in Congress See More Cuts in Arms Budget Reagan Trimmed," *New York Times*, May 5, 1984.
16. Wayne Biddle, "Armed Services Committee in White House Reduces Weapon Budget by Nearly $9 Billion," *New York Times*, April 12, 1984.
17. Steven Weisman, "President Links Control of Arms to MX Missile," *New York Times*, May 15, 1984. For a broader study of the MX debates in Congress, see: Johnson, *Congress and the Cold War*, pp. 268–82.
18. Christopher Andrew and Oleg Gordievsky, *Comrade Kryuchkov's Instructions: Top Secret Files on KGB Foreign Operations, 1975–1985* (Stanford: Stanford University Press, 1993), p. 97; Matlock, *Reagan and Gorbachev*, p. 88.
19. Memo by Donald Fortier, NSC Director of Politico-Military Affairs: "The View from Moscow," November 1983. The Donald Fortier Files, "Soviet Project," RAC Box 14, RRPL.
20. Memo by McFarlane: "U.S.-Soviet Relations: Immediate Prospects," The Robert McFarlane Files, Series I: Subject File, RAC Box 3, Soviet Union: Sensitive File, 1983 (October 21–November 7, 1983), RRPL.
21. Wilson, *The Triumph of Improvisation*, p. 79.
22. Memo by McFarlane: "NSPG Meeting on Soviet Noncompliance with Arms Control Agreements," December 20, 1983, Executive Secretariat National Security Planning Group Files, NSPG 0081, December 20, 1983 (Compliance), Box 2, RRPL.

23. Sven Kraemer to McFarlane, "NSC Meeting on Compliance," January 7, 1984, NSC Executive Secretariat Meeting Files, Box 10, RRPL.

24. Garthoff, *The Great Transition*, p. 517.

25. Matlock, *Reagan and Gorbachev*, pp. 79–80.

26. Interview by the author with Ambassador Jack Matlock, August 30, 2017.

27. McFarlane to Reagan, "U.S.-Soviet Relations: A Framework for the Future," February 24, 1984, The Jack Matlock Files, Series I: Chron File, January 1984–March 1984, Box 3, RRPL.

28. For the text of Reagan's interview with *Time Magazine*, see: Bob Sims to McFarlane, "Time Interview," December 21, 1983, The Robert McFarlane Files, Series II: Chronological Files, Chron (Official) December 1983, RAC Box 6, RRPL. For the planning of the interview, see: Matlock to McFarlane, "President's Interview with *Time Magazine*," December 13, 1983, The Jack Matlock Files, Series I: Chron File, October–December 1983, Box 2, RRPL.

29. Matlock, *Reagan and Gorbachev*, pp. 92–93.

30. Matlock to McFarlane, "Today's Breakfast Meeting," December 3, 1983, The Robert McFarlane Files, Series II: Chronological Files, Chron (Official) December 1983, RAC Box 6, RRPL.

31. Oberdorfer, *From the Cold War to a New Era*, p. 71.

32. Handwritten letter by McFarlane to Reagan, December 18, 1983, The Robert McFarlane Files, Series II: Chronological Files, Chron (Official) December 1983, RAC Box 6, RRPL.

33. Oberdorfer, *From the Cold War to a New Era*, p. 71.

34. Reagan to Andropov, December 23, 1983, The Jack Matlock Files, Series I: Chron File, October–December 1983, Box 2, RRPL.

35. Victor Kohn, "Andropov Reported to be on Dialysis for Serious Kidney Disease," *Washington Post*, December 28, 1983.

36. Mikhail Gorbachev, *Memoirs* (New York: Doubleday, 1996), p. 152.

37. Robin Renwick (Head of UK Chancery, Washington, DC) to John Weston (FCO Defence Department), "Mondale on Defence and Arms Control," January 5, 1984; Mark Pellew (British Embassy, Washington, DC) to Noel Marshall (FCO North American Department), "Mondale Foreign Policy Statement," January 5, 1984, FCO 82–1496, "U.S. Presidential Election 1984," UKNA. For analysis of Mondale's campaign team, see: Diane Granat, "Mondale's Campaign Team: Can It Do the Job?" *Congressional Quarterly*, September 22, 1984.

38. Transcript of speech by Walter Mondale to the National Press Club: "A Safer World," Washington, DC, January 3, 1984, FCO 82–1496, "U.S. Presidential Election 1984," UKNA.

39. Clymer, *Edward M. Kennedy*, p. 350.

40. Michael Getler, "Reagan Optimistic on U.S.–Soviet Relations," *Washington Post*, January 16, 1984.

41. Transcript of Speech by Ronald Reagan: "Address to the Nation and Other Countries on United States-Soviet Relations," January 16, 1984. See: www .reaganlibrary.gov/research/speeches/11684a

42. Cited in: John Lewis Gaddis, *The Cold War* (New York: Penguin, 2005), p. 228.

43. Garthoff, *The Great Transition*, p. 145.
44. Dobrynin, *In Confidence*, pp. 544–45.
45. Garthoff, *The Great Transition*, pp. 160–61.
46. Craig and Logevall, *America's Cold War*, p. 311.
47. Dobrynin, *In Confidence*, pp. 544–45.
48. Memorandum for McFarlane by Charles Hill: "International Reaction to President's Speech on U.S.-Soviet Relations," January 17, 1984, The Jack Matlock Files, Series I: Chron File, January 1984–March 1984, Box 3, RRPL; Hedrick Smith, "Reagan's Address: Trying a New Tactic," *New York Times*, January 17, 1984; Serge Schmemann, "Soviet Press Agency Finds No New Ideas or Proposals in President's Speech," *New York Times*, January 17, 1984.
49. Letter by Massie to McFarlane, January 10, 1984, The Jack Matlock Files, Series I: Chron File, January 1984–March 1984, Box 3, RRPL.
50. Record of a conversation between Reagan and Thatcher at the White House, September 29, 1983. PREM 19–1153, UKNA.
51. Memorandum for McFarlane by Charles Hill: "International Reaction to President's Speech on U.S.-Soviet Relations," January 17, 1984, The Jack Matlock Files, Series I: Chron File, January 1984–March 1984, Box 3, RRPL; Matlock, *Reagan and Gorbachev*, pp. 85–86.
52. Hedrick Smith, "Reagan's Address: Trying a New Tactic," *New York Times*, January 17, 1984.
53. Tyroler (ed.), *Alerting America*, pp. 334–36.
54. Shultz, *Turmoil and Triumph*, p. 1135.
55. Ehrman, *The Rise of Neoconservatism*, p. 173; Craig and Logevall, *America's Cold War*, pp. 330–31.
56. See: Halper and Clarke, *America Alone*, pp. 178–81.
57. "Reagan Issues Report on Soviet Compliance," *New York Times*, January 24, 1984. For internal papers on Soviet (non)compliance issues, see, for example: Interagency Memorandum: "Decision Measures: U.S. Policy Responses to Soviet Violations," January 6, 1984; NSC Memorandum: "Compliance Policy Overview," January 6, 1984; "Talking Points for Mr. McFarlane: NSC Meeting on Soviet Noncompliance with Arms Control Agreements," January 9, 1984. All are contained in: NSC Executive Secretariat Meeting Files, Box 10, RRPL.
58. Garthoff, *The Great Transition*, pp. 145–46. See also: Rowland Evans and Robert Nowak, "The Week Reagan Played His Trump," *Washington Post*, January 18, 1984.
59. "Reagan Issues Report on Soviet Compliance," *New York Times*, January 24, 1984.
60. Memo by McFarlane: "National Security Council Meeting on Mutual and Balanced Force Reductions," January 13, 1984; "NSC Meeting Regarding MBFR," January 13, 1984, NSC Executive Secretariat Meeting Files, Box 10, RRPL.
61. Memorandum for McFarlane by Charles Hill: "Further Reaction to the President's Speech on U.S.-Soviet Relations," January 19, 1984, The Jack Matlock Files, Series I: Chron File, January 1984–March 1984, Box 3, RRPL.

62. Shultz, *Turmoil and Triumph*, p. 467.
63. Shultz to Reagan, "Record of my Meeting with Gromyko," January 18, 1984, The Jack Matlock Files, Series I: Chron File, January 1984–March 1984, Box 3, RRPL. See also: Shultz, *Turmoil and Triumph*, pp. 468–71; Gromyko, *Memoirs*, pp. 301–02; Oberdorfer, *From the Cold War to a New Era*, p. 74.
64. Letter from Andropov to Reagan, January 28, 1984 (delivered on January 30); Shultz to Reagan, "My Meeting with Dobrynin," January 30, 1984, The Robert McFarlane Files, Series I: Subject Files, Soviet Union: Sensitive File, 1984 (January 26–February 13, 1984), RAC Box 3, RRPL.
65. Dobrynin, *In Confidence*, pp. 547–48; Gaddis, *George F. Kennan*, p. 665.
66. Cited in: Ryan, "1984, Regional Crises, and Morning in America: The Predawn of the Reagan Era," p. 279. The memorandum, "Lebanon Report to Congress," was prepared by Robert Kimmit, December 14, 1983.
67. Ibid., pp. 279–81; Charles Brower, "Stranger in a Dangerous Land: Reagan and Lebanon, 1981–84," in *Reagan and the World*, pp. 282–84.
68. National Security Planning Group Meeting, "Talking Points for Robert McFarlane," December 1, 1983. *The Reagan Files*. See: www.thereaganfiles.com/83121-nspg-talking-points.pdf
69. Letter by Rep. Les Aspin and Rep. Lee Hamilton to Reagan, December 14, 1983, The James Baker Files, Series I: Memorandum File, Subseries C, 1984–January 1985, Box 8, RRPL.
70. Memorandum by McFarlane to Reagan, "Talking Points for NSPG on the Next Steps in Lebanon," January 3, 1984, *The Reagan Files*. See: www.thereaganfiles.com/8413-nspg-meeting-talking.pdf
71. Martin Tolchin, "House Leaders Urge New Study of Beirut Policy," *New York Times*, January 3, 1984; Francis Clines, "Reagan and O'Neill Square Off on Beirut Mission," *New York Times*, January 26, 1984.
72. M.B. Oglesby to James Baker, "Hill Attitude Regarding Lebanon," January 3, 1984. The memo includes James Baker's handwritten conclusions. The James Baker Files, Series I: Memorandum File, Subseries C, 1984–January 1985, Box 8, RRPL.
73. Ronald Reagan, "Address to the Nation on Events in Lebanon and Grenada," October 27, 1983. See: www.reaganlibrary.gov/research/speeches/102783b
74. William Taubman, *Gorbachev: His Life and Times* (New York: W.W. Norton, 2017), p. 191.
75. For the Soviet leadership transition between Andropov and Chernenko, see: Brown, *Seven Years that Changed the World*, pp. 50–51; Anatoly Chernyaev, *My Six Years with Gorbachev* (University Park, PA: Pennsylvania State Press, 2000), pp. 5–7; Gorbachev, *Memoirs*, pp. 197–201; Arbatov, *The System*, pp. 266–68; Kotkin, *Armageddon Averted*, pp. 51–53; Zubok, *A Failed Empire*, p. 276.
76. Oberdorfer, *From the Cold War to a New Era*, p. 81.
77. Telegram from Bush to Reagan and McFarlane, February 14, 1984; Memo from the Situation Room to McFarlane, "Vice President's Meeting with Chernenko," February 14, 1984, The Robert McFarlane Files, Series I:

Subject Files, Soviet Union: Sensitive File, 1984 (February 14–February 23, 1984), RAC Box 3, RRPL.

78. Sen. Howard Baker to Reagan, February 17, 1984, The Jack Matlock Files, Series I: Chron File, January 1984–March 1984, Box 3, RRPL.

79. Letter by Chernenko to Reagan, February 23, 1984, The Robert McFarlane Files, Series I: Subject Files, Soviet Union: Sensitive File, 1984 (February 24–March 8, 1984), RAC Box 3, RRPL.

80. Wirthlin to Baker, Deaver, Rollins, and Spencer, "Major Findings from February National Survey (Field Dates February 2–4, 1984)," February 16, 1984. The Michael Deaver Files, Series VI: Political Material, Campaign 1984, Box 67, RRPL. See also: Louis Harris, "Reagan's Foreign Policy Erodes Confidence in Him," *The Harris Survey*, February 27, 1984, The Tip O'Neill Papers, Series II, Subseries A: The Kirk O'Donnell Files, Box 2, The Harris Surveys 1983–84, BCBL; Presidential Job Approval, Ronald Reagan: The Gallup Poll January 30–February 6, 1984, APP. See: www .presidency.ucsb.edu/statistics/data/presidential-job-approval;

81. McFarlane to Reagan, "U.S.-Soviet Relations: A Framework for the Future," February 24, 1984. The memorandum was based on the workings of the "breakfast group" organized by George Shultz. The Jack Matlock Files, Series I: Chron File, January 1984–March 1984, Box 3, RRPL.

82. McFarlane to Reagan, "Checklist of U.S.-Soviet Issues: Status and Prospects," February 24, 1984. The memo was written by Shultz's "breakfast group" on February 18. The Robert McFarlane Files, Series I: Subject Files, Soviet Union: Sensitive File, 1984 (February 14–February 23, 1984), RAC Box 3, RRPL.

83. McFarlane to Reagan, "U.S.-Soviet Relations: Program of Action for 1984," February 1984. The Robert McFarlane Files, Series I: Subject Files, Soviet Union: Sensitive File, 1984 (February 14–February 23, 1984), RAC Box 3, RRPL.

84. Matlock, *Reagan and Gorbachev*, p. 88; Oberdorfer, *From the Cold War to a New Era*, p. 82.

85. Brinkley (ed.), *The Reagan Diaries*, pp. 220–21; Reagan, *An American Life*, p. 592.

86. Memo by Charles Hill to McFarlane, "Gromyko Speech on Foreign Policy," February 29, 1984. Gromyko delivered the speech in Minsk on February 27; Charles Bremner (Reuters), "Chernenko Attacks Washington, Calls for Deeds not Words," March 2, 1984. The Robert McFarlane Files, Series I: Subject Files, Soviet Union: Sensitive File, 1984 (February 24–March 8, 1984), RAC Box 3, RRPL.

87. Matlock to McFarlane, "Conversation with Zagladin," February 20, 1984. The Robert McFarlane Files, Series I: Subject Files, Soviet Union: Sensitive File, 1984 (February 14–February 23, 1984), RAC Box 3, RRPL; "Memcon between Jack Matlock, Vadim Zagladin, and Stanislav Menshikov," Moscow, February 15, 1984. The Jack Matlock Files, Series I: Chron File, January 1984–March 1984, Box 3, RRPL.

88. Memcon between Dr. Lawrence Horowitz, Jack Matlock, and John Poindexter: "Horowitz's Conversations in Moscow," January 26, 1984;

Matlock to McFarlane, "Message from Zagladin," January 27, 1984, The Jack Matlock Files, Series I: Chron File, January 1984–March 1984, Box 3, RRPL.

89. Matlock, *Reagan and Gorbachev*, pp. 93–94; Clymer, *Edward M. Kennedy*, pp. 321–22.

90. Shultz to Reagan, "Conversation with Senators Cohen and Biden on U.S.–Soviet Relations," February 27, 1984. The Robert McFarlane Files, Series I: Subject Files, Soviet Union: Sensitive File, 1984 (February 24–March 8, 1984), RAC Box 3, RRPL; M.B. Oglesby and Pam Turner to McFarlane, Baker, and Deaver, "Arms Reduction Talks," February 21, 1984. The James Baker Files, Series I: Memorandum File, Subseries C, 1984–January 1985, Box 8, RRPL.

91. Letter by Reagan to Scowcroft, March 8, 1984; Letter by Reagan to Chernenko, March 6, 1984. The Robert McFarlane Files, Series I: Subject Files, Soviet Union: Sensitive File, 1984 (February 24–March 8, 1984), RAC Box 3, RRPL.

92. Shultz to Reagan, "My Meeting with Soviet Ambassador Dobrynin," March 7, 1984. The Robert McFarlane Files, Series I: Subject Files, Soviet Union: Sensitive File, 1984 (February 24–March 8, 1984), RAC Box 3, RRPL.

93. Matlock, *Reagan and Gorbachev*, pp. 94–95.

94. Shultz, *Turmoil and Trumph*, p. 474. See also: Shultz to Reagan, "Art Hartman's Meeting with Gromyko on March 11," March 14, 1984. The Jack Matlock Files, Series I: Chron File, January 1984–March 1984, Box 3, RRPL.

95. Letter by Chernenko to Reagan, March 19, 1984. NSC Executive Secretariat Head of State Files; USSR: Chernenko (8401238), Box 39, RRPL.

96. Reagan, *An American Life*, pp. 593–94.

97. Letter by Chernenko to Reagan, March 19, 1984. See Reagan's handwritten note on the first page. NSC Executive Secretariat Head of State Files; USSR: Chernenko (8401238), Box 39, RRPL.

98. Leslie Gelb, "This is 'Sackpig', and it May Never End," *New York Times*, June 6, 1984.

99. Memorandum by Ed Rowny (START Negotiator) to McFarlane, Dam, Ikle, Adelman, George, and Moreau, "Guidelines for a START Agreement," March 16, 1984; Memorandum by Rowny to McFarlane (for the President's reading), "Where to go on START?" March 23, 1984. NSC Executive Secretariat Meeting Files, NSC 104–114, Box 11, RRPL.

100. Memorandum by Kenneth Adelman (ACDA Director) to Reagan: "Arms Control Possibilities in 1984," March 23, 1984. NSC Executive Secretariat Meeting Files, NSC 104–114, Box 11, RRPL.

101. Memorandum by Nitze to Reagan, "Thoughts on an Arms Control Initiative," March 23, 1984. NSC Executive Secretariat Meeting Files, NSC 104–114, Box 11, RRPL.

102. Memorandum by Weinberger to Reagan, "Arms Control Strategy," March 23, 1984. NSC Executive Secretariat Meeting Files, NSC 104–114, Box 11, RRPL.

103. Report by the Directorate of Intelligence: "Soviet Interest in Arms Control Negotiations in 1984," March 23, 1984. NSC Executive Secretariat Meeting Files, NSC 104–114, Box 11, RRPL.

104. Memorandum by Weinberger to Reagan, "Arms Control Strategy," March 23, 1984. NSC Executive Secretariat Meeting Files, NSC 104–114, Box 11, RRPL.

105. Minutes of NSC Meeting, "Nuclear Arms Control Discussions," March 27, 1984. NSC Executive Secretariat Meeting Files, NSC 104–114, Box 11, RRPL.

106. "O'Neill Steps up Criticism of Reagan in TV Interview," *Christian Science Monitor*, April 13, 1984.

107. Remarks by Walter Mondale, Maycrest College, Davenport, Iowa, January 18, 1984, The Walter Mondale Papers, Loc: 153.I.20.7B, Speech Files, December 1983–September 1984, Iowa folder, Manuscripts Collection, MNHS.

108. See: Transcript of speech by Walter Mondale to the National Press Club: "A Safer World," Washington, DC, January 3, 1984, FCO 82–1496, "U.S. Presidential Election 1984," UKNA.

109. Bernard Weinraub, "Mondale Asks for Ban on Arms in Space," *New York Times*, April 25, 1984; Remarks by Walter Mondale, Case Western Reserve University, Cleveland, Ohio, April 24, 1984, The Walter Mondale Papers, Loc: 146.L.9.7B, Platform Briefing Materials Book, Manuscripts Collection, MNHS.

110. Bernard Weinraub, "Mondale Attacks Reagan's Policies," *New York Times*, April 13, 1984.

111. Oliver Wright (British Ambassador) to the UK Foreign Office, "1984 Democratic Party Platform: Foreign Policy," July 6, 1984, FCO 82–1497, "U.S. Presidential Election 1984," UKNA.

112. Waller, *Congress and the Nuclear Freeze*, pp. 295–96.

113. Cannon, *President Reagan*, pp. 516–18; Farrell, *Tip O'Neill and the Democratic Century*, p. 643.

114. Walter Mondale, *The Good Fight: A Life in Liberal Politics* (New York: Scribner, 2010), p. 294.

115. Ryan, "1984, Regional Crises, and Morning in America: The Predawn of the Reagan Era," p. 286.

116. Zelizer, *Arsenal of Democracy*, p. 330.

117. Smith, *The Power Game*, p. 364.

118. Mondale, *The Good Fight*, p. 292.

119. Joseph Kraft, "Back in Contention," *Washington Post*, April 12, 1984.

120. Frances Clines, "James Baker: Calling Reagan's Election Moves," *New York Times*, May 20, 1984.

121. "Themes Meeting: Agenda," April 13, 1984, The James Baker Files, Series I: Memorandum File, Subseries C, 1984–85, Box 8, RRPL.

122. Letter by Nixon to McFarlane, March 29, 1984, The Robert McFarlane Files, Soviet Union: Sensitive File 1984 (March 9–June 20, 1984), RAC Box 3, RRPL.

123. Shultz to Reagan, "My Meeting with Dobrynin," April 6, 1984, The Jack Matlock Files, Series I: Chron File, April–May 1984, Box 4, RRPL.

124. Reagan to Chernenko, April 16, 1984, NSC Executive Secretariat Head of State Files; USSR: Chernenko (8490448, 8490546), Box 39, RRPL.

125. Robert Adelman, *Serious Fun: A History of Spectator Sports in the USSR* (New York: Oxford University Press, 2003), pp. 127–28.

126. Deaver to Peter Ueberroth (President of the Los Angeles Olympic Organizing Committee), May 25, 1984, The Jack Matlock Files, Series I: Chron File, April–May 1984, Box 4, RRPL.

127. Reagan to Chernenko, May 3, 1984; Reagan to Juan Antonio Samaranch (IOC President), May 8, 1984, NSC Executive Secretariat Head of State Files; USSR: Chernenko (8401238), Box 39, RRPL.

128. Dusko Doder, "Soviets Withdraw from Los Angeles Olympics," *Washington Post*, April 9, 1984.

129. Oliver Wright (British Ambassador) to Antony Acland (Head of the British Diplomatic Service, FCO), "The President and the Russians," May 22, 1984, FCO 82–1497, "U.S. Presidential Election 1984," UKNA.

130. Matlock to McFarlane, "U.S. Attempts to Reach Agreements with the Soviets," May 29, 1984. See attached information sheets: "U.S. Proposals and Initiatives toward the USSR since Early January" and "Talking Points: U.S. Initiatives Toward USSR," The Jack Matlock Files, Series I: Chron File, April–May 1984, Box 4, RRPL. See also: Matlock, *Reagan and Gorbachev*, p. 97.

131. Ronald Reagan, *Public Papers of the Presidents of the United States, 1984*, "Conference on U.S.-Soviet Exchanges, June 27, 1984" (Washington, DC: GPO, 1986), pp. 916–18; Garthoff, *The Great Transition*, pp. 156–57.

132. Shultz to Reagan, "Sakharov Plans to go on Hunger Strike," April 18, 1984; Letter by Congressional Wives for Soviet Jewry to Reagan, April 3, 1984; Draft letter, Reagan to Chernenko (undated), attached with Shultz's memo to Reagan on April 18, 1984, The Jack Matlock Files, Series I: Chron File, April–May 1984, Box 4, RRPL.

133. Matlock to McFarlane, "Proposed Presidential Statement: Building Cooperation Between U.S. and Soviet Peoples," May 29, 1984 (see hand-written note for John Lenczowski's views), The Jack Matlock Files, Series I: Chron File, April–May 1984, Box 4, RRPL.

134. John Lenczowski to McFarlane, "Reactivation of U.S.-USSR Environmental Agreement," May 8, 1984. The Jack Matlock Files, Series I: Chron File, April–May 1984, Box 4, RRPL.

135. Matlock to McFarlane, "Proposed Reactivation of U.S.-USSR Environmental Cooperation Agreement," May 29, 1984, The Jack Matlock Files, Series I: Chron File, April–May 1984, Box 4, RRPL.

136. McFarlane to Reagan, "U.S.-Soviet Relations: Toward Defining a Strategy," February 18, 1984, The Jack Matlock Files, Series I: Chron File, January 1984–March 1984, Box 3, RRPL; James Billington, "With Russia After 50 Years: A Time of Danger, an Opening for Dialogue," *Washington Post*, November 20, 1983.
See also: Shultz, *Turmoil and Triumph*, p. 478; Wilson, *The Triumph of Improvisation*, p. 79; Leffler, *For the Soul of Mankind*, p. 361.

137. Ronald Reagan, *Public Papers of the Presidents of the United States, 1984,* "Conference on U.S.-Soviet Exchanges," June 27, 1984 (Washington, DC: GPO, 1986), pp. 916–18; See also: Garthoff, *The Great Transition,* pp. 156–57.

138. "Gallup Reports Reagan Leads Mondale and Hart," *New York Times,* May 31, 1984.

139. Garthoff, *The Great Transition,* pp. 177–78.

140. Dobrynin, *In Confidence,* pp. 554–55.

141. Kenneth Dam (Deputy Secretary of State) to Reagan, "U.S.-Soviet Bilateral Relations: Possible Soviet Policy Decision," The Jack Matlock Files, Series I: Chron File, June–August 1984, Box 5, RRPL.

142. Chernenko to Reagan, June 6, 1984, NSC Executive Secretariat Head of State Files; USSR: Chernenko (8490695), Box 39, RRPL.

143. Reagan to Chernenko, July 2, 1984, NSC Executive Secretariat Head of State Files; USSR: Chernenko (8490757, 8490769), Box 39, RRPL.

144. Nitze to McFarlane, "September Vienna Talks," July 18, 1984, NSC Executive Secretariat System Files, System II, Box 15 (8490785), RRPL.

145. Chernenko to Reagan, July 7, 1984; Dam to Reagan, "Chernenko's Response to Your July 2 Letter on the Vienna Talks," July 7, 1984. NSC Executive Secretariat Head of State Files; USSR: Chernenko (8490757, 8490769), Box 39, RRPL; Chernenko to Reagan, July 26, 1984, NSC Executive Secretariat Head of State Files; USSR: Chernenko (8490829), Box 39, RRPL. See also: Garthoff, *The Great Transition,* pp. 158–59; Newhouse, *War and Peace in the Nuclear Age,* pp. 171–72.

146. Dusko Doder, "Moscow Viewed Space Talks as a Test of U.S. Intentions," *Washington Post,* August 5, 1984.

147. Newhouse, *War and Peace in the Nuclear Age,* p. 382.

148. Oberdorfer, *From the Cold War to a New Era,* p. 85.

149. Memorandum of Conversation between Ronald Reagan and Helmut Kohl in the Oval Office, March 5, 1984, The Jack Matlock Files, Series I: Chron File, January 1984–March 1984, Box 3, RRPL.

150. "Reagan Belittles Effect of Protest," *Associated Press* (reported in *Fort Lauderdale News*), June 11, 1984.

151. See for example: Letter by Rep. Bill Goodling (R-Pennsylvania) to Reagan, 14 May 1984, The Jack Matlock Files, Series I: Chron File, June–August 1984, Box 5, RRPL.

152. Frances Clines, "Baker and Percy Appeal to Reagan for Moscow Talks," *New York Times,* June 13, 1984.

153. Transcript of President Reagan's news conference, June 14, 1984. See: www.reaganlibrary.gov/research/speeches/61484d

154. Matlock to McFarlane, "News Conference Tonight: Summitry," June 13, 1984, The Jack Matlock Files, Series I: Chron File, June–August 1984, Box 5, RRPL.

155. Matlock, *Reagan and Gorbachev,* pp. 102–03.

156. McFarlane to Reagan, "Summitry and the Next Steps in U.S.-Soviet Relations," June 19, 1984 (memo prepared by Matlock), The Jack Matlock Files, Series I: Chron File, June–August 1984, Box 5, RRPL.

157. Shultz, *Turmoil and Triumph*, p. 480.

158. Cannon, *President Reagan*, p. 536.

159. "Reagan Said to Joke of Bombing Russia Before Radio Speech," *New York Times*, August 13, 1984.

160. Garthoff, *The Great Transition*, p. 160; Hedrick Smith, "Reagan's Gaffe," *New York Times*, August 16, 1984; "President's Joke About Bombing Leaves Press in Europe Unamused," *New York Times*, August 14, 1984.

161. Fay Joyce, "Mondale Chides Reagan on Soviet-Bombing Joke," *New York Times*, August 14, 1984; "Storm as Reagan Bombing Joke Misfires," *The Guardian*, August 14, 1984; Remarks by Walter Mondale, George Washington University, Washington, DC, September 25, 1984, The Walter Mondale Papers, Political Papers and Campaign Files, Conventions, Loc: 148.J.17.10F, Manuscripts Collection, MNHS; Simon Miles, "The Domestic Politics of Superpower Rapprochement: Foreign Policy and the 1984 Presidential Election," pp. 281–82, in Johns and Lerner (eds.), *The Cold War at Home and Abroad*.

162. For insight into Gromyko's character, see: McFarlane to Reagan, "Andrei Gromyko: The Consumate Soviet Diplomat," September 14, 1984, The Jack Matlock Files, Series I: Chron File, September–December 1984, Box 6, RRPL. See also: David Remnick, 'Gromyko: The Man Behind the Mask,' *Washington Post*, January 7, 1985.

163. Shultz, *Turmoil and Triumph*, p. 471.

164. Frances Clines, "Reagan, Meeting Gromyko, Asks for Closer Ties," *New York Times*, September 24, 1984.

165. "A Russian Is Coming. Then What?" *New York Times*, September 16, 1984.

166. Memorandum of Conversation between President Reagan and Andrei Gromkyo, September 28, 1984, The Jack Matlock Files, Series I: Chron File, September–December 1984, Box 6, RRPL.

167. For recollections of the meeting, see: Oberdorfer, *From the Cold War to a New Era*, pp. 89–93; Shultz, *Turmoil and Triumph*, pp. 483–85; Dobrynin, *In Confidence*, pp. 555–58; Reagan, *An American Life*, pp. 603–05; Gromyko, *Memoirs*, pp. 306–09; Matlock, *Reagan and Gorbachev*, pp. 100–01.

168. Cannon, *President Reagan*, pp. 535–51; Darman, *Who's In Control?*, pp. 120–33. For Mondale's recollections, see: Mondale, *The Good Fight*, pp. 300–03. See also: Transcript of the Debate between the President and Walter Mondale in Kansas City, October 21, 1984. See: www .reaganlibrary.gov/research/speeches/102184b

169. Zelizer, *Arsenal of Democracy*, p. 330.

170. Brands, *Reagan*, p. 461.

171. Reagan, *An American Life*, pp. 605–06.

172. Matlock to McFarlane, "Controlling Leaks in Dealing with the Soviets," November 23, 1984, The Jack Matlock Files, Series I: Chron File, September–December 1984, Box 6, RRPL.

173. Oberdorfer, *From the Cold War to a New Era*, pp. 98–99; Shultz, *Turmoil and Triumph*, pp. 497–98.

174. Oberdorfer, *From the Cold War to a New Era*, p. 100.

175. Shultz, *Turmoil and Triumph*, p. 504.
176. See National Security Planning Group Meetings: "Soviet Defense and Arms Control Objectives," November 30, 1984; "U.S.-Soviet Arms Control Objectives," December 5, 1984; "Discussion of Geneva Format and SDI," December 10, 1984; "Discussion of Substantive Issues for Geneva," December 17, 1984, System II Files: 91296, RRPL.
177. Robert Kimmitt (NSC Executive Secretary) to Matlock, "Candidates Briefing," August 23, 1984, The Jack Matlock Files, Series I: Chron File, June–August 1984, Box 5, RRPL.
178. Chernyaev, *My Six Years with Gorbachev*, pp. 15–16.
179. Charles Moore, *Margaret Thatcher: At Her Zenith: In London, Washington and Moscow* (London: Alfred Knopf, 2016), pp. 231–42; Aldous, *Reagan and Thatcher*, pp. 170–72; Taubman, *Gorbachev*, pp. 196–201. Thatcher, *The Downing Street Years*, pp. 459–63; Gorbachev, *Memoirs*, pp. 206–08. See also: Record of conversation between Thatcher and Gorbachev at Chequers, December 16, 1984, PREM 19-1394, UKNA.
180. Moore, *Margaret Thatcher*, pp. 242–53; Aldous, *Reagan and Thatcher*, pp. 173–82; Thatcher, *The Downing Street Years*, pp. 463–68; Reagan, *An American Life*, p. 609, Shultz, *Turmoil and Triumph*, pp. 508–09. For Thatcher's report to Reagan on the meeting with Gorbachev, see: PREM 19-1394, UKNA. For the Reagan–Thatcher meeting, see: Memcon between Reagan and Thatcher at Camp David, December 22, 1984, European and Soviet Affairs Directorate, NSC: Records (Thatcher Visit, Dec 1984, Box 90902), RRPL.
181. Shultz, *Turmoil and Triumph*, pp. 505–12; Adelman, *The Great Universal Embrace*, pp. 91–92.
182. Memorandum of Conversation: Shultz–Gromyko Meeting in Geneva, January 7, 1985, The Jack Matlock Files, Series I: Chron File, January–April 1985, Box 8, RRPL.
183. Matlock, *Reagan and Gorbachev*, pp. 103–04; Oberdorfer, *From the Cold War to a New Era*, pp. 104–05; Shultz, *Turmoil and Triumph*, pp. 514–19; Adelman, *The Great Universal Embrace*, pp. 92–94.
184. Matlock to McFarlane, "Organizing for Arms Reduction Negotiations with the Soviets," January 12, 1985, The Jack Matlock Files, Series I: Chron File, December 1984–January 1985, Box 7, RRPL; Matlock, *Reagan and Gorbachev*, p. 104; Shultz, *Turmoil and Triumph*, p. 516.
185. Memcon between Ronald Reagan and Vladimir Shcherbitsky in the Oval Office, March 8, 1985, The Jack Matlock Files, Series I: Chron File, January–April 1985, Box 8, RRPL. See also: Serge Schmemann, "Ukrainian Leader Begins Visit to U.S.," *New York Times*, March 4, 1985.

9 CONCILIATION

1. Reagan, *An American Life*, p. 611; Brinkley (ed.), *The Reagan Diaries*, p. 307.
2. Kotkin, *Armageddon Averted*, pp. 25–28; Zubok, *A Failed Empire*, p. 277.

3. Brown, *Seven Years that Changed the World*, pp. 4–6; 257.
4. Wilson, *The Triumph of Improvisation*, p. 88; Leffler, *For the Soul of Mankind*, p. 376.
5. Matlock, *Reagan and Gorbachev*, pp. 114–15; Craig and Logevall, *America's Cold War*, pp. 330–31.
6. "Reagan to Mrs Elsa Sandstrom," November 25, 1985, in Kiron Skinner, Annelise Anderson, and Martin Anderson (eds.), *Reagan: A Life in Letters* (New York: Free Press, 2003), p. 414.
7. Brands, *Making the Unipolar Moment*, pp. 103–04.
8. Leffler, *For the Soul of Mankind*, pp. 366–74; Kotkin, *Armageddon Averted*, pp. 35–39; Hoffman, *The Dead Hand*, pp. 174–88; Evangelista, *Unarmed Forces*, pp. 260–62; Matlock, *Reagan and Gorbachev*, pp. 136–37. See also: Gorbachev, *Memoirs*, pp. 22–136.
9. Mikhail Gorbachev and Zdenek Mlynar, *Conversations with Gorbachev: On Perestroika, the Prague Spring, and the Crossroads of Socialism* (New York: Columbia University Press, 2002), p. 50.
10. Eduard Shevardnadze, *The Future Belongs to Freedom* (New York: Free Press, 1991), p. 37.
11. Arbatov, *The System*, p. 293.
12. Taubman, *Gorbachev*, pp. 208–09.
13. Gates, *From the Shadows*, pp. 327–30.
14. Report by the Directorate of Intelligence, "Gorbachev, the New Broom," June 1985, The Robert McFarlane Files, Soviet Union: Sensitive File, 1985 (06/16/1985–08/31/1985), RAC Box 3, RRPL.
15. Shultz, *Turmoil and Triumph*, p. 527.
16. Reagan to Gorbachev, March 11, 1985, NSC Executive Secretariat Head of State Files; USSR: General Secretary Gorbachev (8590272, 8590334), Box 39, RRPL.
17. Shultz, *Turmoil and Triumph*, pp. 529–32; Dobrynin, *In Confidence*, pp. 567–68.
18. Oberdorfer, *From the Cold War to a New Era*, p. 110–11; Shultz, *Turmoil and Triumph*, pp. 532–33.
19. "Conference of Secretaries of the CC CPSU, held in the Office of General Secretary Gorbachev," March 15, 1985, Library of Congress, Manuscript Division, Dmitrii Antonovich Volkogonov Papers, 1887–1995, mm97083838, Reel 17, Container 25, WCDA. See: https://digitalarchive.wilsoncenter.org/document/121966
20. Gorbachev to Reagan, March 24, 1985; Shultz to Reagan, "Letter from Gorbachev," March 25, 1985, NSC Executive Secretariat Head of State Files; USSR: General Secretary Gorbachev (8590272, 8590334), Box 39, RRPL.
21. James Markham, "American Officer Killed by Russian in East Germany," *New York Times*, March 26, 1985; Jack Anderson and Dale Van Atta, "Behind an American's Death in Germany," *Washington Post*, January 22, 1988.
22. Garthoff, *The Great Transition*, pp. 209–12.

23. James Markham, "American Officer Killed by Russian in East Germany," *New York Times*, March 26, 1985.

24. See: Talbott, *The Master of the Game*, pp. 255–60; Bill Keller, "Upstaged by Soviet Events, Geneva Arms Talks Fade," *New York Times*, March 14, 1985.

25. Matlock, *Reagan and Gorbachev*, p. 113.

26. Lenczowski to McFarlane, "Soviet Perceptions and the Soviet Political Mind," April 12, 1985; McFarlane to Reagan, "Soviet Perceptions and the Soviet Political Mind," April 12, 1985, The John Lenczowski Files, Active Measures (5), Box 1, RRPL; David Satter, "Don't Talk With Murderers," *Wall Street Journal*, April 12, 1985.

27. Remarks by Secretary Weinberger to the Nashville, Louisville, and Birmingham Councils on Foreign Relations, May 3, 1985, The Jack Matlock Files, Series I: Chron Files, April–June 1985, Box 9, RRPL.

28. Matlock, *Reagan and Gorbachev*, pp. 113–14; Shultz, *Turmoil and Triumph*, p. 535.

29. Bernard Gwertzman, "U.S. Plans to Seek Closer Soviet Ties in Spite of Slaying," *New York Times*, March 27, 1985; Garthoff, *The Great Transition*, p. 210.

30. Shultz, *Turmoil and Triumph*, pp. 533–34.

31. Letter from Reagan to Gorbachev, April 4, 1985 (delivered by Tip O'Neill in Moscow on April 10, 1985), The Jack Matlock Files, Series I: Chron File, January–April 1985, Box 8, RRPL.

32. Garthoff, *The Great Transition*, pp. 213–14; Oberdorfer, *From the Cold War to a New Era*, pp. 114–15; Matlock, *Reagan and Gorbachev*, pp. 115–16.

33. Dobrynin, *In Confidence*, pp. 547–48; Farrell, *Tip O'Neill and the Democratic Century*, p. 662.

34. McFarlane to Reagan, "Speaker O'Neill's Meeting with Gorbachev," April 10, 1985, The Jack Matlock Files, Series I: Chron Files, April–June 1985, Box 9, RRPL.

35. Farrell, *Tip O'Neill and the Democratic Century*, pp. 662–63.

36. Statement of Thomas P. O'Neill in Moscow, April 10, 1985; Summary of Meetings with Gromyko and Supreme Soviet Delegates, April 9, 1985. The Tip O'Neill Papers, Series 6, Subseries D: Press Relations, Box 21, BCBL; O'Neill, *Man of the House*, pp. 293–95. See also: Gorbachev, *Memoirs*, p. 533; Chernyaev, *My Six Years with Gorbachev*, pp. 28–29.

37. Reagan to Gorbachev, April 30, 1985, NSC Executive Secretariat Head of State Files; USSR: General Secretary Gorbachev (8590475), Box 39, RRPL.

38. Brinkley (ed.), *The Reagan Diaries*, p. 317; Reagan, *An American Life*, pp. 614–15.

39. Statements by Thomas P. O'Neill, May 12, 1983 and May 23, 1983, The Tip O'Neill Papers, Series 6, Subseries D: Press Relations, Box 19, BCBL.

40. Letter from Reagan to O'Neill, March 22, 1985; Letter by Shultz to O'Neill, March 25, 1985, The Tip O'Neill Papers, Series 6, Subseries D: Press Relations, Box 19, BCBL.

41. Brands, *Reagan*, pp. 461–62; Brinkley (ed.), *The Reagan Diaries*, pp. 305–08.

42. Michael Weisskopf, "Nitze Unlinks MX Funds, Arms Talks," *Washington Post*, March 14, 1985.
43. Gerard Smith, Clark Clifford, and Paul Warnke, "MX Is Not a Useful Bargaining Chip," *Washington Post*, March 16, 1985.
44. Michael Weisskopf, "Aspin Urges Party to Alter Defense Stand," *Washington Post*, April 18, 1985; Zelizer, *Arsenal of Democracy*, p. 330.
45. Brinkley (ed.), *The Reagan Diaries*, p. 306.
46. Johnson, *Congress and the Cold War*, pp. 280–82.
47. Bill Keller, "MX Debate: It's Not Over," *New York Times*, March 30, 1985; Dorothy Collin, "MX Missile Deal Sought by Reagan," *Chicago Tribune*, May 22, 1985; Steven Roberts, "House Votes Bar on Buying MX Over Next Year," *New York Times*, June 19, 1985.
48. Smith, *The Power Game*, pp. 536–51.
49. Matlock to McFarlane and Poindexter, "State Paper on U.S.-Soviet Relations," April 2, 1985, The Jack Matlock Files, Series I: Chron File, January–April 1985, Box 8, RRPL.
50. Shultz to Reagan, "My Meeting with Dobrynin," April 19, 1985, The Robert McFarlane Files, Soviet Union: Sensitive File, 1985 (01/12/1985-06/15/1985), RAC Box 3, RRPL.
51. Matlock to McFarlane and Poindexter, "Conversation with Dobrynin and Sokolov," May 8, 1985, The Jack Matlock Files, Series I: Chron Files, April–June 1985, Box 9, RRPL.
52. Poindexter to Reagan, May 13, 1985 (see Reagan's handwritten note), NSC Executive Secretariat Chron Files, No. 8590504, RRPL.
53. Shultz, *Turmoil and Triumph*, p. 563.
54. Dobrynin, *In Confidence*, p. 572.
55. For the Shultz–Gromyko meeting, see: Shultz, *Turmoil and Triumph*, pp. 563–65; Nitze, *From Hiroshima to Glasnost*, pp. 409–10; Oberdorfer, *From the Cold War to a New Era*, pp. 115–17; Dobrynin, *In Confidence*, p. 572; McFarlane, *Special Trust*, pp. 308–09.
56. Oberdorfer, *From the Cold War to a New Era*, pp. 117–18.
57. Serge Schmemann, "Baldrige Meets With Gorbachev," *New York Times*, May 21, 1985; Serge Schmemann, "Trade Gain in Soviet Talks Seen," *New York Times*, May 22, 1985; Garthoff, *The Great Transition*, p. 218. See also: Memo: "Baldrige's Report on his Trip to China, India, and the Soviet Union," May 29, 1985, The Jack Matlock Files, Series I: Chron Files, April–June 1985, Box 9, RRPL.
58. Matlock to McFarlane, "Shultz Conversation with Dobrynin on Meeting between the President and Gorbachev," May 29, 1985; Shultz to Reagan, "Conversation with Dobrynin," May 25, 1985, The Jack Matlock Files, Series I: Chron Files, April–June 1985, Box 9, RRPL.
59. Matlock to McFarlane and Poindexter, "Interim Restraint," June 4, 1985, The Jack Matlock Files, Series I: Chron Files, April–June 1985, Box 9, RRPL; Shultz, *Turmoil and Triumph*, pp. 567–70; Matlock, *Reagan and Gorbachev*, pp. 121–22.
60. Talbott, *The Master of the Game*, pp. 226–29.

61. "Reagan Statement on Arms Accord," *New York Times,* June 11, 1985; Shultz, *Turmoil and Triumph,* p. 569; Matlock, *Reagan and Gorbachev,* p. 122. On May 27, 1986, Reagan announced that the United States would no longer abide by the SALT II limits. See: FitzGerald, *Way Out There in Blue,* pp. 334–35; Garthoff, *The Great Transition,* pp. 554–55.

62. Gorbachev to Reagan, June 22, 1985, NSC Executive Secretariat Head of State Files; USSR: General Secretary Gorbachev (8590483, 8590713), Box 40, RRPL; Shultz to Reagan, "My Meeting with Dobrynin on June 24; Gorbachev's Response on Interim Restraint," June 25, 1985; Matlock to McFarlane, "Gorbachev's Response to the President's Letter on Interim Restraint," June 26, 1985, The Jack Matlock Files, Series I: Chron Files, June–August 1985, Box 10, RRPL.

63. "Minutes of a CC CPSU Politburo Session Nominating Gorbachev for General Secretary," March 11, 1985, WCDA. See: https://digitalarchive.wilsoncenter.org/document/120771

64. Zubok, *A Failed Empire,* pp. 278–80; Kotkin, *Armageddon Averted,* pp. 62–67.

65. Report by the CIA Directorate of Intelligence, "Gorbachev, the New Broom," June 1985, The Robert McFarlane Files, Soviet Union: Sensitive File, 1985 (06/16/1985-08/31/1985), RAC Box 3, RRPL.

66. Matlock, *Reagan and Gorbachev,* pp. 135–36. For Yakovlev's recollections, see: Aleksandr Yakovlev Interview, Hoover Institution and Gorbachev Foundation Collection, Box 3, Folder 5, HIA.

67. Service, *The End of the Cold War, 1985-1991,* pp. 128–34; Wilson, *The Triumph of Improvisation,* p. 90.

68. Dobrynin, *In Confidence,* pp. 574–75; The Anatoly Adamishin Papers, Diaries: 1985, 10 Apr. 1985, Box 1, HIA.

69. Shevardnadze, *The Future Belongs to Freedom,* pp. 38–39; Oberdorfer, *From the Cold War to a New Era,* pp. 118–19.

70. Shultz, *Turmoil and Triumph,* pp. 571–72.

71. Dobrynin, *In Confidence,* pp. 575–76.

72. Matlock to McFarlane, "Gromyko's 'Elevation': First Thoughts," July 2, 1985, The Jack Matlock Files, Series I: Chron Files, June–August 1985, Box 10, RRPL. See also: Sestanovich to McFarlane, "Shevardnadze for Gromyko," July 2, 1985, The Donald Fortier Files, U.S. Policy toward the Soviet Union, RAC Box 15, RRPL.

73. Memcon between Shultz and Shevardnadze, July 31, 1985, The Jack Matlock Files, Series I: Chron Files, June–August 1985, Box 10, RRPL; Matlock to McFarlane, "Shultz–Shevardnadze Meeting in Helsinki," August 7, 1985, The Jack Matlock Files, Series I: Chron Files, June–August 1985, Box 10, RRPL; Shultz, *Turmoil and Triumph,* pp. 573–74; Oberdorfer, *From the Cold War to a New Era,* pp. 121–23.

74. "Meeting of the Politburo of the CC CPSU, Regarding Yelena Bonner's Request to Travel and Andrei Sakharov's Situation," August 29, 1985, WCDA. See: https://digitalarchive.wilsoncenter.org/document/115982

75. Bernard Gwertzman, "U.S. Hails Visa for Sakharov's Wife," *New York Times,* October 30, 1985; Philip Taubman, "Soviet Lifts Sakharov

Banishment and Grants a Pardon to Bonner," *New York Times*, December 20, 1986.

76. Interview by the author with Ambassador Jack Matlock, August 30, 2017.

77. "U.S.-Soviet Relations in the Late 20th Century," Official White House Transcript of an Address in Santa Barbara by Robert McFarlane, August 19, 1985; Garthoff, *The Great Transition*, pp. 222–23; Gerald Boyd, "Soviets Must Shift on Major Issues, McFarlane Insists," *New York Times*, August 20, 1985.

78. See for example: Gerald Boyd, "Soviets Must Shift on Major Issues, McFarlane Insists," *New York Times*, August 20, 1985; Hedrick Smith, "U.S. Strategy of Toughness: A Counter to the Russians," *New York Times*, August 23, 1985; David Hoffman, "An Autumn of Confrontation: U.S. Signals Hard-Nosed Approach to November Summit Talks," *Washington Post*, August 22, 1985.

79. Telephone Interview by Lockwood Doty of Washington Broadcast News with Ronald Reagan, August 24, 1985. See: www.reaganlibrary.gov/8248 5b See also: Gerald Boyd, "President Hoping to End 'Suspicions' at Summit Parley," *New York Times*, August 25, 1985.

80. White House News Summary, August 26, 1985, Excerpts from the David Brinkley Show, The Donald Fortier Files, U.S. Policy Toward the Soviet Union, RAC Box 15, RRPL.

81. Wilson, *The Triumph of Improvisation*, p. 95; Reagan, "Interview with Foreign Journalists," April 29, 1985. See: www.reaganlibrary.gov/researc h/speeches/42985g; Reagan, "Radio Address to the Nation on the Strategic Defense Initiative," July 13, 1985. See: www.reaganlibrary.gov/research/sp eeches/71385a

82. Transcript of the President's News Conference, September 17, 1985. See: www.reaganlibrary.gov/research/speeches/91785c

83. "An Interview with Mikhail Gorbachev," *Time Magazine*, September 9, 1985; Oberdorfer, *From the Cold War to a New Era*, p. 128.

84. NSC Meeting, "Soviet Foreign Minister Shevardnadze's Visit," September 20, 1985, NSC Executive Secretariat Meeting Files, Box 12, RRPL.

85. Memcon, "The President's Meeting with Foreign Minister Eduard Shevardnadze," September 27, 1985, The Jack Matlock Files, Series I: Chron Files, August–October 1985, Box 11, RRPL; Gorbachev to Reagan, September 12, 1985, NSC Executive Secretariat Head of State Files; USSR: General Secretary Gorbachev (8590483, 8590713), Box 40, RRPL. See also: Shultz, *Turmoil and Triumph*, pp. 576–77; Matlock, *Reagan and Gorbachev*, pp. 140–43.

86. Shevardnadze, *The Future Belongs to Freedom*, p. 90.

87. Oberdorfer, *From the Cold War to a New Era*, pp. 123–24.

88. FitzGerald, *Way Out There in Blue*, p. 295; Alan Weisman, *Prince of Darkness: Richard Perle: The Kingdom, the Power, and the End of Empire in America* (New York: Union Square Press, 2007), pp. 80–85.

89. Talbott, *The Master of the Game*, pp. 224–25, 231–49; Shultz, *Turmoil and Triumph*, pp. 578–82.

90. Talbott, *The Master of the Game*, p. 245.
91. Shultz, *Turmoil and Triumph*, pp. 578–80.
92. FitzGerald, *Way Out There in Blue*, pp. 290–1; Shultz, *Turmoil and Triumph*, p. 581; Talbott, *The Master of the Game*, p. 248.
93. Reagan to Gorbachev, October 31, 1985, NSC Executive Secretariat Head of State Files; USSR: General Secretary Gorbachev (8591135), Box 40, RRPL.
94. Oberdorfer, *From the Cold War to a New Era*, pp. 126–27.
95. "Conservatives Criticize SDI Reversal," *Baltimore Sun*, October 18, 1985.
96. Caspar Weinberger, "SDI: Realities and Misconceptions," *Christian Science Monitor*, October 18, 1985.
97. Shultz, *Turmoil and Triumph*, pp. 589–95. See also: Oberdorfer, *From the Cold War to a New Era*, pp. 130–39; McFarlane, *Special Trust*, pp. 314–16; Matlock, *Reagan and Gorbachev*, pp. 144–45.
98. Brinkley (ed.), *The Reagan Diaries*, p. 355.
99. Matlock to Reagan, "Background Paper on Soviet Psychology," September 23, 1985. The Jack Matlock Files, Series I: Chron Files, August–October 1985, Box 11, RRPL.
100. See for example: McFarlane to Reagan, "Soviet Instruments of Control," October 1985 (prepared by Jack Matlock). The Jack Matlock Files, Series I: Chron Files, August–October 1985, Box 11, RRPL; McFarlane to Reagan, "Gorbachev's Domestic Agenda," October 1985 (prepared by Jack Matlock). The Jack Matlock Files, Series I: Chron Files, October–November 1985, Box 12, RRPL.
101. McFarlane to Reagan, "Gorbachev and his Geneva Agenda," November 1985 (prepared by Jack Matlock). The Jack Matlock Files, Series I: Chron Files, November–December 1985, Box 13, RRPL.
102. Shultz to Reagan, "What to Expect from Gorbachev in Geneva," November 12, 1985, The Jack Matlock Files, Series I: Chron Files, November–December 1985, Box 13, RRPL; Shultz to Reagan, "Preparing for Gorbachev," September 19, 1985, The Jack Matlock Files, Series I: Chron Files, August–October 1985, Box 11, RRPL.
103. Gates, *From the Shadows*, pp. 341–45.
104. Mann, *The Rebellion of Ronald Reagan*, pp. 90–93; Cannon, *President Reagan*, p. 749; Brands, *Reagan*, p. 507.
105. McFarlane to Reagan, "Gordievsky's Suggestions," October 30, 1985, NSC Executive Secretariat Chron Files, No. 8591139, RRPL.
106. Diggins, *Ronald Reagan*, p. 365.
107. Matlock, *Reagan and Gorbachev*, pp. 150–53.
108. "Weinberger Letter to Reagan on Arms Control," *New York Times*, November 16, 1985.
109. Reeves, *President Reagan*, pp. 281–82. See also: McFarlane, *Special Trust*, pp. 316–17.
110. Shultz, *Turmoil and Triumph*, p. 598.
111. Matlock, *Reagan and Gorbachev*, pp. 149–50. See also: Reagan, *An American Life*, p. 628.
112. "Stories and Anecdotes," The Donald Regan Papers, White House Subject File, Summit: Geneva 1985, Box 215, Folder 3, Manuscript Division, LOC;

Donald Regan, *For the Record: From Wall Street to Washington* (New York: Harcourt Brace Jovanovich, 1988), pp. 304–05. Cannon, *President Reagan*, p. 750; Brands, *Reagan*, p. 510.

113. Memcon: Reagan–Gorbachev Meetings in Geneva, First Private Meeting, November 19, 1985, The Jack Matlock Files, Series I: Chron Files, November 1985–February 1986, Box 14, RRPL; "Summit: The First Private Meeting," November 19, 1985, The Donald Regan Papers, White House Subject File, Summit: Geneva 1985, Box 215, Folder 3, LOC.

114. Memcon: Reagan–Gorbachev, Geneva, First Plenary Meeting, November 19, 1985, The Jack Matlock Files, Series I: Chron Files, November 1985–February 1986, Box 14, RRPL; "Summit: First Private Meeting," November 19, 1985, The Donald Regan Papers, White House Subject File, Summit: Geneva 1985, Box 215, Folder 3, LOC.

115. Memcon: Reagan–Gorbachev, Geneva, Second Plenary Meeting, November 19, 1985, The Jack Matlock Files, Series I: Chron Files, November 1985–February 1986, Box 14, RRPL; "Summit: First Private Meeting, Afternoon Session," November 19, 1985, The Donald Regan Papers, White House Subject File, Summit: Geneva 1985, Box 215, Folder 3, LOC.

116. Memcon: Reagan–Gorbachev, Geneva, Second Private Meeting (Pool House), November 19, 1985, The Jack Matlock Files, Series I: Chron Files, November 1985–February 1986, Box 14, RRPL; "Summit: Pool House Meeting," November 19, 1985, The Donald Regan Papers, White House Subject File, Summit: Geneva 1985, Box 215, Folder 3, LOC.

117. Memcon: Reagan–Gorbachev, Geneva, Third Private Meeting, November 20, 1985, The Jack Matlock Files, Series I: Chron Files, November 1985–February 1986, Box 14, RRPL; "Summit Notes: Second Day; Morning," November 20, 1985, The Donald Regan Papers, White House Subject File, Summit: Geneva 1985, Box 215, Folder 4, LOC; Adelman, *The Great Universal Embrace*, p. 144.

118. Memcon: Reagan–Gorbachev, Geneva, Third and Fourth Plenary Meetings, November 20, 1985, The Jack Matlock Files, Series I: Chron Files, November 1985–February 1986, Box 14, RRPL; "Summit Notes: Second Day; Afternoon," November 20, 1985, The Donald Regan Papers, White House Subject File, Summit: Geneva 1985, Box 215, Folder 4, LOC.

119. "Summit Notes: Dinner," November 20, 1985, The Donald Regan Papers, White House Subject File, Summit: Geneva 1985, Box 215, Folder 3, LOC; Reagan–Gorbachev Meetings in Geneva, "After-Dinner Conversation," November 20, 1985, The Jack Matlock Files, Series I: Chron Files, November 1985–February 1986, Box 14, RRPL; Oberdorfer, *From the Cold War to a New Era*, pp. 152–53; Reagan, *An American Life*, p. 640; Shultz, *Turmoil and Triumph*, pp. 604–05.

120. Brinkley (ed.), *The Reagan Diaries*, p. 370; "Debriefing of President," November 19, 1985, The Donald Regan Papers, White House Subject File, Summit: Geneva 1985, Box 215, Folder 3, LOC.

121. "Storics and Anecdotes," The Donald Regan Papers, White House Subject File, Summit: Geneva 1985, Box 215, Folder 3, LOC; Arbatov, *The System*, p. 320.

122. Reagan, *An American Life*, pp. 634–41; Leffler, *For the Soul of Mankind*, pp. 384–85. For Gorbachev's recollections, see: Gorbachev, *Memoirs*, pp. 526–31. For a more skeptical take on the Reagan–Gorbachev exchanges, see: FitzGerald, *Way Out There in Blue*, p. 309.

123. "Summit Notes: Dinner; Signing Ceremony," November 20, 1985, The Donald Regan Papers, White House Subject File, Summit: Geneva 1985, Box 215, Folder 3, LOC.

EPILOGUE

1. "Summit Finale: The Reaction on Capitol Hill; Transcript of Reagan Report to Congress on Geneva Meeting," *New York Times*, November 22, 1985; Reagan, *An American Life*, p. 641.

2. Reeves, *President Reagan*, p. 294. See also: Bernard Weinraub, "Reagan and Gorbachev Optimistic After Meeting," *New York Times*, November 22, 1985.

3. Brinkley (ed.), *The Reagan Diaries*, p. 371.

4. Gorbachev, *Memoirs*, pp. 524–26.

5. Dobrynin, *In Confidence*, p. 592.

6. Oberdorfer, *From the Cold War to a New Era*, pp. 153–54.

7. Hedrick Smith, "Setting the Post-Summit Tone," *New York Times*, December 8, 1985.

8. "Conference at the Central Committee of the Communist Party of the Soviet Union in preparation for the 27th Congress of the CPSU," December 28, 1985, NSA. See: https://nsarchive2.gwu.edu/NSAEBB/NSAEBB172/Doc27 .pdf See also: "Excerpt from Anatoly Chernyaev's Diary," November 24, 1985, NSA. See: https://nsarchive2.gwu.edu/NSAEBB/NSAEBB172/Doc26 .pdf

9. Letter from Gorbachev to Reagan, December 24, 1985, NSC Executive Secretariat Head of State Files; USSR: General Secretary Gorbachev (8591293), Box 40, RRPL.

10. Chernyaev, *My Six Years with Gorbachev*, pp. 83–84; Anatoly Chernyaev's notes, "Gorbachev's Instructions to the Reykjavik Preparation Group," October 4, 1986, The Reykjavik File, NSA, EBB, no. 203, doc. 5. See: http s://nsarchive2.gwu.edu/NSAEBB/NSAEBB203/Document05.pdf

11. Oberdorfer, *From the Cold War to a New Era*, pp. 189–205. For a full record of the Reykjavik meetings, see: The Reykjavik File, NSA, EBB, no. 203, various meetings. See: https://nsarchive2.gwu.edu//NSAEBB/NSAEBB203/in dex.htm

12. Shultz, *Turmoil and Triumph*, pp. 773–74.

13. Newhouse, *War and Peace in the Nuclear Age*, p. 398.

14. Craig and Logevall, *America's Cold War*, pp. 332–35; Brands, *Making the Unipolar Moment*, pp. 104–05.

15. Brands, *Making the Unipolar Moment*, p. 105; Reagan Remarks to ACDA and State Department Officials, October 14, 1986, Box 142, Papers of the Committee on the Present Danger, HIA.
16. Transcript of Politburo Meeting, "Soviet-American Relations and Negotiations on Nuclear and Space Armaments," February 26, 1987, NSA. See: https://nsarchive2.gwu.edu/NSAEBB/NSAEBB238/russian/Final987-02–26%20Politburo.pdf
17. Leffler, *For the Soul of Mankind*, pp. 399–400; Oberdorfer, p. 245.
18. William Moskoff, "Unemployment in the former Soviet Union," p. 370, in James Millar and Sharon Wolchik (eds.), *The Social Legacy of Communism* (New York: Cambridge University Press, 1994); Kotkin, *Armageddon Averted*, pp. 62–67.
19. See for example: Peter Schweizer, *Victory: The Reagan Administration's Secret Strategy that Hastened the Collapse of the Cold War* (New York: Atlantic Monthly Press, 1994); Caspar Weinberger, *Fighting for Peace: Seven Critical Years in the Pentagon* (New York: Warner Books, 1990); Richard Pipes, *Vixi: Memoirs of a Non-Belonger* (New Haven: Yale University Press, 2003).
20. Melvyn Leffler, "Ronald Reagan and the Cold War: What Mattered Most," *Texas National Security Review*, Vol. I, Issue 3 (May 2018), p. 85.
21. Gates, *From the Shadows*, p. 449.
22. See for example: Archie Brown, "Gorbachev, Perestroika, and the End of the Cold War," pp. 111–24, in Coleman and Longley (eds.), *Reagan and the World*; Zubok, *A Failed Empire*, p. 343; Matthew Evangelista, "Turning Points in Arms Control," pp. 83–103, in Richard Herrmann and Richard Ned Lebow (eds.), *Ending the Cold War: Interpretations, Causation, and the Study of International Relations* (New York: Palgrave Macmillan, 2004).
23. Craig and Logevall, *America's Cold War*, pp. 348–50.
24. Evangelista, "Turning Points in Arms Control," p. 99, in Herrmann and Ned Lebow (eds.), *Ending the Cold War*.
25. Craig and Logevall, *America's Cold War*, pp. 345–46; Melvyn Leffler, "Ronald Reagan and the Cold War: What Mattered Most," *Texas National Security Review*, Vol. I, Issue 3 (May 2018), p. 83; For an excellent study on the role of transnational movements, see: Matthew Evangelista, *Unarmed Forces: The Transnational Movement to End the Cold War* (Ithaca, NY: Cornell University Press, 1999).
26. Brown, *Seven Years That Changed the World*, pp. 3–6, 256–57; Leon Aron, "The 'Mystery' of the Soviet Collapse," *Journal of Democracy*, Vol. 17, No. 2 (April 2006), pp. 22–3.
27. Kotkin, *Armageddon Averted*, p. 171.
28. Brown, "Gorbachev, Perestroika, and the End of the Cold War," pp. 111–24, in Coleman and Longley (eds.), *Reagan and the World*; Brown, *Seven Years That Changed the World*, pp. 3–6.
29. Brown, *Seven Years That Changed the World*, p. 272.
30. Mann, *The Rebellion of Ronald Reagan*, pp. 48–50; Richard Nixon and Henry Kissinger, "A Real Peace," *National Review*, May 22, 1987; Henry Kissinger, "How to Deal With Gorbachev," *Newsweek*, March 2, 1987.

31. Reeves, *President Reagan,* p. 336.
32. See for example: Ehrman, *The Rise of Neoconservatism,* pp. 137–92; Halper and Clarke, *America Alone,* pp. 157–81.
33. Charles Krauthammer, "Gorbachev's Iron Smile," *Washington Post,* April 24, 1987.
34. George Will, "The Opiate of Arms Control," *Newsweek,* April 27, 1987.
35. Weinberger, *Fighting for Peace,* pp. 347–48. See also: Matlock, *Reagan and Gorbachev,* pp. 113–14.
36. Oberdorfer, *From the Cold War to a New Era,* p. 294; Schaller, "Reagan and the Cold War," p. 37, in Longley et al, *Deconstructing Reagan;* R. W. Apple Jr. "Gorbachev a Hit with the American Public," *New York Times,* December 4, 1987.
37. Zelizer, *Arsenal of Democracy,* pp. 350–53.
38. "Quayle Says Gorbachev Is Like Past Soviet Leaders," *Los Angeles Times,* September 6, 1988.
39. Craig and Logevall, *America's Cold War,* p. 345.
40. Melvyn Leffler, "Ronald Reagan and the Cold War: What Mattered Most," *Texas National Security Review,* Vol. I, Issue 3 (May 2018), p. 85; "U.S.-Soviet Relations," June 6, 1986, in Jason Saltoun-Ebin, *The Reagan Files,* p. 426; "Memorandum Dictated by Reagan: Gorbachev," November 1985, in Savranskaya and Blanton, *The Last Superpower Summits,* p. 44.
41. Reagan–Gorbachev Meetings in Geneva, "After-Dinner Conversation," November 20, 1985, The Jack Matlock Files, Series I: Chron Files, November 1985–February 1986, Box 14, RRPL; "Summit Notes: Dinner," November 20, 1985, The Donald Regan Papers, White House Subject File, Summit: Geneva 1985, Box 215, Folder 3, LOC.
42. Gergen, *Eyewitness to Power,* pp. 201–02.
43. Wilson, *The Triumph of Improvisation,* pp. 197–99.
44. See, for example: Memorandum by Weinberger to Reagan, "Arms Control Strategy," March 23, 1984. NSC Executive Secretariat Meeting Files, NSC 104–114, Box 11, RRPL; Matlock to McFarlane, "Proposed Presidential Statement: Building Cooperation Between U.S. and Soviet Peoples," May 29, 1984 (see handwritten note for Lenczowski's views); Lenczowski to McFarlane, "Reactivation of U.S.-USSR Environmental Agreement," May 8, 1984. The Jack Matlock Files, Series I: Chron File, April–May 1984, Box 4, RRPL.
45. Caddell to Carter, "Recent Polls and Implications for Strategy," November 6, 1979, The Hamilton Jordan Files, Box 33, Patrick Caddell [3], JCPL.
46. Robert McMahon, "Toward a Pluralist Vision: The Study of American Foreign Relations as International History and National History," pp. 35–50, in Michael Hogan and Thomas Paterson (eds.), *Explaining the History of American Foreign Relations* (Second Edition) (New York: Cambridge University Press, 2004).
47. Fredrik Logevall, "Domestic Politics," p. 154, in Costigliola & Hogan (eds.), *Explaining the History of American Foreign Relations;* Johns, *Vietnam's Second Front,* p. 2.

48. Cited in: Aaron David Miller, *Too Much Promised Land: America's Elusive Search for Arab-Israeli Peace* (New York: Bantam, 2008), p. 77.
49. Miroslav Nincic, "U.S. Soviet Policy and the Electoral Connection," *World Politics*, Vol. 42, No. 3 (April 1990), pp. 370–96.
50. Daniel Bessner and Fredrik Logevall, "Recentering the United States in the Historiography of American Foreign Relations," *Texas National Security Review*, Vol. 3, Issue 2 (Spring 2020), pp. 40–42.
51. Johns, *Vietnam's Second Front*, pp. 6–7.
52. Bayless Manning, "The Congress, the Executive, and Intermestic Affairs," *Foreign Affairs*, Vol. 55, No. 2 (January 1977).

Index

Cambridge Studies in US Foreign Relations

(continued from page ii)